Liberal Democracy and the Social Acceleration of Time

Liberal Democracy and the Social Acceleration of Time

William E. Scheuerman

The Johns Hopkins University Press
Baltimore and London

© 2004 The Johns Hopkins University Press
All rights reserved. Published 2004
Printed in the United States of America on acid-free paper
9 8 7 6 5 4 3 2 1

The Johns Hopkins University Press
2715 North Charles Street
Baltimore, Maryland 21218-4363
www.press.jhu.edu

Library of Congress Cataloging-in-Publication Data
Scheuerman, William E., 1965–
Liberal democracy and the social acceleration of time /
William E. Scheuerman.
   p. cm.
Includes bibliographical references and index.
ISBN 0-8018-7885-3 (hardcover : alk. paper)
1. Democracy. 2. Liberalism. 3. Decision making. 4. Time pressure.
I. Title.
JC423.S282   2004
321.8—dc22
2003018311

A catalog record for this book is available from the British Library.

For Zoë
daily ally against speed

Contents

Preface

This book was written in a period, at least by conventional U.S. standards, of considerable political upheaval. The appointment of a right-wing candidate to the presidency by the conservative majority on the Supreme Court even though his center-left opponent outpolled him by 500,000 votes; the heinous terrorist attacks of September 11, 2001, followed by a stunning expansion of executive prerogative; the establishment under U.S. auspices of an internment camp for accused foreign terrorists, along with a general attack on the civil liberties of U.S. citizens; a crackdown on immigrants and their precarious liberties; a "preemptive" U.S.-led invasion of a sovereign nation-state, Iraq, inconsonant with international law. These events have unavoidably helped shape the discouraging story about contemporary liberal democracy offered here. For what it is worth, I see my own task as trying to situate recent antiliberal and antidemocratic political trends in a broader conceptual and historical light. The process of social acceleration, whose significance becomes most obvious during moments of political crisis, perhaps can help us do so.

I have incurred substantial intellectual and personal debts while writing this book. First and foremost, the University of Minnesota has provided a supportive intellectual and political environment. By combining the right mix of encouragement and constructive criticism, Mary Dietz and Jim Farr have influenced the final shape of this book in more ways than they probably realize. As many in the field of political theory already know, Jim and Mary are legendary mentors of graduate students, and I now understand why: at many junctures in this project their aid was crucial. I am also indebted to Ed Fogelman, who graciously commented on a number of my arguments. Our intellectually lively and demanding graduate students at Minnesota continue to keep me on my toes, and their criticisms of an early version of some of my initial intuitions spurred me to clarify precisely what I was trying to do. In particular, I learned a great deal at the ongoing political theory colloquia organized and run by them. Finally, John Freeman, Jim Parente, and Steve Rosenstone provided institutional support without which I would never have been able to complete the book.

The meeting of critical-minded political theorists, jurists, and social philosophers, held annually in Prague and ably chaired by Hubertus Buchstein, Jean Cohen, Peter Dews, Alessandro Ferrara, Axel Honneth, and Frank Michelman, has also provided a wonderful forum for intellectual experimentation beyond the usual disciplinary constraints. All of this book's key theses were first tested in Prague, and I am grateful for the extensive criticisms I received from the many friends I have made there over the course of the last decade. Also, my colleagues at the journal *Constellations,* for whom I have presented a number of the book's core theses, have repeatedly offered supportive but suitably critical feedback. In particular, I am indebted to Andrew Arato and Nancy Fraser.

Chapter 1 represents the product of an ongoing dialogue with Hartmut Rosa, whose impact on it, as well as on my use of the concept of social acceleration, has been enormous. Early incarnations of chapter 2 benefited from thorough written comments from David Alexander, Ed Baker, Chris Eisgruber, Jim Farr, Thomas Hueglin, Bert Rockman, and Arlene Saxonhouse. An earlier version of chapter 3 was subjected to the impressive critical acumen of Brian Bix, Jamie Druckman, and Tim Johnson. Chapter 4 was written in response to an invitation from Andreas Kalyvas, who has subsequently commented with his usual incisiveness on the ideas developed here. Chapter 5 gained from the feedback of Harry Arthurs, David Dyzenhaus, Volkmar Gessner, Dirk Martin, Ingeborg Maus, Terry Nardin, Peter Niesen, and Steve Young. Finally, chapter 6 was improved through an ongoing dialogue about the merits of reflexive law with Jean Cohen.

Henry Tom at Johns Hopkins University Press early on encouraged me to pursue the project despite the fact it does not easily fit traditional disciplinary categories. Elizabeth Gratch worked hard to improve my prose.

Of course, we often learn the most from our toughest critics. In this vein Iris Marion Young's deep skepticism about the project repeatedly forced me to rethink my ideas.

I completed the manuscript while in residence at the Center for Human Values, Princeton; I am grateful to Josh Ober, the visiting director, for his support. My visit to Princeton was also partially financed through a sabbatical at the University of Minnesota, and my greatest institutional debt thus goes to the citizens of Minnesota for their abiding commitment to quality public education.

Some segments of the text appeared previously in *Cardozo Law Review, Constellations, Constitutional Commentary, Global Society, Journal of Political Philosophy,* and *Polity.*

The volume is dedicated to my daughter, Zoë, who has been an unflagging source of joy to her father since her birth on July 13, 2002.

Once again, let me also express my thanks—for Zoë and for everything else!—to Julia Roos.

Introduction

Any attempt to make sense of the human condition at the start of the new century must begin with an analysis of the social experience of speed. Advances in information and communications technology now allow vast currents of capital to circuit the globe at the blink of the eye and firms to produce different components of a single commodity in distant corners of the globe. The popular obsession with the Internet and the prospect of ever faster computing—higher baud rates, greater bandwidths—represents the most obvious manifestation of a broader set of social and economic trends having far-reaching implications for the temporal horizons of human existence. Ours is an era in which key forms of activity evince heightened possibilities for change and innovation. No area is left untouched by the resultant speed-up: instantaneous global communications, rapid-fire transnational production and consumption, fast information technologies, as well as high-speed weapons of mass destruction merely constitute different expressions of the accelerated tempo of present-day human activity. At the outset of the twenty-first century unprecedented opportunities for simultaneity and instantaneousness determine the contours of social existence to a degree that would have stunned most of our historical predecessors.

Among social theorists an impressive literature already exists on the phenomenon of social speed or acceleration. Yet political and legal scholars have been hesitant to heed Anthony Giddens's thoughtful advice to give proper "conceptual attention to the timing and spacing of human activities," let alone grapple with the implications of speed.[1] This book undertakes to help fill that lacuna by arguing that speed contains manifold implications for liberal democracy. Social acceleration not only can be described in a conceptually rigorous fashion, but many traditional notions about liberal democracy rest on assumptions about temporality which become increasingly problematic with the heightened pace of social life. Social speed potentially disables familiar liberal democratic models of political decision making, raising difficult questions for those of us committed to revitalizing liberal democracy in the new century. Many conventional preconceptions about the proper operations of liberal democracy are undermined by an empirically verifiable process of acceleration taking place in core areas of social activity. Ours is an increasingly high-speed society, and a high-speed society places a premium on rapid-fire political and legal practices: the widely endorsed conception of the unitary executive as an "energetic" entity best capable of acting with dispatch means that social acceleration often promotes executive-centered government and the proliferation of executive discretion while weakening broad-based representative legislatures as well as traditional models of constitutionalism and the rule of law. Slow-going deliberative legislatures, as well as normatively admirable visions of constitutionalism and the rule of law predicated on the quest to ensure legal stability and continuity with the past, mesh poorly with the imperatives of social speed, whereas a host of antiliberal and antidemocratic institutional trends benefit from it.

A massive body of both popular and scholarly literature already provides an alarming portrayal of a daunting array of policy and institutional challenges to present-day liberal democracy posed by globalization, the ecological crisis, and growing political apathy. Unfortunately, liberal democracy suddenly seems far less of a smashing institutional success than it did just a few years ago, when recent converts, dancing in the streets of Prague and even East Berlin, joyously celebrated its heroic victory over Soviet-style dictatorship. This book argues that a bad situation may be even worse.[2] The fundamental temporal dynamics of contemporary society generate a host of serious dilemmas for liberal democracy no less than growing material inequality, the depletion of the ozone layer and climate change, and unprecedented levels of political alienation. Just as political and legal scholars have been vigorously exerting impressive energy in suggesting how liberal democracy might better deal with these more conspicuous problems, so too must we now focus attention on the far-reaching ramifications of social speed.

My aspiration is not to generate yet another doomsday account of the "crisis of liberal democracy." By now we should understand that liberal democracy is an enormously complex and flexible political form. It has ably withstood many significant challenges in the past, and its fundamental core should be able to survive future ones as well.[3] Only if we pay careful attention to the manner in which the high-speed tempo of contemporary society negatively affects liberal democracy, however, can we hope successfully to refurbish it. Although much of what follows in this book might provide ready ammunition to liberal democracy's foes, my orientation ultimately remains a fundamentally constructive one. Would-be defenders of liberal democracy are in reality false friends if they stick their heads in the sand and downplay or even ignore the countless problems confronting it in the new century. Genuine fidelity to liberal democracy requires taking the critical insights of even its most adamant opponents seriously; as I argue here, far too often it has been liberal democracy's authoritarian critics (most notably, the Italian Futurists and the right-wing German jurist Carl Schmitt) who have presciently underscored, albeit in a normatively problematic and typically hyperbolic fashion, how high-speed temporality threatens liberal democracy. Yet, in contrast to liberal democracy's fair-weather fans, such critics at least recognized that the process of social acceleration poses a significant challenge to liberal democracy, and, even though they irresponsibly relied on notions of social speed to justify heinous dictatorships, those of us who hope to renew liberal democracy—in contrast to mere ideologues for the disappointing political and social status quo—also need to integrate a concept of social acceleration into political and legal analysis. To avoid the terrible path toward right-wing dictatorship such authoritarian theorists of speed pursued, however, we will need to do so with greater conceptual precision as well as normative and political acumen.

Among most contemporary political and legal scholars any study that undertakes to rely on an analysis of social speed or acceleration inevitably generates legitimate skepticism, in part because of the unfamiliar character of the project but also in part because many existing attempts by cultural critics and "postmodern" social analysts to thematize the high-speed contours of contemporary society suffer from serious flaws. Nonetheless, in chapter 1 I argue that we can discuss the phenomenon of social acceleration in a conceptually compelling as well as empirically useful fashion. Borrowing from innovative recent research in German sociology, I define *social acceleration* as constituting a long-term yet relatively recent historical process consisting of three central elements: technological acceleration (e.g., the heightening of the rate of technological innovation), the acceleration of social change (referring to accelerated patterns of basic change in the workplace or family, e.g.), and the acceleration of everyday life (e.g., via new means of high-speed communication or transportation). Chapter 1 also identifies the fundamental institutional driving forces motoring social acceleration, modern capitalism and the dynamics of interstate rivalry which constitute an essential component of the modern state system, explaining how my analysis of the institutional mechanisms behind the emergence of our high-speed society differs from a number of influential existing accounts. While insisting that the core intuition behind the ongoing debate among social theorists about temporality remains valid—basic social and economic processes have indeed been undergoing a long-term process of acceleration which has probably intensified in recent decades—I try to add some necessary conceptual clarity and rigor to existing theoretical accounts. Although ignored by most contemporary political and legal scholars, high-speed social temporality has served as a fertile topic of intellectual interest at least since the nineteenth century, and my own undertaking here arguably represents little more than an attempt to remind political scientists, philosophers, and legal scholars of the far-reaching analytic and explanatory potential of a theme that was relatively commonplace in nineteenth- and early-twentieth-century political and social thought.

Chapter 2 outlines why a proper conceptualization of social acceleration not only sheds new light on many familiar debates in political and legal scholarship but also vividly raises a number of tough questions about the fate of liberal democracy. Its central argument is that traditional liberal democratic ideas about the separation of powers rest on crucial, albeit neglected, temporal presuppositions. In the traditional view of liberal democratic government influential well into the twentieth century, legislation was supposed to be slow going, deliberate, as well as prospective, or future oriented; the executive was generally conceived as "expeditious," or capable of dispatch, and also contemporaneous, or present oriented, when properly fulfilling its core functions; the temporal orientation of the judiciary was generally depicted as retrospective, or past oriented. After retrieving the implicit temporal presuppositions of traditional liberal democratic thinking about legitimate decision making, chapter 2 suggests that the process of social acceleration tends to undermine the expectation that elected representative legislatures should represent the main site for lawmaking while simultaneously tending to strengthen the executive. In order to adapt to the dictates of speed, courts are also encouraged to take on forward-looking legislative tasks for which they typically were poorly designed. The temporal contours of our increasingly fast-paced social and economic world render the chief legislative task of successfully predicting future social trends—in my account a necessary presupposition of the notion of prospective legislation—an ever more uphill battle. High-speed society conflicts with the demand for prospective and stable legislative rules. A growing temporal misfit between the fast-paced contours of social life and the necessarily slow-going texture of broad-based, legitimate, deliberative legislative decision making is likely to have deleterious consequences for the traditional ideal of the rule of law, envisioned here as entailing a commitment to general, clear, relatively stable, prospective general rules.[4]

In contrast, the traditional intellectual association of the executive with dispatch seems to leave the executive especially well suited to tackle the exigencies of our rapidly changing, high-speed universe, and many plausible reasons might lead political actors who accept the traditional liberal democratic temporal image of the separation of powers to augment executive discretion. Unfortunately, the most likely result of this trend, the evolution of traditional liberal democracy into a system of rule in which elected legislatures play second fiddle to powerful executives and courts, potentially conflicts with classical liberal democratic normative and institutional ideals. Although more systematic empirical research is still required to corroborate my institutional expectations about the impact of speed, chapter 2 concludes with a brief summary of some revealing recent debates about the evolution of liberal democracy in order to provide initial empirical support for the claim that social acceleration undermines the temporal presuppositions of the separation of powers, as originally conceived.

The succeeding two chapters proceed to sketch out the far-reaching implications of the ever more weighty difficulties of effective prospective lawmaking in a social order subject to incessant change and rapid-fire human action. In the liberal democratic worldview no form of prospective legislation is more significant—or more ambitious—than constitutional lawmaking. As the law professor Richard Kay has accurately noted, authors of a written constitution are asked to do nothing less than establish fundamental "rules of the game" for "an indefinite but presumably long future."[5] Chapter 3 explains why social acceleration engenders inordinate impediments to the noble traditional idea that constitutional law should be fundamentally stable, constant, and relatively transparent in character. The concept of social acceleration also sheds fresh light on ongoing debates among political scientists and legal scholars about the proper contours of constitutional change in liberal democracy. Chapter 3 formulates an institutionally oriented typology of constitutional change in order to claim that high-speed society is most likely to favor executive-driven constitutional alteration while undermining slow-going but relatively deliberative and democratic modes of constitutional change (most prominently, the system of formal amendment outlined by Article 5 of the U.S. Constitution). I conclude with preliminary empirical evidence supporting my prediction that the temporal dynamics of present-day society tend to privilege normatively problematic and insufficiently democratic forms of executive-based constitutional change.

Chapter 4 argues that social acceleration creates no less severe enigmas for ordinary or statutory legislation than for constitutional law. Liberal democratic legislatures appear to have tacitly responded to social acceleration by trying to hasten the process of political decision making in order to maintain their relevance to our high-speed universe. Unfortunately, legislatures risk doing so at the cost of sacrificing their most attractive institutional virtues, as conceptualized by classical liberal democratic theory. Here, again, we find troubling empirical evidence—in particular, the legislature's tendency to delegate vast and oftentimes poorly defined grants of exceptional or "emergency" decision-making authority—that the executive has tended to benefit from the general speed-up in state activity which accompanies the process of social acceleration.

Carl Schmitt, twentieth-century Germany's most impressive authoritarian right-wing political and legal theorist, was a disturbingly perceptive analyst of the speed-up of legislation, or what Schmitt described as the "motorization" of lawmaking. Chapter 4 therefore devotes substantial attention to a critical analysis of Schmitt's fascinating diagnosis of the motorization (or acceleration) of the legislature. Although oftentimes perceptive, Schmitt's empirical description of the motorization of legislation ultimately rests, however, on a misleading explanation of its fundamental causes. Schmitt's profound hostility to liberalism ultimately prevented him from making proper sense of the sources of legislative motorization, as he wrongly placed the blame for it at the doorway of liberal jurisprudence rather than the general process of social acceleration. In addition, Schmitt's proposed political and institutional responses to it are both empirically inaccurate and normatively unappealing. Schmitt was right to imply that the high-speed temporality of contemporary society potentially threatens liberal democracy. He was wrong to believe that only a right-wing dictatorship, in which the expeditious executive is given full and unlimited reign to tackle the demands of speed, can effectively respond to the imperatives of high-speed society.[6] Chapter 4 also criticizes an influential body of recent U.S. legal scholarship for unwittingly committing intellectual mistakes analogous to Schmitt's. Notwithstanding the huge political and philosophical differences separating recent U.S. jurists from Schmitt, some of them wrongly endorse an insufficiently democratic answer to the pathologies of accelerated legislation which occasionally mirrors the conceptual ills of Schmitt's account. Recourse to Carl Schmitt allows us to highlight the potential dangers of pursuing the court-centered institutional rejoinder to legislative acceleration presently favored by contemporary U.S. jurists who see the revitalization of the common law as the best antidote to the pathologies of statutory legislation.

In the final analysis Schmitt's innovative attempt to grapple with the institutional consequences of speed is most useful as a revealing and arguably paradigmatic example of a political and legal theory of speed which irresponsibly discards liberal democracy. A constructive response to the dilemmas of liberal democracy can nonetheless gain by directly confronting the gauntlet thrown down by Schmitt: its proponents will need to think hard about how speed can serve as an ally, rather than an enemy, of liberal democracy.

Much of this book is devoted to explaining how the concept of social acceleration can help us understand relatively familiar developmental trends (the proliferation of executive discretion, e.g.) at work within nation-state-based liberal democracy. Yet social acceleration is also indispensable for analyzing the widely discussed process of "globalization," a topic necessarily of paramount interest to anyone concerned with liberal democracy's future prospects. Chapter 5 posits that we can only make sense of the "shrinkage," or "compression," of geographical distance by understanding the acceleration of basic social and economic processes which makes it possible in the first place. I also argue that the challenges of social acceleration are especially pronounced at the level of transnational economic relations (e.g., among "global players"), in which the reliance on new possibilities for simultaneous and instantaneous interaction is especially extensive. Any attempt to extend liberal democratic ideals and their traditional institutional moorings to the transnational level must now grapple with a profound process of social acceleration operative in the global economy. Social acceleration—as evinced, for example, by the high-speed pace of transnational production—is a central reason why traditional liberal democratic ideals are even more difficult to institutionalize at the transnational than the domestic level.

My main support for this claim revolves around a discussion of the proper place of the liberal rule of law in the transnational economy. Notwithstanding the expectations of most policy makers in the World Bank, International Monetary Fund, and national governments in the rich North, economic globalization seems surprisingly resistant, in crucial ways, to attempts to buttress it by means of classical rule of law attributes, understood here to require the pursuit of clear, general, and stable prospective legal norms as well as substantial predictability and certainty in international economic law. According to the argument developed in chapter 5, the paucity of rule of law virtues in the global economy derives at least as much from the high-speed pace of contemporary transnational economic life as from a host of more familiar explanations. That paucity is based on the fact that the rule of law's traditional preference for relatively stable and durable norms meshes poorly with the dictates of a global economy subject to constant change and increasingly fast-paced economic activities. Although economic globalization requires legal banisters, the traditional view of an "elective affinity" between capitalism and the rule of law no longer easily obtains in the context of a high-speed capitalism that poses numerous challenges to traditional liberal legal ideas.

In light of the substantial dilemmas generated by social acceleration for liberal democracy both at home and abroad, how might we reform its institutional operations so as to ensure that they are better suited to the dictates of speed? To be sure, the question is a difficult one. Nonetheless, chapter 6 considers a panoply of institutional possibilities for recalibrating liberal democracy while preserving its indispensable normative and institutional core. With proper institutional imagination it should be possible to guarantee that speed revitalizes rather than debilitates liberal democracy. After considering the possibility of making better use of high-speed communication and information technologies for the sake of refurbishing public debate and strengthening deliberative legislatures, I examine provocative recent proposals for modifying the traditional separation of powers as well as instituting new forms of rule making (in particular, "reflexive law") as possible ways by which liberal democracy might respond more effectively to social acceleration. Social acceleration needs to become an integral part of the conceptual paraphernalia of anyone seriously interested in the pressing matter of liberal democratic institutional reform, and political and legal scholars are badly mistaken if they believe that they can tackle the many institutional challenges at hand without paying due attention to the temporal dynamics of contemporary society. In chapter 6

I take an initial stab at showing how social acceleration allows us to think creatively about institutional design.

By now it should be clear that the present study intends to tackle a formidable array of controversial questions. I do so at the risk of intellectual exaggeration and even simplification. For example, my concern with the implications of speed for liberal democracy necessarily means that I typically ignore alternate causal analyses behind some of the institutional trends described here. I do not mean, however, to replace a bland and even one-dimensional refusal to think seriously about temporality with an equally one-sided causal story; if I appear to do so, it is only because temporal factors have been widely neglected by political and legal scholars. It should also be clear that the volume tends to transcend traditional disciplinary divides. Although my main interests lie in political and legal theory, I have found it necessary to make intellectual connections to social theory, institutional questions generally discussed by political scientists and political sociologists, and legal issues typically the province of law professors and international lawyers. This also poses a number of obvious intellectual risks; the relevant specialists will have to determine whether or not I have succeeded in navigating the rocky waters at hand. Nonetheless, it remains my view that any serious endeavor to do justice to the fascinating question of the impact of social temporality on liberal democracy necessarily must break free of the neat disciplinary boxes in which scholars typically build their nests. My hope is that I can encourage others to look beyond the cozy confines of their own nests in order that we might work together to think hard about the consequences of speed for the unfulfilled quest for a free and decent political and social order.

Liberal Democracy and the Social Acceleration of Time

CHAPTER ONE

Social Acceleration

A growing number of popular books posit that ours is an era in which "the acceleration of just about everything" is taking place.[1] The appeal of this literature is that it hits a raw nerve in the contemporary body politic: present-day society indeed is subject to the temporal dictates of speed. If the concept of social acceleration is to prove amenable to rigorous political and legal analysis, however, we need to do better than make vague references to ubiquitous acceleration. In this spirit let me begin by underscoring the significance of recent debates on the temporal contours of contemporary society. Then, on a more analytical and constructive note, I suggest that we have to understand exactly what are the main forms of social acceleration as well as where they occur, before systematically discussing the fundamental sources of social acceleration. After formulating a sufficiently robust concept of social acceleration, I will turn to a discussion of its implications for liberal democracy.

Social Thought and Temporality

It has long been commonplace among historians and social scientists to insist on the social character of human conceptions of time.[2] Unstated assumptions about temporality constitute a fundamental framework for everything we think or do. Yet these assumptions vary tremendously across and even within societies. Notwithstanding striking diversity in the scope of human presuppositions about time, from the perspective of any particular historically situated individual they are likely to take on the "full force of objective facts to which all individuals and institutions necessarily respond."[3] Their socially constructed nature hardly means that they are subjective. On the contrary, presumptions about time tend to become part of the unquestioned background of social life and thus typically appear necessary. We are unlikely to be aware of their historically transitory and socially circumscribed character, despite their tendency to structure the horizons of our experience in profound ways. A peasant in medieval Europe would undoubtedly be surprised to learn that his fundamental preconceptions about temporality—derived chiefly from an agricultural economy in which the pace of economic activity and innovation are relatively slow going—embody little more than the limited institutional possibilities of a particular historical moment. If he could somehow be propelled into a social setting in which high-speed forms of communication and transportation were universal, however, the narrowness of that which previously seemed so self-evident to him might suddenly become manifest.

Different forms of social organization produce correspondingly distinct temporal assumptions. Periods of social transition tend to bring such hitherto hidden differences into the open. In a now classic essay E. P. Thompson described how early industrial capitalism witnessed fierce battles among traditional artisans and craftsmen who initially refused to succumb to industrial capitalism's embrace of a workplace resting on the precise and systematic measurement of neatly quantified, homogeneous, linear units of time. For the traditional artisan the disciplinary time clock of the capitalist workplace represented an alien and threatening intrusion into traditional temporal assumptions that jarred with the imperatives of modern capitalism.[4] Richard Sennett's recent study of the impact of ongoing economic changes on personal character suggests that many present-day employees are undergoing a similarly disorienting transition from the relatively routinized time of welfare state–managed capitalism and its classic institutional expression, the predictable (and oftentimes tedious) industrial assembly line, to the "disjointed time" of contemporary capitalism in which flexibility and the possibility of rapid-fire reactions to fast-paced changes are at a premium. The speed and flexibility of present-day economic life generates a workplace in which disruptive change becomes the norm; character traits suited to earlier forms of capitalism (e.g., the long-term temporal attachment of loyalty) tend to conflict with present institutional imperatives.[5] Recent temporal shifts pose a fundamental challenge to the system of labor regulation which emerged in the context of the welfare state. Correspondingly, key conflicts between labor and capital now concern the most suitable way to deal with heightened demands for flexibility and high-speed reaction times characteristic of workplace life.

Not only do distinct forms of social organization correspond to distinct experiences of time, but different assumptions about time also uneasily coexist at any given historical juncture. The temporal presuppositions of those engaging in physically exhausting forms of traditional low-wage agricultural labor in rural Mexico diverge significantly from those of the Internet entrepreneurs and currency traders located in Mexico City. A currency trader in London engaged in computerized financial transactions with his counterpart in Tokyo operates in a somewhat different set of temporal horizons than the newspaper vendor standing outside the currency trader's office trying to get rid of his daily allotment of the *Financial Times* or the housewife working at home with minimal outside contacts. Temporality is hardly experienced uniformly in urban and rural areas or across social and national divides.[6] Indeed, social existence takes place "in divergent and oftentimes contradictory manifestations of social time."[7] The social experience of temporality is plural, not singular, meaning that different forms of social activity can be related to correspondingly distinct experiences of temporality. One of the most perceptive mid-twentieth-century analysts of the social experience of temporality, Georges Gurvitch, categorically insisted that "every society must attempt to unify, even if only relatively, these multiple manifestations of time and attempt to arrange them in a hierarchy" in order to provide a measure of coherence to social life.[8] As countless historical and contemporary examples attest, however, the process of unifying the pluralism of social times constitutes a ripe source of social and political tension. Even if we question the enigmatic functionalist logic that probably buttresses Gurvitch's insistence on the necessity of unifying temporal experience, it remains the case that the coexistence of different experiences of temporality points to some difficult questions. What are the likely consequences of the potentially antagonistic temporal logics of different institutions and social practices? How can individuals mediate successfully between the tempo of the capitalist economy, for example, and that of liberal democratic politics? The legitimacy of liberal democratic rule is predicated on the necessity of wide-ranging but time-consuming deliberation and debate. If the capitalist workplace privileges temporal efficiency and a capacity for rapid-fire action and reaction, can political institutions traditionally conceived as necessarily based on unhurried practices (e.g., legislatures committed to deliberation and the representation of a broad array of interests) successfully "keep up" with a fast-moving economy subject to incessant change and innovation?

Social scientists and historians have not only successfully underscored the tension-ridden social character of temporality. More recently, they have also struggled to fine-tune Marshall McLuhan's prescient diagnosis of an "acceleration at all levels of human organization."[9] Indeed, the notion that ours is a distinctly high-speed society has become relatively commonplace in recent social theory, with a host of prominent thinkers—most important among them Zygmunt Bauman, Manuel Castells, Anthony Giddens, David Harvey, Reinhart Koselleck, and Paul Virilio—advancing different versions of the basic thesis that the temporal horizons of key elements of contemporary society have undergone substantial acceleration vis-à-vis earlier forms of social organization.[10] Despite sizable intellectual and political distances separating them, recent social theorists generally see dramatic advances in communication, transportation, and information technology as crucial harbingers of social acceleration. Typically depicting the relatively privileged status of capitalism as a central reason for the ubiquity of speed in many facets of contemporary life, they persuasively argue that the imperatives of capitalist production privilege ever faster modes of production, distribution, and consumption which impact on a broad range of noneconomic activities as well. Contemporary social theorists also point out that the rate of scientific and technological innovation seems increasingly impressive. Not only does each new scientific innovation require shorter spans of time, but the rate of its practical technological application and subsequent commercial diffusion appear to be quickening, and the temporal span separating each of these stages continues to decline as well.[11] In addition, many aspects of contemporary cultural experience are undoubtedly characterized by what Thomas Hylland Eriksen, a Norwegian social scientist, has fittingly dubbed the "tyranny of the moment."[12] When fast food is devoured in front of TV screens that offer up fleeting MTV images or thirty-second news "sound bites" and a great deal of serious art, film, and literature is preoccupied with experiences of ephemerality and simultaneity, there are good reasons for suspecting that the temporal horizons of both "low" and "high" culture are undergoing noteworthy transformations as well.

Social theorists are rightly striving to do justice to the enormous complexity of the temporal trends at work in present-day society. Yet they often tacitly endorse Gurvitch's observation that social time is hierarchically ordered, with high-speed forms of activity ascendant. Speed is typically favored in capitalist production, for example, because of its manifold contributions to profitability, while high-speed weaponry as well as speed in transportation and communication often confirm the privileged position of political elites by making it "possible for them to exert more effective control over distant territories, tributaries, and markets."[13] Because of the enormous impact of capitalist production over many arenas of social existence, it should come as no surprise that its temporality has tended to become prevalent as well. Those institutions that constitute the main sites of power and privilege in modern society possess a special position within the hierarchy of social temporalities, and their temporal dynamics oftentimes override those of other social activities.[14] Legitimate skepticism in the face of e-commerce hyperbole at the beginning of the twenty-first century should not lead us to ignore the fact that contemporary society "is characterized by the integration of information technology as a key factor in all kinds of production . . . Whether one is to blast a mountain, build a ship, sell a bag of crisps, investigate a case of arson, perform a heart bypass operation or give a lecture in social anthropology, people in our society are increasingly dependent on computer technology."[15] The ubiquity of high-speed information and communications technologies means that a substantial array of everyday activities now operates at an ever more rapid-fire pace, as both new and more traditional forms of economic activity are being reconfigured by high-speed communication and information technologies as well as novel possibilities for simultaneity and instantaneousness.[16]

To be sure, we are hardly the first generation to find itself excited by a dizzying sense of overcoming traditional temporal limits yet at the same time burdened with an anxious sense of lagging behind a runaway world whose fast pace too often overwhelms us.[17] The perception that ours is an identifiably high-speed civilization has long represented a constitutive feature of modern Western consciousness. In Montesquieu's *Persian Letters* (1721) Rica, a fictional visitor from the Islamic world, remarks that the French "are always in a hurry, because they have important business to do . . . At last, worn out, they go home to rest, in order to resume their tiring duties next day." Rica then wryly notes than an appropriate epitaph for the grave of a typical European would be: "Here rests a man who never rested before."[18] In the 1830s Alexis de Tocqueville transplanted his fellow Frenchman Montesquieu's diagnosis of the temporal proclivities of eighteenth-century France to the shores of North America: for Tocqueville it was the Americans whose way of life was characterized by restlessness and a preference for constant change, whereas France now appeared relatively staid and slow going.[19]

Especially since the advent of industrial capitalism, intellectual discourse has been replete with references to a widely shared awareness that experiences of distance and space are invariably transformed by the emergence of high-speed forms of transportation (e.g., rail and air travel) and communication (e.g., the telegraph and telephone). Remarking on the long-term implications of railroads, an English journalist writing in the *Quarterly Review* in 1839 worried that, as distance was "annihilated, the surface of our country would, as it were, shrivel in size until it became not much bigger than one immense city."[20] A few years later Heinrich Heine, the émigré German-Jewish poet, captured this same experience when he noted: "space is killed by the railways. I feel as if the mountains and forests of all countries were advancing on Paris. Even now, I can smell the German linden trees; the North Sea's breakers are rolling against my door."[21] In 1904 the American literary figure Henry Adams diagnosed the existence of a "law of acceleration," fundamental to the workings of social development, in order to make sense of dramatically increased rates of scientific and industrial innovation as well as concomitant increases in the pace of basic social change. Presciently anticipating the contemporary theoretical fascination with the problem of speed, Adams insisted that modern society could only be properly understood if the seemingly irrepressible acceleration of basic technological and social processes was given a central place in social and historical analysis.[22] Numerous cultural and intellectual innovations dating from the period between 1880 and 1918, including Cubism, simultaneous poetry, ragtime music, and important currents within philosophy and social theory, can also be fruitfully interpreted as constituting responses to a sense of temporal speed-up widespread among Europeans and North Americans at the time.[23]

Many more recent allusions to the high-speed attributes of modern social life can be found in the work of a diverse range of literary and philosophical figures. Although Futurism celebrated the "aesthetic of speed" exemplified by "great locomotives, twisting tunnels, armored cars, torpedo boats, monoplanes, and racing cars" at the outset of the last century, most subsequent intellectuals have been less enthralled by evidence of social acceleration.[24] John

Dewey anxiously described contemporary society's "mania for motion and speed," while Theodor Adorno later complained about the present-day "cult of technical speed," contrasting it unfavorably to the relatively slow pace of nineteenth-century liberal society. Carl Schmitt lamented the "motorization" of legislation which resulted from the attempt to regulate a high-speed society. Hannah Arendt worried about the "onslaught of speed" as well as the "ever-quickening increase in human knowledge and power" in contemporary society. Her former teacher, Martin Heidegger, expressed similar anxieties.[25] Many recent literary notables have also expressed unease about the high-speed texture of contemporary life.[26]

Allusions to the high-speed texture of social life are pervasive in modern consciousness because social acceleration represents a constitutive feature of modernity. Scholars generally agree that the rise of industrial capitalism generated a particularly intense period of social acceleration, and some additional evidence points to a further intensification of social acceleration within recent decades as well—so, at least, runs a plausible line of argumentation now widely endorsed by social theorists.[27] The preference for speed, however, is probably as old as Western modernity. For example, throughout its history modern capitalism has searched for

> new organizational forms, new technologies, new lifestyles, new modalities of production and exploitation and, therefore, new objective social definitions of time and space . . . The turnpikes and canals, the railways, steamships and telegraph, the radio and automobile, containerization, jet cargo transport, television and telecommunications, have altered space and time relations and forced new material practices . . . The capacity to measure and divide time has been [constantly] revolutionized, first through the production and diffusion of increasingly accurate time pieces and subsequently through close attention to the speed and coordinating mechanisms of production (automation, robotization) and the speed of movement of goods, people, information, messages, and the like.[28]

Modern capitalism has always worked to accelerate the course of production and consumption in many ways. Maximizing the economic advantages of speed is a crucial strategy for capitalists to maintain profitability, and hence "the history of capitalism has been characterized by a speed-up in the pace of life, while so overcoming spatial barriers that the world seems to collapse inward upon us."[29] During moments in the economic cycle characterized by intense competition or crisis, businesses that are able to exploit the advantages of developing faster forms of production and consumption may prove most adept at defeating their rivals. Technological innovations generated by capitalism's built-in tendency to accelerate production and consumption—most recently, the increasingly widespread role played by rapid-fire computerization in many areas of the economy—mean that instantaneousness and simultaneity tend to become constitutive features of modern economic life.

Although capitalism has always tended to privilege speed, contemporary manifestations of social acceleration still remain distinctive. In this vein David Harvey has tried to demonstrate that the worldwide economic downturn of the 1970s paved the way for a reorganization of economic life in which fresh possibilities for the successful exploitation of new high-speed information, communication, and transportation technologies, constituting core features of an emerging post-Fordist economy that has replaced many elements of assembly line–centered production, came to play a decisive role. For Harvey post-Fordism is driven by high-speed technologies that place a "premium on 'smart' and innovative entrepreneurship, aided and abetted by all the accouterments of swift, decisive, and well-informed decision making." Those best able to make effective use of new communications and information technology to exploit no less novel possibilities for "flexibility with respect to labor processes, labor markets, products, and patterns of consumption" are now likely to outrace their competitors.[30]

Whatever one makes of the specifics of Harvey's interpretation, the crucial point is that a growing body of evidence suggests that the pace of many facets of economic life has been significantly heightened in recent decades vis-à-vis earlier manifestations of capitalism. Growing reliance on microchips and computers makes it possible, for example, for electronically integrated financial markets to transact billions of dollars in mere nanoseconds.[31] Outsourcing, "small batch" and short production runs, "just in time" production and distribution flows, and subcontracting—each of these increasingly decisive features of present-day capitalism can be interpreted as elements of a broader movement toward accelerating the pace of production and adapting ever more rapidly to fast-changing shifts in consumption. Each also represents a relatively novel manifestation of social acceleration, and each was made possible by recent technological developments (e.g., instant data analysis) which allow firms to minimize the potential economic disadvantages of distance and duration. Dramatically increased rates of commercial, technological, and organizational innovation, evident in a vast range of economic activities, have resulted.[32] The rate of crucial forms of economic exchange, such as world trade, seems to be accelerating as well.[33] When currency traders in Frankfurt can communicate instantaneously via computer with their peers in Singapore, clothing retailers regularly introduce new product lines every few months in reaction to the changing demands of teenagers, and rapid-fire forms of technology make it profitable for corporate managers to undertake the production of components of a single commodity (e.g., an automobile) simultaneously in distant corners of the globe, it is hard to deny that the temporal horizons of economic activity are undergoing significant changes.

Toward a Concept of Social Acceleration

However useful, recent theoretical reflections on the social phenomenon of speed remain unsatisfactory. Can we formulate a more systematic and empirically fungible conception of social acceleration and thereby move beyond the somewhat impressionistic and underdeveloped understanding that tends to haunt most existing accounts?

At the most elementary level social acceleration can be characterized as a decrease in the amount of measurable units of time necessary for a particular activity or experience (e.g., goods produced, messages transmitted, or kilometers covered via automobile). It also refers to a decline in the amount of quantifiable time necessary for what one observer has dubbed "socially relevant" changes.[34] As the German social theorist Hartmut Rosa has perceptively argued, participants in the ongoing debate about speed are describing phenomena that can be fruitfully grouped into three categories. Although the empirical borders between them are typically blurred, and notwithstanding the fact that all three "ideal-types" of social acceleration are causally interrelated as well (and thus can be plausibly interpreted as constituting different elements of a single social trend), conceptual clarity demands that we try to distinguish between and among them.[35]

First, we find extensive evidence for an intense process of *technological acceleration*, according to which key technical processes (particularly in communication, transportation, and production) now take place at a faster pace than in earlier historical periods. Communication transpires between distant geographical points at an unprecedented rate, travel times have been dramatically cut, and the time necessary for the production of even relatively complex commodities gets steadily reduced. Many recent innovations in information technology, such as the Internet, exemplify this facet of social speed. Under this rubric we can also include the heightened pace of scientific and technological *innovation,* as the half-life of many new forms of technology rapidly declines while the number of innovations per unit of time (year or decade, e.g.) seems to increase. In this spirit Hans Jonas pointed out many years ago that modern technology quickly came to embody "a *principle* of innovation itself which made its constant further occurrence mandatory."[36] Technological acceleration can be measured and quantified with relative ease, and its existence can be verified by many empirical cases. For example, the capacity (and thus speed) of microprocessors is typically doubled every eighteen months; transmission speed on the Net is doubled every year; the U.S. telephone system in 1915 was able to handle 3 simultaneous voice calls, within a generation the quantity was 480, and by the 1980s Telstar satellites could handle 100,000 telephone links.[37] Typists once averaged 30,000 keystrokes an hour; today their visual display terminal (VDT) operator successors are expected to achieve 80,000 keystrokes in the same quantity of time.[38] Historians tell us that railway travel in 1845 was three times the speed of stagecoach travel, the introduction of the clipper ship at the beginning of the nineteenth century cut travel time on the high seas in half, and the subsequent emergence of the steamship resulted in no less dramatic decreases in necessary travel time on many sea routes. In the first half of the twentieth century ships required eight days to cross the Atlantic. Today jets traverse the same distance in six hours, and until its final flight in 2003 the Concorde was able to do so in less than one hour.[39] Indeed, one of the most striking—and widely observed—facts of economic life since the industrial revolution is the increasing speed with which products and services are generated, along with the increased pace of scientific and technological innovation that helps make increased velocity in production possible.[40]

Second, the pace of significant *social change or transformation* exhibits evidence of acceleration as well. Relatively far-reaching shifts in economic and social life now take place at a breakneck rate.[41] Forms of economic organization and occupational patterns, for example, change intragenerationally rather than over the course of whole generations. One familiar result of this alteration in the temporal horizons of social life is that our contemporaries may change jobs many times during the life course, whereas our historical predecessors often were destined to follow occupations identical to those of their parents and even grandparents. And even those of us who do not periodically shift jobs are likely to find ourselves in workplace settings where constant organizational restructuring or rationalization constitutes the norm and not the exception. Technological changes can produce relatively dramatic changes in economic and social organization in a short span of time; within a mere two decades new informational technologies have generated far-reaching shifts in many arenas of economic production and consumption. The example of computerization also reminds us that social change or transformation tends to be related to technological acceleration. As the pace of technological innovation increases, the rate of major social and economic change will tend to grow as well, as new forms of technology often lead to experimentation with novel forms of social and economic organization. Maybe this is why some analysts sloppily clump technological acceleration with the acceleration of social change; it is easy to see how one can make a quick transition from describing the relentless revolutionizing of modern technology to a more general discussion of broader forms of social change.[42] Nonetheless, it is necessary to distinguish between them. High-speed transportation, communication, and information technologies, for example, are often closely linked to key forms of social change, but these social changes themselves (e.g., altered workplace structures, changes in family structure, new modes of communication or cultural life) represent distinct phenomena requiring careful study. By ignoring this point and conflating accelerated social change with technological acceleration, we risk succumbing to a crude form of technological determinism.

This second facet of social acceleration is undoubtedly more difficult to study systematically than technological acceleration. Some social change may be insignificant, and, since change arguably constitutes a permanent feature of modern society, we ideally need some way to distinguish between different varieties of change (e.g., in the family, economy, or polity) and their varying degrees or extent. Some social changes (such as the transition from the patriarchal family to alternative forms of family life) are obviously significant, whereas others (such as the introduction of a new flavor of ice cream) may be trivial. Within a single area (e.g., the economy), it would be useful to differentiate between significant and relatively insignificant change (changes at the level of the relations of production vs. relatively minor varieties of industrial reorganization, e.g.). We also need to be able to evaluate and measure the temporal pace of relevant social change more effectively. Such difficulties, however, should not lead us to throw the baby out with the bathwater. Peter Laslett has developed a potentially useful typology that distinguishes between a multiplicity of distinct forms of social change, suggesting plausibly that the rate and basic character of change varies between and among them. Social change at the normative level of belief and religion, for example, seems to lag behind the relatively fast pace of economic change and the rate of technological innovation. Change at the level of the relations of production is probably more slow paced than at the level of technical change in production.[43]

Although more systematic empirical analysis is required, the recent social theory literature nonetheless offers substantial evidence that the pace of relevant social change in core arenas of human existence is undergoing acceleration. The dynamism of contemporary society means that many crucial forms of economic organization, socialization patterns, and cultural trends now tend to become obsolescent at a rapid pace. Along with the example of workplace organization, one might also mention family life, whose half-life seems subject to rapid decline as well: whereas family patterns in agrarian society remained unchanged over generations, it is no longer uncommon for individuals to experience a variety of different family lifestyles over the course of a lifetime.[44] Such experience is only possible, of course, because of increased experimentation in society at large with alternative family lifestyles. Similarly, senior citizens are by no means the only members of contemporary society who sense that linguistic and cultural habits seem to change at a quickening pace. Even those who have reached the age of thirty are likely to be unfamiliar with the techno-jargon employed by teenagers who grew up cruising e-mail chat rooms.[45] Karl Marx's observation that social life seems characterized by "uninterrupted disturbance, everlasting uncertainty and agitation" represents at least as apt a description of the present era as it did of nineteenth-century industrial capitalism.[46]

One familiar manifestation of this trend is the rapid aging of our capacity to gain some sense of certainty about the future. In a social environment subject to incessant change, past experience often proves unreliable in light of the marked discontinuity between the rapidly changing present and earlier experience. Our capacity to gain some sense about what the future is likely to bring suffers from a declining half-life no less than the products we purchase, televisions shows we watch, and job tasks assigned to us at the workplace.[47] Those who were trained to repair computers just a decade ago are often incompetent when asked to cure the latest computer virus; academic colleagues who came of age in the 1960s and early 1970s find themselves looking with disbelief at the behavior of younger colleagues socialized amid the market euphoria of the

1980s and 1990s.[48] In many settings the accelerated pace of social change means that prejudices and opinions derived from previous experiences increasingly offer little guidance for the future and that "all new-formed ones become antiquated before they can ossify."[49]

Finally, the social and economic acceleration of contemporary society includes the *heightened tempo of everyday life*, according to which substantial empirical testimony points to an objectively measurable intensification of experiences and activities that we engage in during a given period of time. Not only is there evidence of a decline in the amount of units of time required by many activities, but social acceleration also entails an increased quantity of experiences or activities actually undertaken during a specific period of time. When the philosopher John Dewey alluded to contemporary society's "mania for motion and speed," it was this element of our social world which he had in mind.[50] More recently, Staffan Burenstam Linder, a Swedish economist, has similarly pointed out that over the past several decades "the pace is quickening, and our lives in fact are becoming steadily more hectic."[51] In recent years this third face of speed has attracted the attention of popular authors who worry that the imperatives of an accelerated everyday existence threaten to overwhelm human capacities for absorbing information and coordinating our lives in a meaningful and coherent manner.[52] It also lies at the base of ubiquitous anxieties about the "pressures" and "scarcity" of time.

We should probably see this final face of acceleration as linked to technological acceleration, which constitutes the immediate fount for the ever faster pace of everyday life: we are able to fill up our lives with a greater variety of activities and experiences than our historical predecessors in part because timesaving devices allow us to do so. The relative rapidity with which broader social and economic patterns of social life now undergo change may, however, also be tied to it. For example, the hectic pace of everyday life undoubtedly derives in part from the widespread sense of trying to "catch up" with a fast-paced world in which we worry incessantly about "falling behind." The widespread obsession with catching up represents an understandable reaction to a social world whose structural elements are subject to fast-paced change.

No necessary link exists between the reduced amount of time required by any given activity and the fact that we now tend to fill our busy lives with more activities and experiences. The mere fact that an assembly line worker at Ford Motor Company is capable of contributing to the production of more automobile parts during an eight-hour workday than her predecessor hardly by itself *requires* her to do so, any more than academics' improved access to high-speed word processing demands of them that they generate more articles and books. Leisure and increased free time very well might result from technological acceleration. The fact that technological acceleration instead seems to generate a quantitative increase in activities or experiences thus cries out for explanation. An obvious starting point for such an explanation would be the structure of the capitalist economy. For example, General Motors' interest in profitability leads not only to the introduction of timesaving devices but also to a quantitative increase in the number of automobiles produced over a given span of time. In addition, powerful economic incentives lead General Motors to encourage consumers to experience as many distinct automobiles as they possibly can during the course of their lives. To the extent that economic growth also generates an increased standard of living among at least some segments of the population, consumers will be able to afford an ever more impressive range of goods and services. The result is a scenario in which firms egg on consumers to buy more goods, with many consumers equipped with the resources necessary to do so. The paradoxical consequence is likely to be a "harried" class of consumers drowning in material goods with which they spend decreasing amounts of time. Consumption itself requires time, and, as it increases, the time available to enjoy individual consumer goods is likely to decline as well.[53]

Time budget studies of basic human activities, long a legitimate scholarly pursuit among social scientists, can be interpreted as providing preliminary empirical evidence for the acceleration of everyday life. Analysts who interpret the huge body of empirical material available differ in their accounts of the precise character and sources of this acceleration, yet they generally agree that the data available confirm the claim that growing numbers of us are trying to cram an ever greater number of activities into smaller units of time.[54] Important studies of the sleep patterns of the fully employed in the rich countries (Germany, Japan, Spain, Sweden, the United Kingdom, and the United States) suggest that we probably sleep less than we did even in the recent past; significant numbers of us now also suffer from sleep-related disturbances.[55] Less time is now spent on a range of "personal needs" (including personal hygiene), with the time devoted to meals at home undergoing sizable decreases in recent years as well.[56] Although the paid workday has tended to decrease since the 1960s, many of us spend more time getting to work, with commutes on the average longer than they were in the recent past.[57] In addition, the total amount of time devoted to unpaid household labor (including childcare) has arguably increased, notwithstanding the automation of domestic activities.[58] Interestingly, our favorite leisure activities reflect, perhaps to a greater extent than in the past, the harried pace of other aspects of our lives: an increased amount of time is devoted to individualized but nonetheless intense and oftentimes high-speed sports (e.g., cycling, tennis, jogging, and working out at fitness studios). One might also mention the blurring of the temporal borders between the weekend and normal workweek, with the weekend becoming less and less distinct, in terms of the activities undertaken then, from the remainder of the week.[59]

Other researchers dispute some of these concrete findings—such as the increases in time devoted to unpaid domestic labor and decreases in sleep time—while nonetheless generally confirming the existence of a speed-up of daily life. In this vein John Robinson and Geoffrey Godbey underscore the paradoxical character of recent temporal trends. Even though Americans engage in less paid and unpaid labor and now enjoy substantially more free time than in 1965, they suffer from a widespread sense of feeling rushed and hectic. Robinson and Godbey identify at least one main culprit: Americans now devote an increasingly substantial amount of their free time to watching TV, and this trend leaves less time for a variety of activities to which their historical predecessors were able to devote more time. American socialize less, engage in less associational activity, read less, and attend fewer cultural events such as sporting events and visits to museums than they did in 1965.[60] Whatever the objective sources of the acceleration of everyday life, at the subjective level the consequences are relatively unambiguous: polling data shows that, in 1971, 22 percent of Americans described themselves as "always feeling rushed," while in 1985 the number was 35 percent; by 1992 the proportion had reached 38 percent. In 1971, 27 percent said they "almost never felt rushed," whereas in 1985 the number decreased to 20 percent and a mere 17 percent in 1995. A recent Japanese survey found that 70 percent of respondents felt similarly pressed for time.[61]

The Sources of Social Acceleration

What, then, are the fundamental driving forces behind social acceleration? Not surprisingly, social theorists thus far have produced different answers to this question. Harvey sees "time and space compression" as determined funda-

mentally by the immanent dynamics of capitalist production. In this materialist vein the analysis of the temporal assumptions of material production not
only provides one of the keys to understanding the dialectics of capitalist social
development, but it also sheds light on the changing distribution of power in
contemporary capitalism.[62] Many others refuse to subscribe to Harvey's Marx-
ism while nonetheless acknowledging the pivotal role that modern capitalism
has played in motoring social acceleration. In this vein Giddens recognizes the
central place of capitalism in explaining shifts in social temporality while
breaking decisively with a narrowly Marxist framework. He emphasizes persuasively how facets of modernity typically ignored by Marxist analysis—for
example, the development of the surveillance capacities of the modern state—
contributed to changed conceptions of space and time.[63] Reinhart Koselleck
analogously suggests that social acceleration can also be linked to the process
of early modern state development and, more specifically, mercantilist policies
that encouraged political elites to cultivate the development of new roads,
canals, and improved transportation technologies for political and military
purposes.[64] Paul Virilio, the most creative postmodern theoretician of speed,
underscores the pivotal role that the development of weapons technology has
played in the compression of space via high-speed warfare. Although markedly
less systematic than either Giddens or Koselleck, Virilio similarly hints at the
limits of Marxist interpretations of social temporality by highlighting interstate competition as a source of social speed.[65]

Social theorists have traced social acceleration to different causes because
there are indeed a number of structural sources at its root. First, the understandable appeal of a materialist approach to social acceleration stems from
the fact that modern capitalism has played a pivotal and perhaps predominant
role in the acceleration of modern society. There is perhaps no greater empirical support for Weber's renowned description of capitalism as "the most fateful force in our modern life" than the multiplicity of ways by which the
temporality of capitalism generates so many different manifestations of social
acceleration.[66] Reducing the time necessary to produce a specific product,
decreasing the turnover time required to turn a profit, accelerating the pace of
technological innovation, speeding up production in order to maximize the
use of labor power, getting goods to distant markets as quickly as possible,
making sure that production adjusts to rapidly changing fluctuations in consumer demand—many familiar features of modern capitalism contribute di-

rectly to the acceleration of basic social and economic activities. Examples of technical acceleration (e.g., the introduction of new labor-saving technologies), the acceleration of social change (e.g., rapid-fire alterations in industrial or workplace organization), and the acceleration of everyday life (e.g., the harried consumer) are immediately linked to the dynamics of modern capitalism. Countless other examples (such as the general sense of a "shortage" of time) are surely related to capitalism's tendency not only to maximize the temporal efficiency of certain activities but also to provide incentives for us to fill our time with as many activities as we possibly can. Is it no wonder that we tend to eat, walk, and talk (or at least communicate) faster than most of our historical predecessors or that we manage to pull this off even though we may sleep less than many of them did?

If social acceleration were simply a manifestation or immediate offshoot of modern capitalism, however, one indeed might legitimately wonder what is gained by focusing on its merits as a conceptual device for making sense of contemporary society. Why not instead opt for a more traditional brand of social theory having a materialist or at least economic orientation? Might not the recent fascination with the temporal contours of social action then prove at best misleading and at worst an ideological obfuscation of more basic structural (i.e., economic) mechanisms? Indeed, if social acceleration rests on more fundamental economic processes, what causal punch could it possibly carry anyway? In light of its origins in more basic economic processes, the category of social acceleration would seem to offer a weak starting point for explaining the causal mechanisms of much of anything.[67]

The easy answer to this question is that social acceleration is a multisided phenomenon with significant noneconomic as well as economic origins. If we miss the noneconomic driving forces behind social acceleration, we necessarily fail to understand it properly and inevitably misconstrue many of its main components. The more complex response is that, even though social acceleration is ultimately connected to familiar structural features of modern society, it nonetheless represents a significant phenomenon in its own right, in possession of far-reaching implications for conventional conceptions of liberal democracy. As I hope to demonstrate in this book, a proper focus on the distinctive attributes of social acceleration allows us to make sense of the weaknesses of our dominant conceptions of liberal democracy in a way that more familiar explanatory approaches fail to accomplish. Social acceleration constitutes a relatively autonomous dynamic, and its thematization by recent social theorists represents an intellectual innovation that political and legal theorists ignore at their own risk.[68]

In this spirit Rosa has plausibly pointed out that the three core types of social acceleration interact to produce a self-propelling feedback cycle. As noted earlier, technical innovation (the introduction of the steamship, e.g., or the Internet) sometimes generates new social patterns and forms of social organization, and technical acceleration is often inextricably tied to the acceleration of social change. Increased rates of technical change, for example, are related to heightened rates of transformation in workplace life and occupational patterns. In turn, the acceleration of social change is wedded to the acceleration of the pace of everyday life. Given the fast pace of basic social change, the "lessons" of earlier experience now tend to become obsolescent at a relatively rapid rate, and practical or normative orientation based on past experience suffers from a declining half-life. The present-day obsession with "moving forward" because "standing still" really means "falling behind" is much more than an idiosyncratic psychological pathology. On the contrary, it represents an understandable, though by no means psychologically or physically costless, reaction to a society subject to incessant change. But how might we best deal with the troubling specter of falling behind? First, by filling up our time with as many activities as we possibly can, since a social environment characterized by permanent change means that it tends to become ever more difficult to predict ahead of time which options are most likely to prove advantageous or useful. Second, by pursuing or at least being receptive to new forms of technical acceleration (and other forms of temporally efficient activity), since timesaving technology would seem to provide the most immediate way to accelerate basic social processes and thereby successfully "catch up" with fast-paced change. The paradox, however, is that new varieties of technological acceleration not only are destined to generate subsequent forms of accelerated social change and a speed-up in the pace of life, but they also ultimately produce a renewed sense of "lagging behind," thereby completing the feedback cycle. In this way the three basic types of acceleration can be interpreted as composing interconnected components of a self-propelling mechanism subject to its own relatively autonomous logic.[69]

Nonetheless, this feedback cycle only operates in the context of broader institutional mechanisms that help set it into motion in the first place. Alongside modern capitalism, a major structural source of acceleration is eminently political in character.[70] The modern nation-state triumphed over an array of competing modes of political organization (empires, city-states, loose networks of city-states) in part because of its superior manipulation of speed. The competition for control over territory and population so pivotal to political success in a dangerous international environment has long constituted a major source of social acceleration. High-speed technologies and forms of social organization make up indispensable tools in the battle for territory and population. The continued operation of many core features of the modern Westphalian system of states means that interstate competition and power rivalry today remain crucial components of political life: in a political universe consisting of territorially distinct sovereign states, where differences with rival sovereign states are ultimately settled by force, states are still forced to develop high-speed technologies and organizational forms in order to augment their coercive capacities.[71] States that fail to make effective use of the potential military and strategic advantages derived from the successful harnessing of speed face the specter of conquest or even elimination.

In the Westphalian system states "must be, and usually are, concerned about their security from being attacked, subjected, dominated, or annihilated . . . Striving to attain security from such attack, they are driven to acquire more and more power in order to escape the impact of the power of others. This, in turn, renders the others more insecure and compels them to prepare for the worst. Since none can ever feel entirely secure in such a world of competing units, power competition ensues, and the vicious cycle of security and power accumulation is on."[72] If we keep in mind that the successful manipulation of speed is a crucial source of power, then it becomes easy to see not only why the modern state system motors the process of social acceleration but also why acceleration in political life ultimately tends to breed even more acceleration, thereby confirming the suspicion that social acceleration is driven by a relatively autonomous developmental logic. The acquisition of power necessitates high-speed weapons and social organization, which in turn typically engender yet more insecurity and thus subsequent attempts to accelerate the tools of organized destruction once again. Because no one is ever secure in this scenario, a vicious cycle of power accumulation via social acceleration likely ensues.

A rich body of classical sociological theory, pioneered by Max Weber and Otto Hintze, puissantly underscores the centrality of war making to political development.[73] The most impressive contemporary representative of this tradition, Charles Tilly, has persuasively argued that the nation-state was ultimately able to outrace competing modes of political organization chiefly because of its superiority at waging and preparing for war. Success in a potentially explosive political universe requires the efficacious extraction of the means of war from domestic constituencies (e.g., by means of rationalized taxation and an efficient system of administration) as well as the capable employment of the means of violence against external foes. Not only are the conflict-laden dynamics of war making and its preparation essential for understanding the present-day predominance of the modern nation-state, Tilly argues, but we can also explain variations in European (and, subsequently, global) political development by means of a proper analysis of the different forms of extraction and means of war making pursued by different political entities.[74]

Unfortunately, Tilly and others working in this tradition tend to neglect the crucial temporal preconditions of war making and its preparation.[75] The modern nation-state's military and administrative prowess has repeatedly gained from the introduction of ever more mobile and rapid-fire forms of military organization and mass destruction. These include high-speed weapons (e.g., cruise missiles that reach their targets in a few moments), the accelerated pace of innovation in military technology (which seems to have become permanent in the twentieth century), and high-speed forms of military organization (such as the introduction of the systematic drill in the seventeenth century, which meant that the soldier's "every movement attained a new level of exactitude and speed").[76] Military rivalry based on interstate competition clearly spawns technical acceleration (e.g., new high-speed technologies developed in the context of war preparations), but it is also easy to grasp its ties to both the acceleration of social change and the acceleration of everyday life. Just to mention one familiar contemporary example: the Internet has its immediate origins in the fierce arms race between the United States and Soviet Union, but it now contributes to innumerable facets of social acceleration in part because of the significant economic and commercial roles it has come to play.

Virilio's aphoristic observation that "speed is violence" undoubtedly obscures the complexity of the relationship between social acceleration and the state's coercive capacities.[77] Nonetheless, Virilio is right to emphasize the inordinate role that the capacity for rapid attack and reaction and high-speed weapons plays in modern warfare. A driving force in modernity behind technological innovation—and technical acceleration—has undoubtedly been the power interests of political and military leaders intent on augmenting their position vis-à-vis restive groups at home as well as competing political units. To be sure, conservative-minded political and military leaders have oftentimes resisted the introduction of technical innovations that accelerated the pace of destruction, just as overly traditionalistic capitalists have been hesitant to undertake required innovations for the sake of accelerating production. Yet history is filled with examples of armies and states that were brutally punished for failing to keep up with novel forms of high-speed military organization or technology.[78] Indeed, in some respects the stakes in interstate competition may be higher than in the economic rivalry that fuels social acceleration under the auspices of capitalist production. Whereas many unsuccessful entrepreneurs were simply forced to join the ranks of the middle or working classes, political and military leaders unable to ward off foreign attack have often faced the specter of imprisonment or worse.

Many of the most important sites of social acceleration that predate industrial capitalism—for example, early modern improvements in transportation, shipping, and roads—are directly linked to the power interests of modernizing state elites faced with the ominous specter of destructive foreign wars. Rational forms of administration and taxation also make up crucial manifestations of social acceleration, and, to the extent that the conflict-ridden imperatives of interstate competition helped initiate modern bureaucracy, the modern state system constitutes a crucial source of social acceleration in this respect as well. For example, in conventional (e.g., Weberian) models of rational bureaucracy, decision making is pictured as based on top-down commands or directives. Administrators are not required to undertake a demanding process of time-consuming deliberative give-and-take, in which a multiplicity of arguments and competing interests are considered, and all affected viewpoints receive a fair hearing. In the classical model administrative activity is thus an efficient timesaving instrument because it minimizes the need for time-consuming deliberation during the implementation of policy. Administrative officials need not engage in ambitious debate or worry about reaching an agreement about the aims of policy, since others have already done so for them. In Weber's account they ideally do nothing more than apply standing general rules and, like "automatons," properly "spill forth the verdict" on any particular issue at hand "with the reasons, read mechanically from codified paragraphs."[79] Modern rational administration potentially represents a contribution to rapid-fire state action no less than the high-speed forms of violence so often sought by military elites.

Modern state competition obviously constitutes a relatively long-term source of social acceleration. Yet some contemporary theorists argue that in this sphere of human endeavor, as in capitalist production, acceleration has been particularly furious in recent decades.[80] The suspicion that social acceleration takes the form of a feedback cycle—with high-speed technology breeding ever more rapid-fire social activity—provides some initial support for this claim: if we are correct to postulate that speed inevitably breeds the need for more speed, then it would make sense that modern society tends to experience ever more intense forms of social acceleration.[81] In any event there can be little question that many recent technological developments responsible for novel forms of instantaneousness and simultaneity have been motored by military rivalry rather than commercial competition. The most traumatic experiences in which the compression of space by means of speed has become especially vivid—German *Luftwaffe* bombings in London in World War II or the First Gulf War, in which millions "tuned in" to watch Allied "smart bombs" do their dirty work—have been essentially military in nature as well. The most alarming manifestations of social acceleration also fall under this rubric. During the Cuban missile crisis both sides had approximately fifteen minutes warning time for nuclear war; a mere decade later the normal warning time was down to several minutes.[82] Just a few years ago major newspapers reported that in 1983 the Soviet early warning system falsely reported an American nuclear attack; the Soviets assumed that they only had twenty minutes to respond. Fortunately, Soviet commanders had sense enough to ignore the information provided to them by their military satellites.[83] In the context of hectic U.S. preparations for a second war against Iraq in 2003, the *New York Times* reported that a "quick tempo can be seen across the military industrial complex. Faster-moving infantry, smarter bombs, newer satellites, pilotless vehicles—are all being propelled by a wartime sense of urgency in what is sure to be a costly quest for speed."[84]

This facet of social acceleration immediately raises tough questions for liberal democracy. What is the proper role of elected deliberative legislatures when fundamental matters of life or death may need to be decided in a few minutes? Indeed, when the "constant progress of rapidity" within weapons technology "threatens from one day to the next to reduce the warning time for

nuclear war *to less than one fatal minute,"* what room is there for any meaningful human reflection and deliberation, let alone the broad public debate and
exchange favored by liberal democratic ideals of decision making, in the face of
sudden military threats?[85] It should come as no surprise that many of the most
fateful foreign policy decisions in the contemporary world—for example, John
F. Kennedy's response to the Cuban missile crisis—have often been made with
little public or even legislative impact and that foreign policy decision making
has regularly fallen into the hands of a narrow set of political elites. Too often,
liberal democracy appears to have been outpaced by the structural dynamics of
a state system that privileges high-speed action.

With similar worries in mind, a Canadian theorist of international relations, Ronald Diebert, recently suggested that the present-day obsession with
velocity means that we now find ourselves subject to a perilous "empire of
speed" which is transforming conventional forms of power and authority and
thereby undermining possibilities for human autonomy.[86]

Speed and Western Modernity

Although substantial work still needs to be done in formulating an adequate
theoretical and empirical account of social acceleration, there are good reasons
why contemporary social theorists from so many different intellectual camps
have chosen to focus on the accelerated tempo of social activity in order to
make sense of both present-day society and modernity as a whole. Discussions
of social acceleration need not succumb, however, to vague speculation or
categorical mushiness. Acceleration can be fruitfully studied by grouping it
into three main types: technical acceleration, the acceleration of social change,
the acceleration of the pace of everyday life. Although social acceleration
possesses a self-propelling logic of its own, it ultimately can only be understood in reference to core institutional features of modern society, the capitalist economy and competitive state system, which have functioned as major
driving forces behind it. In light of the central role that capitalism and the
competitive state system have played in shaping so many aspects of modern
social existence, it should come as no surprise that their high-speed temporalities generally seem predominant as well. A plurality of social temporalities probably continues to exist in contemporary society, but in this
pluralist heaven those who move most quickly enjoy God's favor and thus
determine the pace of most heavenly activity.

The reason Western consciousness has been preoccupied with the phenomenon of social speed is that Western modernity has probably been the main site and birthplace of social acceleration. Of course, non-Western societies have also experienced social acceleration. Yet it was in the West that modern capitalism and the modern state system first made their appearance, releasing an intense process of social acceleration unparalleled in human history before spreading across the globe and thereby gaining a universal significance they previously lacked. Along with many other highly ambivalent achievements of Western modernity, social acceleration constitutes an import to parts of the world which, fittingly, have long been madly rushing to "catch up" to the West.[87] The fact that many of them have already outraced the Western powers lends support to the view that social acceleration represents a self-driven feedback cycle from which an easy escape seems unlikely.[88] Once the genie of speed escapes from the bottle, it becomes unclear how we might ever recapture it, and its presence is now felt as deeply in Tokyo and Hong Kong as in New York and London.

If we can assume that it is more than the usual ethnocentrism to underscore the Western roots of the intense social acceleration that now envelops a large portion of humanity, it also seems appropriate to conclude the discussion with a brief reminder of one of the main intellectual concerns of modern European social theory. Classical social theorists were fascinated with the task of uncovering the cultural and intellectual origins of what appeared to them to be distinctly Western social practices and institutions. So, what cultural traditions and ideals helped pave the way for the process of social acceleration that represents such a striking feature of Western modernity? A number of candidates come to mind. One could easily reinterpret Weber's famous analysis of the religious origins of modern capitalism in light of the analysis of social acceleration provided here: Benjamin Franklin's encapsulation of the spirit of capitalism, "time is money," seems to provide an obvious forerunner to the obsession with temporal efficiency which lies beyond the "continual whirl" of our high-speed society.[89] Modern individualism, whose cultural and ideological roots are probably more multifaceted than Weber occasionally acknowledged, offers a ready cultural basis for the imperatives of a high-speed society. Modern individualism has emphasized the intuition that each one of us possesses the potential to pursue a distinct and original life, a special way of being human which requires us to question preexisting customs or traditions and undertake novel and original action.[90] This emphasis on novelty and originality seems only a short step away from some of the most familiar manifestations of social acceleration: the preference for incessant scientific and technical innovation, for example, or the relative willingness in modernity to experiment with new forms of social organization. If we recall that modern individualism has also included an influential strand according to which a rich and fulfilled life, in which each of us should enjoy a rich variety of activities and experiences, represents the good life, it is easy to see why the cultural terrain of Western modernity provided the requisite motivational and intellectual resources for social acceleration.[91] How better to live the rich and fulfilled life than by loading our calendars with as many activities and experiences as we possibly can and thus doing so in as temporally efficient a manner as possible?

The fact that so many of us now feel rushed and tired by day's end merely reminds us that here, as in so many other arenas of modernity, the highest of cultural ideals helped pave the way for institutional mechanisms having consequences dramatically different from those our historical predecessors had in mind.

CHAPTER TWO

Liberal Democracy's Time

Assumptions about temporality permeate traditional liberal democratic political theory: liberal democracy rests on a temporal separation of powers according to which distinct (legislative, executive, and judicial) functions of government presuppose different temporal horizons. Social acceleration poses fundamental challenges to the temporal fundaments of the separation of powers, potentially disfiguring the original vision of a system of government according to which core decision-making activities should be left in the hands of a representative legislature, whereas the executive and judiciary should only possess narrowly circumscribed opportunities for creative activity. High-speed society tends to favor high-speed political institutions, and traditional liberal democratic assumptions about temporality unwittingly aggrandize executive power and weaken broad-based popular legislatures. Albeit paradoxically, the traditional liberal democratic temporal separation of powers potentially generates antiliberal and antidemocratic results—in particular, the rise of executive discretion and decay of parliamentary legality—amid the intensified tempo of modern social and economic existence.

The Temporal Separation of Powers

Temporal assumptions infuse classical conceptions of liberal democracy. Although scholarship tends to neglect these presuppositions, they are crucial for understanding how our historical predecessors envisioned the proper operations of liberal democracy. Without suitable attention to them, we simply cannot understand the origins of modern liberal democracy.

Perhaps no feature of classical liberal democracy is more fundamental than its commitment to the idea of a separation of powers. At least since Montesquieu, liberal democratic political thought has relied on distinguishing between legislative, executive, and judicial forms of power. Liberal democrats have accepted the notion that legislation refers to the making of new laws, execution means putting those laws into effect, and judicial power entails declaring what the law is in the case of controversies. This familiar tripartite division can be interpreted as resting on three basic ideas. First, it implies the possibility of restraining the exercise of political power by splitting government up into distinct institutional branches and then "giving to those who administer each department the necessary constitutional means and personal motives to resist encroachments of the others."[1] By dividing the exercise of power and guaranteeing that no single institution dominates the operations of government, the impressive power instruments of the modern Leviathan can be internally limited and checked. Closely tied to this first element of the separation of powers is the familiar emphasis in traditional liberal democratic thought on the need for a concomitant separation of persons. When state power is placed in the hands of distinct actors with different institutional interests, training, and professional background, ambition is "made to counteract ambition," and potentially troublesome concentrations of power in the hands of narrow political cliques can be warded off.[2] Finally, the idea of a separation of powers typically presumes a distinction between fundamental governmental functions or operations, whereby legislation, execution, and adjudication are conceived as composing dissimilar activities in possession of distinct internal logics. Because of functional differences between them, an influential strand in the liberal democratic tradition underscores the virtues of locating them in separate institutional sites. Because the legislature and executive are concerned with the divergent undertakings of deliberation (*deliberare*) and action (*agere*), for example, it seems sensible to create an institutional division of labor between them while simultaneously entrusting them to different actors.[3]

Why was the separation of powers so vital to the intellectual architects of modern liberal democracy? According to the traditional view, the separation of powers alone provides for the possibility of realizing an identifiably liberal democratic vision of freedom. As Montesquieu famously observed, liberty is found "only where there is no abuse of power," which requires that in the operations of government "power should be a check to power."[4] Only then can legal security, or what *The Spirit of the Laws* aptly describes as "tranquility of mind arising from the opinion that each person has of his safety," gain effective protection.[5] "There would be the end of everything, were the same man or the same body, whether of the nobles or of the people, to exercise those three powers, that of enacting laws, that of executing the public resolutions, and of trying the causes of individuals."[6] Alongside this commitment to a characteristically liberal quest to limit state power and thereby ensure legal security to the individual, the ideal of the separation of powers can also be plausibly interpreted as contributing to the rise of modern democracy. The modern view of self-legislation as constitutive of political freedom was probably implicit in the idea, widely endorsed even by early modern advocates of the separation of powers otherwise hostile to democracy, that representative legislatures rightly constitute the main site for lawmaking.[7] The insistence on a clear delineation of legislative rule making from executive or judicial application of the law was a necessary institutional presupposition of the predominance soon accorded elected representative legislatures within liberal democracy.[8] For many of the intellectual forerunners to liberal democracy, legislation undertaken by elected representatives offered an effective realization of the (implicitly democratic) intuition that the legitimacy of legislation requires the free and universal consent of the governed.

To be sure, idealized portrayals of the classical conception of the separation of powers are always potentially misleading: no real-life system has ever successfully instantiated a "pure" version of the separation of powers. The presidential veto in the United States, for example, represents an obvious deviation from the core notion that lawmaking should be placed in the hands of representative assemblies. The impressive power now possessed by some constitutional courts similarly underscores the intellectual dangers of relying too heavily on an idealized interpretation of the separation of powers.[9] Nonetheless, the history of modern liberal democracy can be plausibly interpreted as constituting a series of experiments with different possible interpretations of the proper relationship between these three elements of state power. Even though the deceptively simple tripartite structure of the doctrine risks masking the vastly more complex institutional outcomes engendered by it, it remains essential for understanding liberal democracy. Every contemporary version of liberal democracy ultimately builds on the "celebrated theory" of the separation of powers as "expounded by Locke and more especially Montesquieu," and it arguably remains indispensable to a proper analysis of both its parliamentary and presidential progeny.[10]

The traditional liberal democratic separation of powers also includes a decisive temporal subtext: legislation is prospective, or future oriented; judicial activity is fundamentally retrospective, or past oriented; and the executive is contemporaneous, or present oriented in its fundamental orientation.[11] The separation of powers exhibits a temporal division of labor no less than it does a quest to divide the modern state into distinct institutional units, bodies of personnel, and functional activities for the sake of rationalizing the exercise of political power. Any account of its temporal qualities should acknowledge the dangers of an overly idealized depiction of its operations as well, since its distinct temporal functions have overlapped in "real-life" liberal democracy no less than other facets of legislative, executive, and judicial authority. By understanding liberal democracy's fundamental temporal division of labor, however, we not only can place many of its familiar facets in a fresh light, but we can also begin to understand the challenges posed by social acceleration to traditional interpretations of its proper operations.

Legislation is future oriented because it requires state actors to engage in a forward-looking process of trying effectively to plan or coordinate future state activities and, albeit to a more limited extent, future social trends.[12] In this vein John Locke's *Second Treatise* describes the proper tasks of prospective legislators as aspiring to "foresee, and so by laws to provide for, all accidents and necessities that may concern the public."[13] Clear, prospective, general statutes are thus to provide determinative guidelines for future state action. Although always necessarily based on the past and present experiences of those who promulgate them, statutes are supposed to provide future state actors (e.g., judges and administrators) with clear direction about the proper scope of their undertakings. In effect, present lawmakers aim to predetermine subsequent state activity, and they are asked to do so with as much foresight as they can realistically muster. The future-oriented character of legislation also means, however, that lawmakers are inevitably forced to make predictions about the likely course of a potentially significant array of succeeding social trends. If a statute concerning a particular type of economic endeavor is to remain useful down the road and not just in the immediate future, for example, legislators must foresee, to the greatest extent possible, future "necessities" in the relevant area of the economy.

Of course, legislators often fail to perform this task effectively. Statutes may turn out to be irrelevant or even obstructive to potentially desirable future trends; the history of modern legislation is filled with countless examples of mediocre lawmaking. One reason for this common problem is precisely the fact that effective legislation requires impressive capacities of foresight: prospective legislation ideally demands of lawmakers that they do nothing less than look into a crystal ball in order to glean reliable predictions about future events. As long as laissez-faire ideology limits government's activities, the predictive tasks at hand remain relatively limited in scope, though by no means insignificant; even laissez-faire governments waged wars, colonized distant lands, and provided a basic legal framework for domestic social and economic development. A minimal state committed to nothing more than providing for the common defense and supplying basic public services (e.g., building roads and canals) still requires of legislators that they try to forecast a complex array of future trends: is economic development most likely to be buttressed by building a road between City A and City B or, instead, City C? Which military innovations seem destined to dominate war making in the future and thus constitute a legitimate public investment?

However difficult to achieve, prospective statutory rule making also helps generate legal security by providing fair warning about the most likely path of future state activity. The liberal democratic quest for legal security builds directly on the idea of future-oriented legislation. Since Locke, the ideal of the rule of law has entailed a preference for legislation that is not only supposed to be prospective but relatively stable as well, because only a relatively unchanging body of legal norms is thought to be capable of preserving sufficient legal security and predictability. The intimate connection between the future-oriented temporal horizons of legislation and legal stability is captured nicely by legal theorist Richard Fallon, who notes that "law should be stable in order to facilitate planning and coordinated action over time."[14] Only a statute that successfully predicts future trends is likely to remain relevant for a lengthy period of time and thus contribute to legal stability; only relatively unchanging or stable norms possess a reasonable chance of allowing individuals subsequently to plan and coordinate their activities with some chance of success. From one perspective a stable statute is nothing more than a successful interpretation, and corresponding codification, of future public necessities by present-day lawmakers. By requiring lawmakers to determine ahead of time how and when they will act (as specified in a farsighted statute), competent prospective legislation helps ensure that nonstate actors operate in a relatively stable and predictable legal environment and thus can navigate future undertakings with some degree of confidence.

This future-oriented notion of legislation rests, however, on a fundamental paradox. Although demanding of lawmakers that they coordinate future state activities and calling for meaningful predictive talents, it simultaneously rests on an interpretation of the future as distinguished by fundamentally open-ended temporal horizons. Stability within the law can never be perfect; even the best laws may require future modification.

Recall that the liberal democratic idea of legislation builds on a radical break with older notions of political decision making, according to which lawmaking bodies merely applied pre-given customary law, typically conceived in terms of an eternal "good old law" that was fundamentally static and unchanging in nature.[15] In this older model legislation was past oriented to the extent that it ideally represented a mere application of past legal practices. Familiarity might lead us to miss the radical character of the modern notion of statutory legislation as a creative process of future-oriented activity, in which state actors engage in self-consciously innovative efforts to predict the exigencies of the future. In part the genius of this evolutionary development lies in its implicit acknowledgment of the social and economic dynamism of modern society. The insight that the future represents a potential break with the past probably only became plausible in the context of a historical setting subject to relatively significant forms of social and economic change.

In the traditionalistic conception of legislation dominant in the West for centuries, adaptability to change was only allowed by political institutions to the extent that decision making could be packaged as a plausible application or restoration of customary law. This emphasis in the traditionalist notion on legislative fidelity to unchanging or absolute norms meshes poorly with legislative creativity and innovation, however, and it clearly limits the range of acceptable political decisions. In contrast, the future-oriented character of the modern idea of legislation sets lawmakers free to undertake novel forms of state activity, in part by acknowledging that the future is more than a mere repetition of the past: the modern conception of legislation gives state actors a free rein to coordinate future trends because it understands that the future may pose legislative challenges that no longer can be tackled by appeal to customary legal ideas derived from an "immemorial past" seen as constituting the main fount of political wisdom.[16] Yet it simultaneously leaves lawmakers with the unenviable task of undertaking to foresee a future whose potential novelty represents a core presupposition of the creative legislative authority they now possess. Legislators are asked to make use of creative power for the sake of minimizing future uncertainty and unpredictability in political and social affairs, even though the relatively freewheeling legislative power now wielded by them is predicated on an implicit acceptance of the difficulty of using past experience in order to predict the future. The cognitive burdens placed by traditional liberal democratic thinking on legislators are weighty: we demand of them that they try to foresee the future, but we only given them the requisite authority to do so with the understanding that the most useful guide humans possess for predicting the future, past and present experience, easily fails us.

No easy resolution to this paradox is available at either the level of theory or practice. Nonetheless, it is revealing that one of the traditional justifications of majority decision making at least takes note of the paradox. The liberal democratic temporal division of labor asks of legislators that they coordinate the future. If future generations are to enjoy the same privilege, the possibility of correcting or reversing present majority decisions must be available to them as well. Thus, majority rule making is only legitimate if present minorities possess a reasonable chance to make up part of a future majority. Why should a political participant accept the principle of majority rule if she were destined to remain part of a permanent minority? As Elaine Spitz has noted, majority rule presupposes the possibility of subsequent revisions of present-day majority decisions. In contrast, if the proposals of a contemporary majority can be rendered permanent, they threaten to undermine the normative presuppositions of majority rule: "Plans for the future must provide for choice. No blueprint can be so comprehensive and so financed or organized that those who inherit it have no viable options about its retention. A chance to revise what has been done is essential."[17] Otherwise, majority rule risks becoming majority tyranny, and there is no longer sound reason for a prospective minority to assent to majority decision making. When understood in this light, we can see how majority rule represents one potential institutional device for negotiating the congenital tensions of modern prospective legislation. Present legislative majorities are asked to coordinate the future. Yet they do so with the knowledge that the future nonetheless remains open-ended and that their capacity to offer detailed plans for the future is necessarily limited. Legitimate majority rule making provides for future-oriented legislation while simultaneously presuming that rules promulgated in the present may have to be revisited in the future.

The familiar differentiation between statutory and constitutional lawmaking also represents an implicit effort to grapple with the paradox of trying to foresee the future while concurrently recognizing the improbability of producing all-encompassing blueprints for it. Whereas traditional liberal thinkers occasionally concede the limited predictive capacities of normal legislatures, they are more hesitant to do so in the sphere of constitutional lawmaking, thereby tacitly conceding that some forms of prospective legislation may be more susceptible to change and flux than others. Locke, for example, suggests that normal acts of the legislature should become "null and void" after one hundred years, while the "fundamental constitutions" he proposed for colonial Carolina not only lack amendment procedures but also were to "remain the sacred and unalterable form and rule of government of Carolina forever."[18] Both statutory and constitutional law should strive for long-term stability; constitutional law possesses a better chance to do so. Of course, advocates of liberal democracy quickly modified this deeply static view of constitutionalism, as the American Revolution successfully introduced the noteworthy innovation of constitutional amendment procedures.[19] Nonetheless, Locke's obsession with stability in constitutional law continues to haunt contemporary constitutionalism: the inordinately complex and demanding amendment rules of Articles 5 of the U.S. Constitution render fundamental political change via constitutional amendment exceedingly difficult in the United States.[20]

As an effort to grapple with the tension-ridden character of prospective legislation, the differentiation between statutory and constitutional law generates as many dilemmas as it successfully resolves. Written constitutions represent an especially demanding type of prospective legislation. Like legislators promulgating statutes, constitution makers are supposed to foresee future trends for the sake of effectively funneling the operations of state authority. In some contrast to acts of regular legislation, traditional liberal democratic theory typically suggests that they should aspire to do so for "an indefinite but presumably long future."[21] Statutes may fall into disuse or require modification, whereas constitutions should last forever—or at least as long into the future as mortal beings are able to conceive. Constitutional lawmaking thus requires potentially awesome foresight and powers of prediction, since we call on constitutional lawmakers to do nothing less than achieve stable and reliable "rules of the game" for an innumerable number of future settings likely to be radically different from those in which the constitution was first promulgated. The main normative and political reasons behind the traditional emphasis on the unchanging character of constitutional law seem persuasive enough. How better to avoid a crude partisan instrumentalization of the basic political rules of the game while simultaneously ensuring far-reaching legal stability? Nonetheless, attributing to constitutional lawmakers the predictive skills called for by the promulgation of constitutions for "an indefinite but presumably long future" rests uneasily alongside the modern acceptance of the necessity of creative lawmaking as the best way to deal with potential novelty of the future.

Beside this future-focused conception of legislation, the intellectual forerunners to modern liberal democracy articulated a complementary temporal model of the judiciary as retrospective, or past oriented. In the conventional liberal democratic view of the judiciary widely endorsed well into the early twentieth century, judges were to engage chiefly in "retroactively oriented reasoning," and their activity was to be characterized by a "marked orientation to the past," since they would ideally be concerned exclusively with the ascertainment of past events and the relationship of those events to legal precedents or statutory rules that already have been declared valid.[22] Until recently, even common lawyers typically downplayed the creative and thereby future-oriented character of their rulings, insisting that past precedents provided the main justification for their actions. In the simplest terms: judges should follow standing (or past) rules or precedents, simply determining whether some more recent (but, of course, also past) activity accords with them. Whereas legislators are asked to predict and foresee future developments, judges engage in a distinct form of historical, or past-oriented, excavation whose boundaries are determined by pre-given legal materials and practices. Notwithstanding the fundamental temporal differences between legislation and adjudication, proper retrospective adjudication, like effective prospective legislation, makes an indispensable contribution to legal security and stability. Since judges are chiefly concerned with applying past political and legal accomplishments, embodied in standing legal materials, to more recent (but nonetheless past) developments, they help ensure legal continuity with the past and thus a stable and secure legal environment. However arduous, judicial activity lacks the fundamentally creative merits of prospective legislation. Because it chiefly concerns settled legal materials stemming from political and legal struggles that have come (albeit perhaps only provisionally) to a conclusion, the traditional view infers that retrospective judicial activity, when properly practiced, would tend to be less partisan or controversial than future-oriented legislation, in which legislators are asked to cooperate in shaping a hitherto undisclosed future that citizens will soon inhabit.

The profound hostility to judicial discretion which characterizes the mainstream of the liberal legal tradition from John Locke to Jeremy Bentham rests on myriad historical and philosophical sources.[23] Yet one significant intellectual basis is arguably the intuition that the judiciary is best able to contribute to legal stability and security by leaving the creative, future-oriented tasks of state activity in the hands of elected representatives, chosen by means of relatively frequent periodic elections. What better way to guarantee the judicial pursuit of continuity with the legal past than by removing future-oriented legislative tasks from the auspices of the courts while simultaneously placing the most creative and, typically, most controversial and immediately "partisan" element of decision making, prospective legislation, in the hands of an elected legislature subject to immediate political pressures? Despite its widely noted failings as a realistic description of judicial activity, the classical view of the separation of power between legislatures and courts presumes the plausible intuition that future-oriented state activities should be institutionally separate from those that are past oriented. When unelected and oftentimes unrepresentative expert jurists are allowed to engage in the creative activity of trying to coordinate future state activities, an obvious danger appears: judges may find themselves forced to mask innovative (legislative) activity in tortured interpretations of legal precedent or standing rules.[24] Future-oriented promulgation is then disingenuously allowed to masquerade as "mere" retrospective application of standing law. From the standpoint of classical liberalism it thus made eminent normative and institutional sense to distinguish clearly between judicial and legislative activity while minimizing the potentially future-oriented and creative (as well as potentially controversial) facets of judicial decision making. Decent government needs both future-oriented (innovative) legislation and a modicum of legal continuity secured by a (past-oriented) judiciary. Yet, because the different temporalities of these two forms of state activity call for corresponding differences in institutional practice, orientation, and training, we need to insist on an identifiable separation between them. Successful innovative or creative (future-oriented) politicians and competent (past-oriented) jurists who follow legal precedent or the "letter of the law" are likely to represent two very different decision-making creatures; for this reason it also makes sense to situate future-oriented legislative and past-oriented judicial personnel in distinct institutional sites.

Legislators promulgate norms for the sake of grappling with an uncertain future; judicial actors contribute to legal continuity by applying precedent and settling conflicts on the basis of previous legislative decisions; the executive enforces or puts law into effect in the here and now. Although the history of liberal democratic ideas about executive power is complex and multifaceted, the present-oriented, or contemporaneous, temporal contours of modern executive power make up a vital strand of that tradition. Citizens may violate standing laws, in which case present action or immediate "execution" is called for (e.g., an arrest by a police officer). Similarly, foreign foes may suddenly pose a life-or-death challenge to the political community and the legal system in its entirety, and thus prompt executive action is required in response as well. Montesquieu's seemingly odd observation that "the executive power is generally employed in momentary operations" probably has to be interpreted in light of these oftentimes unstated temporal presuppositions.[25] The executive typically displays its distinctive temporal attributes in action designed to counteract a present threat, and its operations are "momentary" in the sense that it swings into motion in the face of concrete or immediate dangers that appear during a contemporary temporal conjuncture or moment.

Of course, the duration of executive activity is likely to be determined by the length of time necessary to subvert the immediate threat at hand; the difficulty of counteracting such a threat often means that executive action is more than short-term, or momentary, in duration. In addition, a competent executive obviously worries about how best to ward off foreign dangers and guarantee the preservation of domestic order in the future as well as the present.[26] Thus, the executive's fundamental task of counteracting dangers to legality not only requires immediate operations potentially extending for a lengthy period of time but also a future-oriented approach to prospective dangers which might seem to blur the temporal divide between legislative and executive power. Indeed, in presidentialist variants of liberal democracy in which the executive possesses significant independent legislative authority, this temporal boundary is undoubtedly obscured to a greater degree than in its parliamentary rivals. According to some versions of early liberalism, however, the future-oriented core of legislative activity implies that elected representatives are nonetheless institutionally best suited to deliberate about and determine the most appropriate course of state activity in the face of potential future threats. In this by no means insignificant strand of traditional argumentation, executive action should typically be momentary not only because it takes place in the present instant but also insofar as its scope and duration might be dramatically curtailed, particularly in comparison to the practices of "reason of state" which early modern liberalism criticized. If legislators prove competent at foreseeing future needs, executive action typically should not entail anything more than brief and clearly circumscribed acts of implementation and enforcement. From this traditional perspective Montesquieu's apparent conflation of *immediacy* with *momentary* represents an apt expression of why the contemporaneous nature of the executive is linked intimately to a broader quest to limit the scope of executive power altogether.[27]

Other voices in the liberal tradition have expressed more skepticism about the possibility of radically minimizing the scope and duration of executive activity. This skepticism occasionally results from understandable doubts about the capacity of representative legislatures to demonstrate the impressive predictive capacities that the modern concept of prospective legislation requires. Along these lines Locke conceives of legislative power as future oriented in the sense that laws are supposed to foresee future necessities. As noted earlier, law is prospective because only rules announced beforehand can provide legal security but also because legislation in its very nature is concerned with the task of predicting and coordinating future needs.[28] The "exigencies of the times" are "impossible to foresee" with perfection, and thus legislative power is inherently limited.[29] Prospective legislation suffers from a temporal Achilles' heel—namely, the improbability of legislatures consistently promulgating sensible statutes for the future as well as the present. According to Locke's *Second Treatise,* the most reasonable answer to the legislative power's tendency to commit mistakes in predicting the future is to place "power in the hands of the prince to provide for the public good, in such cases, which depending on unforeseen and uncertain occurrences, certain and unalterable laws could not safely direct."[30] The executive's contemporaneous orientation leaves it best equipped to tackle unforeseen circumstances that no legislator could have successfully predicted and whose novelty necessarily makes them an unlikely object of successful (past-oriented) adjudication. The necessity of executive prerogative to act beyond and even against the law thus derives not merely from the need to acknowledge the limitations of inflexible and rigid legislative statutes but from an even more fundamental need to make sure that the present is free from an unduly slavish dependence on the dictates of the past. The rigidity of law is merely a manifestation of the domination of the present by the past. Although future-oriented, legislative activity inevitably generates rules that soon represent (past) predictions about the present and future. Because "things of this world are in so constant a flux, that nothing remains in the same state," however, Locke believes that we need to envision institutional devices capable of correcting for our limited ability to predict the future.[31] Given that the legislature "is usually too numerous, and too slow," only the present-oriented executive is likely to prove able effectively to break with the letter of the law for the sake of rapidly adjusting legislative authority in accordance with immediate or present political needs.[32]

The temporal division of labor implicit in the liberal democratic separation of powers sheds light on many other familiar institutional ideals as well. Since Locke and Montesquieu, liberal political thought has relied on a series of striking contrasts between legislative and executive activity. Legislative politics is typically conceived as resting on a process of freewheeling deliberation involving a rich sample of public opinion, and liberal thinkers have repeatedly emphasized the necessarily measured and unhurried prerequisites of a legitimate process of reasonable debate in which participants possess a fair chance to express distinct political views and defend a multiplicity of interests. Deliberation allows legislators to determine which interests are worthy of government endorsement in the first place. It also serves as a cognitive test of the reasonableness and well-considered character of proposed legislation: only deliberative legislation can approximate the core liberal democratic intuition that lawmaking rests on the free and equal consent of the governed.[33] In light of the temporal presuppositions of prospective legislation described earlier, the orthodox emphasis on the deliberative and potentially rational character of representative legislatures seems especially desirable. The legislature's responsibility to coordinate and predict the future, especially when forced to concede its basically open-ended character, calls for the mobilization of an impressive arsenal of cognitive tools. In addition, the fact that legislatures undertake the most creative and potentially contentious element of state power—namely, the task of formulating policies for the future—implies that they should be subject to especially wide-ranging political debate and contestation. Notwithstanding Locke's anxieties about the temporal limitations of legislative power, many liberal thinkers thus argue convincingly that only ambitious deliberative exchange in broadly based political bodies, involving the representation of a rich diversity of interests and ideas, possesses a reasonable chance to accomplish the arduous and unavoidably controversial cognitive tasks at hand. Revealingly, even those writers skeptical of popularly elected legislatures, in part because of the alleged irrationality of popular debate, often find themselves forced to describe the relatively slow and deliberate character of legislative debates as constituting one of their virtues: Alexander Hamilton writes in Federalist 70 that the inevitable "differences of opinion" and "jarring of parties" or interests characteristic of legislative politics means that in the legislature "promptitude of decision is oftener an evil than a benefit."[34] Although Hamilton famously believed that the "personal firmness" requisite for competent political leadership was most likely to be found in the executive, even he acknowledged that a time-consuming process of deliberative give-and-take was indispensable if proper circumspection were to be achieved within representative assemblies.[35]

On one level Hamilton and others in the liberal tradition thereby merely underscore the point that debate within any but a tiny group, regardless of its cognitive quality, is destined to be time-consuming solely because of its sequential character. Given that "two speakers at an assembly cannot both be heard by everyone if they try to speak simultaneously," even a relatively unimpressive deliberative exchange in a parliament consisting, for example, of a mere one hundred representatives is likely to seem slow going.[36] On another level liberals typically defend the relatively slow character of legislative exchange as a necessary precondition for ensuring its high quality. In this view the fact that the legislature is "taking its time" provides prima facie evidence that its deliberations are suitably thorough in character and thus of the legitimacy of the legislature's special status as the main site for prospective lawmaking. This temporal assumption expresses the considerable weight placed by Enlightenment liberalism on freewheeling rational deliberation as a source of effective legislation. The Enlightenment faith in the emancipatory potential of human reason played a central role in liberalism's conceptualization of elected legislatures as requiring robust—and necessarily unrushed—rational debate.[37]

The unhurried character of legislative debate is typically contrasted with the executive's capacity for expeditious action. The association of the executive with "dispatch" is virtually universal in modern liberal democratic theory. Harvey C. Mansfield Jr. has tried to trace this view to implicitly Machiavellian features of the modern executive, in accordance with which the suddenness of action is essential if a ruler is to impress his capacities for *virtu* on an intimidated and fundamentally passive populace. In this interpretation the emphasis on executive speed possesses eminently pre-democratic and antiliberal connotations. In fact, liberals have indeed followed Machiavelli, but instead chiefly by endorsing Machiavelli's mundane observation that a unitary executive can act with high-speed *agere* and thus efficiently, whereas large and numerous legislatures often cannot.[38] The fact that the executive consists, most fundamentally, of a single actor, means that it can act quickly; because some facets of political decision making require speed, a swift executive necessarily makes up a core component of any sensible system of political rule. In this vein Montesquieu's famous observation that a plural executive would inevitably undermine one of the chief functions of executive power—namely, its ability to act with dispatch—soon became a dogmatic article of faith among liberals.[39] Those who challenged the notion of a singular and thereby unitary executive— for example, the Anti-Federalists—consistently found themselves relegated to the status of obscure footnotes in the history of liberalism.[40] Although slow-moving deliberation ensures a high measure of reasonableness within government, lawmaking ultimately requires a single actor able to actualize its imperatives in an efficient and timely manner; a plural executive might unduly and inefficiently replicate the (time-consuming) process of debate that already took place within the legislature and thus unnecessarily reduce government's ability to act not only in accordance with the results of reasonable deliberation but effectively as well. In this widely held view representative government requires both reasoned circumspection and expeditiousness. The separation between the legislature and executive in part merely offers a sensible institutional embodiment of the (complementary) division of labor between these two fundamental prerequisites of good government. Just as a proper understanding of the legislature's future-oriented tasks implies the virtues of slow-going, freewheeling deliberation, so too can we grasp the need for a high-speed executive by understanding its contemporaneous temporal orientation. How better to grapple with contemporary or immediate threats to the polity than by means of an executive evincing flexibility and capable of rapid-fire action?

The intimate connection between the unitary executive and speed contains far-reaching implications for determining the proper scope of executive power in the liberal model. Most immediately, it permits us to make sense of the substantial leeway early liberalism tended to grant the executive when, as Locke noted in his famous defense of executive prerogative, "flux" and the constantly changing "exigencies of the times" require an immediate rapid-fire response that large representative assemblies are unlikely to achieve. In Locke's influential account prerogative power to act outside and sometimes even against the law when abnormal or unusual "accidents may happen, wherein a strict and rigid observation of the laws may do harm (as not to pull down an innocent man's house to stop the fire, when the one next to it is burning)," is thus best left in executive hands.[41] Similarly, Locke argues that the executive's foreign policy powers (in his terminology, the "federative" power) cannot "be directed by antecedent, standing, positive laws . . . and so must necessarily be left to the prudence and wisdom of those whose hands it is in, to be managed for the public good." Far-reaching executive discretion is necessitated by the "variation of designs and interests" in foreign affairs, in which the unpredictability and fast-paced character of events require swift and unhindered executive action.[42] War "admits not of plurality of governors," in part because the slow and deliberate character of prospective legislation meshes poorly with the temporal imperatives of a dangerous foreign realm.[43] Prospective legislation is of limited value in the foreign sphere because the fundamental unpredictability of interstate conflict simply contradicts the prospective legislative quest for long-term predictions and plans. Retrospective adjudication is similarly inadequate because of the legally underdeveloped character of the international arena, deriving in part from the unavoidable failure of the legislative power to promulgate statutes for the foreign realm. In contrast, the executive's built-in capacity for speed and rapid-fire action leaves it well equipped to grapple with an ever-changing international environment, where expeditious undertakings in accordance with the present or immediate moment are at a premium.[44]

Yet how, then, can intelligent executive action be ensured beyond the boundaries of standing law? History is filled with the annals of expeditious but irresponsible and adventuresome rulers. Precisely those temporal virtues that render the executive best suited to rapid-fire action in foreign affairs arguably leave it badly adapted to achieving reasonableness and intelligence in decision making. If even multiheaded deliberative legislatures are sometimes overwhelmed by the cognitive demands of lawmaking, how, then, could the single person of the executive ever successfully tackle the complex tasks of foreign policy in a dangerous and variable political universe? Interestingly, the traditional answer to this question includes a decisive temporal component. Although the solitary character of the executive implies that its undertakings potentially lack the breadth and richness of legislative deliberation, the executive should be able to compensate for this weakness by means of gaining substantial experience. For this reason an important strand in traditional liberalism argues for extending the duration of the executive's term of office vis-à-vis the legislature: only a chief executive able to coordinate foreign policy for a relatively lengthy period of time has a reasonable chance of gaining the "personal firmness" requisite to an intelligent use of its temporal capacities for dispatch.[45] When the executive acts unilaterally, its possession of many years can compensate, or so it seems, for the lack of many voices.

The judiciary occupies an uneasy intermediate position in this component of the liberal democratic temporal separation of powers. Liberal theorists quickly grasped that an effective independent judiciary needs potentially time-consuming procedures and formalities, and that delay in the administration of justice often correctly serves "the end that the people may grow calm and give their judgment coolly."[46] Although distinct from the tasks of legislation, retrospective legal reasoning similarly requires thoughtful and temporally demanding deliberation in reference to legal precedents and statutes. If we are to ensure that legal decisions are not based on "false reasonings or the momentary churning of a judge's humors," judicial institutions thus should function to slow down the process of decision making for the sake of heightening its overall reasonableness.[47] Especially in legal systems in which juries possess substantial authority, judicial decision making, unlike executive rule, is also likely to involve more than a single or small group of professional actors. Yet the body of key judicial actors is still likely to be significantly less numerous than representative legislatures, thereby reducing the overall temporal burdens of deliberative sequentiality in comparison to those of large popular assemblies. Furthermore, the general tendency in classical liberal legal thought to subscribe to a simplistic mechanical conception of judicial activity led many theorists to neglect the cognitive—and potentially time-consuming—difficulties of legal interpretation. If the "judiciary is in some measure next to nothing" compared to the legislature and executive and judges are "no more than the mouth that pronounces the law," there is no pressing reason to worry too much that its activities are all that deliberate and thereby slow going.[48] Indeed, if judicial activity represents nothing more than the mechanical activity of pronouncing the law, then it might seem reasonable to expect judges to act in an expeditious manner while nonetheless successfully preserving basic legal protections. Perhaps this is why, in striking contradistinction to its innumerable excursions on executive dispatch and deliberate legislation, references to the temporality of the judiciary are scattered and underdeveloped in Enlightenment political thought. Key theoretical influences on liberal democracy sometimes awkwardly underline the virtues of "promptness" in judicial activity as much as they do delay and caution.[49]

The subtext of a temporal division of power also haunts many other significant features of liberal democracy. For example, the U.S. Federalists asserted that their proposed rendition of the separation of powers would produce an effective and energetic government, in contrast to the division and gridlock forecast by harsh critics of the separation of powers—most prominently, Thomas Hobbes. Interestingly, the Federalist argument derives in part from the extensive authority their proposals bestowed upon the unitary executive, which they envisioned as providing direct institutional expression to the political necessities of high-speed action. In this view the U.S. version of the separation of powers would succeed in enabling rather than disabling decisive state decision making by making sure that possibilities for executive dispatch occupied a prominent place in the overall political scheme.[50] Alternately, bicameralism has been widely interpreted as a tool aimed at decelerating legislative decision making for the sake of heightening its cognitive merits. In this account a selective upper legislative house works to counteract what James Madison described as the potential for "all single and numerous assemblies to yield to the impulse of sudden and violent passions."[51]

The early liberal preoccupation with circumventing irrationality in popular politics exemplified by Madison's defense of the U.S. Senate also meshes with the basic temporal assumptions described earlier. Well into modern times, intellectual forerunners to liberal democracy endorsed the traditional view that meaningful participation and self-government could only be realized on a small scale in part due to the necessities of time-consuming travel and communication in geographically large states. Modern thinkers soon challenged this dogma, however, by arguing that deliberative elected representative institutions might successfully resolve the temporal dilemmas intrinsic to direct popular rule in large and populous states. In Montesquieu's view, for example, the temporal difficulties of popular deliberation in a geographically large state render direct participation there unrealistic, thus necessitating representative government because the "people collectively are extremely unfit" for discussing public affairs, especially "in large states."[52] Elective representative institutions may seem slow going when compared to the unitary executive. Yet they constitute a practical, timesaving institutional device for gaining a sense of the interests and views of the community as a whole in geographically large communities where direct democracy would be impossible in part because of its manifest temporal inefficiency.[53]

In some contrast to Montesquieu, Locke's *Second Treatise* suggests that precisely the temporal inefficiency of mass or popular deliberation represents a possible virtue: in his famous discussion of the "dissolution of government" he argues that the inherent slowness of popular politics is one of the reasons why a tyrannized people is only likely to overthrow its leaders after a "long train of abuses."[54] The reasonableness of popular politics is accentuated by its slow-moving character, and procrastination—so Locke claims—heightens the rationality of mass politics and helps make sure that, when organized political authority fails to perform its appointed tasks, revolutionary popular politics potentially offers a sensible alternative. In Federalist 10 Madison follows Montesquieu by accepting the need for a representative system, in part because he similarly understands the practical and temporal impracticalities of direct democracy in large states. Yet Madison simultaneously reformulates Locke's plausible intuitions about the possibility of a sufficiently slow-paced, deliberate mode of popular politics: the large size of the proposed American republic should help protect it from the familiar pathologies of republican government in part by decelerating the pace of popular political exchange. Small republics allow for rapid communication and thus are subject to the whims of "temporary considerations" inconsistent with the long-term interests of free government, whereas communication "is always checked" in a large republic, thereby reducing the ills of faction. The large size of the American republic potentially contributes to the reasonable character of popular politics. For this reason, Madison concludes, traditional defenses of republican government are badly mistaken in their hostility to geographically large, pluralistic polities.[55]

Temporal Challenges to Liberal Democracy

How is social acceleration likely to impact the temporal separation of powers? At first glance classical liberal democracy would seem well equipped to deal with the challenges of acceleration described in chapter 1. The liberal democratic conception of positive legislation breaks with traditional ideas of a customary "good old law," thereby opening the door to far-reaching legislative creativity, an indispensable prerequisite of political decision making in a social context subject to significant change and novelty. In addition, this conception of legislation acknowledges the open-ended texture of the future, thereby tacitly acknowledging the social and economic dynamism of modernity. The accelerated pace of technological innovation and social change means that the future, to a greater extent than ever before, is destined to look fundamentally different from the past. Nonetheless, traditional liberal democratic theory's answers to social acceleration are ultimately insufficient. Although liberal democracy's intellectual forerunners anticipated the challenges posed by social acceleration, they ultimately failed to presage their full significance. This failing is hardly unexpected in light of the thinking of recent social theorists who have plausibly argued that social acceleration tends to intensify during the course of modernity. Social acceleration was still a relatively underdeveloped process when Locke, Montesquieu, and Madison formulated their paradigmatic theoretical contributions to liberal democracy. Not surprisingly, their institutional responses to it were incomplete as well.

What classical writers failed to foresee is that social acceleration potentially undermines core features of the temporal separation of powers, disfiguring liberal democracy as initially conceived. In particular, social acceleration presents a direct threat to the notion of prospective, or future-oriented, legislation, tending to undermine the paramount position of legislative rule making in the traditional liberal democratic temporal division of labor. As I hope to show here and in succeeding chapters, the ways by which political systems have tackled the imperatives of social acceleration have been complex and even contradictory. Nonetheless, the most likely beneficiary of recent shifts in the temporal horizons of human activity is the unitary executive, whose contemporaneous and high-speed temporal contours appear to leave it especially well suited to decision making in a corresponding high-speed social environment. High-speed society privileges high-speed institutions, and in the liberal democratic worldview it is typically the executive who is viewed as an especially energetic institutional agent. In contrast, deliberative representative legislatures risk getting left at the wayside, as the ever faster pace of social and economic life conflicts with the conventional emphasis on the legislature's necessary reliance on careful, wide-ranging, and time-consuming deliberative exchange. The judiciary is also likely to undergo significant transformation, as the classical temporal vision of a retrospective, or past-oriented, court system leaves it no less poorly suited than the legislature to the dictates of a high-speed social and economic world subject to incessant change.

Whether social acceleration can help explain changes in the institutional operations of contemporary liberal democracy raises difficult empirical questions requiring careful scrutiny. For now I merely ask readers to follow a series of thought experiments, whereby we consider different ways by which the general process of social acceleration likely influences the temporal separation of powers described earlier. In my view it is perfectly legitimate to outline the presumptive influence of social acceleration on the temporality of liberal democracy before proceeding to inquire about possible empirical substantiation for our expectations. One might also legitimately question whether a useful discussion of liberal democracy should start with eighteenth- and nineteenth-century political thought given that contemporary liberal democracy hardly represents a carbon copy of Locke's, Montesquieu's, Madison's, or even Mill's ideas. Nevertheless, the assumptions about temporality discussed in the previous section of this chapter unquestionably exercised a major influence on the genesis of liberal democracy, and they continue to impact contemporary political practice in many ways as well. The contrast between a deliberate legislature and expeditious executive, the notion that law should be prospective and stable along with the closely related view of constitutions as entailing long-term temporal commitments, as well as the assumption of the reversibility of majority decisions remain influential features of the liberal democratic worldview. Although elements of the temporal separation of powers may seem at most tangentially related to contemporary liberal democratic practice, many of its core components continue to shape both popular and academic views of liberal democracy.[56]

So, what are the presumptive consequences of social acceleration for the traditional liberal democratic notion of legislation? As we saw earlier, that model was always latently tension ridden since it required lawmakers to foresee the future while concurrently taking note of the difficulties of doing so. Ideally, legislators would be in possession of a crystal ball allowing them to make prospective laws adapted to future trends. Yet classical authors also recognized the impossibility of legislative omniscience in light of the future's open-ended nature. Social acceleration seems destined to exacerbate this basic tension. Social acceleration implies an intensification of the rate of relatively significant forms of social change, thereby concomitantly heightening the already sizable difficulties of predicting a fundamentally open-ended future. The more or less permanent change that comes to characterize many facets of modernity makes the tasks of competent prospective legislation ever more toilsome in part because the future, in fact, increasingly becomes a stage for the unforeseen and unprecedented. Modernity has always entailed a heightened status for novelty in innumerable facets of social experience. Social acceleration exacerbates this trend: the pace of technological innovation increases dramatically, economic organization is constantly reshuffled, and new methods of production are introduced at a stunning rate; new forms of social interaction multiply exponentially elsewhere as well. As the experience of novelty becomes ubiquitous, successful prospective lawmaking is probably destined to become an ever more uphill battle.

Recall that the legislature was conceived as the central site for lawmaking in part because freewheeling debate and deliberation provided its activities with a normative legitimacy lacking in the executive, whose chief function was to undertake energetic action in applying general legislative norms to individual scenarios, as well as the judiciary, in which decision making was supposed to take a retrospective and even mechanical form. As the ever more rapid pace of social and economic life conflicts with the necessarily unhurried characteristics of freewheeling deliberative legislation, a fundamental temporal misfit emerges. Legislators are required to "take their time" in order to struggle with the burdensome duty of generating norms suitable to future developments. Yet the ever more hectic pace of change in the social and economic universe which lawmakers are supposed to coordinate seems oblivious to the prerequisites of sensible legislation. Because one fundamental purpose of legislation is to grapple with the side effects of precisely those forms of social change whose temporal contours seem especially rapid (e.g., economic disruptions generated by an increasingly fast-paced capitalism), lawmakers are left with the strenuous job of foreseeing change not only where it seems least predictable but also where its tremors are often most unsettling.

As social change becomes pervasive, lawmakers, grappling with a greater variety of sticky policy dilemmas, legislators may be overwhelmed by the awesome temporal burdens of reaching consensus on a multiplicity of complicated time-consuming issues. The intensification of social acceleration connotes an increased likelihood that legislatures simply will not have sufficient time to respond competently to a cacophony of legitimate demands for state action. The most immediate peril is that the distinctive normative attributes of elected representative legislature—namely, patient and oftentimes slow-going debate for the purpose of reasonable decision making and interest mediation—consequently suffer. Legislators may find themselves debating complex issues and potential objects of regulation which suddenly alter before their eyes, dramatically augmenting the hardships intrinsic to consensus building in the context of complex policy issues. They may finally succeed in pursuing a series of legislative initiatives only to discover that the social and economic presuppositions underlying their policy choices have already shifted. Even when lawmakers succeed in hammering out an agreement about the proper direction of policy, their legislative resolutions risk becoming out-of-date and anachronistic as rapidly as social change itself. Here, too, as long as laissez-faire ideology circumscribed government regulation of social and economic affairs, these dilemmas may have seemed insignificant. When government becomes actively involved in social and economic life, however, the underlying temporal dilemmas become crystal clear: popular assemblies are expected to do nothing less than react effectively to a multiplicity of rapid-fire changes in social and economic life while simultaneously maintaining fidelity to the traditional notion of its legitimacy as resting on wide-ranging forms of unhurried debate.[57]

The profound dilemmas of prospective legislation in the context of social acceleration are especially evident at the level of the most ambitious form of future-oriented legislation, constitutional lawmaking. Even the most well-conceived constitutional document unerringly lags behind the course of social and economic development, and it is only a matter of time before there must be some express departure from the original constitutional framework. This basic enigma gains in significance as social acceleration intensifies. A political system that endorses Locke's hostility to constitutional amendment powers merely aggravates it. Of course, a constitutional court may take upon itself the task of adapting constitutional norms to social and economic change; the illustrious history of the U.S. Supreme Court suggests that the judiciary can play a stabilizing role in the quest to make sure that constitutional norms are well suited to contemporary conditions. But we should have no illusions about the potential normative price to be paid. Covert constitutional rule making by the courts may undermine the traditional liberal aspiration to develop a legal system resting on relatively clear and transparent norms accessible to a broad array of democratic publics. When constitutional courts disguise constitutional reform as mere interpretation of rules already present within the founding document, constitutional jurisprudence is likely to become enormously complex. The resulting inability to predict which norms of constitutional jurisprudence may be applied in a given case raises serious problems for the normative commitment to a relatively predictable and stable system of law as well as for the traditional juridical function of preserving legal stability.[58] From the perspective of the classical temporal separation of powers, fundamental constitutional amendment via constitutional courts mistakenly conflates two distinct functions of state authority, prospective legislation and retrospective legislation. Consequently, neither competent adjudication that guarantees legal stability nor good lawmaking based on wide-ranging deliberation and interest mediation is likely to result. How can a narrow and relatively unrepresentative group of judicial experts successfully exercise the awesome tasks of prospective constitution making?

Faced with legislative dilemmas stemming from social acceleration, how might we expect institutional actors socialized in the liberal democratic worldview to respond? A variety of conceivable institutional responses come to mind, the most immediate one being that overburdened lawmakers seek aid from other institutional sites. Where are they most likely to turn for aid? It seems implausible that legislators would consciously opt for the judiciary, given its traditional association with retrospective decision making as well its necessary focus on individual cases, both of which leave courts poorly suited to producing future-oriented general rules. The judiciary's past-oriented temporal character, as exemplified by its preoccupation with precedent and standing rules, typically leaves it even less adept at dealing with new and unprecedented issues than the legislature. In contrast, confronted with the contradictory demands of responding to a panoply of rapid changes while aspiring to preserve freewheeling forms of time-consuming debate, parliaments might delegate lawmaking duties to an executive pictured by classical liberal theory as best equipped to tackle fast-moving social and economic developments that call for an immediate response. Given the arduous chore of successfully regulating an ever-changing variety of fast-paced social arenas, along with the traditional association of the executive with dispatch and expeditiousness, classical liberal democratic theory might legitimately be interpreted as affirming the virtues of handing over the coordination of fast-paced problems to the "energetic" unitary executive.

Conventional liberal democratic temporal assumptions might also imply that it makes sense to provide the executive with far-reaching discretionary legal authority to do so, because the fast-changing character of the material at hand means that any clearly formulated legislative norm or standard may soon appear obsolescent. As social acceleration makes it difficult for lawmakers to develop stable and binding norms capable of guiding state action well into the future, legal norms will decreasingly conform to the traditional liberal democratic requirement that statutes take a clear, prospective, general, and relatively predictable form. Faced with a barrage of novel and unexpected social and economic trends, legislators are likely to embrace flexible and open-ended legal forms in order to provide the executive with a fair chance of effectively responding to constant change. Action beyond and even outside the scope of parliament's general rules will be called for. The traditional conception of the rule of law as entailing a commitment to government action in accordance with clear, general, stable, and prospective rules would soon seem quaint and anachronistic, as the legal order struggled to accommodate a vast range of vague and open-ended standards delegating substantial discretionary power to the executive.

As Locke's *Second Treatise* anticipates, the scope of executive discretion turns out to be intimately connected to the legislature's ability to foresee social and economic trends. Social acceleration curtails parliament's ability to coordinate future activities; the scope of discretionary executive authority thereby expands as well. In our high-speed social world the legislature's inability "to foresee, and so by laws to provide for, all accidents and necessities, that may concern the public" risks becoming a significant source of executive discretion.[59] Scholars have long debated the precise character of executive prerogative in Locke's theory. When read in this light, the scope of the Lockean prerogative depends significantly on assumptions about social temporality. If Locke is best interpreted as advancing a static and fundamentally traditionalist conception of social and economic life, executive prerogative would seem destined to remain an exceptional political instrument, to be employed exclusively during occasional "accidents" or crises. On this first reading Locke is merely reformulating a fundamentally traditional defense of temporary emergency powers, necessary in the face of emergencies in which strict observance of the law would aggrandize a life-or-death threat to the political community. In this interpretation prerogative powers are temporally limited, and the ordinary rule of law can successfully coordinate political action during the predominant portion of political life. On a second reading, in which we instead emphasize Locke's apparent intimation of modernity's social dynamism and built-in preference for permanent change and innovation, his account of executive prerogative appears in a different light. If the main function of execu-tive prerogative is (1) to compensate for legislative norms whose imperfections are impossible to predict, and (2) the constant "flux" of modernity means that the scope of these imperfections is likely to increase dramatically, then (3) executive prerogative would seem destined to permeate political life. To the extent that modernity is characterized by social acceleration, then that institu-tional mechanism best suited to the dictates of high-speed change would probably have to take on unprecedented significance. Despite Locke's own express preference for government action in accordance with clear, general, stable, and prospective laws, his conception of executive prerogative, along with his anticipation of the temporal dynamics of modernity, thereby antici-pates a situation of permanent prerogative, in which far-reaching executive discretion becomes preeminent in many areas of state activity.[60]

The temporal presuppositions of the liberal democratic separation of pow-ers underscore the considerable appeal of this institutional adaptation, not-withstanding its probable flaws, in another fashion as well. Recall again the traditional view of the legislature as prospective, the executive as contempo-raneous, and the judiciary as retrospective. How might the general process of social acceleration shape each of these distinct temporal perspectives? Both technical acceleration (e.g., the increased tempo of technological innovation) and the acceleration of social change tend to render the past-oriented orienta-tion of the courts immaterial to the necessities of political decision making, because past experience is decreasingly likely to be useful in a world where novelty becomes ubiquitous. Judicial precedents or standing rules become ever more inapposite to the panoply of new dilemmas judges face when social acceleration becomes intense. We have also noted that social acceleration dis-ables the predictive capacities of prospective legislators. In sharp contrast, the present-oriented character of the executive appears to outfit it with precisely the right temporal orientation required by social acceleration. In Montes-quieu's telling phrase, "the executive power is generally employed in momen-tary operations," and one of the most striking facets of social acceleration is the proliferation of novel experiences and trends (new technologies, e.g., or sud-den shifts in economic or military affairs) which not only occur at an increas-ing pace but do so abruptly and unexpectedly. Because the energetic executive is traditionally conceived as best able to swing into motion at a moment's notice, it oftentimes naturally seems most adept at dealing with a range of sudden and fast-paced events—a foreign policy crisis, for example, or a sudden economic downturn—which even the most prescient body of lawmakers was unable to foresee. Indeed, to the extent that interstate competition represents a key source of social acceleration, the traditional view of the executive as institutionally best capable of navigating the perilous and legally murky waters of foreign affairs seems conducive to a general expansion of executive decision making authority. As interstate competition results in speed and velocity playing an ever greater role in foreign affairs, the political community might very well turn, to a greater degree than in the past, to that institutional site conventionally conceived as best able to undertake action no less rapid-fire and fast paced than the international universe in which we increasingly find ourselves.

Although unmindful of its ambivalent consequences for the rule of law, John Stuart Mill can be plausibly reinterpreted as anticipating the broad outlines of such an institutional response to acceleration, as demonstrated by his well-known discussion in *Considerations on Representative Government* of the necessity of far-reaching delegations of legislative authority to a "committee of very few persons."[61] The rise of the modern administrative state requires reinterpretation in light of the concept of social acceleration. Commentators on Mill's work often focus on his flattering assessment of the virtues of a well-trained group of administrative experts, thereby neglecting his perceptive observations about the significance of the time horizons of legislative activity. Mill understood that the traditional model of a time-consuming deliberative lawmaker threatened to render parliaments ineffective in the face of modern social and economic demands. If legislators take their duties seriously and strive to achieve well-crafted legislative statutes only after having engaged in measured debate, "the mere time necessarily occupied in getting through bills, renders Parliament more and more incapable of passing any, except on detached and narrow points."[62] Conscientious legislators increasingly face the "sheer impossibility of finding time to dispose of" their lawmaking activities properly given the prerequisites of modern government.[63] The slow-going character of deliberative legislatures increasingly leaves them poorly suited to the fast-paced imperatives of modern social life, and only by providing substantial decision-making autonomy to a corps of expert officials can modern legislatures hope to tackle the ever more arduous task of laying out the course of future state activity.

Unfortunately for Mill, social acceleration also implies that the "distinction between controlling the business of government," the proper task of parliament, "and actually doing it" is necessarily less tidy than his remarks suggest.[64]Acceleration infers that it increasingly becomes difficult for actors to acquire reliable insights about the likely course of many future social trends. When policy goals accordingly remain at least somewhat unclear and open-ended or when policy goals are clear but bureaucratic and technical experts (as well as interested private groups) understandably disagree about the best way to achieve the aims at hand in a rapidly changing world, however, an arduous process of consensus building will have to take place within administrative bodies. If that process is going to achieve more-or-less satisfying results, it too will have to be subject to the constraints of relatively time-consuming deliberative exchange and interest mediation. Forcing administrative actors to rush their decisions is sure to generate irrational and undesirable results no less than in the case of overhasty legislatures.[65]Although legislators may delegate decision-making authority to administrative bodies in order to save time, the increasingly unpredictable character of the future ultimately renders that strategy problematic as well. Legislative delegation transplants the enigma of identifying realizable future policy goals in a rapidly changing world from the legislature to the administration but by no means necessarily overcomes it.

To be sure, one might legitimately wonder whether the modern executive in fact possesses the capacity for dispatch ascribed to it by the classical temporal separation of powers. The experience of the modern administrative state quickly reminds us, notwithstanding the traditional metaphor of the single executive, that the executive itself is a complex and multiheaded creature, composed of a host of (oftentimes competing) bureaucratic units, whose members are no less numerous than other branches of government. Disagreement and interest conflict are no less a part of our many-headed executive than our elected legislatures.[66] Revealingly, the notion of the unitary executive was formulated for the most part prior to the maturation of some of the core features of the modern state: when Machiavelli or even Locke and Montesquieu sketched out the virtues of a singular executive, modern bureaucracies, the professionalization of officialdom, rational systems of tax collection, modern forms of military organization, as well as many features of the modern administrative state remained underdeveloped or nonexistent. So, the influential notion of the unitary high-speed executive arguably fails to do justice to crucial features of contemporary political reality.

Although plausible, this rejoinder misses a crucial point. For now we are merely trying to reconstruct how liberal democratic politicians and officials struggling with the consequences of social acceleration might adapt accordingly. Whatever their empirical merits, traditional liberal democratic ideas about executive power could easily lead political actors to conceive the executive as best suited to grappling with the flux and incessant change that make up core elements of social acceleration. Remember as well that a classical justification for the privileged place of executive decision making in foreign affairs was the latter's presumed unpredictability and the resulting need for executive dispatch and flexibility; in this vein Locke believed that war "admits not of plurality of governors." An immediate offshoot of the general process of social acceleration is a heightened unpredictability in prospective domestic lawmaking as well. It requires no great stretch of the liberal imagination to conclude that the increased difficulty of gauging a fast-moving future in the domestic arena might require a substantial accretion of executive discretion there as well; the sizable influence of Locke's conception of executive prerogative in the history of liberal democracy provides preliminary support for this expectation.[67] Moreover, even if there are solid empirical grounds for questioning the doctrinaire association of the executive with dispatch, there are still sound reasons for accepting one element of the traditional view: parliament or congress "as a collective organization takes definitive action through the legislative process, which is cumbersome, difficult to navigate, and characterized by multiple veto votes," whereas the executive—especially in presidential and semi-presidential systems—"can often make the first move."[68] This ability to initiate or act first admittedly composes only one feature of what traditional liberal democratic thinkers had in mind when elaborating the idea of an energetic unitary executive. Yet its continued empirical plausibility lends credence to the expectation that the temporal presuppositions of the traditional separation of powers doctrine will often lead liberal democrats to turn to the executive when faced with the need for swift state action.

Perhaps this argument is still too rigid in light of the familiar fact that institutional adaptation is typically a messy process, with cautious tinkering, trial-and-error experimentation, and conscious institutional design operating alongside one another in a complicated and oftentimes inconsistent manner. For example, legislators might find themselves, probably more unwittingly than via conscious choice, trying to tackle the difficulties generated by social acceleration by minimizing some of the core differences between the legislature and executive. If the unitary executive is best adapted to high-speed society, might not elected representative bodies understandably interested in maintaining their paramount position in decision making modify their practices so that they tend to approximate those of the executive? General legislative debate would be shortened and thereby sped up; strict time limits could be predetermined for legislative debate, with conceptions of accelerated (or "fast-track") legislation gaining in popularity; deliberation itself might be reduced, with the real work of parliament taking place in small collegial bodies or committees in which the burdens of deliberative sequentiality can be substantially minimized; legislators would grudgingly sacrifice the quaint liberal preference for clear, prospective, and stable statutes, openly admitting that parliament is destined to issue highly specialized laws reminiscent of the individual "decrees" or "orders" traditionally undertaken by the executive as a way of confronting immediate, or momentary, political threats; legislators might also concede the impossibility of statutes remaining valid for the lengthy period sought by early modern political theorists.

The right-wing authoritarian German theorist Carl Schmitt diagnosed crucial components of this institutional possibility in a disturbing 1950 discussion of what he polemically describes as the "motorized legislator." Later I argue that Schmitt's account accurately chronicles many of the most disturbing trends in recent lawmaking: well before recent social theorists tackled the phenomenon of social acceleration, Schmitt grappled seriously with ongoing changes in the temporal horizons of human activity, and, despite his own unacceptable authoritarian political preferences, Schmitt understood that present-day legislatures bent on replicating the unitary executive risk abandoning those normative attributes that justify their preeminent institutional position. A synchronization of high-speed social and economic life with lawmaking might culminate in the abrogation of both freewheeling parliamentary deliberation and the rule of law. Operating in the context of an accelerated (*beschleunigt*) world where speed is at a premium, Schmitt argues, legislatures increasingly take the form of "an ever faster" and simplified apparatus in which "summary proceedings"—not unhurried debate—became commonplace.[69] For Schmitt this reduction of the liberal democratic legislature to a mechanical instrument for coordinating fast-moving social and economic affairs derives from liberalism's congenital misunderstandings about politics; as we will see in chapter 4, Schmitt wrongly posited that the inherent contradictions of liberal jurisprudence inevitably engender high-speed motorized legislatures. Yet Schmitt's diagnosis also accurately suggests that accelerated lawmaking results from the indisputable need for rapid-fire state action amid the temporal contours of contemporary capitalism. Notwithstanding liberal democracy's commitment to the ideal of the deliberative legislature, the rise of the motorized legislature heralds the disintegration of the classical attributes of liberal democratic lawmaking. Functioning as a technical device for overseeing high-speed affairs, liberal democratic lawmaking increasingly consists of vague and open-ended legal resolutions, exceptional and emergency norms delegating vast discretionary power to the executive and various administrative bodies, and poorly crafted statutes possessing a limited half-life. Each of these legal trends represents a decisive yet ultimately unsuccessful attempt by liberal democracy to accelerate lawmaking in order to respond to the altered temporal conditions of contemporary social life.

Schmitt's prescient 1950 essay also briefly intimated the possibility of the judiciary reinventing itself along similar lines. Although the retrospective orientation of the traditional judiciary makes it a poor candidate for successfully passing the novel temporal tests at hand, social acceleration is likely to lead legislatures to issue pliable open-ended statutes that inevitably help transform judicial functions. Open-ended legal materials lend themselves to no less creative, open-ended forms of adjudication; this is precisely why Enlightenment jurists concerned with the perils of judicial arbitrariness were so preoccupied with semantic clarity and coherence in the law.[70] When parliament promulgates vague laws, however, it sometimes grudgingly concedes the impossibility of effectively predicting future social needs. If a statute or precedent is not only fundamentally open-ended in character but also arguably cries out for subsequent judicial adaptation, the judiciary no longer legitimately need maintain an exclusively retrospective orientation. Some open-ended statutes not only allow for judicial creativity but also represent a legislative plea for help from the courts in updating state activity in order to make sure that it corresponds to contemporary needs.[71] In this vein the Legal Realist Jerome Frank observed many years ago that the traditional liberal democratic model of adjudication becomes problematic given the multiplication of settings in which legal rules inevitably encounter an ever greater variety of "permutations and combinations of events . . . which were never contemplated when the original rules were made." Describing core elements of the process of social acceleration analyzed in chapter 1, Frank pointed out that

> new instruments of production, new modes of travel and of dwelling, new credit and ownership devices, new concentrations of capital . . . all of these factors of innovation make vain the hope that definitive legal rules can be drafted that will

forever after solve all problems. When human relationships are transforming daily, legal relationships cannot be expressed in enduring legal form. The constant development of unprecedented problems requires a legal system capable of fluidity and pliancy. Our society would be strait-jacketed were not the courts . . . constantly overhauling the law and adapting it to the realities of ever-changing social, industrial, and political conditions.[72]

Whereas Locke had conceived of the executive as best suited to the task of compensating for the limited foresight of legislatures faced with the dilemma of predicting future necessities, Frank grasped not only that this corrective function would likely undergo a sizable increase in the contemporary world but also that courts might perform it. As the legislature's capacity for generating clear, binding statutes capable of effectively guiding future action decays, courts might step into the resultant gap by compensating for the limited predictive talents of a legislature confronted ever more directly with the imperatives of social acceleration. However attractive from a normative standpoint, the classical dream of an airtight legal code in which judicial discretion is rendered unnecessary tends to be systematically undermined by acceleration and its resultant increases in the "speed of movement of goods, people, information, messages, and the like."[73]

Unfortunately, Frank's profound hostility to traditional liberal jurisprudence led him to obscure the failings of this possible judicial answer to social acceleration. Not only would courts necessarily abandon the circumscribed retrospective role ascribed to them by classical jurisprudence, but they also might gain extensive discretionary authority if they were continually to overhaul law for the sake of updating it in accordance with the realities of ever-changing social conditions. Because Frank openly celebrated the prospects of a judiciary liberated from the purportedly anachronistic ideals of classical liberal legal theory, he ultimately downplayed the dangers of a freewheeling judiciary whose activities might become perilously similar to the executive prerogative promoted by Locke as one plausible institutional answer to slow-moving legislatures and their rigid statutory creations. Although the judiciary, in contrast to the executive, would still lack control over the impressive power instruments of the modern state (e.g., the police and army), in order to ensure their synchronization with high-speed society its activities would now be similarly free from formalistic legal restraints. But how, then, might the judiciary successfully realize its original purpose of preserving stability and predictability?

What would prevent courts from becoming a new source of illegitimate forms of discretionary power?[74] Like parliament, the judiciary might imitate the executive and thereby streamline its tempo in accordance with social acceleration but only at the cost of abandoning its special normative and institutional attributes.

What, then, of the traditional quest to heighten the quality of popular deliberation by decelerating it? As noted earlier, this endeavor played a major role in the temporal framework of classical liberal democratic thought. Alas, the Madisonian hope that geographically large republics would be free of irrational bouts of quick and unseasoned popular debate seems quaint in an age featuring widespread possibilities for simultaneity and instantaneousness in human communication and interaction. Social acceleration means that Madison's belief that "communication is always checked" in a large republic is now surely less tenable than in the past. Perhaps it is no accident that contemporary concerns about the failures of contemporary liberal democracy to make effective use of recent technological innovations for the sake of strengthening possibilities for thoughtful popular debate echo Madison's expectation that rapid communication in small republics tends to benefit narrowly interested factions. In this vein political theorist Benjamin Barber points out that new information technologies possess enormous potential for improving the texture of democratic debate. Yet "teleconferencing, videotex, and the interaction possibilities of this technology are being systematically exploited in the commercial world by corporations bent on enhancing efficiency through enhancing information and communication."[75] Unless we develop adequate institutional mechanisms allowing democratic citizens to take advantage of the new technologies, Barber notes, new forms of simultaneity and instantaneousness are likely to serve a narrow set of privileged economic interests rather the common good. We thus find ourselves confronted with a question that surely would have been familiar to Madison, despite the intellectual distance separating Madison's relatively modest faith in popular politics from our more robust contemporary democratic commitments: how can we channel new high-speed technologies so as to heighten their deliberative merits and advance the common good, rather than leave them to the whims of selfish factions?

Even though political scientists have long recognized that Madison's ideas about the advantages of large republics no longer easily obtain for contemporary liberal democracy,[76] they have barely begun to scratch the surface of the normative and institutional questions raised by this realization. For example, how can autonomous publics emerge and achieve some minimal level of staying power amid the high-speed pace of social and economic change? Public life probably presupposes an ability to undertake relatively long-term projects as well as some capacity for mutual trust and commitment; effective action in concert with fellow citizens is probably impossible otherwise. How are the requisite character traits to be cultivated amid a social context privileging short-term perspectives, adaptation to constantly changing tasks, and episodic institutional and even personal ties? Is contemporary high-speed capitalism, for example, sufficiently supportive of the long-term temporal attachments required by democratic politics? Unfortunately, some evidence suggests that the "new economy" buttresses temporal orientations that pose serious problems for achieving such attachments.⁷⁷ Without them it becomes difficult to see how public life can be successfully sustained. Discipline, the capacity for acquiring skills over time, and long-term commitments are required "if one is to play Chopin, grow outstanding orchids, or learn to craft furniture," let alone attend (oftentimes tedious and time-consuming) political meetings regularly or try to gain a grasp of oftentimes complex political issues. One hardly need depend on exaggerated expectations about democratic participation in order to understand that effective citizenship requires at least some patience and capacity for long-term commitments. Yet recent social scientists tell us that one of the more familiar facets of the increased pace of everyday life is that we "are becoming more likely to avoid activities that require patience, learning, and total commitment."⁷⁸ It requires little imagination to see why the continued erosion of such temporal traits might further aggravate the elected representative legislature's already fragile position in contemporary political life: impatient citizens who expect quick answers to difficult questions are unlikely to appreciate the niceties of time-consuming parliamentary procedure and debate.⁷⁹

To their credit, many recent political thinkers—most prominently, cultural conservatives—address this dilemma by worrying about the lack of constancy and stability plaguing contemporary social life. But the traditionalist overtones characteristic of this line of argumentation—in particular, a tendency to privilege largely unchosen commonalities of history, belief, and culture—leave it poorly suited to acknowledge the advances wrought by high-speed society. Social acceleration is an ambivalent and in crucial respects irreversible process; the real question is how we can harness it for the sake of refurbishing public life and, more generally, liberal democracy. One can easily conceive of manifestations of social acceleration that a decent society might sensibly discard. By the same token it is difficult to see why a dynamic and energetic society would want to dispose of every facet of social acceleration. High-speed information and communication technologies, for example, represent indispensable achievements that any prospective political and social order will need to employ properly. As Dewey noted long ago in *The Public and Its Problems*, it is always easy to "lay the blame for all the evils" of modern society's "mania for motion and speed" and "restless instability" at the doorstep of a scapegoat. Cultural conservatives have certainly identified a number of candidates for that scapegoat.[80] But we still face a difficult question: "how can a public be organized . . . when literally it does not stay in place? Only deep issues or those which can be made to appear such can find a common denominator among all the shifting and unstable relationships . . . [Political attachments] are bred in tranquil stability; they are nourished in constant relationships. Acceleration of mobility disturbs them at their root. And without abiding attachments associations are too shifting and shaken to permit a public readily to locate and identify itself."[81] We need to confront the normative and institutional difficulties raised by incessant motion and speed without succumbing to a misplaced nostalgia for static and impervious forms of social life.

Speed and Institutional Change

Although I can only offer preliminary evidence for the grand claims sketched out here, the vantage point of political theory provides us with a useful starting point for highlighting where subsequent empirical research should focus. Since the nineteenth-century liberal democracies have undergone major transformations in response to a rich variety of factors; it would be silly to see social acceleration as the sole or even main causal factor driving the institutional shifts that have taken place. For that matter there are good reasons for doubting the possibility of any universal theory of liberal democratic institutional transformation, in light of the spacious roles played by the particularities of historical context, national political tradition, and accident. While offering initial evidence that certain key institutional shifts in liberal democracy are in fact explicable in terms of the account provided here, I primarily aim in this section at rendering empirically plausible the possibility that social acceleration has played a meaningful role in liberal democratic institutional change. Only further research can ultimately determine whether the expectations about institutional change described in the earlier sections of this chapter hold water.

Nonetheless, it is striking that a substantial body of research meshes with the predicted impact of social acceleration on liberal democracy proffered here. In correspondence with Jerome Frank's expectations, courts have long aggressively abandoned the retrospective temporal perspective favored by traditional jurisprudence, and the tendency toward creative judicial activity and interpretation is now well nigh universal in the liberal democratic universe. A recent collection of essays aptly entitled *The Global Expansion of Judicial Power* documents what is already evident to most careful observers of judicial development in the last fifty years: "the phenomenon of judges making public policies that previously had been made or that, in the opinion of most, ought to be made by legislative and executive officials appears to be on the increase" almost everywhere, raising difficult normative and institutional questions as courts take on broad legislative tasks for which they were never designed. The volume's editors rightly mention the "mounting influence of American jurisprudence and political science," which have typically endorsed a U.S.-style constitutional court, as one source of the rise of powerful creative judiciaries that increasingly hope to do much more than maintain stability and continuity in the law.[82] Yet their account also correctly refers to institutional trends that potentially corroborate the analysis of social acceleration provided here: "ineffective majoritarian [legislative] institutions" and "willful delegation" of legislative power represent two key sources of growing judicial decision-making authority in many liberal democracies.[83] Of course, it would be mistaken to claim that the rise of openly creative, forward-looking courts represents nothing less than a victory for unmitigated judicial discretion along the lines drawn by Jerome Frank; the institutional trends at hand are far more complicated. By the same token it is striking that the central intellectual preoccupation of recent jurisprudence—namely, the dilemma of legal indeterminacy—can be interpreted at least in part as an attempt to make sense of heightened institutional possibilities for discretionary adjudication.[84] Progressive legal scholars often celebrate the open-ended character of judicial decision making, whereas their conservative peers typically lament it, yet both camps recognize that freewheeling judicial power is now a significant facet of contemporary political life. From the conceptual perspective outlined here, the present-day scholarly fascination with legal indeterminacy arguably represents an acknowledgment both of the increasingly legislative character of the judiciary as well as of the potential dangers to liberal jurisprudence stemming from the judiciary's abandonment of a traditional retrospective temporal orientation.

Although the scholarly literature on parliamentary decay rarely directly addresses questions of temporality, the characteristic emphasis on the limited deliberative quality of contemporary legislatures, repeated claims that modern legislators are overwhelmed by a vast array of tasks for which they lack sufficient time, as well as widespread concerns about the slow-going and inefficient character of parliament potentially confirm the prediction that social acceleration poses serious risks for liberal democratic legislatures. Even though it would be unfair to criticize contemporary legislatures by comparing them unfavorably to idealized models of their nineteenth-century predecessors, there can be little doubt that the elected legislature's role in our political systems today is more modest than that originally sought by the mainstream of classical liberal theory.[85] The precise causal mechanisms at work are complex, yet social acceleration has probably helped transform representative bodies into their present institutional rendition, in which freewheeling deliberation is not only less ambitious than hoped for by many classical writers, but parliament now also seems bent on enigmatically streamlining its activities. Recent empirical work confirms many of Schmitt's expectations about the ongoing speed-up, or "motorization," of parliamentary legislation. Contemporary lawmaking bodies are asked to handle significantly more legislation than their historical predecessors, but less time is available for general debate, and legislation is considered more quickly, even though legislatures now typically meet for longer periods of time than their nineteenth- and early-twentieth-century predecessors. It is now common practice among legislative bodies to suspend rules requiring general ("floor") consideration of legislation, and much of the work of the legislature takes place in specialized committees. Yet "time constraints that are so prominent for the House [of Representatives] as a whole are prominent in the committee room as well," and some evidence suggests that time for meaningful deliberation has also declined there.[86] No wonder that political scientists complain about a "crisis of ungovernability."[87] The push for fast-track trade legislation, which allows Congress to circumvent traditional legislative procedures in order to empower the executive to undertake swift action in the economic arena, represents the logical culmination of broader long-term legislative tendencies. Like many other decision-making trends in our legislatures, fast-track authority potentially helps synchronize lawmaking with the fast-paced imperatives of contemporary society. Unfortunately, as Schmitt prophesied, it also risks sacrificing traditional legislative power.

Schmitt also suggested that the motorization of lawmaking would engender a vast range of vague delegations of open-ended authority to the executive and administration, exceptional and emergency norms, as well as poorly crafted statutes possessing a limited half-life. In fact, executive and administrative agencies now exercise vital decision-making functions, and bureaucratic decrees sometimes take on greater significance than general legislative statutes. Albeit extreme, a recent example from South America illustrates some of the troubling tendencies at hand: "Peru is considered a democracy because it elects a president and parliament. In the five years after an election, though, the executive has been known to make 134,000 rules and decrees with no accountability to the congress or public. After elections, no ongoing relationship exists between those who make decisions and those who live under them."[88] Analysts of the U.S. polity have similarly chronicled a dramatic twentieth-century expansion of rule by executive order, according to which presidential decrees and proclamations are declared legally binding. Although the executive typically claims statutory or constitutional authority for its orders, the legal basis for executive decree is often suspect, notwithstanding the profound impact that decrees have had on a vast array of policy arenas. From the interpretive perspective outlined earlier in this chapter, it is revealing that one recent commentator describes executive orders as "quick, convenient, and relatively easy mechanisms" that allow presidents to avoid time-consuming legislative formalities. Because some forms of unilateral execution action in the United States are exempt from procedural tests that alternative forms of administrative rule making must pass, rule by executive decree at least holds out the promise of speedy decision making.[89]

In light of the temporal analysis provided earlier, the vast outpouring of literature on antiformal trends in both public and private law appears in a fresh light as well. Much law consists of vague and open-ended statutes delegating far-reaching discretionary authority to the executive and administration, and a great deal of twentieth-century legal scholarship has been devoted to the task of explaining why law decreasingly conforms to the classical liberal democratic model.[90] Although temporal issues are generally neglected in this debate as well, the fact that legislatures in the last century often delegated vast decision-making authority to the administration based on a belief in its supposedly superior "efficiency" fits well with the temporal argument to the extent that efficiency is typically associated with swift decision making. The argument developed here implies that the tendency to delegate legislative authority—oftentimes poorly defined and highly discretionary[91]—follows in part from the traditional liberal democratic vision of the temporal horizons of decision making. Too often, legislatures have thrown their hands in the air in frustration when faced with social acceleration and abandoned their lawmaking duties to institutional instances envisioned as better able to tackle speed.[92] The results have been ambivalent: open-ended legal forms have helped pave the way for the regulation of the capitalist economy as well as the undeniable achievements of the welfare state, but they have also sometimes generated legal irregularity and even arbitrariness.

The pressures of acceleration probably also help explain why judicial and legislative efforts to oversee the administrative state often prove unsuccessful, whereas the executive repeatedly gains the upper hand in institutional battles for control of the state bureaucracy. The administrative state raises complicated questions for the traditional tripartite separation of powers, since classical liberals envisioned neither the scope nor scale of contemporary government activity. Accordingly, many legal scholars now speak of the "fourth branch" of government. Yet traditional preconceptions about the executive continue to encourage institutional actors and their scholarly allies to posit that it alone can serve as the legitimate master of the burgeoning administrative machinery. Subjecting the administrative state to the legislature or judiciary, they argue, conflicts fundamentally with the imperatives of executive unity. Even more telling for our purposes here, the need for temporal efficiency, or "energy," in government purportedly requires an administrative state with the executive at the helm.[93] Whereas judicial and legislative inroads into the administrative state tend to be clumsy and temporally inefficient, an administrative apparatus dominated by the single person of the executive allegedly means that the modern administrative state can act with no less energy and "personal firmness" than the single person of the classical executive. The administrative state can partake of executive speed or energy, proponents of this view claim, but only if legislative and judicial controls over it are reduced to a minimum.

By depending on statutes that expressly limit their validity to a clearly delineated time span, many parliaments now also expressly concede that legislative norms can only possess a short half-life.[94] Locke's suggestion that we can reasonably expect statutes to provide effective guidance for an entire century would undoubtedly strike many present-day legislators as no less quaint and anachronistic than his old-fashioned Enlightenment faith in the possibility of a neatly codified, airtight system of clear, prospective, stable general norms. Most dramatic, the stunning proliferation of exceptional and emergency powers in contemporary liberal democracy seems to confirm the Lockean inference that constant "flux" tends to augment executive prerogative. One way in which legislatures have grappled with the high-speed temporality of contemporary social life is by surrendering traditional modes of legislation in favor of vast delegations of discretionary power to the "energetic" executive. Legislatures thereby opt for flexible open-ended legal authority arguably better attuned to the ever-changing demands of dynamic capitalist production and the no less fast-moving temporality of interstate competition and conflict. In high-speed arenas of both domestic and foreign policy, the heightened difficulties of successful prospective legislation play into the hands of an executive traditionally conceived as best suited to the management of speed and unpredictability.

Far too few scholars have bothered to reflect on the disturbingly commonplace reliance on exceptional and emergency powers by even the most successful liberal democracies. Many political scientists and legal scholars would probably still be surprised by the opening statement of a revealing U.S. Senate report from 1974, in which the bipartisan Committee on National Emergencies and Delegated Emergency Powers summarized its finding by concluding that the United States had on "the books at least 470 significant emergency powers statutes without time limitations delegating to the Executive extensive discretionary powers, ordinarily exercised by the Legislature, which affect the lives of American citizens in a host of all-encompassing ways. This vast range of powers, taken together, confer enough authority to rule this country without reference to normal constitutional processes."[95] As the report systematically outlines, a vast range of open-ended emergency delegations of power to the executive concern not only the familiar arenas of foreign affairs and war preparedness but also many areas of economic regulation. Even during peacetime the American president since 1945 has exercised substantial discretion to settle strikes, initiate price controls, limit exports, deal with the exigencies of the so-called drug wars, and counteract unwanted immigration. Nor have more recent developments witnessed a reversal of the trends that encouraged Senators Frank Church and Charles Matthias to conclude their report with the observation that "emergency government has become the norm" within the United States.[96] In fact, the American senators probably downplayed the extent of the problem by excluding a detailed comparative analysis of other liberal democracies from their report: what makes the trend toward rule by exceptional power all the more disturbing is how pervasive it has become within liberal democracy. Substantial comparative evidence describes similar trends at work in many other liberal democracies, despite major differences in legal culture and institutions.[97] Poorly defined grants of executive-based emergency or prerogative authority covering a wide range of policy matters constitute a key institutional attribute of many present-day liberal democracies.

Is it merely speculation to claim that the growth of executive-centered government can be linked to traditional temporal assumptions about the executive? The historical record includes innumerable cases of executives openly appealing to those preconceptions in order to justify expanded discretionary authority. For now I mention only a few paradigmatic examples from the history of the twentieth-century U.S. presidency, which most observers believe has gained vast lawmaking powers unforeseen and unintended by the nation's founders.[98]

Franklin Delano Roosevelt's New Deal programs, which engendered ample executive lawmaking powers under the auspices of doing battle with the Great Depression and then Germany and Japan, were justified by Roosevelt's revealing 1933 declaration of the need for "undelayed . . . Executive power to wage a war against the emergency, as great as the power that would be given to me if in fact invaded by a foreign foe."[99] Linking the economic crisis of the 1930s to foreign invasion, Roosevelt's famous inaugural address appealed to the traditional Lockean notion that unpredictable, rapidly unfolding foreign crises demand swift executive power and at least a temporary departure from the "normal balance of Executive and legislative authority."[100] In 1936 the Supreme Court relied on the same vision of rapid-fire executive authority in order to approve extensive executive discretion in international commerce: Justice George Sutherland referred to traditional liberal democratic notions of executive dispatch in order to argue for executive preeminence in foreign relations.[101] Not surprisingly, President Roosevelt's advisors soon made a habit of citing Justice Sutherland's statement from the landmark case of *United States v. Curtiss-Wright Export Corporation* in order to help legitimize executive prerogative.[102] FDR himself also made a point of referring to the heightened tempo of contemporary life—for example, his reference to the "lightning speed" of world events in a famous 1939 address to Congress—to vindicate the dramatic expansion of executive power which took place under his watch.[103]

To be sure, the Great Depression and World War II did constitute genuine emergencies, and, whatever its legal failings, executive discretion undeniably served good purposes in warding off the Depression and two deadly wartime foes. So, perhaps it is more revealing to note that Roosevelt's successors, amid political scenarios far less perilous than 1933 or 1940, have regularly appealed to the image of the swift executive in order to augment executive authority. The political scientist Theodore Lowi has perceptively argued that both the American Right and Left have helped prepare the way for expanded executive discretion in the postwar era by concurrently endorsing an accelerated model of decision making, which he describes as beholden to "secrecy, unilateral action, energy . . . decisiveness, where time is always of the essence," contrasting it to the "slow track" of the traditional liberal democratic separation of powers.[104] American liberals have favored the expansion of presidential power because of their belief in the "*need* for presidential power to get America going, to keep America going, to coordinate the highly pluralistic parts of the American democracy," in order to bring about overdue social and economic reform.[105] According to this "domestic emergency model" of decision making, only the swift unitary executive is capable of leading the way amid a series of dire domestic crises (most important, periodic economic downturns and racial unrest) which threaten to paralyze the republic.[106] For their part conservatives have responded to the liberal version of the fast-track presidency with a "war model" defense of executive prerogative, according to which they "assume a condition of war—or constant threat of some sort to national security—that makes aggrandizement of the presidency urgently necessary."[107] The "war against communism," in contrast to the liberal "war against poverty" and racial injustice, provided the main ideological justification for the right-wing embrace of presidential power well into the 1980s. Despite the manifest differences between the two models of executive power, both nonetheless build on the traditional idea that the executive is best suited to the management of fast-moving events, and both presuppose the traditional association of the executive with dispatch.

Recent observers of the British polity have described similar trends toward a "quiescent Parliament" operating in a "system of government that rests so much power in the executive branch."[108] The general trend toward presidential and semi-presidential regimes in many parts of the world potentially perhaps stems at least in part from pathologies of social acceleration I have tried to recount.[109]

Refurbishing Liberal Democracy?

In this chapter I have underscored the substantial challenges posed by social acceleration to traditional conceptions of liberal democracy: social accelera- tion helps transform liberal democracy into a system very different from that envisioned by its original theoretical architects. Of course, Montesquieu, Locke, Madison, and Mill are hardly deserving of our unthinking intellectual fidelity, and many elements of their theories have rightly been subjected to harsh criticism.[110] Even if we acknowledge the failings of classical ideas about the separation of powers, however, it remains the case that legislative decay, concomitant expansion of executive rule, ubiquity of legal discretion, and proliferation of emergency powers should worry us. Because the classical sepa- ration of powers doctrine makes up a core component of a distinctive liberal democratic vision of freedom, its disintegration is hardly a trend whose nor- mative implications can simply be dismissed out of hand as an expression of backward-looking (let alone politically conservative) intellectual nostalgia. We can easily mock some of the more naive ideals of classical liberal democratic theory—for example, its mechanical vision of judicial decision making—but the last laugh will be on us if we fail to take seriously the enigmatic facets of institutional change within liberal democracy.

The sad truth is that, while real-life liberal democracies have tacitly ac- knowledged many offshoots of social acceleration, liberal democratic political theory has offered little in the way of constructive guidance because it has rarely identified, let alone grappled with, the fundamental temporal dilemmas at hand. On the contrary, liberal democracy's harshest critics too often have dominated intellectual debate about the relationship between speed and poli- tics. Earlier I mentioned Carl Schmitt's telling account of the motorized legis- lature. We should also recall Italian Futurism's celebration of speed as well as the pivotal role played by it in the Futurist embrace of fascism. While praising "great locomotives, twisting tunnels, armored cars, torpedo boats, mono- planes, and racing cars," the Italian poet Filippo Tommaso Marinetti pro- claimed a new "aesthetic of speed," announcing in his characteristically over- heated fashion that "the world's magnificence has been enriched by a new beauty, the beauty of speed."[111] "Human energy centupled by speed will master

Time and Space."[112] Unfortunately, Marinetti directly linked the aesthetic of speed to fascism. In place of the "noisy chicken coops" of sluggish, slow-going deliberative liberal parliaments, Marinetti sought rule by "innovating, swift men" in an authoritarian government committed to taking "novelty, speed, [and] record-setting" seriously.[113] Since liberal democratic parliaments purportedly are run by "old men whose role is to rein in power, [and] slow the maturation of plans," only fascism's deeply rooted enmity to liberal representative government supposedly offered a suitable answer to the structural imperatives of the high-speed pitch of contemporary existence.[114] For Marinetti, Mussolini's "swift temperament" and ability to sway the crowd "like a swift antisubmarine boat, an exploding torpedo" made him the perfect antidote to a decadent liberal democracy unsuited to the dictates of speed.[115] Building uncritically on the modern conception of the executive as best adapted to the challenges of speed, Marinetti's celebration of velocity inevitably culminated in his enthusiastic embrace of executive-centered dictatorship.

Notwithstanding its one-sided and hyperbolic character, the Futurist celebration of speed at least succeeds in underscoring how the experience of social acceleration might join forces with traditional temporal preconceptions about the separation of powers to generate an explosive mix of ideas: embrace that institutional constellation (executive-centered rule, preferable unrestrained by traditional liberal democratic restraints) deemed by the mainstream of modern political thought consistently most adept at grappling with the imperatives of speed while disposing of those institutions (most important, deliberative legislatures committed to the rule of law) which appear to conflict with modern society's built-in preference for permanent change and innovation. If the challenge of speed is now omnipresent, why not turn to a legally unbound high-speed executive to tackle it? The fact that the Futurists considered speed a ubiquitous feature of the modern world implied for them that any executive-centered emergency regime would now have to be a permanent and potentially unlimited affair: a high-speed social world requires a no less high-speed political system, and only a full-fledged emergency dictatorship can hope successfully to match the demanding bill of goods at hand.

If it were the case that social acceleration necessarily outstrips the fundamental preconditions of liberal democracy, those thinkers who have emphasized the tragic quality of modernity would finally have gained an irrefutable confirmation of their prophesies: human history culminates in social and economic conditions that no longer can be meaningfully controlled by free and equal individuals, engaging in reasonable deliberation. Human beings would have created a world that is simply too fast for their own good, and liberal democratic visions of autonomy would soon be nothing more than an odd reminder of a bygone past, of nostalgic interest in the same way that political thinkers lamented the demise of the Greek polis long after it had left the historical scene.

Unfortunately, the tendency of social acceleration to debilitate the core institutions of liberal democracy too often provides sustenance enough for this pessimistic scenario. By thinking hard about how speed might be successfully transformed into an ally rather than an enemy of liberal democracy, we will need to consider the possibility of circumventing this pessimistic scenario.

CHAPTER THREE

Constitutionalism in an Age of Speed

At the turn of the twentieth century the political and legal scholar James Bryce presciently described a fundamental dilemma in his essay "Flexible and Rigid Constitutions": "As conditions never remain long the same in this changeable world, constitutions need to be amended. Yet a principal merit of those which belong to the rigid type is to give steadiness and permanence to the government carried on under them, which they cannot do if they are frequently altered. Here, therefore, is a constant difficulty, which can be overcome only by wisdom in statesmen, by patience and self-control in the people."[1] The difficulty has gained in significance over the course of the last century. The rapid-fire pace of social and economic life calls for constitutional change and adaptation, and flexibility in constitutional law would seem especially well suited to the temporal imperatives of our era. Yet constitutional flexibility risks undermining the steadiness and permanence that liberal democratic defenders of constitutionalism traditionally sought from it, since frequent constitutional alteration seems inconsistent with the quest for constitutional stability. How, then, can we preserve a necessary modicum of stability in constitutional law while simultaneously institutionalizing the flexibility required by our high-speed age?

An impressive body of political and legal thought already addresses the nexus between constitutions and social and economic change. In the United Stares both Progressive Era intellectuals and the Legal Realists harshly criticized the U.S. Constitution for its seeming inability to adjust effectively to twentieth-century social and economic conditions.[2] Since the late nineteenth century advocates of social reform have repeatedly attacked Article 5, arguing that its burdensome amendment procedures undermine possibilities for constitutional adaptation required by the changing realities of social and economic life. The left-wing journalist Daniel Lazare's recent characterization of the U.S. political system as subject to an anachronistic "frozen constitution" fundamentally inimical to reform is only the latest salvo in a series of harsh reviews of U.S. constitutionalism previously proffered by suffragists, supporters of a constitutional ban on child labor, and New Dealers who sought a formal amendment codifying the welfare state.[3] Contemporary liberals in the legal academy often tout the merits of an elastic "living constitution," arguing that only flexibility in legal exegesis can keep the constitution attuned to the challenges of social and economic dynamism. They consider the literalist and originalist modes of interpretation propounded by conservative rivals wrongheaded in part because such views allegedly obscure constitutionalism's temporal presuppositions: written constitutions are intended to remain a source of binding law for "an indefinite but presumably long future," but constitutions can fulfill this function only if we interpret their norms flexibly in order to allow for adaptability amid rapid social change.[4]

It might therefore seem presumptuous to assert that scholars have failed to focus sufficiently on the challenges posed by social acceleration to constitutionalism: students of constitutionalism have wrestled with many of the temporal shifts described in chapter 1. Nonetheless, they have generally failed to do so with the requisite conceptual thoroughness. Although it includes innumerable references to social change and the problems posed by it for constitutional law, legal scholarship typically obscures the multipronged character of social acceleration as well as its underlying structural dynamics; vague references to social change fail to capture the complexity and significance of the social processes described earlier. Because of this socio-theoretical lacuna, constitutional scholars too often miss the novelty of the intellectual and institutional tasks we face. To claim, for example, that social change is universal and the problem of constitutional change is thus by no means altogether new risks ignoring the lessons of recent social theory work on temporality. Not only is it possible to analyze the core temporal trends of contemporary society in a systematic manner, but we also need to recognize that the pace of social innovation continues to increase at a dizzying rate. Even though the question of constitutional change is a familiar one, social acceleration nonetheless forces us to place that question at the fore of any discussion of constitutional government. Social acceleration means that one of the peripheral concerns of traditional constitutional scholarship necessarily takes center stage: any defensible vision of constitutionalism must rest on a normatively and institutionally plausible theory of constitutional change.[5]

The Dilemma of Constitutional Obsolescence

How does social and economic acceleration impact constitutionalism? As noted in chapter 2, written constitutions represent exacting forms of prospective lawmaking, according to which constitution makers are asked to predict future social and economic trends in order to channel state power as effectively as possible. Of course, ordinary legislators are also asked to foresee future social patterns. Special about written constitutions, however, is that their architects typically aspire to do so for "an indefinite but presumably long future."[6] Statutory legislation may require relatively frequent alteration or fall into disuse, as evinced by the growing reliance on sunset laws and other devices that implicitly concede their limited half-life.[7] But constitutional lawmakers traditionally are expected to realize stable rules of the game well suited to myriad future events. Recall that John Locke, one of the intellectual forces behind modern liberal constitutionalism, went so far as to argue that the "fundamental Constitutions of Carolina" should "remain the sacred and unalterable form and rule of government of Carolina for ever."[8] Anyone who peruses Locke's "fundamental Constitutions" will search in vain for amendment procedures. Locke's preference for a fundamentally unchanging body of constitutional law long exerted a weighty influence on the mainstream of liberal democratic constitutionalism.[9]

Later generations fortunately modified Locke's extreme notion of an unalterable constitution and also challenged his preference for a detailed, code-like constitutional document.[10] Many written constitutions contain relatively abstract language ("due process," e.g., or "cruel and unusual punishment"):

this innovation has served as a useful mechanism for constitutional architects struggling to achieve a successful legally binding set of norms able to guide future generations. In the U.S. case, as in many others, "the very language of the Constitution suggests that the Framers . . . recognized that the Constitution is . . . a majestic charter for government, intended to govern for ages to come and to apply to both unforeseen and unforeseeable circumstances."[11] Yet even elastic constitutional language is supposed to help guide and bind the activities of subsequent political and legal actors. Constitutional lawmakers are still expected to possess impressive powers of foresight. Abstract constitutional language must have some meaningful relationship to future social and economic events if it is to help later generations wrestle effectively with their challenges. Most constitutional architects take care to craft constitutions with great care, in part because they sensibly presuppose that constitutional language can and should shape the course of future events. Their political contemporaries often treat the process of constitution making with reverence, thereby similarly acknowledging the momentousness as well as the potential quandaries of the ambitious prospective legislative tasks at hand. They appreciate that writing a constitution should be much more than a strategic "game" pitting narrow-minded partisans seeking immediate gain: successful constitution making requires political actors to look beyond the narrow temporal horizons of present-day political life and envision the basic outlines of a desirable shared future.

Social and economic acceleration conflicts with the traditional expectation that constitutional legislators can be expected to predict future trends with some measure of competence. The foresight of even the most adept constitutional architect suffers in the context of an environment subject to the dictates of acceleration, as the scope of "both unforeseen and unforeseeable circumstances" expands dramatically. The half-life of every original constitutional agreement is subject to decay in a social and economic environment in which intense change becomes pervasive. Rapid alterations in the social and economic circumstances presupposed by even the most farsighted constitutional lawmakers exacerbate the hardships of their already difficult tasks. Not even the most abstract language appropriate to its status as a "majestic charter" can circumvent the necessity of fundamentally updating the constitution in order to adjust to social and economic change. As the legal scholar Richard Kay rightly notes, "human history tells us that sooner or later every constitution will begin to chafe," and fundamental departures from an original constitutional agreement inevitably occur.[12] At some juncture an unmistakable "misalignment between the constitution and the social and political realities which any system of government must take into account" appears; even the most pliable constitutional language may need to take on novel and unexpected meanings in order to allow for fundamental ruptures with the constitutional status quo.[13] Social and economic acceleration provides the familiar dilemma of constitutional obsolescence with heightened significance. Core facets of social and economic acceleration include the intensification of technological and economic innovation, as well as the closely related process whereby broader patterns of social and economic life (occupational patterns, for example, or workplace organization) increasingly tend to undergo relatively rapid transformations. Any constitutional system that intends to employ state authority effectively for the sake of tackling the exigencies of social and economic life faces the problem that constitutional lawmakers, to a decreasing degree, can realistically succeed in anticipating the vast unprecedented shifts likely to confront future generations. In relatively static social and economic settings, the specter of constitutional obsolescence typically remained distant; perhaps this is why early modern political and legal thinkers tended to conceive of written constitutions as fundamentally timeless documents, unlikely to require amendment or alteration. Like so many other features of our high-speed world, however, constitutions risk becoming "out-of-date" at an ever more rapid rate. No constitution can remain unchanged for long in a world in which "all fixed, fast-frozen relations, with their train of ancient and venerable prejudices and opinions, are swept away, all new formed ones become antiquated before they can ossify. All that is solid melts into air, all that is holy is profaned."[14]

  If the diagnosis sketched in chapter 1 is correct, social acceleration also includes the heightened frequency of relatively substantial forms of social and economic change: we now find ourselves in a social and economic world in which far-reaching transformations in many arenas of human activity occur at a rapid-fire pace. Along with technological acceleration, the acceleration of basic social change represents a constitutive feature of our high-speed society. Thus, the enigma at hand is not merely that we require constitutional systems to provide a modicum of flexibility so that future generations can tinker with their basic structure in order to adapt to minimal forms of social change. Constitutions increasingly must accommodate frequent and relatively far-reaching social and economic transformations. Yet fundamental social alterations oftentimes require no less frequent shifts in constitutional practice. Just as alterations in the assumptions about factual social and economic circumstances underlying any given statute threaten to render it obsolescent,[15] so too does the dramatically heightened pace of change in core features of social and economic life suggest an increased possibility of constitutional obsolescence. Every constitutional system is intimately intermeshed with the course of social and economic life, and the acceleration of the latter requires adaptation by the former. Constitutional law "is not some 'reflection' of, or 'superstructure' hovering above capitalist property and market relations; it is an essential mode of existence . . . of those relations. When those relations are undergoing substantial change, so will law."[16] As the pace of social and economic activity accelerates, so, too, the tempo of necessary constitutional change increases. Social and economic acceleration implies the need for a relatively dynamic mode of constitutionalism able to adapt to continual and intense social and economic change.

Constitutional lawmakers are supposed to achieve a relatively coherent document able to provide a basis for some, however minimal, measures of stability and clarity in the law. For the moment we can bracket the difficult questions of how much stability or clarity is required, the appropriate legal character they should take, as well as the substantive aims and goals infusing them. Nonetheless, the very idea of a written constitution is predicated on the idea that its norms should bind and thereby coordinate social and political actors with some degree of constancy if they are to serve as a meaningful source for a standing body of jurisprudence concerned with the fundamental rules of the game. Acknowledging this point hardly requires fidelity to naive originalist legal ideas or a cramped brand of legal formalism.[17] Written constitutions are also conceived as cogent public statements providing "fair warning" and orientation to political and legal actors about the basics of political life. Although himself an admirer of the "unwritten" British constitution, even Bryce conceded that written constitutions were better attuned to the democratic temper of contemporary life: "the democratic man . . . is pleased to read and know his Constitution for himself. The more plain and straightforward it is the better."[18]

Without presupposing some version of these conventional ideas, it becomes unclear why we need written constitutions in the first place. Alas, contemporary conditions require constitutions exhibiting enormous flexibility; they now must leave room for a vast and constantly expanding range of novel social and economic experiences, many of which are likely to prove unsettling. Although social and economic acceleration thus calls for heightened constitutional adaptability, it is by no means self-evident how we can simultaneously achieve a sufficient dose of stability and clarity in constitutional law. A permanently altering, highly adaptable constitutional system risks opening the door to legal inconstancy and opaqueness. It not only threatens the permanence and steadiness long seen as indispensable to constitutional law but also potentially undermines publicity in constitutional law.

Two rejoinders to these preliminary reflections come immediately to mind. First, it might seem as though the specter of constitutional obsolescence only concerns systems dedicated to the pursuit of expansive forms of state activity in the economy. Constitutions based on "free market," or laissez-faire, ideals might be relatively immune to constitutional obsolescence to the extent that they are less committed to regulating fast-paced forms of social and economic activity and thus would be less subject, for example, to the impermanence of our high-speed capitalist economy. This argument gains some initial empirical support from the fact that constitutional systems expressly supportive of far-reaching state intervention in the economy are precisely those in which the problem of obsolescent norms and clauses has long been most intensely discussed. For example, U.S. state constitutions provided a legal framework for active intervention relatively early on (i.e., by the mid-nineteenth century). Yet an impressive body of scholarship suggests that the easy amendability of state constitutions burdened them with detailed norms concerning economic policy, many of which (e.g., specific provisions concerning railroads and the nitty-gritty of commerce and trade) soon were out-of-date. In short, those constitutional documents most intimately tied to the tasks of economic regulation appear subject to more or less constant amendment.[19] Nonetheless, this rejoinder is ultimately unconvincing. Constitutional systems committed to free market ideals also require adaptation to the ever-changing contours of social and economic change. Governments supportive of free market policies engage in significant forms of state activity in economic and social affairs; Thatcher's United Kingdom and Pinochet's Chile both sought a "strong state," albeit one quite different from the welfare state. Even a diehard libertarian judge who pursues free market interpretations of a specific constitutional clause (such as due process) will find herself forced to adapt the clause to social and economic change, and she is likely to engage in series of creative reinterpretations in order to ensure its relevance to the breakneck pace of social and economic life. Laissez-faire constitutional systems operate within, and thus must react to, the challenges of social and economic acceleration, no less than constitutional systems committed to the welfare and regulatory states.[20]

Second, perhaps we should see constitutions as expressive of broadly defined set of abstract moral principles, along the lines proposed by the legal philosopher Ronald Dworkin and others who take seriously the fact that written constitutions often consist of open-ended, moralistic clauses strikingly different from the code-like general rules favored by defenders of a traditional model of legality.[21] From this perspective founding fathers (and mothers) do not intend their offspring to be interpreted in the same way as conventional legal rules or statutes. The argument presented here thus fails to do justice to the special features of constitutional law: constitutions should be read as elastic "living" documents, offering statements of abstract principle which should prove relatively immune to changing social and economic conditions, rather than as a neatly codified set of legal rules. Of course, the ban on "cruel and unusual punishment" may imply a different set of concrete legal answers in 2089 than 1789. Nevertheless, at the level of abstract principle *cruel and unusual punishment* possesses a sufficient degree of moral and legal coherence and stability according to which constitutions can maintain the requisite measures of constancy and clarity over time. From this angle the dilemma of social and economic acceleration turns out to be a pseudo-problem because constitutions consist of abstract principles able to guarantee their identity and legally binding force for "an indefinite but presumably long future."

Even if we concede the view that we should read constitutions, at least in part, as embodying abstract moral principles, the phenomenon of temporal acceleration can hardly be disposed of so quickly. At the very least social and economic acceleration implies that interpretations of abstract constitutional principles will be forced to change at a no less high-speed rate than social and economic life itself. The intensified rate of technological change, for example, points to the likelihood of regularly reinterpreting what *cruel and unusual punishment* means in policy and legal terms, as new technologies potentially allow for no less novel forms of state brutality. In a similar vein the guarantee of "due process" in the criminal law will require different constraints on state actors when high-speed surveillance instruments supplant the truncheon as the most dangerous weapon available to the police. The legal implications of a constitutional "right to privacy" will also have to be constantly revised in the face of permanent innovation in information technology. From the bird's-eye view of the legal or moral philosopher, "cruel and unusual punishment," "due process," and the "right to privacy" may seem to embody relatively unchanging principles; from the perspective of the legal or political actor "on the ground," the necessity of constantly reinterpreting them tends to represent the more noteworthy facet of the enigma at hand. Social and economic acceleration requires a speed-up of the process by which constitutional norms undergo reinterpretation probably no less intense than the general acceleration in social and economic affairs at large.

At some point constitutional interpretation necessarily shades off into fundamental constitutional alteration. Even the most abstract constitutional principle forecloses some set of imaginable interpretations, and one hardly must endorse an unduly narrow model of legal interpretation in order to recognize the virtue of maintaining a distinction between the interpretation of a preexisting constitutional principle and the invention or creation of a new one. Moreover, we can readily concede that the line between constitutional interpretation and alteration is hard to draw in legal praxis while maintaining that there are good normative and institutional reasons for preserving it. We can also admit that there are legitimate differences of opinion about the best theoretical account of the distinction between constitutional interpretation and alteration. Nonetheless, formal constitutional amendment procedures presuppose the possibility of drawing a distinction between constitutional interpretation and modification. Stripped of this distinction, the constitutional commitment to formal amendment—a core feature of most modern constitutional systems—makes no sense.[22]

As suggested earlier, social and economic acceleration heightens the need for relatively frequent fundamental constitutional change. The rapid-fire pace of major social and economic transformation means that the imperatives of constitutional change increasingly tend to explode the confines of legal interpretation. Abstract constitutional principles will have to undergo relatively frequent fundamental alteration in order to adapt effectively. Judicial actors who adjust constitutional norms to novel social conditions may claim that their decisions represent examples of "mere" legal interpretation. A closer examination, however, is likely to reveal that their rulings often entail fundamental constitutional alteration.

This is no mere thought experiment. It is now something of a cliché among legal scholars that constitutional courts periodically engage in constitutional lawmaking arguably as ambitious as original acts of constitutional founding. Under the auspices of interpreting the Fourth and Fifth Amendments of the

U.S. Constitution, for example, many dramatic twists and turns have occurred in the fundamental understanding of criminal procedure, in part as responses to rapidly changing social conditions. The general focus of the Fourth and Fifth Amendments, "the idea that the Constitution places great value on one's ability to keep information out of the government's hand," has been subject to a rich diversity of restatements, and a careful analysis of constitutional history belies robust claims about their purported constancy over time.[23] Some constitutional courts undertake what legal scholar Robert Lipkin aptly describes as "revolutionary adjudication," in which judges engage in fundamental reinterpretations of the basic constitutional rules of the game so as to alter core elements of the political system's legal and political identity.[24] Constitutional courts take on the authority of the constituent power by initiating ambitious forms of fundamental constitutional alteration. Traditional (generally politically conservative) legal commentators often attribute the exercise of the constituent power by courts to power-hungry judges or the endorsement of problematic models of flexible legal interpretation.[25] From the vantage point of the diagnosis developed here, however, matters look more complicated. Whatever its normative and legal faults, the universal tendency for powerful courts to undertake frequent constitutional alteration represents a practical adaptation to a fundamental institutional dilemma: how can we achieve the frequent constitutional change called for by the breakneck pace of social and economic acceleration?

Constitutional Adaptation in an Age of Speed

Activist constitutional courts represent only one possible institutional adaptation to social and economic acceleration. In this section I offer a preliminary typology of constitutional change, aimed at demonstrating that the experience of social speed sheds fresh light on some of its most widely discussed dilemmas.[26] Social acceleration underscores the existence of a paradox at the heart of contemporary constitutionalism: social speed risks favoring insufficiently democratic mechanisms for constitutional adaptation, and democratic modes of constitutional change appear to mesh poorly with the imperatives of acceleration, thereby potentially robbing constitutionalism of the legitimacy that its most persuasive defenders rightly consider indispensable. The most well-trod paths of constitutional change have entailed institutional adaptation primarily via (1) the "dualistic" system of formal amendment initiated by the

U.S. founders; (2) the courts; (3) legislatures (most famously, the UK system of constitutional reform via parliamentary statute); and (4) the executive.[27] Two caveats should be kept in mind. First, constitutional change typically involves a variety of institutional and political actors, and any conceptual typology risks obscuring the messy empirical realities of real-life constitutional alteration. Political actors typically require the cooperation or at least acquiescence of other institutional players. Nonetheless, the typology offered here should better allow us to make sense of the core institutional and temporal dynamics of constitutional adaptation. Second, the social theory debate described in chapter 1 suggests not only that social acceleration represents a long-term process but also that the speed-up of social life continues to intensify. Although I cannot adequately buttress this empirical claim here, recent work in social theory provides initial grounds for believing that the dilemmas posed by social acceleration for constitutionalism have increased in the last century and are likely to continue to do so. Because the temporal quagmires outlined in the following discussion are thus likely to gain in significance in the years to come, it is incumbent on those of us concerned with preserving constitutional government that we tackle them head on.

(1) Bruce Ackerman has recently reminded us of what arguably was the greatest invention of the U.S. framers—namely, a system of constitutional dualism in which the activities of ordinary lawmaking are separated from higher constitutional legislation. In this view the U.S. founders abandoned Locke's notion of a basically unchangeable constitution, but they simultaneously insisted that fundamental constitutional reform would be required to take an arduous and time-consuming path.[28] Higher legislation involves making "supreme law in the name of the People," and it does so by ensuring a greater level of democratic legitimacy than typically found in the ordinary course of political decision making. Constitutional reform should not take place at the level of everyday politics, because the heightened democratic legitimacy required for constitutional lawmaking simply cannot be demonstrated by a single victory at the polls, for example, or the domination of one branch of the government by one political party or the election of an individual candidate. In order for constitutional change to be legitimate, it "must take to the specially onerous obstacle course provided by a dualist Constitution for purposes of higher lawmaking,"[29] because the U.S. founders believed that fundamental change to the constitutional system should exhibit a high degree of popular consensus. For this reason they placed enormous burdens on the

process of formal constitutional amendment: future generations would be permitted to alter the original constitutional compact, but they would have to do so in accordance with the tough procedures outlined in Article 5 of the U.S. Constitution.

Not only does constitutional dualism minimize the perils of leaving the authority to change the fundamental rules of the game to those immediately involved in the political game (e.g., legislators), but it is simply mistaken to assert "that the winner of a fair and open election is entitled to rule with the entire authority of We The People."[30] No single institution (Congress, e.g., or the Supreme Court) can legitimately claim to speak for "the people" as a whole, and we can only reasonably determine that a proposed change to the constitutional system possesses the requisite democratic legitimacy if it has successfully withstood a lengthy series of institutional tests. Of course, alternative liberal democratic models of constitutional change also presuppose that fundamental constitutional change should rest on a high degree of democratic legitimacy. Noteworthy about the U.S. innovation, however, is the intuition that the achievement of a sufficient democratic basis for constitutional reform presupposes a relatively lengthy period of intense political debate and mobilization as well as expresses support from a broad range of political institutions and that it encourages passage of a series of time-consuming institutional tests in order to ensure that popular support for constitutional amendment is sufficiently deliberate and well considered.

Social acceleration defies the temporal preconditions of this admirable vision of constitutional reform. A key desideratum of higher lawmaking is that "it proceed slowly and deliberately," and toilsome amendment procedures were clearly intended by the framers to decelerate popular debate and exchange in order to ensure its reasonable character.[31] They envisioned Article 5 as requiring that constitutional reform would be subject to a series of temporally drawn-out institutional checks, in part because they believed that a modicum of rationality in popular debate and exchange could only be achieved by guaranteeing that it offered a fair hearing to a rich diversity of views as well as a meaningful opportunity to acknowledge the pluralism of interests found in modern society. Practiced in anything more than a small group, however, this meant that deliberation would have to be a slow-going affair.[32] Within the U.S. system the process of ordinary legislation thus includes a number of mechanisms (bicameralism, e.g., and the executive veto) aimed in part at decelerating decision making and thereby contributing to its deliberative merits.[33] From the perspective of the U.S. founders it made no less sense to create amendment procedures significantly more complex and time-consuming than the rules of everyday legislative politics. How better to ensure the correspondingly higher level of reasonable democratic consensus called for by the vastly weightier tasks of higher lawmaking than by dramatically decelerating the process of constitutional change via cumbersome obstacles to formal amendment?

The result of the founders' reflections was a system of amendment now widely seen as one of the most inefficient in the world.[34] The framers were so effective at decelerating constitutional reform via formal amendment that they arguably helped paralyze the U.S. system of formal amendment altogether; a vast range of scholarly studies describes the virtual impossibility of undertaking meaningful constitutional reform in the United States via Article 5.[35] The diagnosis of contemporary society outlined earlier helps shed fresh light on this familiar quagmire. Social acceleration implies that the formal amendment procedures of the U.S. Constitution increasingly have operated in the context of a social and economic universe characterized by rapid-fire change and innovation. Our high-speed social and economic world conflicts with the time-consuming procedures outlined in Article 5, generating a misfit between the temporal horizons of formal constitutional amendment and social and economic affairs. Of course, much of the existing critical literature on the U.S. model of constitutional amendment laments its laggard character. What that literature obscures is that "slowness" per se is no failing, particularly in a system of constitutional dualism in which deliberateness is indispensable to higher lawmaking. Indeed, for the U.S. founders as for the mainstream of Enlightenment political thought, slowness was generally a virtue to be aspired to in popular deliberation, whereas rapidity in mass politics typically could be taken as prima facie evidence of its irrationality.[36] Institutional slowness only becomes a handicap in a social and economic world in which speed is at a premium and social alterations take place at an ever more intense pace.

Not surprisingly, the deliberate process of democratic constitutional reform outlined by Article 5 has long suffered from neglect.[37] Social and economic acceleration means that political actors repeatedly find themselves forced to adapt the constitutional system to incessant and oftentimes substantial social and economic change, and the procedures of Article 5 understandably appear to strike many of them as little more than a quaint leftover from a simpler world fundamentally irrelevant to the real-life institutional tasks of contemporary politics. Accordingly, some of the most blunt assessments of the temporal misfit between Article 5 and contemporary society have come from perceptive politicians. During the heyday of the New Deal, proposals to pursue a formal amendment in order to establish a sturdy constitutional basis for the emerging welfare state generated a terse response from President Roosevelt: referring to the lengthy time period it would surely take to alter the Constitution, Roosevelt seems to have anticipated the temporal flaws of Article 5 when he announced, "We can no longer afford the luxury of twenty-year lags."[38] Why waste scarce political energy on a fight for a formal amendment whose advantages might only accrue decades down the road?

To be sure, Article 5 outlines an unusually laborious set of amendment procedures, and the fundamental core of constitutional dualism is undoubtedly consistent with somewhat less time-consuming methods of formal amendment. By the same token it would probably be a mistake simply to chalk up the temporal misfit between formal constitutional amendment and contemporary society to the idiosyncrasies of the U.S. Constitution or to suggest that alternative systems for formal amendment might easily overcome the dilemmas posed by social and economic acceleration. Social acceleration implies that every system of formal amendment resting on dualistic constitutional principles— and thus committed to broad-based, time-consuming popular deliberation via lengthy institutional tests—is likely to find itself forced to deal with the temporal misfit described here. For example, Australia, whose Constitution requires that proposed amendments be approved by both houses of parliament, or by one house twice, and then ratified by a nationwide majority of voters as well as majorities in four of six states, appears to suffer from temporal pathologies akin to those plaguing formal constitutional change in the United States. Somewhat reminiscent of the U.S. tendency to ignore Article 5 in order to bring about constitutional reform, dissatisfaction with the Australian Constitution seems widespread; its rendition of constitutional dualism similarly appears to mesh poorly with present-day temporal pressures.[39] Moreover, to the extent that contemporary society rests on a built-in intensification of social acceleration, even those constitutional systems possessing amendment procedures less cumbersome than those in the United States may be destined to struggle, to an increasing degree, with problems akin to those long plaguing constitutional adaptation in the United States.

Perhaps this is why there has not only been a significant revival of scholarly interest in the question of constitutional change but also why so many legal scholars today seem unconvinced that any formal amendment could ever serve as an adequate device for achieving peaceful constitutional change.[40] At the very least, social acceleration raises difficult questions for those of us sympathetic to the worthy notion that constitutional adaptation via formal amendment not only should take a deeply democratic form but that we need to ensure its deliberate and well-considered character by means of time-consuming institutional tests.

(2) Courts also update the constitutional system in accordance with changing social and economic realities. As noted earlier, social acceleration implies the necessity of continuously reinterpreting constitutional norms as well as frequent alterations to key elements of the constitutional system. Not only does social speed help muddy the border we might draw between "law" and "politics," but constitutional courts also will probably tend to modify the constitution and take on the role of stealth constitution-making or constituent power.[41] The U.S. innovation of judicial review has provided institutional possibilities for constitutional change which undoubtedly would have surprised the founders: U.S. Supreme Court decisions have impacted more profoundly on the fundamental operations of the political system than most formal amendments promulgated via Article 5.[42]

In 1921 Justice Benjamin Cardozo captured the underlying rationale for this path to constitutional change when he observed that in contemporary society "nothing is stable. Nothing is absolute. All is fluid and changeable. We are back with Heraclitus." For Cardozo the "perpetual flux" of social and economic relations defies formalistic modes of constitutional exegesis.[43] Jurists would do well to offer a "more plastic, more malleable" reading of the U.S. Constitution in order to guarantee its relevance to the changing exigencies of the times.[44] Judges should minimize the impact of precedent in order to allow themselves room for creative readings of the law; the fidelity to the past intrinsic to stare decisis decreasingly makes sense given the profound fluidity and alterability of twentieth-century social and economic affairs.

A few decades earlier astute observers of the U.S. system had already attributed the striking tendency among American jurists to engage in creative constitutional interpretation to the weaknesses of Article 5. In his influential essay on "Flexible and Rigid Constitutions" Bryce grouped the United States under the latter rubric, arguing that American judges overcome the problem of constitutional rigidity, deriving in part from Article 5, by pursuing open-ended interpretations of constitutional law which their more formalistic British legal peers found unsettling. The case of the American Republic suggested that rigidity in formal amendment procedures might be compensated for by flexibility within constitutional exegesis.[45]

From the perspective of social and economic acceleration, constitutional adaptation via judicial interpretation exhibits a number of advantages vis-à-vis formal amendment. It allows for the recurrent reinterpretation of constitutional norms; since many of these reinterpretations do not possess the status of fundamental modifications or alterations to the constitution, this practice performs a vital function for a political system faced with continual and intense change. By not burdening constitutional adaptation with the time-consuming procedures called for by formal constitutional amendments, flexible constitutional exegesis permits courts to respond more quickly to many difficult constitutional conflicts. To be sure, decision making by higher courts is hardly a paragon of speed or efficiency, and their deliberate character is guaranteed by slow-going legal procedures only moderately less arduous than formal amendment. Nonetheless, in many situations the judiciary seems better suited than formal constitutional amendment to the temporal imperatives of our high-speed world. As Cardozo anticipated in 1921, the widespread tendency among twentieth-century jurists to pursue supple constitutional interpretation and downplay precedent has often provided jurists with the flexibility called for by a constantly changing social and economic environment.

Echoing earlier critics of the antiformalistic course of twentieth-century American jurisprudence, the legal theorist Brian Bix correctly notes that the most influential present-day U.S. legal philosopher, Ronald Dworkin, "emphasizes the possibility of revision too much and the likeliness of settledness too little . . . [His theory] celebrates the notion of the great individual judge rethinking whole areas of the law."[46] Even more pointedly, present-day jurists who insist on emphasizing the original meaning of constitutional language criticize Dworkin and other defenders of flexible constitutional exegesis for ignoring the more traditional ideas of legal interpretation embraced by Enlightenment jurisprudence. Such critics may be right to worry about the tendency to morph constitutions for the sake of adjusting them to rapidly changing social and economic circumstances. Unfortunately, however, they too often simply assume that the inevitable misfit between constitutional lawmaking and social experience can simply be ignored by kowtowing to the original constitutional architects.[47] Whatever its faults from the standpoint of traditional liberal jurisprudence, Dworkin's theory meshes nicely with the structural dictates of a no less dynamic social and economic world. Indeed, the same can probably be claimed for many of the antiformalistic trends influential in twentieth-century American legal thought. The universal phenomenon of social acceleration may be one of the reasons why both the U.S. innovation of judicial review and U.S. legal thought have proven so influential abroad in the last half-century.[48] Social and economic speed generates difficult institutional challenges for every political system, and the U.S. example of powerful courts engaging in flexible interpretation offers proven devices for grappling with its consequences. For fledgling democracies hoping to ensure future possibilities for significant political reform via peaceful constitutional means, constitutional change via a U.S.-style constitutional court understandably appears to offer a model worthy of imitation.

However well trodden, the court-driven path of constitutional adaptation to social acceleration suffers from serious flaws. Despite its temporal Achilles' heel, constitutional lawmaking via formal amendment is conducive to relatively impressive levels of legal constancy and clarity. Higher lawmaking by means of formal amendment not only implies that constitutional norms are unlikely to change rapidly, but major constitutional shifts will have to be achieved via express constitutional lawmaking, in which a relatively broad set of political constituencies debates and gains familiarity with the issues at hand. In addition, higher lawmaking typically results in a relatively clear and unambiguous alteration to the constitutional document, thereby contributing to the preservation of the crucial legal virtues of clarity and publicity. In contrast, the tendency to minimize precedent and condone flexible constitutional interpretation indicates likely reductions in legal constancy, and the practice of continuously adjusting constitutional norms to social and economic conditions risks diminishing the clarity of constitutional law as well. U.S. experience suggests that judges will tend to mask even fundamental constitutional reform as conventional legal interpretation; a highly complex and even obscure body of constitutional jurisprudence is the most likely consequence. The enhanced difficulty of predicting beforehand which constitutional norm is applicable to a specific legal scenario poses tough questions for those who take the notion of a written constitution seriously.[49]

Just as troubling, constitutional change via judicial action suffers from democratic deficits. We hardly need endorse a simplistic majoritarian conception of democratic politics in order to worry about the specter of constitutional courts regularly acting as the constituent power or the potential dangers to popular accountability when courts are so overwhelmed by social and economic change that they are unable to distinguish between constitutional interpretation and fundamental constitutional alteration in the first place. Nor does the unavoidably narrow case-centered character of judicial decision making always leave courts "well suited to confront many of the constitutional problems of modern life."[50] To be sure, there are many solid normative and institutional reasons supporting judicial review. Whether present-day institutional versions of judicial review are well suited to the enormous tasks of constitutional adaptation posed by our high-speed world, however, remains unclear. Constitutional dualism resists the notion that any single institution should speak in the name of the people. The fact that social and economic acceleration probably has helped transform too many constitutional courts into a "kind of Constitutional Assembly in continuous session" should worry us.[51]

(3) Elected legislatures often serve as the institutional focus for constitutional change, either by dominating the process of formal constitutional amendment or by discarding the distinction between ordinary and constitutional legislation altogether. Examples of the former include political systems in which formal amendment procedures place special emphasis on a positive (oftentimes supermajority) vote of the central legislature, while the United Kingdom represents the classical example of the latter.[52] From the perspective of constitutional dualism, parliament-motored constitutional adaptation represents an ambivalent normative and institutional response to social acceleration. By undertaking fundamental alterations to the constitutional system, legislatures risk succumbing to the illusion that they can effectively stand in for the people as a whole. By the same token their broad-based representative character arguably makes elected legislatures better suited to many relatively mundane aspects of constitutional adaptation than courts, and the fact that they need not focus on resolving individual legal disputes often provides their activities with the general scope missing from judicial rulings.

No less ambiguous are the temporal qualities of parliamentary constitutional change. A century ago Bryce vigorously defended the British model of constitutional change via ordinary legislation by underscoring its capacity for flexibility in the face of conditions that "never remain the same in this changeable world."[53] More recently, political scientists Stephen Holmes and Cass Sunstein have upheld parliament-centered constitutional adaptability for the emerging democracies of Eastern Europe, arguing that in the context of dramatic social and economic transformations, "a good deal of [constitutional] flexibility and 'ad hockery'" represent the sine qua non of political survival.[54]

Given the turbulence of social and economic affairs in the new democracies, "a general presumption in favor of flexible amending procedures dominated by the established powers, especially the legislature," is necessary to ensure a sufficient level of institutional adaptability.[55] For our purposes Holmes and Sunstein's view is revealing for two reasons. First, there is no need to downplay the manifest severity of the political and institutional enigmas faced by the Eastern Europeans in order to acknowledge that Holmes and Sunstein's suggestive comments implicitly underscore a more general dilemma: as we have seen, social acceleration indicates that constitutional systems everywhere require heightened adaptability.

Second, there are indeed good reasons for claiming that elected legislatures may respond more adeptly to social acceleration than some competing institutional mechanisms. Nonetheless, we should avoid overstating the temporal virtues of the legislative mode of constitutional change. In chapter 2 we saw that liberal democratic political thought has typically envisioned legislative politics as predicated on a wide-ranging process of deliberative exchange involving the expression of a relatively diverse and representative sample of public opinion and competing interests; liberal writers have repeatedly underscored the unhurried prerequisites of deliberate (and thereby legitimate) legislative decision making. Only if the legislature "takes its time" by engaging in a relatively lengthy period of freewheeling deliberation is it deserving of the privileged place rewarded it by traditional liberal democratic theory: in accordance with this basic intuition, Federalist 70 notes that the "differences of opinion" and "jarring of parties" found in elected legislatures mean that "promptitude of decision is oftener an evil than a benefit" there.[56]

Real-life legislatures may very well succeed in rapidly adjusting the constitutional system to quickly changing social and economic realities. The traditional view implies, however, that they risk doing so at the price of sacrificing those slow-going deliberative attributes that justify their privileged status in the first place. The less-than-stellar record of legislative-based constitution making in many parts of the world suggests that this anxiety deserves to be taken seriously.[57] In addition, parliamentary constitutional adaptation may ultimately prove less flexible than Holmes and Sunstein assume. They acknowledge that the parliamentarization of constitutional adaptation obscures the distinction between higher and ordinary law. Yet they miss the most obvious temporal dilemma generated by the tendency to reduce constitutional lawmaking to a subset of statutory legislation. An immediate danger of easy legislative amendability is that constitutions are likely to be filled with provisions no less detailed than those found in statutory law. From one perspective this trend seems advantageous, since it potentially indicates that constitutional law is undergoing an express public revision of its fundamental norms in accordance with evolving social and economic realities. Yet the easy parliamentary amendability of constitutional law is likely to engender a troubling unintended consequence. Statutory law books are already filled with badly out-of-date rules and standards, in part because the half-life of ordinary legislation tends to decline in the face of social acceleration. The legislative path to constitutional adaptation risks exacerbating the general problem of legal obsolescence by allowing for rapid-fire amendments to a constitutional document which increasingly will be pictured by lawmakers as nothing more than an extension of ordinary legislation. The paradox is that the constitution's easily alterable character simultaneously increases the likelihood of a legal system unduly burdened by legal norms that may soon appear far less relevant to social and economic conditions than they did at the time of their promulgation. Parliament-based constitutional change inadvertently loads the constitutional system with norms embodying quick legislative interventions whose significance may very well prove short-lived. In this fashion the parliamentary road to constitutional adaptation tends to increase the complexity and opaqueness of constitutional law, which hardly bodes well for the quest to preserve legal stability and clarity.

Notwithstanding his preference for Great Britain's "flexible constitution" over the rigid U.S. system, Bryce was at least forthright enough to suggest that easy legislative constitutional changes engender a comparably complicated and even "mysterious" system of constitutional law.[58] Contemporary defenders of the parliamentary road to constitutional adaptability typically ignore this peril, despite the fact that social acceleration seems likely to increase its likelihood. Again in some contrast to contemporary authors such as Sunstein and Holmes, Bryce also underscored the potentially antidemocratic tenor of constitutional change via parliament. Worried that the British model, in contrast to U.S. constitutionalism, failed to include adequate institutional devices for generating deliberation and thoughtfulness in constitutional lawmaking, Bryce argued that British constitutional flexibility could only continue to flourish by preserving what he unabashedly described as the "aristocratic" temper of nineteenth-century parliamentary life: "It needs a good deal of knowledge, skill and experience to work a flexible constitution safely, and it is only in the educated classes that these qualities can be looked for."[59] Britain had thus far successfully warded off the perils of excessive constitutional inconstancy, but, if the "uninstructed" propertyless masses gained control of parliament, they would inevitably employ the flexible constitution rashly and ineptly in order to satiate their emotional "class passions." Representative bodies shaped by the "wealthier and so-called upper classes" remained best able to provide a "moderating factor" necessary to check "ill-considered action" likely to be sought by prospective working-class parliamentary majorities.[60]

Regardless of his class prejudices, Bryce was right to imply that defenders of flexible constitutions need to explain how constitutional change will be undertaken with sufficient deliberation, particularly in light of their lack of time-consuming formal institutional mechanisms expressly established for the sake of guaranteeing thoughtful constitutional amendment. The fact that Bryce located the requisite capacity for constitutional deliberation in a privileged class of educated property owners underscores the fact that contemporary defenders of constitutional change via parliament still need to show how their model can provide the political wisdom indispensable to good constitutional lawmaking. Bryce also accurately prophesied that parliaments dominated by the privileged and educated were soon destined to become a thing of the past. In part because of fundamental temporal and spatial changes in human experience,

> these assemblies are now changing their character, as the countries in which they exist have changed. The progress of science has, through the agency of railways and telegraphs, of generally diffused education, and of cheap newspapers, so brought the inhabitants of large countries into close and constant relations with one another and with their representatives, that the conditions of a small city-state are being reproduced . . . The same news reaches all the citizens at the same time, the same emotion affects all simultaneously, and is intensified by reverberation through the press. The nation is, so to speak, compressed into a much smaller space than it filled three centuries ago, and has become much more like a primary assembly than it was then . . . [If representatives become] rather delegates under instruction than men chosen to speak and vote because they are deemed trusty and intelligent, much of the moderative value which the representative system has possessed will disappear.[61]

As Bryce accurately presaged, the democratization of elected representative bodies, as well as the shift toward high-speed forms of political exchange and interaction, fundamentally transforms parliamentary bodies long dominated by privileged social constituencies of a cautious and conservative political temperament. But how, then, can legislative bodies still legitimately claim the awesome powers of constitution making when citizens legitimately no longer believe that their representatives constitute an educated "aristocracy"? Why assume that twenty-first century contemporary legislatures possess the political competence and farsightedness necessary for fundamental constitutional lawmaking? Pale restatements of Bryce's defense of the political and intellectual superiority of nineteenth-century legislature will not suffice.[62]

(4) Recent history includes numerous cases of executive-driven constitutional change. Unfortunately, political theorist Hannah Arendt was right when she observed, "Napolean [*sic*] Bonaparte was only the first in a long series of national statesmen who, to the applause of the whole nation, could declare 'I am the *pouvoir* constituent.' "[63] The most infamous twentieth-century example directly spawned Arendt's own interest in explaining the instability of Continental European constitutionalism vis-à-vis its U.S. counterpart: even before Hitler's rise to power, popularly elected executives in Germany discarded core features of the Weimar Constitution, as it exploited the immobility of the socially and politically polarized German Reichstag in order to justify a constitutionally dubious transformation of the Weimar political and social system.[64] An examination of the sad history by which many interwar democracies became quasi-authoritarian states by 1939 offers analogous examples of executive-motored constitutional change.

This path of constitutional alteration has by no means always necessarily generated authoritarian outcomes, however. In the United States fundamental constitutional changes have taken place in the context of legislative-executive relations concerning foreign policy, with the president now in possession of treaty and war-making powers about which his nineteenth-century predecessors could only have fantasized. Accounts of this shift typically highlight the predominant role played by the executive, supplemented by legislative and judicial acquiescence, in undermining previous constitutional limitations on executive power in foreign affairs.[65] In 1958 President Charles de Gaulle not only disregarded the parliament-centered Fourth French Republic's procedures for constitutional amendment in order to dismantle it and establish a presidential regime, but he also made sure to gain novel amendment procedures that ensured executive supremacy in the amendment process.[66] Even more recently, Russia's President Boris Yeltsin in 1993 effectively demoted parliament to a junior partner in government by unilateral constitutional change (subsequently ratified by a constitutionally suspect popular referendum),[67] while Argentina's President Carlos Menem in 1994 single-handedly brought about a major alteration of the Argentine political system permitting him to seek an additional term in office.

Carl Schmitt, who advised the Weimar government during the republic's final crisis-ridden hours, argued that in socially and politically divided political systems only a popularly backed executive typically proves capable of generating major constitutional reform. Amid crisis scenarios in which the need for fundamental constitutional change becomes pressing, amendment procedures are typically reduced to easily manipulated partisan political weapons, constitutional courts mask their fundamentally political preferences in the disingenuous language of the rule of law, and deeply split legislatures find themselves unable to decide on anything meaningful whatsoever. Only a mass-based executive, ruling on the basis of a plebiscite consisting of "an unorganized answer, which the people, characterized as a mass, gives to a question which may be posed by an authority whose existence is assumed," is likely to possess the institutional integrity required by the weighty tasks of constitutional reform.[68]

Schmitt was so enamored of this path because he believed that it could help dismantle the liberal democratic institutions he so loathed.[69] The fact that many who disagree fundamentally with his normative and political preferences concede that executive-based constitutional alteration is often hostile to liberal democracy suggests that he may unfortunately have been onto something. Constitutional dualism reminds us that no single political institution can legitimately speak in the name of the people as a whole. As noted earlier, parliament-centered constitutional reform is inconsistent with constitutional dualism. Yet the executive's attempt to claim the mantle of the constituent power is typically even more dubious: whereas a broadly based, multivocal legislature can sometimes plausibly represent a sizable portion of the diverse views and interests found in contemporary society, a single univocal executive regularly cannot do so.[70] In addition, executive-driven constitutional reform is often accompanied by the specter of political violence, as other political organs are forced to cede their formal authority over constitution making and accept purely advisory roles. Political sociologist Andrew Arato rightly wonders whether any elected legislature that allows the executive to monopolize constitution-making authority would reasonably do so as "anything other than an implicit response to the threat of force."[71] The crisis situations that function as the most common terrain for executive-based constitutional change rarely prove conducive to broadly based popular deliberation and reflection. On the contrary, the executive justifies clamping down on civil liberties and minimizing parliamentary participation because the dictates of the emergency conflict with the luxury of time-consuming deliberation.

The crisis rhetoric often exploited by would-be executive constitutional reformers is revealing in other respects as well. Executive power has been intimately associated in the modern political tradition with the possibility of rapid-fire *agere* in juxtaposition to slow-going *deliberare:* Hamilton in Federalist 70 notes that only by placing executive authority in the hands of "one man" can we ensure that government action is "conducive to energy" as well as the requisite "decision, activity, secrecy, and dispatch."[72] In fast-paced crises in which standing rules arguably no longer offer effective political guidance, does it not make sense to turn to the temporally contemporaneous executive, allegedly best equipped to deal with the unexpected and unforeseen? The traditional image of the present-oriented executive as most capable of acting with "dispatch" (or speed) remains a crucial feature of recent liberal democratic thinking as well: President George W. Bush repeatedly appealed to it in the aftermath of the September 11, 2001, terrorist attacks in order to garner vast emergency authority.[73] In a landmark 1936 U.S. Supreme Court decision that supported an executive-based effort to enhance presidential authority in foreign policy, Justice Sutherland described the president as the only institutional actor who "can energize and direct policy in ways that could not be done by either Congress or his own bureaucracy. His decision-making processes can take on degrees of speed, secrecy, flexibility, and efficiency that no other governmental institution can match."[74] Reiterating the traditional view, Sutherland claimed that the executive's distinct institutional attributes justify far-reaching discretion in many arenas of foreign policy. Executives who aspire to undertake major constitutional reform obviously have much to gain by using, simulating, or even manufacturing crises, given that emergencies cry out for rapid-fire responses and the present-oriented executive is purportedly best suited to initiate such responses. In each of the examples mentioned here an emergency (the severe economic downturn of the 1930s; the French war in Algeria; profound economic troubles in Yeltsin's Russia and Menem's Argentina) not only provided an immediate justification for executive-motored constitutional change but also allowed the executive to suggest that its capacity for dispatch and efficiency offered the only serious alternative to further political or economic decay.[75]

Revealingly, Hamilton also linked the unitary executive to effective democratic oversight of its activities. "The public opinion is left in suspense about the real author" of a specific political action when plurality in the executive allows its members to shift blame and obscure their responsibility for political mistakes, whereas the unitary executive offers the public a genuine "opportunity of discovering with facility and clearness the misconduct of the persons they trust."[76] Not only is the unitary executive best equipped for initiating rapid-fire action, Hamilton argues, but its unitary character also means that the public possesses a real chance to identify, in a temporally efficient manner, which political actors should be held responsible for a particular action. During an emergency this institutional attribute becomes particularly valuable. Members of a plural executive tend to "pass the buck" when undesirable results follow from their actions, requiring the public to engage in an unnecessarily time-consuming game of figuring out who is to blame for incompetent or ineffective action. Amid the fast-moving temporal imperatives of the crisis situation, such temporally costly deliberations prove extravagant and potentially disastrous.

Hamilton was no apostle of executive-driven constitutional change. Nevertheless, it is easy to see how his influential vision of the temporal superiority of the unitary executive could mistakenly lead some to envision executive-based constitutional change not only as speedy and efficient and thus best suited to moments of crisis but in possession of superior democratic legitimacy as well. Yet those who implicitly build on Hamilton's ideas in order to justify executive-dominated constitutional reform conveniently ignore the fact that the mind-boggling institutional complexity of the modern executive makes it much easier for political actors to pass the buck than Hamilton's argument anticipates; examples of present-day executive actors scrambling to blame their administrative rivals for unpopular policies are legion. Politically precocious politicians, of course, have manipulated the reality of our institutionally complex (and arguably "plural") executive to their personal advantage on many occasions.[77] Like other key facets of the traditional liberal democratic temporal separation of powers, Hamilton's picture of the superior democratic credentials of the executive is at least partially anachronistic: the contemporary executive oftentimes fails to live up to the Hamiltonian promise of ensuring popular accountability by allowing publics to link state action to particular political personalities in a quick or speedy fashion.

Fundamental constitutional alteration obviously represents a key aspect of constitutional change. Constitutional norms are also adapted to social acceleration, however, in less dramatic ways. Social acceleration risks transforming the executive into a privileged site for constitutional adaptation, fundamental or otherwise. Earlier in this chapter I noted that social acceleration implies the necessity of a more or less permanent reinterpretation of constitutional norms as well as frequent alterations to the fundamental rules of the constitutional system. I also posited that speed makes it increasingly difficult to draw a clear line between constitutional interpretation and fundamental alteration. These points are also important for understanding executive-driven constitutional adaptation. If I am not mistaken, there are solid reasons for expecting the executive to gain most from the process of social acceleration. Our traditional preconceptions about executive power imply that executive-based constitutional adaptation is best suited to social acceleration. If (1) the executive is institutionally best equipped to undertake rapid-fire action and (2) ours is a social world in which the need for rapid-fire responses to sudden changes in social and economic realities is at a premium, then (3) the executive would seem especially well adapted to many facets of constitutional adaptation. To the extent that social acceleration implies both incessant reinterpretations and frequent alterations to the constitutional system, substantial doses of executive-driven constitutional change might seem to represent a perfectly sensible institutional adaptation, notwithstanding its potential normative and political ills. Just as the distinction between interpretation and fundamental alteration so often becomes unclear in judicial practice, so, too, the difficulty of distinguishing between the executive's reinterpretation of the constitutional rules of the game and its fundamental modification or alteration of these rules is likely to grow.

As noted earlier, the acceleration of the pace of everyday life constitutes a crucial component of social acceleration. A broad range of data documents the existence of a pervasive sense of feeling "rushed" and "short on time" in contemporary society, along with widespread worries about "falling behind" in a social environment subject to incessant changes. This has encouraged some analysts to speculate that a well-nigh universal impatience with slow-going activities represents an understandable attitudinal and psychological reaction to the dictates of high-speed society.[78] To be sure, the political implications of surveys about anything as imprecise as impatience require careful scrutiny. Yet, if high-speed society indeed breeds a general impatience with slow-going processes and activities, is it no wonder that executive-driven constitutional change looms so large in our era? Appealing to traditional notions about the swiftness of the unitary executive, executives would seem well positioned to exploit such attitudes for the sake of delegitimizing alternative sites for constitutional change. Of course, political scientists and sociologists have long sought empirical explanations for the broad appeal of executive-centered plebiscitarianism. Perhaps the social psychology of our high-speed society, working in conjunction with traditional preconceptions about executive power, can help solve some of the remaining riddles.

Only further systematic empirical research can demonstrate whether social acceleration actually contributes to the amplification of executive authority in constitutional lawmaking so familiar from the history of recent liberal democracy. Nonetheless, the dangers at hand are real. Especially in foreign policy, the presumed necessity for dispatch functions as a ready justification for undertaking substantial executive-driven alterations to the constitutional status quo. Economic crises, and even the relatively ordinary tasks of economic management, also risk increasing the scope of executive prerogative, since the executive seems best equipped to provide the rapid-fire institutional responses required by the high-speed dynamics of contemporary capitalism. In light of the rapidity, scope, and intensity of social and economic change, the traditional association of the executive with speed potentially paves the way for unparalleled exercises of executive power.

Revitalizing Constitutionalism?

In this chapter I have argued that social acceleration undermines normatively attractive visions of constitutional change (e.g., constitutional dualism) while favoring hyperpresidentialist "*autogolpe* or a revolution from above."[79] Speed also seems complicit in the trend toward excessive complexity and opaqueness in constitutional law, which risks undermining the noble vision of a "plain and straightforward" constitution accessible to democratic publics. In short, constitutionalism seems vulnerable to the depressing temporal dynamics of liberal democratic transformation described in chapter 2.

Is there no path beyond this bleak state of affairs? How might we combat the tendency of social acceleration to dismantle stability and clarity in constitutional law as well as privilege insufficiently democratic modes of constitutional adaptation?

A number of institutional proposals on the table suggest that we need not throw our hands in the air in desperation. Most prominently, Ackerman argues for reconfiguring the existing U.S. rendition of dualist constitutionalism, chiefly by streamlining the U.S. system of formal amendment by minimizing the authority provided state governments by Article 5 of the U.S. Constitution. In his proposal a successfully reelected president would be authorized to initiate amendments, which would then be subject to congressional ratification as well as popular approval by means of referenda taking place in the following two presidential election years.[80] While unshackling the U.S. system of a key source of its extreme laggardness—namely, the necessity for ratification by a supermajority of state legislatures or constitutional conventions, Ackerman aspires to preserve the basic contours of constitutional dualism. In this view it is possible to achieve a less time-consuming yet nonetheless normatively more satisfying model of constitutional dualism than that enshrined in Article 5 while simultaneously preserving the valuable insight that constitutional alteration should require approval by a multiplicity of political tests based in distinct institutional sites. One can interpret Ackerman's proposals as a thoughtful attempt to recalibrate constitutional dualism in accordance with the temporal dictates of social acceleration. Although specifically concerned with the U.S. case, Ackerman's general institutional insights conceivably might be applied elsewhere.[81]

Unfortunately, this discussion suggests a possible flaw with Ackerman's proposal: the decisive place of the executive in it raises the specter of precisely the sort of plebiscitarianism which has so often proven destructive of constitutional government in the past. Ackerman's reliance on the U.S. case, in which presidentialism has functioned with relative success, leads him to downplay the possible dangers of presidentialism and, more specifically, executive-dominated constitutional change in other political and social settings. Substantial negative experience with exports of U.S. presidentialism suggests that we should hesitate before pursuing them to a greater extent than Ackerman acknowledges.[82]

Potentially more fruitful are various proposals to reshape constitutional dualism in a less plebiscitary fashion. Like Ackerman's as well as the existing U.S. version of formal amendment, such proposals are predicated on the need for multiple institutional tests in order to ensure meaningful deliberation and reflection as well as convincing evidence that "we the people" have spoken clearly. Nonetheless, they do so while reducing the extreme delays plaguing existing institutional renditions of constitutional dualism. Legal scholar Sanford Levinson suggests changing the U.S. system so that "congressional majorities *plus* presidential approval plus ratification by sufficient states to comprise a majority of the population *or* popular ratification" would suffice to pass a formal amendment. In the case of presidential opposition a congressional supermajority would be required.[83] Political scientist Donald Lutz considers a reduction in the number of states required for ratification as well as considering the possibility of national constitutional referenda as a replacement for some existing institutional trials.[84] By maintaining core components of dualist constitutionalism, such proposals also rightly strive to maintain sufficient clarity and publicity in constitutional law: constitutional change via a revised system of formal amendment would still require broad public debate on proposed constitutional amendments, thereby contributing to a system of constitutional law subject to far-reaching public scrutiny.

On a less parochial (i.e., U.S.-centered) note, Arato praises the new democracies of Eastern Europe for institutionalizing formal amendment rules whose temporal requirements position them between the "extremely rigid American or totally flexible British constitution" in order to ensure a healthy balance between legal stability and adaptability.[85] Recent constitutional framers have perceptively tried to avoid the excessively static character of the U.S. system of formal amendment as well as the potential ills of undue constitutional fluidity. Arguing that the U.S. needs to borrow from recent constitutional innovations abroad, Arato advocates differentiated amendment rules allowing for easier changes to political institutions while insulating certain features of the constitutional system (e.g., civil liberties and judicial independence). A differentiated amendment mechanism would allow for greater institutional adaptability while also protecting elements of the constitutional system for which easy amendability is probably disadvantageous. By exposing constitutional courts to heightened possibilities of override, an additional virtue of Arato's proposal is its potential prowess as a check on their problematic tendency to act as constituent power.[86] More flexible amendment procedures would not only allow for robustly democratic constitutional alteration but also more effectively permit "we the people" to overrule unacceptable appropriations of the constitution-making power by the courts.

Whatever their particular merits, proposals of this type illustrate how we might begin to retool constitutionalism for our high-speed world. A central implication of the argument offered here is that any serious discussion of constitutionalism needs to tackle the implications of social acceleration. Even the most worthy normative and institutional ideas about constitutionalism remain of limited value unless we can demonstrate their suitability to our high-speed world.

If such institutional reflections are to bear fruit, however, they will also have to reexamine a traditional pair of liberal democratic temporal assumptions. Chapter 2 identified the presupposition, widely shared among classical theorists, that deliberation involving anything more than a small number of individuals is necessarily time-consuming: when a relatively substantial group of participants engages in cognitively sophisticated deliberation in which a broad array of views is formulated and a no less rich array of interests expressed, deliberation will have to be measured and unhurried. In order to take a reasonable and thereby legitimate form, deliberation takes time, and this holds for both political life at large (e.g., among publics in civil society) and for those formal institutions (most important, the legislature) intended to be representative and broad based in character. This assumption is indispensable for understanding the U.S. innovation of constitutional dualism as well as the model of formal amendment deriving from it; the framers of the U.S. Constitution burdened subsequent generations with the demanding procedures of Article 5 in part because they wanted to encourage a high level of circumspection in higher constitutional lawmaking. It is also crucial for understanding the manifest failure of the existing U.S. instantiation of constitutional dualism to deal adequately with social acceleration; as noted earlier, formal amendment has been neglected in part because of its profound temporal misfit with social acceleration. Many institutional attempts at constitutional adaptation (via courts, the legislatures, and the executive) can be fruitfully understood as compensatory adjustments to that temporal misfit.

As noted, the orthodox picture of the "energetic" executive as capable of rapid-fire action continues to play a significant role in liberal democratic thinking. Assumptions about the energetic executive potentially open the door to an executive-dominated system of constitutional adaptation, because appeals to the executive's high-speed character typically justify its impressive powers. The dictates of speed cry out for flexible, rapid-fire institutional responses, and the classical temporal portrait of the executive will lead many political and legal actors to deem the executive best attuned to tackling the imperatives of constitutional adaptation.

Yet perhaps the traditional contrast between slow-going *deliberare* and high-speed *agere* no longer makes sense? What if we need presuppose neither a misfit between popular and legislative deliberation and social acceleration nor the superior suitability of the executive to the imperatives of speed? After all, the contemporary executive is a complicated institutional entity, made up of a rich variety of (oftentimes conflicting) bureaucratic units: the emphasis in traditional reflections on the unitary and even solitary nature of the executive badly obscures the empirical realities of both the administrative state and present-day executive decision making. Even when the executive branch acts unilaterally, seemingly straightforward undertakings can prove toilsome and time-consuming, as anyone familiar with the less-than-efficient operations of the modern executive can attest. Executive-centered dictatorships often implicitly appeal to the dogma of the swift unitary executive when promising rapid responses to domestic and foreign crises; revealingly, they often fail to act either quickly or effectively.[87] Uncritical reliance on an overly concretistic and historically anachronistic description of the executive as "one man" meshes poorly with the decision-making realities of modern executive power and the modern administrative state.[88]

In classical liberal democratic theory the dogma of the high-speed unitary executive has also been intimately linked to the metaphor of a "body politic" operating in a hostile "state of nature," according to which only the single person of the executive is best capable of guaranteeing swift and effective self-defense in the face of immediate physical threats against the political community.[89] Yet this conceptual support for the high-speed executive is now surely anachronistic. To be sure, we can easily see why the metaphor of a body politic seemed so tenable to early modern political thinkers. Writing amid the extreme political upheavals that plagued the European political world between 1500 and 1700, they witnessed the elimination of countless political units unable to protect themselves effectively against more advanced forms of bureaucratic and military organization.[90] When many political entities (e.g., the city-states of sixteenth-century Italy) confronted the real possibility of political and legal extinction, the notion that political units should be modeled on the metaphor of a physically vulnerable body politic, against which even a seemingly modest physical assault might pave the way for profound peril, closely matched political realities. This metaphor now clashes with the contours of our relatively stable contemporary state system, however, in which the legal, let alone physical, elimination of competing state units is rare. Wars obviously can be even more destructive than they were in early modern Europe. Yet even the bloodiest of them no longer typically result in the extinction or territorial appropriation of competing states. Implicit representations of the state as a fragile body, for which physical assault can quickly become a fundamental threat to self-preservation, obscures crucial facets of contemporary international relations. The traditional intuition that foreign threats call for free-wheeling executive discretion clearly requires reconsideration as well. Despite the familiar weaknesses of the existing international legal system, picturing that system as a lawless state of nature misconstrues international legal relations at least since the founding of the United Nations.[91] If executive prerogative is justified by the legal unpredictability of the international arena, that justification no longer obtains as readily as in the past.

Similarly, traditional temporal accounts of popular politics require reexamination. For example, early modern discussions of popular deliberation arguably presuppose underdeveloped forms of transportation and communication: well into the nineteenth century, elected representatives were forced to engage in time-consuming travel in order to meet their colleagues, and correspondence or news might require weeks or even months to reach its target. In an age of instantaneous communication and high-speed travel the temporal presuppositions of popular deliberation are dramatically different than in the days of Hamilton or even Mill, as new technologies potentially allow huge numbers of people to exchange views at unparalleled speed. The association of popular deliberation with "slowness" no longer deserves the self-evident character that it possessed for so many of our historical predecessors. Although social acceleration too often has functioned to undermine the rightful place of popular politics while unduly strengthening authoritarian trends, there is no a priori reason for precluding the possibility that novel possibilities for instantaneousness and simultaneity in human experience might instead serve the cause of freewheeling deliberation either in elected representative institutions or among democratic publics.[92]

I make no claim that there is an easy technological fix for liberal democracy's present-day pathologies. Yet novel information and communication technologies arguably provide untapped possibilities for improving broad public deliberation. Democratic theorist Ian Budge is not only right to observe that high-speed interactive technology "has made it easier to have frequent popular votes with supporting discussion," but he is also correct to suggest that liberal democracy has barely begun to make productive use of the potential advantages of new interactive technologies.[93] In deliberative politics "fast is often bad, [and] slow sometimes good," given the fact that legitimate deliberation and interest mediation should encompass a broad range of views and interests.[94] At the same time, there is no reason why unnecessary or excess slowness, deriving purely from the contingencies of a particular spatial and temporal context, might not be legitimately discarded. To the extent that existing forms of popular politics too often are outraced by the fast pace of events, the reduction of surplus laggardness might prove useful in revitalizing the noble liberal democratic ideal of government by freewheeling discussion and debate. The misfit between the fast-paced course of social and economic life and the relatively slow-going texture of popular politics need not constitute an unchanging feature of political life. Geographical distance—as noted by James Madison in Federalist 10—has traditionally been a source of the time-consuming character of mass deliberation. Yet "the existence of electronic communication means that physical proximity is no longer necessary" for relatively direct forms of political interaction.[95] The sequential character of deliberation, whereby speakers take turns participating in particular political forums (a town meeting, e.g., or legislative assembly), is another.

Of course, deliberative politics will always necessarily entail a process of reciprocal give-and-take, and thus some element of sequentiality remains intrinsic to it. But sequentiality can take a very different concrete form in the context of interactive communication and information technologies allowing for mass debate at a breathtaking pace. Because new technologies "can enhance lateral communication among citizens, can open access to information to all, and can furnish communication links across distances that once precluded direct democracy," many traditional temporal and spatial restraints on popular deliberation now no longer obtain.[96] Any remaining restraints derive from the core presuppositions of a normatively acceptable model of political deliberation—in particular, the need to preserve openness and reciprocity among participants. There is no self-evident reason for presupposing that the fundamental normative presuppositions of public deliberation, however, are necessarily inconsistent with political exchange via high-speed technology.

These concluding observations raise countless unanswered questions, not the least of which concerns the precise role for high-speed communication and information technologies in a revised model of legitimate constitutional change. But they also point to the prospect that social acceleration contains positive implications for liberal democracy neglected in the account developed thus far. Although social acceleration risks disabling democratic modes of constitutional adaptation and contributing to the decay of constancy and clarity in constitutional law, it may also open up new possibilities for renewing liberal democratic constitutionalism. If liberal democracy is to become a progressive and forward-looking force for the future, we will need to continue to think hard about how the age of speed not only threatens constitutionalism but potentially points the way to its revitalization as well.

CHAPTER FOUR

The Motorization of Lawmaking

The dilemmas of social acceleration are no less severe in the sphere of ordinary or normal legislation than in constitutional law. In 1950 Carl Schmitt observed that contemporary legislatures are increasingly prone to a disturbing process of "motorization" whereby they calibrate their activities in accordance with the high-speed temporality of contemporary society. According to Schmitt, "law making procedures become ever faster and more circumscribed, the path towards the achievement of legal regulation shorter, and the share of jurisprudence smaller."[1] Legislative and judicial proceedings tend to approximate summary proceedings but hardly the instantiations of careful debate and exchange envisioned by Enlightenment thinkers and their nineteenth-century liberal progeny. Legislatures generate vast quantities of statutes at an ever more rapid pace, typically doing so in a rushed and hectic manner. The constant barrage of new laws renders the traditional quest to achieve clarity and stability in the law untenable. Statutes undergo a structural transformation that bodes poorly for conventional conceptions of the rule of law. Forced to adapt to a vast array of constantly changing political and economic challenges that cry out for speedy resolution, legislatures often hand over expansive grants of poorly defined authority to nonlegislative bodies. Statutes decreasingly comport with conventional models of general, clear, public, and prospective norms, instead taking the form of vaguely defined delegations of legislative authority to executive and administrative bodies. Laws increasingly amount to "constantly alterable orders [*Anordnungen*] oriented towards the rapidly changing concrete situation" at hand.[2] Administrative "orders" or decrees represent paradigmatic examples of "motorized law" because their growing importance in the decision-making apparatus follows naturally from the acceleration of lawmaking and its tendency to undermine statutory clarity and generality. No less striking is the proliferation of exceptional or emergency powers as well as their surprising extension to novel arenas of lawmaking. As early as 1931, Schmitt correctly identified the widespread tendency within contemporary liberal democracy to equate economic and financial crises with military attacks and armed insurrections, thereby justifying executive recourse to sweeping emergency powers as a means of coordinating economic activity. As Schmitt accurately observed, declarations of "economic-financial states of emergency" become increasingly commonplace in the face of omnipresent threats of economic instability.

Schmitt's analysis of motorized legislation constitutes part of his lifelong quest to discredit liberal democracy and its principled commitment to broad-based elected representative legislatures. Notwithstanding Schmitt's own unacceptable normative and political goals, his observations offer a useful starting point for making sense of phenomena that indeed suggest that lawmaking has been undergoing an intense acceleration. Recent empirical research confirms Schmitt's temporal diagnosis: most debate in the halls of parliament is now rushed and hectic, legislatures are busily streamlining their activities in accordance with the temporal demands of our high-speed society, and legal regulation decreasingly accords with classical liberal models. Schmitt's empirical account of the pathologies of rule by high-speed legislative bodies is not only disturbingly perceptive, but Schmitt was right to suggest that legislative acceleration poses difficult questions for those of us, adamantly opposed to his own authoritarian political choices, who are committed to guaranteeing elected representative bodies a decisive role in political decision making. A substantial body of recent U.S. scholarship confirms many of Schmitt's observations about the distinctive legal pathologies of motorized legislation, and contemporary legal and political scholars have been grappling with legal dilemmas that constitute manifestations of the speed-up of legislation diagnosed by Schmitt over a half-century ago.

The first section of this chapter turns to the proliferation of economic emergency powers, both the most neglected and arguably most arresting manifestation of motorized lawmaking. Although the empirical story is a complicated one, substantial evidence suggests that the scope of economic emergency powers has increased significantly in many liberal democracies since the nineteenth century. Initially a mere supplement to wartime emergency authority, executive-dominated emergency economic regulation now represents a more or less permanent feature of political life in many liberal democracies. I then examine Schmitt's contribution, in many ways unsurpassed, to a theory of economic emergency powers. Schmitt was correct to trace the proliferation of emergency economic authority to fundamental changes in the nature of legislative activity. Yet he failed to provide a satisfactory explanation for those changes. In my alternative account the motorization of the lawmaker accurately described by Schmitt is best explained with reference to the process of social acceleration. I also argue that Schmitt's concerns about legislative motorization have also been substantially confirmed by legal scholarship detailing the pathologies of contemporary statutory lawmaking. Recourse to Schmitt is illuminating for the light he sheds on present-day proposals to counteract the pathologies of what legal scholars now describe as "statutorification." At times strikingly reminiscent of Schmitt, recent U.S. legal scholars have argued that the only effective answer to the ills of contemporary statutory legislation lies in a fundamental overhaul of contemporary lawmaking, according to which statutory rule making should cede its predominant position and long-neglected aspects of customary law regain the privileges they possessed before the twentieth century. The lacunae of Schmitt's own appeal to customary law, however, help highlight the fundamental weaknesses of recent answers to legal dilemmas generated by legislative acceleration. Even though present-day U.S. scholarship on statutory lawmaking seems blissfully unaware of Schmitt or his ambivalent intellectual legacy, it risks reproducing the political and conceptual flaws of his original attack on legislative motorization.

Economic Emergency Powers

Let me start with some general observations about the economic state of emergency. First, the phenomenon of liberal democratic regimes relying on emergency institutions and procedures to undertake economic regulation is far more common than generally acknowledged.[3] Virtually unknown before the twentieth century, the practice rapidly became a ubiquitous facet of political life during the interwar years in stable democracies such as Great Britain and the United States as well as in Weimar Germany, France, and many other ill-fated European democracies.[4] Politicians have probably always relied on the rhetoric of crisis to initiate legislative changes. In the twentieth century, however, they often did so in order to abrogate or even abandon normal legislative procedures. Particularly during the darkest days of the Depression, it became commonplace to associate economic crises with traditional justifications for outfitting the executive with exceptional powers. Franklin D. Roosevelt was only one of many elected leaders during this period to demand and gain "broad Executive power to wage a war against the emergency, as great as the power that would be given to me if we were in fact invaded by a foreign foe."[5] Throughout this period liberal democratic states "waged war" against the capitalist economic crisis by means of generous grants of discretionary authority to the executive akin to those previously condoned only during war or civil insurrection.

However problematic, the temporal presuppositions of the traditional liberal democratic separation of powers described in chapter 2 readily allow us to understand the broad appeal of this institutional strategy. No less than wars or natural disasters, severe economic crises indeed constitute potential threats to political stability. Since deliberative legislatures are purportedly unable to act with the requisite expeditiousness, what better way to ward off economic threats than by outfitting the swift unitary executive with far-reaching discretionary economic authority? Abrupt crises that seem to strike economic actors unaware invite a quickened political response that presumably only the contemporaneous, or present-oriented, executive can effectively provide. The additional fact that the specter of economic instability has oftentimes been effectively linked to foreign affairs, in which calls for executive discretion seem most persuasive, provides a supplementary justification for those who consider the expansion of executive power the best answer to economic crisis.

In some interwar polities reliance on executive-centered emergency devices proved effective, while in others (notably France and Weimar Germany), "the unlimited decree-rule of a constitutional government with a dubious popular or parliamentary basis serve[d] only as an intermediate station on the road to complete authoritarianism."[6] Despite this mixed record, the stabilization of liberal democracy in the postwar years in Western Europe and North America hardly resulted in a cessation of all economic states of emergency. Even in the United States, presidents since 1945 have relied on a broad range of emergency delegations of impressive power to conclude strikes, control international trade, and even to reshuffle the rules of the international monetary system.[7] In this vein President Richard M. Nixon declared a national emergency in order to end the postal strike in 1970, while his successors have relied on the broad authority granted the executive by the International Emergency Economic Powers Act (1979) to limit business conducted with Cuba, Libya, and Iran.[8] Most recently, emergency authority has served as an instrument for implementing controversial neoliberal economic policies and so-called shock therapy in many newly democratized countries in Latin America and Eastern Europe. Argentine legislators outfitted President Carlos Menem with awesome exceptional powers to undertake "emergency regulatory power to overcome the present situation of collective risk caused by the serious economic and social circumstances the nation is undergoing," while Russian President Boris Yeltsin was similarly empowered by the Duma to issue any decree necessary for the protection of "social security." Neoliberalism and relatively open-ended delegations of exceptional legislative authority to the executive, justified by reference to the specter of economic instability, have been political bedfellows in fledgling liberal democracies from Moscow to Buenos Aires.[9]

Second, traditional emergency legal institutions and practices obviously vary from country to country. Such institutional and legal differences, however, have had at most a limited impact on the real-life practices of the economic state of emergency. Despite legal and institutional variations (e.g., Anglo-American models of martial law vs. French-inspired conceptions of a state of siege), virtually all twentieth-century liberal democratic polities have been willing to declare economic emergencies before delegating generous (and oftentimes poorly defined) discretionary authority to the executive for the sake of tackling economic problems. The alleged superiority of traditional Anglo-American constitutionalist notions failed to prevent President Nixon from declaring a "national emergency" resulting in the imposition of supplemental duties to deal with a balance of payments crisis or the American Congress from authorizing him "to issue such orders and regulations as he may deem appropriate to stabilize prices, rents, wages, and salaries" by delegating "the performance of any function under this title to such officers, departments, and agencies of the United States as he may deem appropriate."[10] Squabbles about the pros and cons of competing legal instruments of emergency power risk obscuring the strikingly similar manner in which liberal democracies have expanded the definition of an emergency situation to include economic instability in order to legitimize far-reaching forms of executive-dominated economic management.

Third, it is striking that both left- and right-wing governments have made use of emergency economic powers, and a surprising diversity of economic policies has been pursued under their auspices. During the interwar years in Germany, France, and Britain and again during the last twenty years in Eastern Europe and Latin America, balanced budgets, dramatic cuts in the salaries of public employees, and many other deflationary policies have been aggressively undertaken by orthodox-minded governments making use of emergency economic powers; both the relatively cautious welfare state policies of Franklin D. Roosevelt and more ambitious pro-labor policies of Scandinavian social democracy were also advanced by emergency economic instruments.[11] Contrary to the argument of free market theorist Friedrich A. Hayek, only limited empirical evidence can be adduced to support the thesis that an inexorable movement toward an "economic dictatorship"—Hayek's term for the growth of emergency economic authority—is inextricably linked to the expansion of the welfare state and appearance of proto-socialist economic policies.[12] On the contrary, emergency economic powers entailing generous executive and administrative discretion in fact often have served as a powerful weapon for those, such as Hayek, hoping to slash the welfare state and maintain fidelity to the principles of nineteenth-century economic liberalism.

Indeed, the pervasiveness of emergency economic power makes it difficult to draw any easy causal links between it and a host of other conceivable factors. It is true that emergency delegations of economic policy making to the executive have been generated by highly fragmented legislatures in which hostile social and class groupings face-off in an explosive manner, thereby paralyzing legislative decision making and paving the way for executive dominance (most infamously, Weimar Germany between 1930 and 1933).[13] Yet extensive emergency economic powers also have been delegated to executives enjoying strong support within the legislature and the political community at large (such as FDR in 1933). Both parliamentary (e.g., Italy in recent decades) and many presidential systems (e.g., France and present-day Russia) rely on enabling laws and emergency authority within the economic realm.[14] Admittedly, the fact that emergency economic power was so rare in the nineteenth century but so common in our own century might lend support to a more general interpretative scheme according to which its ascent can be traced to the decline of economic laissez-faire, or (in the Marxist rendition of the same argument) the displacement of "competitive capitalism" by "monopoly" or "organized capitalism."[15] Later in this chapter I will show that ongoing structural changes in the capitalist economy do play a pivotal role in the dramatic recent growth of emergency economic power. Yet any argument that underlines broader economic trends obviously needs to avoid two familiar failings. First, this kind of argument too often relies on an idealized and even mythical picture of the nineteenth-century liberal past, and, second, its implicit attempt to categorize social and economic development into distinct stages (e.g., competitive or laissez-faire capitalism vs. monopoly capitalism) risks obscuring the far messier realities of social and economic development.

For now we would do well to avoid forcing the problem of emergency economic power into any predetermined conceptual or ideological scheme. Before trying to develop a general explanation of its origins and subsequent development, we need to take a closer look at the underlying dynamics of its evolution within modern liberal democracy. At the obvious risk of historical simplification, let me try to take a preliminary stab at that indisputably complex task. The definition of what constitutes an "emergency" seems to have taken on broader contours since the nineteenth century. For most of the nineteenth century the employment of emergency powers (in the Anglo-American tradition, martial law) was generally limited to the task of counteracting a direct and unmediated physical threat (e.g., war or rebellion). But this definition has been expanded to include situations in which actual military conflict or violent disorder is absent. In this vein emergency powers are now widely deployed as an instrument of economic management even during peacetime. If I am not mistaken, the story of emergency economic power exhibits a surprising pattern. Emergency economic powers initially functioned as a weapon employed widely against one of the most immediate offshoots of a crisis-ridden modern capitalist economy, the workers' movement, before evolving into an instrument for the direct management of the economic crisis itself. Later emergency economic authority became a device for preempting or preventing the reemergence of economic instability. Most recently, emergency economic powers have come to constitute a more or less permanent instrument of economic management in countries struggling to make the transition from dictatorship to liberal democracy.

Battling the Workers' Movement

Before the twentieth century emergency intervention in the economy was relatively commonplace during wartime or rebellion. Even during the American Revolution the colonists justified a vast range of otherwise unconventional forms of state economic coordination with reference to the exceptional conditions of revolutionary politics; the Civil War provides many similar examples of exceptional wartime economic regulation.[16] Nevertheless, the exercise of emergency authority for the sake of overcoming an economic crisis per se seems to have been rare. For most of the nineteenth century the use of emergency powers was generally limited to situations in which the polity faced a relatively direct physical threat—for example, invasion, rebellion, or civil war.[17] The story is complicated, however, by the fact that emergency authority soon widely served as a powerful weapon against labor and socialist unrest.[18] Karl Marx famously described how constitutional emergency clauses from the French Revolution were transformed into a weapon of reactionary politics and bourgeois class privilege in nineteenth-century France.[19] A perceptive contemporary analyst of parallel trends in the United States early on pointed out that by the end of the nineteenth century martial law's main purpose was to function as a "household remedy" in the battle to squelch an incipient labor movement.[20] Typically employed on the state level by eager governors anxious to ensure a healthy business climate while simultaneously demonstrating their fidelity to "law and order," martial law was widely used in the United States to smash unions and strikes during the seventy-five years between the Civil War and the New Deal.[21]

This more or less universal tendency among elites to ward off challenges to their economic and political privilege by recourse to emergency power proved far more decisive to twentieth-century developments than generally recognized. Discussions of the problem of the economic state of emergency generally see vast delegations of emergency economic authority to the executive during World War I as the immediate driving force behind the innumerable peacetime declarations of an economic emergency in the 1920s and 1930s. For example, many commentators point out that Franklin Roosevelt, as a former assistant secretary of the navy, himself was a veteran of the economic mobilization of World War I.[22] There is no question that wartime experiences of economic coordination played a major role in the proliferation of economic states of emergency both in Europe and North America. From a broader historical perspective, however, this interpretation probably risks overstating the novelty of wartime emergency economic power in the twentieth century while understating the manner in which emergency power as a weapon against the labor movement anticipated crucial features of subsequent developments. On the one hand, the use of emergency power to squelch labor or socialist unrest built, albeit tenuously, on an earlier, more limited understanding of an emergency situation: labor disputes and unrest often involved violent conflict, even if a main cause of labor bloodletting often was the employment of emergency power itself; from the perspective of privileged economic and political elites, labor and socialist unrest always smacked of civil insurrection. At the same time, emergency authority as a political instrument against the laboring classes foreshadowed the open employment of emergency power during peacetime for the sake of grappling with the crisis tendencies of a modern capitalist economy. After all, the appearance of class-based labor radicalism represented an unambiguous challenge to early liberal visions of a harmonious market economy predicated on the promise of prosperity and well-being for all, and the emergence of militant labor movements virtually everywhere constituted the most immediate real-life manifestation of industrial capitalism's underlying limitations and pathologies. Even if we ignore the many direct links between the emergence of the workers' movement and the first great economic crises of industrial capitalism in the 1840s and 1870s, emergency power as an instrument for "cracking down" on the labor movement clearly anticipated future use of emergency authority as a tool for tackling, in a relatively unmediated way, one of the more familiar failings of modern capitalism—namely, its tendency to suffer from periodic economic crises.[23]

From this perspective the British Emergency Powers Act of 1920 is especially illuminating. With the remembrance of wartime emergency provisions fresh in mind, Prime Minister David Lloyd George's postwar Cabinet succeeded in pushing through regulations granting it substantial exceptional authority to limit strike activity interfering "with the supply and distribution of food, water, fuel, or light, or with the means of locomotion."[24] By combining the three "moments" in the historical story just recounted, the act provides a microcosm of the entire history of economic emergency power between the mid-nineteenth and mid-twentieth centuries: its proximity to the wartime context linked it to an earlier tradition in which emergency power chiefly functioned as a tool against violent uprisings and foreign invasions; its anti-strike thrust tied it closely to the widespread tendency to rely on emergency authority against the labor movement; finally, the act's forthright concern with guaranteeing the "supply and distribution of food, water, fuel, or light" clearly pointed the way toward the employment of emergency authority for peacetime economic coordination.

Managing the Economic Crisis

Whatever its precise sources, by the 1920s and 1930s the notion of the emergency situation was increasingly separated from any evidence of military conflict or armed rebellion whatsoever. The dire economic abnormalities of the 1920s and 1930s were placed, virtually everywhere, on the same par with invasions and insurrections, and Roosevelt's famous 1933 equation of the exigencies of the economic depression with an attack "by a foreign foe" merely gave express form to a trend already at work in other liberal democracies. As early as 1923–24, the Stresemann and Marx governments in Weimar Germany relied on the emergency clauses of Article 48 and a series of open-ended enabling laws to deal with the economic cataclysms facing their country; in 1924 the Poincaré government in France tried to use emergency laws to prevent the imminent collapse of the franc but was thrown out of office before succeeding in doing so.[25] Within a few years such practices became a part of "normal" political life throughout a crisis-torn Europe. In line with this novel view of the legitimacy of far-reaching forms of peacetime emergency power as an instrument of economic management, important early New Deal legislation was passed by means of the 1917 Trading with the Enemy Act—an emergency provision left over from World War I providing substantial room for executive prerogative in the economy yet unrelated to the purposes for which Roosevelt and his congressional allies employed it. Anticipating a pattern repeatedly imitated since the 1930s, a piece of emergency economic legislation dating from wartime functioned as a convenient statutory basis for vast peacetime exercises of exceptional economic authority which its authors clearly did not have in mind.[26] This step was in part eased in many settings by characterizations of the economic crisis as deriving, to some extent, from foreign sources. In a backhanded way the global character of the economic crisis was thereby acknowledged but chiefly for the sake of providing the executive with authority traditionally enjoyed only in foreign and military affairs.[27]

Preempting Economic Instability

Since the middle of the twentieth century an additional trend can be identified as well. Both in the United States and elsewhere some forms of emergency economic regulation stemming from the Depression and then World War II became virtually permanent after 1945. Continued reliance on exceptional powers within the economic realm typically was legitimized in the postwar years as a way of warding off a repeat of the disastrous capitalist crisis of 1929, and the extension of emergency economic programs was conceived as essential to the prevention of future economic crises.[28] Here, too, the empirical story is obviously a complex one, but at least two of its features deserve special attention.

First, the Cold War clearly played a pivotal role, though in some national settings more than in others, in perpetuating emergency policies and programs conceived in the dark days of the 1930s. The widespread perception in the 1950s and 1960s that superpower rivalry and the specter of nuclear holocaust had blurred the traditional distinction between peace and war functioned to legitimize continued reliance on emergency economic powers, along with the creation of a vast range of new forms of emergency Cold War economic regulation. Many of these programs, like their predecessors from an earlier era, granted far-reaching discretionary authority to the executive and administration.[29] As noted, even during the interwar years the international character of capitalist economic instability occasionally was emphasized in order to expand the sphere of executive prerogative. The Cold War built on this legacy as well: from the perspective of elite groups in many countries, it rendered the tasks of warding off foreign enemies (especially Soviet communism) and demonstrating the superiority of capitalist liberal democracy, in part by avoiding an economic crisis along the scale of 1929, as intimately related.

Second, it would be a mistake to ignore the innumerable ways in which postwar democracies tried to "regularize" emergency economic powers by subjecting them to a host of novel legal and institutional controls. The "permanent emergency" institutionalized in some of the rich and most stable democracies after 1945 was always hemmed in by a more or less effective range of institutional mechanisms; those living in the relatively robust liberal democracies of Western Europe and North America did not come to reside in the "economic dictatorship" polemically described by Hayek. In an important discussion of the Norwegian Labor Party's reliance on sweeping enabling acts during the late 1940s and early 1950s, Francis Sejersted notes that their acceptance ultimately was predicated on "better and 'safer' procedures for decision-making in the public administration," including the establishment of the much-imitated ombudsman and an Administrative Procedures Act.[30] In many other settings, too, stable postwar liberal democracies strove to contain the potential dangers of generous delegations of emergency power by initiating new forms of executive and administrative oversight.

Nonetheless, the widespread quest to tame emergency economic authority has generated at best mixed results even in the most stable liberal democracies. Recall again the conclusion of a 1974 United States Senate report that the United States had "on the books at least 470 significant emergency statutes without time limitations delegating to the Executive extensive discretionary powers, ordinarily exercised by the Legislature, which affect the lives of American citizens in a host of all-encompassing ways."[31]

As the report outlines, delegations of emergency power to the executive addressed not only war preparation and natural disasters but also many facets of economic life. Unfortunately, more recent commentators have generally confirmed the anxieties that led U.S. Senators Church and Matthias in the 1970s to launch a noteworthy but ultimately ineffective battle against the proliferation of ill-defined emergency powers.[32]

Emergency Powers and Neoliberalism

Yet the ills of emergency economic authority in stable liberal democracies such as Norway and the United States pale in comparison to the problems posed by its spread within the newly democratized postcommunist and Latin American countries. As political scientist Guillermo O'Donnell points out in a recent essay, typical for many of these countries is a style of rule based "on the premise that whoever wins election to the presidency is thereby entitled to govern as he or she sees fit, constrained only by the hard facts of existing power relations and by a constitutionally limited term of office." Part and parcel of this system of "delegative democracy" is the permanent use of a broad array of sweeping delegations of economic authority to the executive which typically are poorly defined and even more poorly restrained by legislatures and courts. As O'Donnell correctly points out, democratizing postcommunist and Latin American countries confront economic problems on a scale that rivals those faced by the rich democracies in the 1930s: "Very high inflation, economic stagnation, a severe financial crisis of the state, a huge foreign and domestic public debt, increased inequality, and a sharp deterioration of social policies and welfare provisions are all aspects of this crisis."[33] Moreover, economic globalization means that "foreign" contributions to economic instability seem more evident than ever before. Hence, executive requests for discretionary powers to fight what even Roosevelt in 1933 characterized in terms of a "foreign foe" are likely to seem even more plausible than during the global crisis of the 1930s, especially in those countries dependent on the fate of decisions made by the International Monetary Fund or World Trade Organization. Not surprisingly, such regimes have rushed to make use of emergency economic devices such as those embraced by France, Great Britain, Weimar Germany, and the United States during the 1920s and 1930s. Yet a decisive difference is that the exercise of emergency economic power in the new democracies is rarely effectively constrained by the legal and institutional checks that have generally conditioned the exercise of emergency authority in the stable, rich democracies of Western Europe and North America; weak judiciaries in Russia and Latin America often fail, for example, to rein in the more egregious abuses of executive prerogative in the economic realm.[34] The scenario is exacerbated by the existence of significant present-day international and domestic pressures on political leaders in the new democracies to pursue neoliberal policies destined to generate economic discomfort among substantial segments of the populace. Continued dependence on emergency economic power, by means of which executive and administrative discretion is maximized and meaningful public debate minimized, seems to provide a short-term political solution for leaders seeking to pursue painful or unpopular economic policies.[35] Whether or not this risky course of action will help stabilize liberal democracy, or instead serve "as an intermediate station on the road to complete authoritarianism" as it did in many parts of Europe between the wars, remains an unanswered question.

Speed and the Emergency Situation

Throughout his long career Carl Schmitt devoted a considerable portion of his intellectual energy to the task of analyzing the dilemmas posed for liberalism by dire crises or emergencies. A significant part of this analysis highlights disturbing legal trends suggesting that liberal democracy has increasingly blurred the dividing line between ordinary legislation and exceptional or emergency powers. Students of contemporary political thought are now generally familiar with Schmitt's theoretical discussion of the problem of the emergency situation as well as the fact that his reflections on emergency power played a pivotal role in his defense of an authoritarian alternative to the Weimar Republic.[36] Scholarship has tended to obscure Schmitt's provocative discussion of emergency economic power, however, as well as Schmitt's argument, formulated in a series of publications between 1931 and 1950, that the imperatives of emergency economic authority demonstrate the fundamental bankruptcy of liberal democracy. In Schmitt's account its preference for the separation of powers, the supremacy of elected legislatures, and the rule of law allegedly render it incapable of dealing with the necessities of the economic state of emergency. Too often, liberal democracies respond to the need for enormous grants of delegated economic authority with halfway measures and bad faith institutional compromises inconsistent with basic liberal principles. By the mid-1930s, Schmitt openly argued, only a National Socialist alternative to liberal democracy was suited to the tasks of the economic emergency.

Nonetheless, Schmitt correctly recognized that emergency economic power had become virtually universal in the liberal democratic political world, observing that its expansion had occurred in many different countries during periods of both war and peace and under the auspices of left- as well as right-wing governments.[37] Already in the 1931 *Guardian of the Constitution,* Schmitt accurately identified the most likely institutional implications of this trend: the growth of far-reaching discretionary executive and administrative power and the concomitant decline of elected legislatures.[38] This trend has also been described by more recent observers who hardly share Schmitt's hostility to liberal democracy. Schmitt also foresaw the possibility that emergency economic powers might lead to new burdens on the judiciary, along lines problematic from the perspective of classical liberal jurisprudence. As he noted in a detailed 1936 discussion of emergency economic powers in Britain, France, Germany, and the United States, liberal democratic governments would likely deal with vast delegations of legislative authority to the executive and administration by initiating new judicial controls over executive authority. Anticipating one of the most striking institutional trends within liberal democracy during the last fifty years, Schmitt suggested that this would probably augment the political influence of the judiciary: given the vast, open-ended character of so many emergency delegations of economic authority, courts would likely gain authority as they were called on to determine the exact limits of delegated legislative authority left unspecified by elected representative bodies.[39] Abandoning the limited retrospective functions granted them by classical liberal jurisprudence, courts increasingly would struggle with the politically explosive task of engaging in the forward-looking coordination of complex economic activities.

What drives the growth of emergency economic power? Unfortunately, Schmitt's favorite explanation is also his weakest. Liberal jurisprudence culminates in the virtual hegemony of legal positivism, as represented most clearly by Schmitt's main intellectual rival, Hans Kelsen.[40] Positivism prepares the way for the acceptance of vast delegations of emergency economic authority to the executive. *The Guardian of the Constitution* criticizes positivists for sacrificing traditional liberal jurisprudence's emphasis on the virtues of clear, prospective, and general legal norms, thereby paving the way for nontraditional legal forms. Poorly defined grants of exceptional economic authority represent a natural outgrowth of this dramatic shift in liberal legal thinking. In addition, positivists such as Kelsen discredit traditional conceptions of state sovereignty. In the process they legitimize a parceling out of state authority to huge agglomerations of hostile political and social constituencies. The resulting "pluralist party-state" contributes to the decline of parliament as an effective lawmaking body and its replacement by a system in which the executive rules by means of sweeping grants of delegated authority.[41] Schmitt's postwar *Situation of European Jurisprudence* (1950) develops this line of inquiry in an even more pointed fashion. The rise of legal positivism, dating from the revolutionary upheavals of 1848, unavoidably generates a "crisis of legality." Positivism's preference for statutory legislation, hostility to natural law, and aversion to judicial interpretation and creativity means that it tends to reduce jurists and legal experts to the passive playthings of an unrestrained motorized legislative demiurge permitted to issue "constantly changing, positive instructions."[42] By undermining the legitimacy of an autonomous legal "estate" [*Stand*] possessing a meaningful role within the legal order, positivism destroys the preconditions of legal expertise on which the achievements of Western legal development rest. Simultaneously, positivism's preference for parliamentary lawmaking leaves it unprepared to ward off the dangers posed to its own existence by omnipotent legislative bodies now free to delegate their authority elsewhere. Legal positivism is fundamentally nihilistic: it sets into motion a process destined to extinguish the centerpiece of its own model of law, the legislative statute, by encouraging parliament to abandon the functions of traditional lawmaking in favor of broad delegations of decision-making power to executive and administrative bodies.[43]

Whatever its merits as a contribution to the history of legal ideas, Schmitt's critique of legal positivism hardly suffices as an empirical explanation for the emergence and growth of emergency economic powers. It is hardly self-evident that positivism has been as intellectually hegemonic or practically influential as Schmitt would have us believe. Even if we were to accept the gist of Schmitt's tendentious characterization of it, positivism's real-life impact has been far more limited than he tends to suggest. Moreover, any attempt to deduce complex, real-life institutional trends from the alleged contradictions of a particular intellectual system should meet with a healthy dose of skepticism. Far too often, Schmitt assumes that history accords with political and legal theory: the internal conceptual limits of liberal theory explain liberalism's real-life political ills. Just as parliament's real-world ills allegedly can be traced to the built-in intellectual failings of liberal views of parliament, so, too, is the proliferation of emergency economic authority in our century supposedly based in the ills of liberal legal thinking.[44]

To his credit Schmitt tentatively points to a competing explanation for the rise of emergency economic powers. Beginning with the 1930s, he sketches a provocative account of why state intervention in the capitalist economy seems intimately linked to liberal democracy's growing dependence on exceptional economic authority. Contrary to economic liberalism, Schmitt argues, far-reaching intervention in the contemporary capitalist economy is essential if political stability is to be assured. By necessity, effective economic management is now an indispensable feature of successful governance. Not surprisingly, modern liberal democracy comes to associate economic crises with military attacks and armed insurrections; dire economic crises do in fact constitute threats to stability.[45]

But why must economic management necessarily entail open-ended delegations of exceptional power to the executive? And why does the practice of emergency crisis management tend to become permanent in character? Schmitt argues that liberal jurisprudence's preference for fixed, codified general norms, along with a strict separation of powers, exacerbates the problem of a time lag within the structure of political and legal decision making. Liberals separate the practices of lawmaking and law application; the former involves the generation of fixed, general norms, and the latter entails their subsequent application to complex individual situations. For liberal jurisprudence statutes always represent a static "fixation" of a legislative act that, by necessity, occurred well before a judicial or administrative actor subsequently applies it. Although liberal legal praxis is thereby "oriented to the past" (*vergangenheitsbezogen*), the dictates of modern interventionist politics cry out for a legal system conducive to a present- and future-oriented "steering" of complex, ever-changing economic scenarios. Liberal statutes "freeze" past experience by making it the basis for a general legislative statute, whereas intervention in the economy means that state actors now face ambitious tasks of both coordinating contemporary economic trends and guiding the future course of economic life. Unfortunately, the temporal gap separating legislation and law application means that judges and administrators are always a step removed from the original experience that inspired legislators to come up with a particular statute in the first place. Liberal judges and administrators "always come too late": they always base decisions about the complex dynamics of contemporary economic conditions on legal relics from an often distant past.[46]

How, then, can this dilemma be solved? Schmitt argues that we need to abandon the traditional liberal conception of the fixed, general statute as well as liberalism's strict delineation of lawmaking from law application, a core element of the traditional notion of the separation of powers; only then can the temporal distance between legislation and legal application be reduced and the enigma of a time lag minimized. One initial step taken by liberal states in this direction entails delegating broad decision-making authority to the executive and administration. For Schmitt emergency economic powers are a particularly dramatic example of this trend. In his view this increasingly common practice points the way toward a long-overdue abrogation of the elements of liberal legalism which render it excessively "oriented to the past." Emergency economic authority represents an attempt to overcome the fundamental dilemma of a time lag plaguing liberal law. Liberalism, however, is unlikely to accomplish the tasks at hand. Writing in 1935, Schmitt asserts that no better example of the liberal failure to deal with the legal imperatives of the modern interventionist state can be identified than the U.S. Supreme Court's hostility to the New Deal. In Schmitt's interpretation Franklin Roosevelt's conservative opponents on the Court were correct to see the open-ended, highly discretionary legislative products of Roosevelt's declaration of an economic emergency as inconsistent with the fundaments of liberal jurisprudence. At the same time, Schmitt notes, Roosevelt was also right to demand economic emergency powers. For Schmitt the New Deal constitutional conflicts underline the impossibility of synthesizing liberalism and emergency economic power. We must choose one over the other, and Schmitt believes that political "realism" in the age of the interventionist state requires us to surrender the intellectual core of legal liberalism.[47]

Thus, the Nazis are praised by Schmitt for finally "crossing the Rubicon" by systematically sacrificing outdated liberal conceptions of the legal statute and separation of powers. Allegedly, National Socialism—which Schmitt enthusiastically embraced in 1933—is most likely to prove adept at grappling with the exigencies of economic management because "law for us is no longer an abstract norm referring to a past act of volition [*auf einen vergangenen Willen bezogene Norm*], but instead the [immediate] volition and plan of the *Führer.*"[48] By getting rid of the distinction between lawmaking and law application, National Socialism allegedly overcomes the problem of a time lag that undermines liberal democratic forms of political and legal decision making. No evidence is produced to support the implausible assumption in Schmitt's argument that Hitler necessarily possesses the awesome cognitive capacities required by the enormous tasks of contemporary economic and social regulation; Schmitt simply appears to assume this. The fact that National Socialism is no longer "past oriented" suffices to render Hitler a "better legislator" than any every known to liberal democracy.[49] Nor does Schmitt concede the obvious point that Nazism thereby makes a legal virtue out of a necessity: having earlier criticized contemporary liberal jurisprudence for abandoning traditional liberal ideas about clarity and generality in statutory lawmaking hardly prevents Schmitt now from praising the Nazis for doing so in a far more ruthless and disturbing manner.

Despite the propagandistic character of his thinking from the mid-1930s, Schmitt still manages to underline a potential problem for traditional liberal jurisprudence. Recent liberal theorists have analogously noted that clear, general legal rules always necessarily "force the future into the categories of the past" in a way that may soon render them inappropriate.[50] Every legal rule codifies a series of expectations drawn from the experiences of legislators, and past history is necessarily used to draw up general norms intended to function as a guide to the future. Yet previous or present experience is a poor guide when political and legal actors confront novel problems. Moreover, the proliferation of delegations of exceptional authority lends some empirical plausibility to the claim that the problem of a time lag diagnosed by Schmitt has proven more troublesome in our century than many liberal jurists have been willing to admit. How might the contemporary steering of economic life exacerbate liberal legalism's built-in time lag? Relatively far-reaching intervention in economic and social affairs was commonplace even in the nineteenth century.[51] Yet the growth of emergency economic powers, as noted earlier, is fundamentally a twentieth-century phenomenon. By itself the appearance of state economic intervention does not suffice as an explanation for the rapid growth of emergency economic authority. So, what is it about recent economic and social life which seems to make the problem of a time lag so pervasive, thus driving liberal democratic states everywhere to delegate emergency economic authority to executive and administrative bodies?

Schmitt tentatively alludes to one source of this development. His 1950 discussion of the "motorized legislator" suggests that the problem at hand is not the interventionist state per se; instead, it stems from an interventionist state driven to engage in rapid-fire regulation. Speed is at a premium in the contemporary world, and one immediate consequence is that state economic intervention is forced to take an ever faster, "accelerated" (*beschleunigt*) form.[52] Liberalism promises legal constancy and relatively stable general norms, whereas the dictates of contemporary motorization entail constant legal change and dynamism. The problem of a time lag within liberal law becomes endemic because ours is a universe in which the time horizons of human activity are incessantly revolutionized. Even liberal states have responded to this trend by embracing novel legal forms (e.g., emergency economic authority) providing heightened flexibility to executive and administrative decision makers; a constant barrage of economic policy dilemmas cries out for a maximum of decision-making flexibility.

Unfortunately, Schmitt's lifelong obsession with combating legal positivism ultimately forecloses an adequate elaboration of this alternative, potentially more fruitful account of the structural roots of the proliferation of emergency economic power. Just when he begins to hint at features of contemporary social life arguably responsible for generating unforeseen problems for liberal jurisprudence, he short-circuits his inquiry by again returning to his polemics against legal positivism; Schmitt makes legal positivism responsible, in the final instance, for the motorization and "technization" of legislative activity that culminates in a ubiquitous recourse to emergency power as an instrument of economic regulation.[53] Yet might not the source of this problem lie elsewhere than legal positivism? At one point Schmitt himself observes that "new accelerations [of lawmaking] derived from the order of a market economy and state coordination of the economy."[54] Chiefly concerned with discrediting liberalism rather than engaging in a critical-minded examination of contemporary economic and social conditions, Schmitt never takes this distinctive explanatory option seriously enough.

Recall David Harvey's apt description of modern capitalism as a "revolutionary mode of production, always searching out new organizational forms, new technologies, new lifestyles, new modalities of production and exploitation and, therefore, new objective social definitions of time and space . . . The capacity to measure and divide time has been revolutionized, first through production and the diffusion of increasingly accurate time pieces and subsequently through close attention to the speed and coordinating mechanisms of production (automation, robotization) and the speed of movements of goods, people, information, messages, and the like."[55] Capitalism's underlying structural imperatives constantly alter the temporal contours of economic activity: "the history of capitalism has been characterized by a speed-up in the pace of life."[56] The decline of turnover time (in production, distribution, and consumption) allows capitalists to maintain profitability; only those capitalists able to exploit faster turnover times are likely to outpace their rivals. Technological innovations produced by capitalist competition transform previously rare possibilities for simultaneity and instantaneousness in human experience into indispensable attributes of present-day economic activity. Intense social acceleration and the resulting "shrinkage of the world"—generated by railroads, automobiles, airplanes, wireless telegraphs, telephones, and computers—have played a decisive role in modern social development, and social acceleration seems to have taken particularly far-reaching forms in the last 150 years; not surprisingly, intellectuals as varied as Marx and Marinetti have offered diagnoses of our era in which the experience of social speed occupies a significant location. Empirical evidence also suggests a continued intensification of social acceleration, as perhaps best demonstrated by recent bouts of innovation in information, communication, and transportation technologies which produce a special emphasis "on 'smart' and innovative entrepreneurship, aided and abetted by all the accoutrements of swift, decisive, and well-informed decision-making," resulting in greatly increased rates of commercial, technological, and organizational change.[57]

A social theory of acceleration potentially offers a superior starting point for properly understanding the social and economic forces fueling the motorization of the lawmaker described by Schmitt. If Harvey is correct, it becomes easy to see why liberal democratic legislatures increasingly have been overwhelmed by the tasks of economic management in our century. Given the demands of a capitalist economy that to an ever greater extent requires fast, constantly changing forms of state intervention in accordance with the rapid-fire dictates of economic life, it is no surprise that even liberal democratic polities tend to hand over vast open-ended authority to executive and administrative bodies widely seen as best suited to the tasks of quick and immediate action. Even in relatively rationalistic versions of Enlightenment political thought, the executive was typically characterized by *agere*, that is, rapid action attuned to the special requirements of the immediate situation at hand. If the exceptional moment is best defined as "comprised of sudden, urgent, unusually unforeseen events or situations that require immediate action, often without time for prior reflection and consideration—i.e., without allowed for preplanned responses," then our increasingly high-speed capitalism, with its sudden downturns and constantly changing, oftentimes unpredictable contours, might seem to require forms of executive-centered political and legal intervention modeled on the logic of the exception.[58] In addition, an explanation that takes the dynamism of modern capitalism seriously possesses the immediate virtue of helping to explain the pervasiveness of emergency economic authority as well as its dramatic proliferation. Even though it would be a mistake to obscure the role played by individual factors within particular political systems in generating an increased dependence of emergency economic power, the ubiquity of emergency economic authority needs to be taken seriously. An analysis that places sufficient weight on general structural trends in contemporary society can succeed in doing so.

The concept of social acceleration also fruitfully contributes to a more general account of the growing significance of emergency powers, economic or otherwise. After all, as Schmitt was well aware, emergency powers have not simply concerned economic management; the tasks of waging and preparing for military conflict have played a central role in the swelling of executive power in the last century. Whereas Marxists such as Harvey have tended to neglect this side of the story, others—including Giddens and Virilio—have correctly suggested that interstate rivalry in the modern state system contributes to the acceleration of social activity. Faced with a vast array of frightening high-speed foreign challenges (e.g., the specter of high-speed warfare), many legislatures seem willing to delegate emergency powers to the executive in the sphere of foreign policy as well. The traditional vision of the high-speed contemporaneous executive described in chapter 2 predisposes policy makers to opt for this institutional path; the proliferation of high-speed activities and instruments in international relations then helps lead them down it. Even more fundamental perhaps, social acceleration contributes to the "compression," or shrinkage, of space noted by perceptive social analysts at least since the nineteenth century.[59] A familiar example underscoring the role of acceleration in weapons technology illustrates the basic dilemma at hand: throughout much of modern history the English Channel functioned as an effective natural defensive barrier for Britain; in World War I German bombers were able to penetrate British airspace but were unable to do much damage; by World War II Nazi planes wreaked havoc on Britain; by the 1960s nuclear technology meant that officials would only be warned a few minutes before enemy nuclear missiles obliterated Britain. When high-speed instruments of mass destruction potentially render traditional political divides irrelevant, traditional liberal democratic modes of decision making may be threatened as well. The compression of our world means not only that national borders have lost some of their original functions as frontiers serving defensive purposes but also that legal forms traditionally considered appropriate to the tasks of overcoming external military threats have been allowed to take on an ever greater role within the everyday operations of liberal democracy. Just as the traditional distinction between the domestic and foreign has been blurred by military technology, so, too, does the classical delineation of emergency from normal legal devices risk losing much of its original clarity and significance. Political philosopher George Kateb has noted that "there can be no genuine democracy so long as foreign policy figures decisively in the life of a society that aspires to be democratic."[60] Yet one enigma we face today is that the compression of distance via high-speed activity tends to obscure the difference between domestic and foreign policy.[61]

Old-fashioned executive usurpations and political hysteria have played a decisive role in the expansion of military-related emergency powers; I do not mean to suggest that the excrescences of emergency rule represent nothing more than an unavoidable consequence of social acceleration. By the same token it would be naive to ignore the fact that many worrisome institutional trends derive from temporal tendencies that are easily exploited by the executive. In an international context in which the "constant progress of rapidity" in weapons technology "threatens from one day to the next to reduce the warning time for nuclear war *to less than one fatal minute*," an executive conceived as best equipped for rapid-fire action is likely to garner substantial opportunities to claim, legitimately or otherwise, that emergency powers are the only effective antidote to the threat at hand.[62]

In fairness to Schmitt he surely anticipated the manner in which interstate relations undergo profound transformations in the context of high-speed weapons technologies.[63] Nonetheless, his obsession with discrediting legal positivism and, more generally, liberal jurisprudence ultimately prevented him from grasping the full significance of his underdeveloped insights about the changing temporal contours of contemporary human existence, and he probably would have resisted a reworking of his picture of a motorized legislature along the lines defended here. Perhaps the conception of social acceleration outlined in chapter 1 can provide a more fruitful explanatory starting point for those of us struggling to understand the disturbing proliferation of emergency powers while rightly hesitant about scrapping liberal democracy.

Statutorification? Carl Schmitt Meets the Common Lawyers

The recent debate among U.S. jurists about statutorification similarly corroborates key features of Schmitt's discussion of legislative motorization. According to a sizable scholarly literature, the last century has witnessed a dramatic increase in the quantity of legislative statutes and a no less considerable boost in the tempo with which legislative bodies promulgate them. Legal scholar Grant Gilmore echoes Schmitt when he notes, "the once leisurely pace of legislative activity had [in the last century] accelerated enormously. In a polarizing society in which crisis had become endemic," legislatures rush to issue statutes in the face of incessant demands for fast-paced legislative action.[64] The result has been a disruptive "orgy of statute making" whose shadows continue to haunt the legal system, along with a dramatically reduced role for traditional forms of judge-centered common law.[65] A no less notable figure in the U.S. legal academy, Guido Calabresi, has also identified integral ties between the increased pace of statutory lawmaking and the widespread perception that legislative norms are better attuned than the common law to the dictates of a high-speed world. For Calabresi, as for Gilmore, both the ascent and the heightened pace of legislative rule making can be traced to trends predating the twentieth century. Nonetheless, since the Progressive Era and New Deal "the speed with which perceived economic crises have followed upon economic crises has brought forth legislative responses" because of "the perceived need for laws that are . . . more immediate than could be afforded by judicial decisions."[66] Lawmakers responded to a crisis-ridden century with bursts of statutory production, and an ambivalent process of "statutorification has occurred at an increasing pace."[67] Although the ascent of the legislative statute ultimately derives from long-term "technological and sociopolitical changes that made slow, accretional, lawmaking unsatisfactory," the major crises of the twentieth century (the world wars, economic depression and resulting movement toward the welfare state, the Cold War) played a major role in speeding up the promulgation of statutory norms.[68] Despite his own unabashed enthusiasm for the common law, even Calabresi is forced to admit that sometimes "courts are not capable of writing speedily enough most of the rules that a modern society apparently needs."[69] Judge-centered case law too often fails to provide the fast-paced action called for by a social and political order subject to incessant acceleration.[70]

The thesis that the intensification of statutory lawmaking is intimately linked to relatively recent shifts in the temporal preconditions of political and social activity is worthy of careful consideration. Sociologists and legal historians have long argued that the increasingly dynamic character of modern society, as evinced with special clarity by the emergence of modern capitalism and its profound impact on the temporal contours of social and economic life, played a pivotal role in the long-term decline of the common law.[71] In a social order in which incessant change becomes common, along with a political order fundamentally committed to providing fast responses to the aggravated pace of social change, any body of law ultimately conceived as embodying "immemorial custom" will probably have to seem suspect.[72] Of course, one would do well not to caricature the common law, which has proven vastly more resilient and adaptable than many critics acknowledge.[73] Nonetheless, its emphasis on precedent and tendency to privilege continuity with the past means that common law jurisprudence ultimately conflicts with social and economic dynamism. Where "all fixed, fast-frozen relations, with their train of ancient and venerable prejudices and opinions, are swept away, all new formed ones become antiquated before that can ossify. All that is solid melts into air, all that is holy is profaned,"[74] the fidelity to past legal practice indispensable to the identity of the common law increasingly seems out-of-date. The ever more dynamic character of many areas of social life requires future-oriented regulations that arguably render "courts . . . less and less competent to formulate rules for new relations which require regulation. They have the experience of the past. They have but one case before them, to be decided by the principles of the past,"[75] when instead we require genuinely prospective rules predicated on the insight that the experience of the past is of limited value given the novel, ever-changing challenges at hand. In an age of speed even a relatively open-ended understanding of the common law doctrine of *stare decisis* is likely to prove unsatisfactory.[76]

The untrammeled, high-speed production of statutes is also related to the decay of natural law.[77] The association of natural law with "invariable foundations" and unchanging "absolute values" means that it similarly conflicts with the dynamic and fast-paced tempo of modern life, along with growing calls for no less fast-paced state action.[78] When Max Weber famously observed that "all metajuristic axioms in general have been subject to ever continuing disintegra-

tion and relativization," he should have more clearly related the disenchant-
ment of natural law to what he elsewhere described as the "extraordinary
acceleration" and high-speed tempo of modern capitalism.[79] Social acceleration represents a no less crucial source of the virtually universal skepticism
about a purportedly invariable natural law than the "judicial rationalism and
intellectual skepticism" offered by Weber as a primary explanation.[80] The decay of natural law means that many traditional restraints on positive lawmaking become controversial: legislatures now deem it legitimate to promulgate a
rich diversity of statutes in arenas that their historical predecessors would have
considered off-limits. As Niklas Luhmann observed, the decline of natural law
generates a scenario in which the only criterion for the legitimacy of a proposed legal change is found within (alterable) positive law itself; recourse to
extralegal natural law axioms conceived as fundamentally unalterable and
permanent is no longer required.[81] In this simple but decisive manner the
universal tendency to provide a privileged status to alterable forms of positive—and especially statutory—lawmaking renders it well suited to modern
social conditions.

Like Schmitt, however, recent U.S. legal scholarship sees a close link between accelerated legislation and a host of contemporary legal pathologies: the
widely celebrated "age of statutes" turns out to be a self-destructive age
of statutorification (*Vergesetzlichung*).[82] Early defenders of statutory legislation promised to liberate legal practice from what Bentham polemically
described as the irrational "Egyptian hieroglyphics" of the common law.[83]
Instead, untamed high-speed statutory lawmaking threatens to undermine
clarity, stability, and predictability in the law, ultimately destroying its own
legal foundations.

Recent theorists of statutorification implicitly endorse Schmitt's notion of
an intimate connection between accelerated legislation and the proliferation
of vague and open-ended legal standards inconsistent with traditional notions
of the rule of law. In Calabresi's account, for example, rushed statutes created
during moments of crisis are likely to be poorly crafted and thereby aggravate
the dilemma of statutory obsolescence, according to which legal systems are
now "choking" on rapidly promulgated and no less rapidly out-of-date laws
"that would not and could not be enacted today, and . . . not only could not be
reenacted but also do not fit . . . the whole legal landscape."[84] Yet the danger at
hand goes well beyond harried legislators, overwhelmed by calls for quick
legislative action, who are simply unable to fulfill their duties properly. Pre-

cisely because future social and economic trends are so much more difficult for statutory drafters to predict in a dynamic and fast-paced world, legislators may consciously opt in favor of "statutes which are loose, ambiguous, vague" in order to provide subsequent actors with the requisite leeway to adjust to changing conditions and needs.[85] The semantic structure of the statute undergoes fundamental alteration in response to the temporal challenges of present-day social and political action: executive and administrative agencies are now expected to interpret open-ended statutes so as to make them consonant with "everyday realities" that undergo significant transformations during the life course of the statute. Flexibility in the executive and administrative application of statutes is an important innovation widely employed by political systems struggling with the rapid pace of social and economic transformation. In effect, state agencies are intentionally outfitted with substantial discretion in order to allow them to compensate for the limited predictive capacities of elected lawmakers.[86] Buttressing Schmitt's expectation that motorized legislatures undermine core liberal aspirations, the literature on open-ended law and increased executive and administrative flexibility, however, is also filled with anxious discussions about their implications for conventional models of legislation. Calabresi worries that delegations of flexible rule-making authority to administrative bodies for the sake of updating state action are often inconsistent with fundamental liberal legal ideals. Administrative rule making sometimes fails to preserve sufficient measures of consistency and coherence in the law as a whole, and attempts at adapting statutes to altered social conditions undermine basic rule of law virtues.[87]

John Locke argued that legislative rules could reasonably be expected to remain valid for a century.[88] The burgeoning literature on statutory obsolescence shows that contemporary legal and political scholars are far less optimistic in their estimates of statutory perseverance.[89] In accordance with Schmitt's analysis of motorized legislatures, many statutes now rapidly become just another waste product of a political and social order obsessed with novelty and change. The half-life of even the most well-crafted statute seems destined to decline substantially in the context of intense social acceleration. The expansion of statutory lawmaking is accompanied by a dramatic growth in outdated and oftentimes irrelevant statutes. This trend bodes poorly for clarity and stability in the legal system; it also defies the decision-making position of the legislature, as judges and administrators find themselves forced to apply outdated statutory norms inconsistent with the actual needs of the situation at hand. In order to ensure effective action, judges and administrators are likely to search for ways of avoiding traditional modes of statutory exegesis, instead opting to engage in creative forms of interpretation which risk shifting decision-making authority away from the legislature and into their own hands. As Calabresi notes, "much of the current criticism of judicial activism . . . can be traced to the rather desperate responses of our courts to a multitude of obsolete statutes in the face of the manifest incapacity of legislatures to keep those statutes up to date."[90] How else but by means of flexible interpretation can judges be expected to come to grips with statutes that seem at best tangentially related to contemporary policy needs? Prominent legal scholars now advocate some variety of what William Eskridge dubs "dynamic statutory interpretation," according to which both statutory language and legislative intention can be legitimately discarded when judges apply relatively old and open-ended statutes. The dynamic and constantly changing character of present-day society means that many statutes on the books are not only likely to age at an accelerated rate but also that the only real chance to make sure that outdated statutes can be applied effectively so as to accord with the "present societal, political, and legal context" is by allowing judges to ignore traditional exegetical approaches to them.[91] In this view judges should flexibly "adapt" obsolescent statutes in order to guarantee their relevance to a constantly changing society.

Recent pleas for dynamic interpretation can be easily interpreted as last-gasp efforts to respond to the dilemmas diagnosed by Schmitt. The general speed-up of legislative activity not only produces a barrage of (oftentimes vaguely formulated) statutes delegating far-reaching authority to nonlegislative authorities, but it also forces other institutions to accelerate their activities accordingly in order to deal with the weighty decision-making burdens now placed in their hands. No less so than the legislature, the judiciary struggles to provide expeditious responses to a vast array of complex policy arenas. Just as Schmitt prophesied in *The Situation of European Jurisprudence*, accelerated lawmaking not only disfigures liberal democratic models of legislation, but it also raises basic questions about the integrity of an identifiably liberal democratic vision of jurisprudence. In a political order in which speed and legislative "output" are at a premium, what place is left for a body of legal experts committed to careful courtroom deliberations and proceedings? Can the institutionally cautious instincts of jurists, as exemplified by the traditional emphasis on preserving stability in the law, survive a political era predicted on rapid-fire decision making?[92] Indeed, legal institutions presently appear subject to a highly problematic motorization reminiscent of similar trends observable in elected legislatures.[93]

Recent empirical research suggests that growing demands on U.S. federal courts to act expeditiously are why many cases now never make it to trial in the first place, for example, and federal judges are much more willing than in the past to grant notices of dismissal and motions for summary judgments. Recourse to relatively informal modes of conflict resolution (e.g., plea bargaining), widely considered less time-consuming than traditional formal legal mechanisms, is on the increase. When cases do make it to trial, temporal pressures mean that core facets of the judicial process are streamlined. Both the length and frequency of oral argument is curtailed, and judges feel pressured to rush the decision-making process in many other problematic ways as well. Judges overwhelmed by the need to act quickly, for example, tend to delegate the authorship of decisions to clerks, and the result is probably a decline in the craftsmanship and deliberativeness of written judicial rulings.[94] Just as the motorization of the legislature risks deforming traditional legislative tasks, so, too, does the motorization of the judiciary pose difficult questions for traditional visions of the legal profession. Is it feasible for judges expected to adapt statutory law to changing social conditions simultaneously to preserve the necessary minimum of constancy and stability demanded by traditional notions of the rule of law? And might not pressures on the courts to streamline their activities undermine the "leisured and learned deliberation" indispensable to competent legal decision making?[95]

Not only is Schmitt's diagnosis of motorized legislation mirrored by recent U.S. legal scholarship, but contemporary criticisms of statutorification parallel his proposed response to it as well. *The Situation of European Jurisprudence* argues that the only suitable answer to the nocuous high-speed statutorification plaguing contemporary law is to revitalize elements of customary legal praxis now widely considered passé: the "breathless hurry" (*atemlose Eile*) characteristic of present-day statutory lawmaking needs to be countered by an approach to law in which the proper role of "leisurely growth" (*ruhiges Wachstum*) is acknowledged.[96] Deceleration is the best antidote to the pathologies of acceleration, and it represents the only chance of preserving the increasingly precarious fundamentals of the Western legal tradition (e.g., the legal virtue of stability).

How, then, might deceleration in the legal system be achieved, and where might we find its most suitable institutional carriers? In order to answer these questions *The Situation of European Jurisprudence* appeals to the nineteenth-century jurist Friedrich Carl von Savigny, a central figure in the Historical School of Law and arguably nineteenth-century Germany's most outspoken defender of customary law. Schmitt praises Savigny for distancing himself from the fetish of codification and the blind faith in statutory lawmaking which so many nineteenth- and twentieth-century jurists naively shared. Although conceding that many aspects of Savigny's legal theory are clearly untenable today, Schmitt heaps praise on Savigny's critical gloss on positive statutory lawmaking, repeatedly describing Savigny as a praiseworthy intellectual model for any contemporary quest to subvert legislative motorization.[97] In Schmitt's interpretation Savigny was presciently aware of the unrealistic character of nostalgic attempts at a full-fledged restoration of a system of customary law. Nonetheless, Savigny was right to distance himself from the modern obsession with positive statutory lawmaking and its embodiment of a hectic "actionism" whose spirit, Schmitt declares, now destructively haunts the operations of contemporary lawmaking.[98] In Schmitt's reading Savigny early on recognized the hazards of any attempt to outfit statutory legislation with a monopolistic status; he was also justified in reminding his nineteenth-century German peers of the implicit virtues of indigenous modes of customary law threatened by the Napoleonic Code and the rush to imitate it throughout Europe.

Although sympathetic toward Savigny's quest to salvage elements of customary law, Schmitt interprets Savigny first and foremost as a defender of the legal profession or estate (*Rechtsstand*).[99] Since jurists constitute the proper professional basis for an effective counterattack against legislative motorization, Savigny is praised for understanding that lawyers and judges represent the most salient "guardians" of legal tradition.[100] Schmitt does not place much stock in Savigny's view of customary law jurists as an "organ of popular consciousness."[101] Yet he endorses Savigny's view that practicing jurists are more likely than legislators to prove effective at ensuring law's core identity. Because only professional jurists embody an instinctual understanding of principled decision making, due process, legal logic and proportion, as well as fundamental legal concepts and institutions, they are best positioned to help preserve indispensable legal virtues and thereby help ward off the perils of legislative motorization.[102] In addition, professional jurists exhibit a praiseworthy caution when bringing about modifications to preexisting law, whereas elected legislators typically pursue impatient and inept legal change. By implication only a legal system in which jurists play a preeminent role can succeed in providing a successful alternative to the pathologies of *Vergesetzlichung* (statutorification). Even though a plausible alternative to the statute-dominated status quo cannot realistically offer a perfect replica of the pre-statutory legal past, Schmitt contends, we would do well to take Savigny's call for a renewal of traditional modes of customary legal praxis seriously. Consequently, we need to refit jurists with the substantial authority unfairly taken away from them by the rise of statutory legislation. Whatever its other faults, customary law provided proper scope to the professional capacities and training of legal practitioners, whom Schmitt describes in *The Situation of European Jurisprudence* as constituting the main driving force behind modern occidental rationalism.[103] A legal system in which jurists' intrinsic skills and talents are properly acknowledged alone can hope to establish authentic legal stability, and not just the superficial "mechanical security" promised by positivist defenders of statutory legislation.[104]

The contemporary debate about statutorification repeatedly echoes this response to legislative motorization. Reminiscent of Schmitt's appeal to Savigny and customary law, Calabresi and others argue that the best answer to the "orgy" of statutory legislation is to recapture features of common law praxis obliterated by twentieth-century political development.[105] Like Schmitt, Calabresi warns his peers of the perils of an exaggerated nostalgia for the pre-statutory legal past while simultaneously insisting that the most sensible response to the ills of high-speed statutorification is to recapture core elements of traditional common law praxis.[106] Modern social and economic conditions preclude a full-scale revival of the common law. Nonetheless, substantial room remains for the common law to function as an effective check on the ills of high-speed statutory legislation. In this view the special status of statutory lawmaking in many arenas of judicial practice requires reconsideration. Given the manifest ills of statutory legislation, there is no principled reason why courts should favor it over the vast range of long-standing norms and practices constitutive of the common law. In order to correct for problems such as legislative obsolescence, judges should be given far-reaching authority to reinterpret and even nullify outdated statutes. Common law courts are to be granted "the power to treat statutes in precisely the same way that they treat the common law. They can . . . alter a written law or some part of it in the same way . . . in which they can modify or abandon a common law doctrine or even a whole set of interrelated doctrines. They can use this power either to make changes themselves or, by threatening to use the power, to induce legislators to act."[107] Courts should again make use of "the entire range of common law techniques to statutory rules, to strike down or revise existing rules, to construct or borrow new rules, to threaten to change rules, and to leave particular areas of the law without rules for a time."[108] If pursued, this approach would undoubtedly engender a hefty increase in the lawmaking authority of courts, along with a likely reduction in the overall political significance of elected legislatures. According to Calabresi and other recent critics of statutorification, however, such a shift is precisely what is required by the weighty task of combating pathological high-speed statute making.

The underlying justification for this proposal recapitulates many of Schmitt's ideas as well. For Calabresi, as for Schmitt, a court-centered deceleration of lawmaking represents a proper antidote to legislative motorization. Because "a slow judicial development of a new rule is still acceptable and even desirable," Calabresi observes, common law courts often are best able to generate legal change while maintaining a requisite dose of stability and continuity.[109] Along with their widely touted flexibility,[110] the cautious character of the common law courts makes them especially well suited to the task of reforming a legal system burdened with obsolete statutes. Advocates of judicial nullification of obsolete statutes also interpret legal experts immersed in the traditional methods and mores of the common law as the most suitable guardians of legal tradition. Because jurists (and especially common law judges) possess an intuitive sense of whether rules "fit" the overall texture of the law, they are generally most adept at guaranteeing coherence in the law as a whole. Far more so than either elected legislators or administrators, their training and practical experience in the common law provide them with a fundamental understanding of the underlying principles operative in the legal order. Second to none when it comes to discerning whether legal materials—statutory or otherwise—mesh with the overall "legal landscape" or "legal fabric," jurists are most likely to do a competent job determining which statutory rules should be modified or discarded for the sake of maintaining a principled and coherent system of law.[111] In this view jurists also make up the sturdiest bulwark against the ongoing erosion of traditional legal ideals generated by legislative motorization, because their instincts and professional training conflict fundamentally with the alarming facets of legislative motorization—most important, the rush to promulgate poorly crafted, open-ended, constantly changing norms.

For Calabresi as well as other recent legal scholars the legal profession—and especially the figure of the common law judge—constitutes what Schmitt in 1950 similarly described as a "final refuge for legal consciousness" in a universe increasingly hostile to basic legal virtues.[112]

Contemporary scholarship also mirrors Schmitt in favoring a far-reaching expansion of the decision-making power of those legal experts properly attuned to the ideal of a stable and consistent body of law, based on a more or less coherent set of fundamental principles. As federal judge Abner Mikva observes, the practical result of the proposal advocated by Calabresi would be to "allow the judiciary to revise laws ranging from a statute's outright inconsistency with other statutory, common law, or constitutional provisions to a statute's failure to become a fixed enough part of the legal firmament to exercise" a meaningful "gravitational force of its own" on the legal system.[113] Calabresi and his allies repeatedly claims that it would be mistaken to exaggerate the countermajoritarian implications of their proposals, in part because legislatures would retain a right to overrule common law rulings about out-of-date statutes.[114] But this is an unconvincing response, in light of the fact that Calabresi claims that legislatures are already overwhelmed by the tasks of lawmaking. If legislatures are incapable of updating statutes on their own effectively, why expect them to supervise an array of courts to be outfitted with far-reaching authority to modify or discard statutes?

Slow Judges versus Fast Legislatures: Decelerating Motorized Lawmaking?

What, then, does the example of Carl Schmitt teach us about contemporary common law–based proposed correctives to statutory obsolescence? To his credit Schmitt seems skeptical of attempts to justify the revival of a traditionalistic judge-centered model of law with appeals to democratic political ideals. His exegesis of Savigny pointedly neglects the latter's claim that jurists can successfully embody "popular consciousness," and Schmitt thereby at least implicitly accepts the criticism that Savigny's vision of customary law hardly meshes well with recent ideas of democracy.[115] Schmitt thus aligns himself with a broad body of twentieth-century scholarship unswayed by claims about the purportedly popular or democratic origins of customary or common law.[116] In contrast, recent discourse on statutorification strains to highlight the democratic virtues of common law review of statutory legislation, notwithstanding weighty evidence suggesting that the "common law has never been a beacon of democracy" for the average citizen.[117] Even if we concede the (hardly uncontroversial) point that common law judges typically are adept at guaranteeing coherence and consistency in the law as a whole, such traits hardly suffice to demonstrate their democratic credentials. Principled legal decision making and a commitment to the idea of treating like cases in a like manner are noble features of the Western legal tradition worth preserving. They do not, however, constitute core attributes of modern conceptions of popular sovereignty. Calabresi argues that legal adaptation via common law jurisprudence "usually required the concurrence of many judges over a long time," and thus "such an allocation of accretional lawmaking authority [to common law courts] could not ultimately be considered undemocratic."[118] Since no single judge can abruptly alter the overall texture of the law and because judicial action is hemmed in by common law procedures and ideals (including *stare decisis*), long-term shifts in the legal fabric typically approximate shifts in popular consciousness. In this (neo-Burkean) view changes in the texture or landscape of the law will only result after a time-consuming series of rulings by many different judges, and thus there is good reason to expect a legal order dominated by common law judges to express "manifestations of popular desires."[119]

Calabresi's argument here represents an attempt to restate the traditional but highly suspect view of the common law as an embodiment of the popular will. This is not an appropriate place to reopen the debate about the common law's purportedly popular credentials, which has occupied countless legal scholars at least since Sir Matthew Hale challenged Thomas Hobbes's critical account of the common law.[120] For Calabresi's argument to obtain, however, we need more evidence that the common law courtroom offers compelling possibilities for freewheeling political deliberation and debate by relatively substantial portions of the citizenry. In many cases this condition clearly is not met by common law courts, which often fail to provide satisfactory forums for popular debate and exchange. Useful deliberation and effective interest mediation are still more likely to occur in broad-based elected representative legislatures. The democratic interpretation of judicial power requires proof that the process of judicial selection offers meaningful possibilities for sufficient popular deliberation about a significant range of policy choices, because Calabresi's proposal means that judges would gain substantial lawmaking authority. Yet here as well there is legitimate room for skepticism. Finally, Calabresi's own tendency to emphasize the intricacies of the common law, and thus the gravity of cultivating specialized legal training and skills, conflicts with the democratic credentials of his proposals. One need not insist on a naive model of the rule of law to worry about the improbability of democratic citizens gaining a reasonable chance of understanding the judge-dominated model of law sought by Calabresi. Bentham was surely unfair in his polemic about the Egyptian hieroglyphics of the common law. But he was fundamentally right to worry that its enormous complexity poses difficult questions for those committed to the democratic ideal of a government accountable—and thus relatively transparent—to citizens and their legal advocates. Calabresi's willingness to outfit judges with vast power to reinterpret and even discard statutes risks heightening legal complexity and making it more difficult for ordinary people to control their government.

By recalling Schmitt's earlier defense of a customary law-based corrective to statutory legislation and its present-day wills, we can identify two additional flaws in the contemporary discussion of the pathologies of rapid-fire statutory lawmaking. First, it is striking that Schmitt's description of precisely what binds judicial rule making in his proposed corrective to statutorification remains ambiguous. As noted, he praises jurists' propensity for principled decision making and their commitment to due process and procedural fairness. Even if Schmitt is empirically correct in this assessment of legal experts, however, it remains unclear whether their possession of these traits could suffice to limit and effectively circumscribe judicial decision making. In U.S. constitutional history, for example, appeals to due process have opened the door to freewheeling judicial legislation; possession of the fundamental legal traits described by Schmitt turn out to be consistent with relatively far-reaching exercises of judicial discretion. One of Savigny's contemporaries accused him of endorsing rule by "juristic Brahmins . . . who would like to mark themselves out as the teachers of laws and morals."[121] Schmitt's ideas in *The Situation of European Jurisprudence* occasionally point in a similar direction. Notwithstanding Schmitt's claim that jurists constitute a "final refuge" for traditional legal virtues, these legal virtues do not seem to include the praiseworthy rule of law commitment to consistent judicial action in accordance with relatively cogent general legal norms or rules. Schmitt tends to dismiss this pivotal element of modern rule of law thinking as a rationalistic excess of a naively "normativistic" mode of legal thought unsuited to contemporary political needs.[122]

Revealingly, the same Achilles' heel plagues recent demands for enhanced common law restraints on legislative rule making. Calabresi argues that judicial nullification of outdated statutes hardly entails unmitigated judicial discretion; judges are merely supposed to modify or overrule outdated statutes that are inconsistent with the broader legal system as a whole. Unfortunately, the likelihood of Calabresi's test of whether a statute "fits" the legal landscape or fabric effectively constraining judicial action seems minimal. For Calabresi *legal landscape* not only refers to existing common law rules and other statutes but also "scholarly criticisms (both in law and derived from such related fields as philosophy, economics, and political science), jury actions that nullify or mitigate past rules, even administrative determinations, all can be appropriate reports of changes in the landscape in response to changed beliefs or conditions."[123] Needless to say, there are good reasons for doubting the capacity of most judges to pull off the strenuous and probably superhuman task of mastering all of these legal (and extralegal) materials effectively, as Calabresi himself occasionally concedes.[124] But, even if judicial decision makers were able competently to compare potentially problematic statutes with the vast range of materials making up the legal fabric, why assume that these materials would provide meaningful direction to judges?[125] Particularly in pluralistic and conflict-laden societies, the legal and extralegal materials described by Calabresi are likely to be multifaceted and even contradictory and thus unlikely to provide clear guidance to judicial decision makers.

Second, both Schmitt and recent common lawyers assume that the relatively laggard pace of traditional judicial practice constitutes a remedy for the excessively fast-paced course of legislative rule making. Although openly acknowledging that the "persistence of this sluggishness of the common law" is one of the original reasons for its fragility, both also believe that a judge-centered deceleration can still serve as an effective antidote to legal pathologies resulting from legislatively based acceleration.[126] Nonetheless, their analyses also suggest that the origins of legislative acceleration oftentimes lie in a more fundamental series of political and social trends to which legislatures have found themselves forced to react; Schmitt refers in *The Situation of European Jurisprudence* to the "new accelerations [in law] derived from the order of a market economy and state coordination of the economy," while Gilmore and Calabresi refer to the political and economic crises (World War I and II, periodic economic downturns, the Cold War) as immediate sources of rushed, or motorized, legislation. So, at least some of the sources of legislative acceleration are located outside the legislative process itself.

In both versions of the argument it remains unclear how a revival of judge-centered traditional legal praxis might succeed in counteracting those causes of the general speed-up of lawmaking derived from broader political and social trends. Both Schmitt and recent U.S. jurists are vulnerable to the criticism that their proposals merely tackle the legislative symptoms of a broader and more profound social process—namely, a far-reaching acceleration of crucial forms of human activity—rather than the root causes of the process itself. It is also unclear why we should expect recourse to either Savigny's customary law or Anglo-American common law to resolve the dilemmas at hand. To the extent that traditional forms of judge-centered legal practice are indeed cautious and time-consuming, they would seem ill fitted to the imperatives of social acceleration. At the very least the misfit between the high-speed tempo of social and economic life and the slow-going pace of lawmaking would probably be even greater under the rule of common law courts than under elected legislatures.

Plausible normative and legal reasons might lead us to prefer the gradual "accretional" ethos of the common law to motorized legislation operating in sync with our fast-paced social universe. Nevertheless, the temporal misfit between the (slow-paced) common law and (fast-paced) social and political life would seem destined to generate severe legal pathologies of its own. Why expect the slow-moving common law to respond efficiently to the rapid-fire changes now so ubiquitous in our dynamic political and social universe? Would not increased dependence on common law justices just as likely exacerbate the dilemma of legislative obsolescence as counteract it? "Courts in the heyday of common law rules were not notoriously energetic about updating. Sometimes centuries passed without more than glacial movement."[127] In light of this experience it seems improbable to expect common law courts to modify statutory legislation so as to ensure its relevance to the rapid-fire tempo of contemporary social and economic affairs.

This conceptual ambiguity generates an additional weakness. The debate about statutorification seems torn between situating its origins in social and political factors outside the legislature and core attributes of modern popularly elected legislatures. To the extent that the latter is underscored as the main causal driving force behind present-day statutory lawmaking, however, the diagnosis of legislative motorization risks representing little more than an updated reformulation of the overstated hostility to popular government so commonplace in Western political thought well into modernity. Especially in Schmitt's account of contemporary legislatures, many elements of the traditional animosity to popularly elected legislatures are easily detected. For Schmitt majority rule making in representative legislatures is typically an irrational affair lacking in adequate deliberativeness; statutory lawmaking by elected representatives tends to take a hectic and impatient form, and its crude and impulsive "deliberations" thus inevitably result in no less sloppy and thoughtless statutes. From his perspective legislatures undergo acceleration in part because popular debate and exchange always risks succumbing to "temporary considerations" inconsistent with long-term perspectives and the common good.[128] The pathologies of legislative motorization are congenital to the extent that they constitute necessary consequences of any attempt to place decision-making authority in the hands of elected representatives inherently unsuited to the dictates of well-considered and truly deliberative decision making.[129]

Not only is this version of the idea of legislative motorization normatively problematic in light of its reliance on a knee jerk hostility to popular government, but it also forecloses any possibility of meaningful reform of the legislature as an instrument for overcoming the pathologies described by Schmitt and recent U.S. jurists. If rule by popularly elected legislatures is flawed from the outset, then the ills of high-speed legislatures probably represent unavoidable and incorrigible offshoots. An answer to those ills, if achievable, will have to be found outside the elected legislature. As we have seen, however, the price to be paid here may be too high. Schmitt does not mind paying that price, since he is hostile to modern liberal democracy and popularly based legislative rule making. Unfortunately, the far less onerous common law response to legislative motorization endorsed by recent U.S. jurists also risks undermining the noble idea of a system of popular legislation primarily "reserved for elected representatives and for their constituents."[130]

Is there an alternative path along which we might salvage statutory legislation while grappling with the pathologies diagnosed by Schmitt and recent U.S. jurists? If the main sources of legislative motorization chiefly lie outside the legislature, there might be. As Schmitt and Calabresi both admit, the fundamental origin of many of the pathologies of contemporary lawmaking lies in the proliferation of "rapid changes in society" which surely would have stunned many of our historical predecessors.[131] Where social acceleration is especially intense, crucial forms of social activity evince enormously increased possibilities for change and innovation; not surprisingly, we now require our political institutions to respond in a correspondingly swift manner to rapid-fire shifts now so commonplace in society at large. One unfortunate result of the long-term trend toward an increasingly dynamic society has been a growing temporal disjuncture between fundamental social and economic processes and elected legislatures badly equipped to grapple effectively with fast-paced social and economic processes. Temporal shifts in fundamental social processes require adaptation by our political institutions. The widespread tendency in recent scholarship to neglect what legal philosopher Jeremy Waldron aptly describes as the "dignity of legislation" means that political and legal thinkers have simply considered questions of this type fundamentally uninteresting. "Not only do we not have the normative or aspirational models of legislation that we need, but our jurisprudence is pervaded by imagery that presents ordinary legislative activity as deal-making, horse-trading, logrolling, interest-pandering, and pork-barreling—as anything, indeed, except principled political decision-making."[132] No wonder we lack a satisfactory account of how legislative rule making might be reformed so as to make it better attuned to the temporal dictates of a social world radically different from that of our historical predecessors.

To be sure, unavoidable "differences of opinion" and the "jarring of parties" essential to decision making in large representative bodies imply that "promptitude of decision is oftener an evil than a benefit" in elected legislatures.[133] We do not want a rapid-fire legislature if it means sacrificing freewheeling debate and exchange required by thoughtful and well-considered legislative decision making. Nonetheless, there is no a priori reason for excluding the possibility of updating our legislatures while maintaining either satisfactory levels of legislative deliberativeness or sufficient fidelity to fundamental legal virtues. In this vein we would do well to pursue a systematic examination of the relatively widespread reliance in recent decades, both at the state and federal level, with "sunset" legislation.[134] Sunset provisions offer no easy answer to the dilemmas of legislative obsolescence. When properly employed, however, they might function as part of a broader answer to the challenges of legislation in a dynamic social environment. They seem especially well suited as a corrective device during moments of emergency or crisis, in which pressures on legislators to deal quickly with novel tasks whose significance they have barely had time to grasp can lead to poorly crafted statutes. Similarly, we might experiment more ambitiously with lawmakers making "specific and limited delegations of the updating power to courts, as Congress has done with regard to the Federal Rules of Civil Procedure."[135] Given the rapid pace of present-day social change, certain courts and administrative bodies should be allowed to update legislative rules. Although it has long been utopian to insist on an absolute legislative monopoly over rule making, fidelity to the noble traditional idea of the elected legislature as the central lawmaker requires that such delegations take a relatively limited and clearly circumscribed form. In contrast to Calabresi's unsatisfactory proposals, legislatures should play a paramount role in determining the scope of this "updating power."

Despite his many errors, Carl Schmitt was right to see accelerated legislation as constituting a formidable normative and institutional challenge to liberal democracy. His analysis of motorized legislation not only offers a valuable starting point for understanding many present-day legal pathologies, but its surprising argumentative parallels to recent debates in the U.S. legal academy help underscore why one proposed cure for statutorification, the revitalization of the common law, risks sacrificing important liberal democratic commitments. We will need to do better than either Carl Schmitt or his unwitting common law allies if we are to combat the ills of motorized legislation. By pointing to possible reforms that might leave liberal democracy well equipped for the exigencies of speed, we can counter Schmitt's hostile attack.

CHAPTER FIVE

Globalization and the Fate of Law

Few notions within modern political and legal theory have been more widely embraced than that capitalism and a legal order embodying the classical rule of law virtues of generality, publicity, clarity, prospectiveness, and stability, in conjunction with relatively formalistic modes of judicial activity, necessarily go hand in hand. Liberal theorists from John Locke to Max Weber argued convincingly that market economies best flourish when resting on a system of legality characterized by a relatively substantial degree of consistency, transparency, and stability; in Weber's famous phrase an "elective affinity" obtains between modern capitalism and "formally rational administration and law."[1] Friedrich Hayek's influential attempt to weld a traditional model of the rule of law directly onto a defense of free market capitalism is merely an exaggerated statement of certain themes already found within the mainstream of the liberal tradition.[2] Liberalism's opponents have also presupposed the existence of an intimate kinship between a market economy based on private property and the liberal rule of law. No less so than Locke or Weber, Marx believed that the formalities of "bourgeois" law were closely allied to modern capitalism, while "post-Marxist" radical jurists (e.g., proponents of Critical Legal Studies) now similarly reproduce the traditional view of a special relationship between capitalism and rule of law.[3] The main difference between the liberals and their critics is that the latter typically rely on the notion of an elective affinity between capitalism and the rule of law in order to discredit both institutions, whereas the former still see market capitalism as indispensable to minimal guarantees of legal security. Contemporary lawyers, policy advisors, and politicians who see market reforms (e.g., in China or Eastern Europe) and the rule of law as two sides of the same coin are simply building on the orthodox view that capitalism and the rule of law require each other.[4]

In light of this surprising consensus, as well as an impressive body of historical scholarship documenting the intimate links between economic and legal liberalism in modern history, it might seem odd to try challenge the idea of a kinship between capitalism and the rule of law.[5] Yet in this chapter I hope to do just that. In my view the traditional belief in an elective affinity between economic liberalism and the rule of law obscures the manner in which the ongoing process of economic globalization threatens core features of the rule of law. Contemporary capitalism is different in many ways from its historical predecessors: economies driven by huge transnational corporations that make effective use of high-speed communication, information, and transportation technologies represent a relatively novel development. The relationship of capitalism to the rule of law is thereby transformed as well. A hitherto unrecognized dialectic has been at work in modern capitalism: by incessantly revolutionizing the temporal horizons of economic action, capitalism tends to diminish its reliance on a robust model of the rule of law. As high-speed social activity "compresses" distance, the separation between domestic and foreign affairs erodes, and the traditional vision of the executive as best suited to the dictates of rapid-fire foreign policy making inadvertently undermines basic standards of legality in the domestic sphere as well. Capitalism contributes to an intense process of social acceleration which ultimately works to limit its dependence on traditional rule of law virtues. The legal infrastructure of contemporary economic globalization suggests that this historical dialectic is now coming to fruition, as traditional modes of liberal law decreasingly figure in the operations of the global economy. Crucial facets of international economic law remain, to a surprising extent, "soft law," disproportionately beneficial to the most privileged "global players"; international business arbitration is still relatively antiformal and nontransparent in character; the World Trade Organization rests on a legal agreement that even today remains plagued by innumerable exception clauses; at the domestic level executive and administrative discretion are especially far-reaching in foreign economic policy. Notwithstanding the orthodox view of the nexus between markets and law, the legal substructure of economic globalization typically exhibits too few classical liberal legal virtues. As I hope to show here, the phenomenon of social acceleration can help explain this surprising state of affairs.

Speed and Globalization

Why address globalization in a study devoted to the impact of speed on liberal democracy? Is doing so merely another example of the inevitable pull of academic bandwagons—in this case, the fashionable topic of globalization?

Two reasons suggest otherwise. First, globalization can be plausibly interpreted as a direct consequence of social acceleration. Social acceleration is not only indispensable to a proper understanding of globalization, but globalization represents an offshoot of the acceleration of social activity described earlier. Careful readers will have already noted that at previous junctures in this study trends widely associated with the process of globalization were briefly mentioned. Earlier reference was made, for example, to the fact that nineteenth- and early-twentieth-century analysts of social speed observed that the acceleration of social activity compresses geographical distance, dramatically transforming our experiences of space or territory. I also provided recent illustrations of this phenomenon: the international character of many economic crises, as well as high-speed warfare that renders national borders porous, help pave the way for a well-nigh universal recourse to disturbing forms of exceptional or emergency law. My earlier discussion of social acceleration inevitably anticipated the present-day debate about globalization because of the intimate connection between the two phenomena.[6] At the most basic level globalization refers to interconnected changes in the temporal and spatial contours of human existence, according to which the significance of space or territory experiences major shifts in the face of a no less dramatic acceleration in the temporal structure of crucial forms of human activity. Geographical distance is typically measured in time. As the time necessary to connect distinct geographical locations is reduced, distance or space undergoes compression or "annihilation." The human experience of space is intimately connected to the temporal structure of those activities by means of which we experience space. Changes in the temporality of human activity generate altered experiences of space or territory. The high-speed temporality of contemporary society ultimately works to undermine the importance of local and even national boundaries in many social activities, thereby engendering a host of phenomena now widely grouped under the rubric of globalization.

Contemporary social theorists rightly associate globalization with deterritorialization, according to which a growing variety of social activities takes place irrespective of the geographical location of participants. As Jan Aart Scholte observes, "global events can—via telecommunication, digital computers, audiovisual media, rocketry and the like—occur almost simultaneously anywhere and everywhere in the world."[7] In this view globalization refers to increased possibilities for action between and among people in situations in which latitudinal and longitudinal location seems immaterial to the social activity at hand. Even though geography remains crucial for many undertakings (e.g., farming to satisfy the needs of a local or regional market), deterritorialization manifests itself in a growing array of social spheres. Businesspeople on different continents engage in electronic commerce; television allows people situated anywhere to observe from the comfort of their living rooms the impact of terrible wars being waged; academics make use of the latest video conferencing equipment to organize seminars in which participants are located at disparate geographical sites; the Internet permits people to exchange greetings with one another despite vast geographical distances separating them. Territory in the traditional sense of a geographically identifiable location no longer makes up the whole of "social space" in which human activity takes place.[8]

Nonetheless, an exclusive focus on deterritorialization offers a misleading picture of globalization. Because the vast majority of human activities remains tied to a concrete geographical locality, the more decisive facet of globalization concerns the manner in which distant events and forces impact local and regional endeavors.[9] Thus, globalization also refers to the growth of social interconnectedness across geographical and political boundaries. For instance, the insistence by powerful political leaders in the First World that the International Monetary Fund (IMF) or World Bank require Latin and South American countries to commit themselves to a particular set of economic policies may result in major changes in everyday life in Lima or Buenos Aires. Analogously, the latest innovations in information technology in India could quickly transform business practices in New York or Tokyo. Globalization concerns "processes of change which underpin a transformation in the organization of human affairs by linking together and expanding human activity across regions and continents."[10] Globalization is also a matter of degree, because any given social activity might influence events more or less far away; even though a growing number of activities seem intermeshed with events on distant continents, certain human activities remain primarily local or regional in scope. Also, the magnitude and impact of the activity might vary; geographically removed events could have a relatively minimal or, alternately, an extensive influence on events at a particular locality. Finally, we might consider the degree to which interconnectedness across frontiers is no longer merely haphazard but, instead, becomes predictable and regular.

Neither deterritorialization nor interconnectedness can be properly conceived, however, without reference to the speed or velocity of social activity. Deterritorialization and interconnectedness initially seem chiefly spatial in nature. Yet it is easy to see how these spatial shifts are directly tied to social acceleration. The proliferation of high-speed transportation, communication, and information technologies constitutes the most immediate source of the blurring of geographical and territorial boundaries which farsighted social thinkers have diagnosed at least since the mid-nineteenth century. The compression or even annihilation of space presupposes increasingly rapid-fire forms of technology; shifts in our experience of territoriality depend on concomitant changes in the temporality of human action. Yet high-speed technology only represents the tip of the iceberg. The linking together and expanding of social activities across borders is predicated on the possibility of relatively fast flows and movements of people, information, capital, and goods. Without these fast flows it is hard to imagine how distant events could possibly enjoy their present influence. High-speed technology plays a pivotal role in the velocity of human affairs. Many other factors, however, contribute to the heightening of overall pace of human activity as well. The organizational structure of the modern capitalist factory offers one example, while certain contemporary habits and inclinations, including a general "mania for motion and speed," represent others.[11] Deterritorialization and social interconnectedness are thus inextricably tied to acceleration, which takes different basic forms (technological acceleration, the acceleration of social change, and the acceleration of everyday life). For this reason, too, we can easily see why globalization is always a matter of degree. The velocity of flows, movements, and interchanges across borders can vary no less than their magnitude, impact, or regularity.

Second, globalization provides a laboratory for testing this study's core thesis that social acceleration threatens liberal democracy. More specifically, the ongoing process of economic globalization rests directly on pronounced forms of social acceleration. Given the many tensions between social acceleration and liberal democracy analyzed earlier in this book, it should come as no surprise that liberal democratic institutions are proving vastly more fragile in the global economy than the orthodox view of a special alliance between capitalism and the rule of law would lead us to expect.

Globalization is best conceived as a multipronged process, since deterritorialization and social interconnectedness manifest themselves in many different (economic, political, and cultural) arenas of social activity. It makes sense to distinguish analytically and empirically between the globalization of the economy, for example, and the globalization of the mass media or political life. Although each facet of globalization is ultimately linked to general trends toward deterritorialization and social interconnectedness, each consists of a complex and relatively autonomous series of empirical developments, requiring careful examination in order to uncover the causal mechanisms specific to it. Each manifestation of globalization also generates distinct conflicts and dislocations. Yet the social theory debate discussed in the opening chapter implies that acceleration, and thus also the elements of globalization based on it, will tend to be most acute where structural mechanisms motoring social speed are correspondingly intense. In support of this expectation, deterritorialization and social interconnectedness are indeed especially far-reaching in the capitalist economy, which privileges speed and plays a central role in generating social acceleration. Economic globalization builds directly on new possibilities for speed in production and consumption which tend to render national borders anachronistic.

Particularly among the global players so prominent in the contemporary economy, new technologies and organizational forms dramatically heighten the experience of instantaneousness and simultaneity, offering rich possibilities for "flexibility with respect to labor processes, labor markets, products, and patterns of consumption" which surely would have astonished earlier generations of entrepreneurs.[12] Transnational enterprises have proven especially adept at making use of new opportunities for speed as well as exploiting their economic advantages. Cross-border economic flows and exchange, as well as the emergence of directly transnational forms of production by means of which single commodities are manufactured simultaneously in distant corners of the globe, depend on high-speed technologies and organizational approaches. The emergence of "around-the-world, around-the-clock" financial markets, in which major cross-border financial transactions are made in cyberspace in the blink of an eye, represent the most familiar example of the alliance between social speed and economic globalization: global financial markets would be inconceivable without recent innovations in information and communication technology, as would a host of no less decisive facets of economic globalization. Subcontracting, outsourcing, "small batch" and short production runs, "just-in-time" inventory flows and delivery systems—each of these innovations accelerates the pace of production and allows firms to adjust rapidly to changes in consumption patterns, and each has been made feasible by dramatic technological developments that make it possible for business enterprise to maximize velocity and thereby minimize the economic significance of geography. The half-life of many products has been dramatically cut in recent decades, impacting production to the extent that enterprises often exhibit "low equipment dedication" and economic facilities may require more or less constant rationalization; the half-life of productive facilities is reduced as well.[13] This is one reason why it often proves profitable to shift economic activities to new localities, thereby directly contributing to the increased mobility of capital which so fascinates observers of the contemporary global economy. By collapsing the "future" into the "present," social acceleration concurrently undermines the distance between "there" and "here." When rapid-fire forms of communication make it profitable for CEOs to oversee the production of different components of a single commodity in far-flung corners of the globe or currency traders in London to communicate simultaneously with their peers in Tokyo, the temporal—and thereby also spatial— horizons of economic activity necessarily undergo dramatic transformations.

Of course, the bourgeois adage of "time is money" has always played a significant role in capitalism. Yet this "old" bourgeois adage seems to be taking on heightened significance amid economic globalization. To be sure, economic globalization includes many trends that hardly seem to express an obsession with "the new, the fleeting, the ephemeral."[14] Multinational corporations rarely vanish overnight from the global stage to be replaced by new upstart firms; investors still need assurances from host states that their property rights are likely to remain secure down the road; businesses often have an economic interest in cultivating good long-term relations with exchange partners. Yet, even those facets of contemporary capitalism exhibiting stability and a "long-term" orientation now operate in a broader economic environment, in which speed and rapid-fire adaptation take on profound and perhaps unprecedented importance. Multinational firms need to figure out how to accelerate production and maximize flexibility; foreign investors require enforceable contracts to protect their property, but they simultaneously operate from the assumption that they may be forced to shift their activities to another location within a relatively short span of time, and the constant fluctuations of the market drive them to seek contracts that ensure extensive opportunities for flexibility; the cultivation of cordial business relations with economic partners by no means detracts from the advantages generated by relatively speedy, unproblematic transactions and forms of dispute resolution likely to facilitate such transactions.

Elective Affinities?

The rule of law is best defined as requiring that state action should rest on norms that are relatively general, clear, public, prospective, and stable. According to the mainstream of modern liberal democratic theory, only norms of this type ensure a minimum of certainty and determinacy within legal decision making, contribute to achieving equality before the law, guarantee the accountability of power holders, and promote fair notice. The rule of law renders the activities of power holders predictable and thereby makes an indispensable contribution toward ensuring the liberty of the private individual as well as the public citizen.[15] Although often ignored by its critics, a commitment to the ideal of the rule of law hardly requires fidelity to a crude *hyperformalism* according to which the rule of law allegedly implies that there is only one determinate answer to every legal question and every manifestation of judicial or administrative autonomy represents an attack on the principle of legality.[16] Even the most cogent legal rule can be interpreted in relatively distinct ways, and it sometimes makes sense to delegate decision-making authority to courts or administrators. Yet, even if legal materials often fail to determine a single correct answer, clear and cogent legal norms provide a framework in which a relatively limited set of acceptable legal answers is delineated. A firm commitment to the rule of law helps guarantee that delegations of decision-making power will be clearly circumscribed and thus accountable to citizens and their elected representatives. A measure of indeterminacy in the law is probably unavoidable, but indeterminacy can be contained and managed by legal norms possessing the attributes of generality, clarity, publicity, prospectiveness, and stability. In short, the rule of law is consistent with what we might describe as the *limited indeterminacy thesis,* according to which defenders of the rule of law need not endorse exaggerated conceptions of legal certainty or predictability.[17]

Nor does the concept of the rule of law as employed here require subscribing to the basic tenets of legal positivism, at least if positivism is seen as necessarily entailing a strict delineation of legality from morality. As Judith N. Shklar noted many years ago, "It is . . . one thing to favor the ideal of a *Rechtsstaat* above all ideological and religious pressures, and quite another to insist upon the conceptual necessity of treating law and morals as totally distinct entities."[18] Within the history of modern legal thought many authors committed to a traditional model of the rule of law in which judicial and administrative discretion were supposed to be kept to a minimum refused to endorse an airtight separation of law from morals. For our purposes the continuing battle between positivists and their critics is of secondary importance, given the fact that both positivists and anti-positivists, though for different reasons, can consistently endorse a model of law as ideally possessing the attributes described earlier.[19] Both positivists and anti-positivists should also be able to identify sufficient reasons to worry about the pervasive antiformal trends within global economic law which I describe later in this chapter.

Space restraints prevent me from offering a detailed survey of the myriad ways in which modern political and legal thought conceived of a special relationship between a capitalist economy and the rule of law. Yet it does make sense to try to recall three core arguments underlying the notion of an elective affinity between the two.

The calculative ethos of the modern capitalist enterprise constitutes one source of the kinship between capitalism and the rule of law. In a line of argumentation developed most richly by Max Weber, "exact calculation" is conceived as reigning supreme within modern capitalism. Characterized most basically by a "systematic utilization of goods or personal service" in which "calculation underlies every single action of the partners," modern capitalism depends on highly developed forms of accounting and bookkeeping, the separation of business from household activities, and formally free labor, each of which makes a vital contribution toward achieving predictable forms of economic activity promising maximum control over the natural world.[20] For Weber the modern entrepreneur is a sober, bourgeois character, embodying a rigorous "asceticism [that] was carried out of monastic cells into everyday life."[21] The discipline of the entrepreneur corresponds to the imperatives of an increasingly calculable and predictable economic universe in which "the technical and economic conditions of machine production . . . determine the lives of all the individuals who are born into this mechanism . . . with irresistible force."[22] In Weber's account, in the premodern "capitalism[s] of promoters, speculators, concession hunters . . . above all, the capitalism especially concerned with exploiting wars," entrepreneurial activity was often "irrational" and adventurous, as capitalists pursued profit by reckless speculation, piracy, or even force. In earlier forms of capitalism (for Weber an economic system having many distinct historical variants) the principle of exact calculation was anything but supreme.[23] But in modern rational capitalism the entrepreneur allegedly trades in his more romantic traits for the self-possession of the cautious, calculating businessman. Just as modern capitalism relies on the principle of exact calculation, so too does its leading figure, the modern entrepreneur, come to embody a disciplined, systematic, and calculative ethos.

In light of this picture of the "ascetic" modern capitalist entrepreneur it is easy to see why Weber, and so many influenced by him, believed that modern capitalism requires the rule of law.[24] Just as modern capitalism makes exact calculation supreme, only modern rational legality—defined by Weber as resting on general, clear, and well-defined legal concepts and norms—provides for optimal legal calculability. Modern capitalism aspires to achieve maximum predictability in economic affairs; a legal order devoted to ensuring maximal calculability represents its natural institutional complement. In Weber's famous account of modern law, legal decision makers ideally were to approximate "an automaton into which legal documents and fees are stuffed at the top in order that [they] may spill forth the verdict at the bottom along with the reasons, read mechanically from codified paragraphs."[25] The machinelike character of modern rational legality corresponds directly to the predictability of modern capitalist "machine production." Despite its obvious exaggerations, Weber's account of modern law's "mechanical" features captures the gist of the conventional liberal view that the rule of law counters unnecessary unpredictability. Generality within law protects against irregularity by demanding that like cases are treated in a like manner. Clarity and publicity serve the same function, for vague and incoherent laws often are applied and enforced in inconsistent ways. Stability similarly helps achieve calculability: rapid or confusing changes in the law contribute to unpredictability and uncertainty in its application and enforcement.

Virtually all forms of organized economic activity exhibit some minimum of calculability and regularity, since it is hard to imagine how regular, ongoing economic activity would be possible without some element of orderliness and predictability. Even a pirate ship probably rests on a normative order and a measure of rule-like behavior. But special to modern capitalism is that it makes the quest for predictability and calculability all-important: "It is not enough for the capitalist to have a general idea that someone else will more likely than not deliver more or less the performance agreed upon on or about the time stipulated. He must know exactly what and when, and he must be highly certain that the precise performance will be forthcoming. He wants to be able to predict with certainty that the other units will perform."[26] For Weber the capitalist preference for "precise performance" in economic relations leads him to prefer an equally precise legal environment maximizing the chances that his expectations will be satisfied. His desire to "predict with certainty" makes him an ally of legal forms (e.g., clear, calculable contracts) which reduce economic uncertainty.

Although often ignored, it is striking that this view relies on a specific—and probably controversial—model of the capitalist enterprise and its key figure, the entrepreneur. If the capitalist entrepreneur could rest satisfied with a rough or approximate sense that his expectations were to be fulfilled, legal forms procuring something less than the absolute, machinelike certainty promised by modern rational legality might suffice for him. A somewhat less airtight, predictable system of law than that offered by a formalistic model of the rule of law might serve the capitalist well enough; maybe capitalism and traditional legal forms exhibiting a limited degree of systematization and formal rationality would be able to coexist successfully.[27] Of course, Weber probably rejected this possibility, in part because of the weight he placed on the role of growing predictability and calculability within his broader vision of the "rationalization" of Western modernity.[28] Even his account of the common law hence underlines the manner in which it embodies "rational" elements structurally similar to those found within the formalistic legal codes of the European Continent. Like their rivals in France and Germany, common law systems allegedly underwent a systematization that provides the calculability required by modern capitalism.[29]

A second defense of the notion of an elective affinity emphasizes the protective functions of the rule of law for the modern entrepreneur. Long engaged in a fierce battle with the legacy of European Absolutism, early modern political theorists (including Locke, Montesquieu, Beccaria, Voltaire, and Kant) conceived of the rule of law as a puissant weapon against political despotism and economic paternalism. Legally unregulated, arbitrary government was typically pictured as posing a threat to individual liberty. Nonetheless, early liberalism's tendency to conceive of the individual chiefly as a proprietor often led it to place a special emphasis on the dangers of political and economic despotism to commercial life. In this view political arbitrariness is simply incongruent with the successful operations of a modern commercial economy. Inconsistent and irregular state activity makes it difficult for proprietors, for example, to engage in necessary forms of long-term private planning, in which economic expectations have a reasonable chance of gaining satisfaction. Why invest when the specter of unforeseen state activity risks wiping away any economic advantages to be gained by doing so? Similarly, when property rights or contracts are unsettled as a result of an unreliable state administration, even simple economic transactions become unsettled and unduly problematic as well.

It is hard to deny the underlying strength of this early liberal insight. In the aftermath of the emergence of the modern state and its awesome monopoly on organized violence, no institution has posed a greater threat to the quest for economic certainty than the state's administrative apparatus. Contrary to some versions of laissez-faire ideology, classical liberalism was not in principle opposed to state action within the economy per se; throughout the history of capitalism the state has played a substantial role in economic affairs. But liberalism understandably was opposed to forms of state action likely to generate unnecessary economic uncertainty and unpredictability. Clarity and publicity within law ensure that entrepreneurs gain fair notice of when and how governmental officials are to intervene. Secret or retroactive legal norms make it difficult for entrepreneurs to know how state agents are likely to act, and thus a liberal legal order best steers clear from them. Generality and stability similarly contribute to the accountability of power holders by helping make sure that they at least act in a consistent way. When Hayek famously wrote in *The Road to Serfdom* that "stripped of all technicalities this [the rule of law] means that government in all its actions is bound by rules fixed and announced beforehand—rules which make it possible to foresee with fair certainty how the authority will use its coercive powers in given circumstances, and to plan one's individual affairs on the basis of this knowledge," it was primarily this protective function of the rule of law which he probably had in mind.[30]

Finally, the plausibility of the idea of an elective affinity between capitalism and the rule of law can be traced to the temporal horizons of economic action within modern capitalism. To be sure, explicit references to the problems posed by the temporal context of economic action are rarely found in modern political and legal thought. Yet implicit assumptions about the temporal preconditions of economic activity play a crucial role in traditional thinking about the rule of law.

Let us recall the seemingly trivial fact that economic action in the history of modern capitalism often entailed risky forms of time-consuming exchange. Distance potentially generates real uncertainty; think of the difficulties posed by the long-distance transport of goods before the advent of high-speed technologies (e.g., the steamship, railroad, automobile, and airplane). Experiences of time and space are inextricably linked, and a slow-paced social universe entails correspondingly limited possibilities for the successful economic management of geographical distance. For the moment imagine a merchant trading in the backwoods of North America in the late eighteenth century, whose business relied on long and risky voyages from a port city on the coast (Boston or Charleston perhaps) to the frontier (present-day Kentucky or Ohio). From the perspective of our early capitalist merchant one way to reduce economic uncertainty would be to make sure that laws impacting on his business remained unaltered during the lengthy span of time it took him to complete his trek and return home from the rural hinterlands. It would make economic sense to seek tax laws unlikely to change during the course of his travels, a stable system of contracts, and many other relatively predictable legal norms and practices. Quick or sudden changes in the tax code—for example, new taxes on products traded by him—would be undesirable to the extent that they unnecessarily heightened economic uncertainty and made it difficult for him to plan his actions in a rational manner. Clarity and transparency in law would promote his understanding of the code and reduce economic insecurity. Its generality would work to prevent him from being discriminated against in relation to similarly situated merchants and traders. In short, familiar features of the rule of law would serve as a powerful tool for counteracting uncertainties generated by the distance and duration of economic exchange. A liberal legal system would facilitate capitalist exchange not only by securing private property and a system of free contracts but also by dramatically reducing insecurities deriving from the temporal and spatial horizons of the merchant's economic environment. The slow pace of his activities, as well as the limited possibilities for annihilating distance, would likely lead the merchant to favor a host of traditional rule of law virtues.

Perhaps the point can be illustrated by drawing a parallel to a widely documented shift in the history of mapmaking and time measurement. In premodern Europe maps and clocks were clumsy and imprecise devices, less concerned with a rational calculation of time and space than serving didactic moral and religious purposes. Only in the Reformation and Enlightenment do we see the proliferation of maps and clocks based on a disenchanted view of nature as an object of conscious human manipulation and control. Revealingly, this quintessentially modern attempt to improve the rational management of the physical environment was inextricably linked to ever more precise, systematic modes of time and space measurement: increasingly exact and reliable systems of measurement based on quantifiable, homogeneous, linear units of time (culminating in modern mechanical watches and clocks), as well as maps in which space was conceived in terms of abstract, uniform grids, lacking the elements of fantasy and religion which once had been paramount in the minds of medieval mapmakers.[31] This seemingly mundane innovation nonetheless contained revolutionary implications: the dramatic shift in the time and space horizons of European civilization, given concrete form within the history of modern cartography and time measurement, played a crucial role in early modern economic development as well as the European conquest of the non-European world.

The development of modern law exhibits remarkably similar structural characteristics. In modern Europe the legal system was more and more conceived in terms of a set of abstract, formal, and general propositions, making up a systematic code to an increasing extent free of traditional moral and religious overtones. Just as modern clock and mapmakers carved time and space into homogeneous units possessing an ever more precise and systematic character, so, too, did modern legal reformers imagine a complementary legal universe consisting of rationally ordered, uniform, abstract concepts and norms as well as formalistic modes of decision making no less mechanical than the operations of a modern clock or more reliable than a good map. Enlightenment intellectuals often brought these related strands within modern thought together. For example, Voltaire was not only fascinated by the possibilities for rational urban planning inspired in part by a conception of space as consisting of abstract, uniform units, but he famously fought to modernize law by basing it on transparent, abstract, universal propositions.

In light of this striking parallel, would it be too far-fetched to suggest that not only modern cartographers and clockmakers but modern jurists as well hoped to improve humanity's instrumental mastery of time and space by means of their contributions to modern culture? For now my point is a modest one. Like rational maps and clocks, the modern rule of law implicitly rested on the aspiration to render both time and space rationally manageable. One crucial way in which it achieved this task was by functioning to reduce economic uncertainty based on the distance and duration of commercial exchange.

Law in Our High-Speed Global Economy

Motoring a general process of social acceleration which ultimately revolutionizes the face of human existence, capitalism incessantly transforms its own temporal horizons. Capitalism's internal dynamics lead it to embrace faster forms of production, consumption, and exchange. The capitalist quest for profits also plays a pivotal role in the introduction of "turnpikes and canals, the railways, steamships and telegraph, the radio and automobile, containerization, jet cargo transportation, television and telecommunications," which transform the phenomenological horizons of human activity.[32] High-speed capitalism annihilates space by reducing the gap between once distant geographical points: the world of the high-speed jet, electronic communications, and instantaneous computerized business exchange is in fact "faster" and thereby "smaller" than that of the stagecoach and pony express. Capitalism makes the experiences of simultaneity and instantaneousness constitutive features of modern life. If villagers in a rural community in Norway can experience the same thing at the same time (e.g., a financial transaction) as city dwellers in Toronto or a taxi driver in Mexico City can watch, via television, as the stock market in London experiences a sudden downturn, then "they in effect live in the same place, space has been annihilated by time compression."[33] Of course, space is by no means literally compressed. But the speed-up and resulting shrinkage of economically relevant geographical distance points to significant shifts in the horizons of human experience.

Social acceleration contains profound implications for all three sources of the elective affinity between capitalism and the rule of law described here. Even if a kinship between capitalism and the liberal rule of law obtained throughout much of the history of modern capitalism, economic globalization suggests that it no longer readily does. To be sure, economic globalization requires significant legal banisters: Political scientist Martin Shapiro aptly describes an ongoing "globalization of law," according to which "the whole world [increasingly] lives under a single set of legal rules."[34] The harmonization and unification of some areas of international economic law seem to have advanced in recent years,[35] legal practice is increasingly transnational in scope, international business arbitration is flourishing,[36] and a host of global institutions (most prominently, the World Trade Organization) functions to provide an emerging legal framework for global economic law. Of course, national legal systems continue to play a decisive role in anchoring economic globalization. Nonetheless, the "set of rules" making up the legal infrastructure of globalization bears surprisingly little resemblance to the liberal model of the rule of law and its commitment to the legal virtues of generality, clarity, publicity, prospectiveness, and stability. As the most impressive study of global business presently available concedes, "the rule of law is not as influential in global regulatory regimes as it is in liberal nations . . . International regulation is not characterized by a rule of law which constrains."[37] The effectiveness of traditional liberal legal devices becomes problematic precisely in those areas of the present-day economy in which social acceleration is especially acute. Core features of the legal basis of economic globalization remain, to a substantial degree, soft law lacking in key rule of law virtues. We can only hope to make sense of the emerging system of global economic law by acknowledging the existence of a mismatch between the temporal horizons of traditional forms of liberal law and economic activity in the global economy.

Legal Consequences of Social Acceleration

Recall that the rule of law in part traditionally served as an instrument for reducing insecurities stemming from the distance and duration of economic activity. Yet social acceleration means that some of these uncertainties now have already been dramatically reduced, especially in economic sectors in which transactions rely on high-speed information, communication, and transportation technologies. Speed facilitates at least some of the functions performed in an earlier phase in the history of capitalism by a liberal legal code consisting of clear, general, and relatively stable norms. Take, for example, the case of a present-day currency trader on Wall Street. Merely by pressing a few keys on her computer, vast amounts of currency are immediately exchanged within a few nanoseconds. Does our Wall Street currency trader experience the same need for a robust rule of law as her historical predecessors? For her colo-

nial predecessor legal stability was a tool for counteracting uncertainties resulting from the distance and duration of his business. Computerization drastically reduces that source of uncertainty; the contemporary currency trader
may vary well consider her eighteenth-century predecessor's old-fashioned
insistence on the virtues of a relatively unchanging, stable legal code quaint.
Even when contemporary motorized legislatures initiate rapid changes in the
legal code, our financial trader, operating at lightning speed, is likely to have
more than enough time to adjust her practices accordingly. Speed provides her
with creative opportunities to negotiate the legal and regulatory terrain about
which her historical predecessors could only have fantasized. Rapid-fire transactions with her peers in Frankfurt or Singapore are unlikely to be faultily dis-
rupted even by quick changes in the law because her transactions are computerized, whereas legislation, thus far, is not. She may experience rapid changes
in the law as inconvenient but probably not the immediate peril they posed to
the eighteenth-century merchant whose business relied on long and risky
voyages. And new possibilities for high-speed action provide her with ways of
making sure that she is always a step ahead of lawmakers: this, at least, is
strongly suggested by the scholarly literature on statutory obsolescence, which
underscores the extent to which positive lawmaking lags behind the rapid-fire
pace of economic transformation.

   This example is intended as more than an academic thought experiment. In
fact, the legal substructure of international finance and banking is remarkably
underdeveloped, characterized for the most part by a set of recommended
"best practices" exhibiting limited formality. The main sites for the regulation
of international banking thus far have shown a striking preference for open-
ended, flexible guidelines, in part because of the diversity of banking practices
worldwide but also in deference to the high-speed "casino capitalism" now
commonplace in the financial world.[38] Working from the assumption that
traditional forms of legality mesh poorly with the dynamic, ever-changing
contours of global finance, contemporary Group of Ten (G-10) central bank
authorities have abandoned the traditional model of imposing "strict, uniform, quantitative limits on the activities of the banks" in favor of flexible
forms of self-regulation.[39] G-10 regulations also remain clouded in secrecy,
generating obvious problems for outsiders hoping to evaluate them: the G-10
committee responsible for making banking regulations "produces little in the
way of public documentation, and no record of its internal meetings."[40] Even
though a growing number of commentators and politicians are now express-

ing reservations about the dangers of the present system,[41] international bankers have hardly been aggressively demanding a system of transnational coordination based on clear, general, and stable state-backed norms. To the contrary, they often have greeted attempts to develop such a system with skepticism, considering it a recipe for heavy-handed state regulation likely to prove inflexible as well as ineffective in light of present-day economic needs. If my analysis here is accurate, there is at least one reason for this unexpected challenge to the traditional view of an elective affinity between capitalism and the rule of law: social acceleration tends to minimize the dependence of certain entrepreneurs on classical liberal law. Particularly within financial and capital markets, simultaneity and instantaneousness reduce the economic agent's reliance on the rule of law as an instrument for counteracting uncertainty stemming from the duration and distance of commercial life, and thus it is no surprise that legal trends there conflict with the traditional liberal model. Although the soft character of global financial regulation accords well with the fast-moving temporal dynamics of financial globalization, however, it also allows global bankers to minimize meaningful possibilities for effective public control and scrutiny of their practices.

Computerized currency trading is probably an extreme example within the global economy, since simultaneity and instantaneousness play an especially prominent role there. By the same token social acceleration is likely to affect an increasingly broad range of commercial activities, as technological innovations diminish economic insecurity stemming from the duration and distance of economic exchange. Legal trends presently visible within the financial and banking sectors—most important, a preference among economic actors for porous, open-ended law—may represent a foreshadowing of the basic contours of an increasingly significant range of legal arenas.[42]

Unfortunately, recent theorists of the rule of law have had relatively little to say about the temporal horizons of liberal law, let alone the implications of recent alterations in the time horizons of economic activity for legality.[43] This is probably one reason why analysts of the legal substructure of economic globalization have been so hesitant to recognize the novelty of the trends at hand. Nonetheless, some prominent legal theorists could be interpreted as providing a starting point for explaining why a high-speed economy is likely to threaten the rule of law.

In his classic *Morality of Law*, for example, legal theorist Lon Fuller observed that the pace of economic activity helps determine the suitability of traditional modes of liberal adjudication. In accordance with the mainstream of modern liberal jurisprudence, Fuller was committed to the view that private economic activity best takes places "within a framework set by the law," which he defined in this context as a system in which "adjudication must act through openly declared rule or principle, and the grounds on which it acts must display some continuity through time."[44] A relatively stable system of legal norms, along with basic property rights and a functioning system of contracts, constitute an indispensable basis for capitalism as long as legal materials possess a relatively substantial degree of those qualities making up what Fuller described as the "inner morality of law," which was Fuller's term for the classical rule of law virtues recounted earlier. Fuller was also in tune with the mainstream of modern liberalism when he insisted that certain forms of economic activity nonetheless "cannot and should not be conducted in accordance with anything resembling the internal morality of law." The operations of a firm are based on "one general principle, that of obtaining maximum return from limited resources," and this principle conflicts fundamentally with the underlying spirit of the "inner morality of law." The economic decisions of a corporate manager necessarily must be subject to quick reversal or alteration when novel conditions appear, whereas "the judge . . . acts upon those facts that are in advance deemed relevant . . . His decision does not simply direct resources and energies; it declares rights, and rights to be meaningful must in some measure stand firm through changing circumstances."[45] Any attempt to determine wages and prices by legal means and then allow courts to rule on wages and prices according to traditional forms of adjudication, is thus destined to "result in inefficiency, hypocrisy, moral confusion, and frustration."[46] When undertaking to deal in an unmediated manner with tasks of economic allocation, it soon becomes self-evident that "courts move too slowly to keep up with a rapidly changing economic scene."[47] Whereas a legal order based on traditional rule of law virtues can successfully provide a framework for economic action, any attempt to expand the scope of adjudication to include activities directly concerned with the coordination or allocation of economic materials is doomed to fail.

Fuller also seems to have believed that we could use temporal criteria to delineate those economic areas in which traditional legal instruments are likely to prove effective from those in which they are destined to prove counterproductive. Some facets of economic life require "rapid" adaptation (e.g., the day-to-day management of a firm), and thus an ambitious reliance on traditional legal devices may prove more of a hindrance than an aid there. Meanwhile, other facets of economic life are relatively constant and stable (e.g., the entrepreneur's expectation that a particular set of time-consuming commercial transactions is likely to take place as promised), and traditional legal devices (a system of stable contracts) can play an effective role there in successfully buttressing economic interaction. Fuller also noted that the distinction between "nonallocative" tasks (in part defined by their relative constancy) and "allocative" tasks (determined to some extent by their reliance on rapid, ever-changing action) could easily be blurred: "I do not mean to imply ... that there are no gradations in the distinction between allocative and nonallocative tasks." In addition, the gradations between such economic tasks vary historically: "tasks that were only incidentally allocative may become more directly so with a change in circumstances."[48] By implication the proper scope of adjudication may very well alter as both the character and pace of the activities at hand also undergo change.

Economic globalization places Fuller's neglected remarks in a fresh light. To the extent that contemporary manifestations of economic globalization rest on a dramatic speed-up in the time horizons of economic activity, Fuller's comments about the historical variability of the limits of traditional forms of adjudication seem directly relevant to the legal analysis of economic globalization. Perhaps it was in part the relatively slow pace of earlier forms of capitalism which helped give Weber's notion of an intimate kinship between capitalism and rule of law real substance, whereas contemporary high-speed globalizing capitalism may be shedding much of its dependence on formal law. Might we take the relatively antiformal character and inconstancy of so much global economic law as a confirmation of Fuller's observation that traditional forms of liberal law are likely to prove inadequate in the context of a "rapidly changing economic scene"? Is it conceivable that high-speed economic globalization renders some traditional legal instruments problematic there as well?

Prominent representatives of Fuller's intellectual nemesis, legal positivism, point the way to a similar conclusion. Frederick Schauer notes, for example, that clear, general legal rules always necessarily "force the future into the categories of the past" in a manner that may soon render them anachronistic.[49] Every rule builds on predictions about the future drawn from past and present experience. Given a relatively high degree of constancy and stability in a particular economic arena, few immediate problems are likely to result from "forcing the future" into a legal framework based on past and present experience. In those areas of the economy characterized by high-speed forms of action and incessant change, however, these problems are destined to become more serious. As noted earlier, liberal jurists have long underscored the manner in which traditional forms of formal adjudication rest on a "marked orientation to the past": judges engage in "retroactively oriented reasoning" to the extent that they are primarily concerned with the establishment of past events (e.g., guilt).[50] But, in the context of economic sectors in which existing rules may seem outdated even before they have made their way into the law books, continuity with the legal past may instead appear to be an impediment to successful economic action. When economic transactions require lightning-fire responses and enormous flexibility, traditional forms of stable general law are just as likely to prevent actors from adjusting nimbly to the dictates of the global economy as they are likely to underpin such action. To a growing degree traditional forms of stable general law soon seem like a "dead" leftover from the past fundamentally incongruent with contemporary economic necessities.

The Impact of Speed on the Protective Functions of the Rule of Law

What, then, of the rule of law's classical protective functions? Notwithstanding its manifest strengths, this traditional idea similarly obfuscates the ways in which economic globalization potentially renders some of its core protective elements anachronistic as well.

Perhaps the most immediate institutional manifestation of capitalism's drive to overcome the limitations of space and time is the ascent of the mammoth transnational corporation (TNC), operating simultaneously in many parts of the world and capable of producing goods and services across national borders at high velocity. TNCs have not only effectively exploited new possibilities for simultaneity and instantaneousness, but their own cross-border character constitutes an immediate embodiment of the broader process whereby social acceleration undermines traditional geographical boundaries. One way by which high-speed capitalism alters the spatial horizons of economic activity is simply by generating faster and bigger transnational firms. According to some accounts, globalization is deepening economic concentration in the world economy, in part because of the exorbitant start-up costs entailed by advanced technology.[51] Increasingly in possession of more economic muscle than all but the richest members of the international state system, TNCs are also managing to outfit themselves with legal authority rivaling that of the nation-state itself. Many of the substantive norms of international business law are directly determined by the huge "industry leaders" who dominate the market, and a growing number of interstate economic agreements point in the direction of placing private businesses and nation-states on a level playing field in terms of legal status. States soon may no longer be the sole bodies in possession of legally recognized "sovereign" power in the international order: corporations increasingly exercise sovereign powers of lawmaking while possessing legal "rights" no less impressive than those of the nation-state, the traditional carrier of sovereignty in modernity.[52]

The growing importance of TNCs to economic life means that an ever more impressive range of economic activities is necessarily intrafirm in character.[53] Yet intrafirm decision-making structures exhibit "more flexibility, and . . . less regard for decision-making consistency that might be acceptable for legal relations."[54] For example, the voluntary "codes of conduct," now widely touted by the global business community as an alternative to traditional nation-state-based legal regulation, too often provide a pseudo-legalistic window dressing for the mistreatment of labor in poor countries.[55] Rarely do they include clear or effective procedures for tackling violations, and only a miniscule proportion of them provides for independent monitoring or third-party enforcement. According to an International Labor Organization (ILO) survey, those most likely to be affected by the codes—especially managers and workers in foreign plants operated by TNCs—are often unaware of their existence in the first place; TNCs presently seem more interested in publicizing the codes to consumers in the rich countries than to those who might benefit from them. The ILO also notes that the voluntary codes are generally vague and imprecise, typically consisting of little more than hortatory declarations (promising "fair and adequate compensation," "just and fair wages," and "good and safe working conditions") but weak on specifics or the details of implementation. No wonder that the ILO concluded its survey of voluntary codes of conduct by claiming that the "current lack of standardized principles and procedures hinders" quality implementation of their stated goals.[56]

Although contractual relations may formally exist between distinct component units of a TNC, such contracts often are no more than managerial orders written up in legal form, in reality lacking the minimal attributes of the classical consent-based free contract.[57] British legal scholar P. S. Atiyah's observation that classical liberal forms of contract have declined over the course of the last century in part as a result of the increasingly prominent role of massive corporations, in which "relationships are conducted by administrative procedures and not by market contracts," takes on heightened significance given the grow-ing role of massive global players in the world economy.[58] In short, even if we ignore the obvious institutional differences between privately owned TNCs and nation-states, it is difficult to claim that the internal structure of TNCs displays minimal features of legality. As TNCs take on an ever more prominent place within economic life, classical liberal legal forms once essential to inter-firm exchanges between economic competitors risk being deprived of some of their previous significance as well.

The problem of intrafirm economic relations is, however, only the tip of the iceberg. Few countries today can afford to brush off the prospect of foreign investment, and the decisive role of the TNCs within the global economy (in particular, their virtual monopoly on advanced technology) generates fierce competition among nation-states forced to bend over backward in order to attract and keep foreign business.[59] It is now widely acknowledged that the relative mobility and vast size of the TNCs sometimes allow them to neutralize the regulatory capacities of the nation-state. Less appreciated is that nonclassi-cal legal forms typically serve as an indispensable instrument for TNCs in their quest to do so. The structural advantages enjoyed by the TNCs in the global political economy sometimes permit them to turn the tables on the nation-state and its once impressive arsenal of legal instruments. Large capitalist enterprise's reliance on the classical protective functions of the rule of law declines as well.

Two examples of this trend have to suffice for now. TNCs are notoriously undertaxed today, in part because they astutely exploit discrepancies among and between national tax codes. International business taxation exhibits ex-traordinary unevenness and disorder, and TNCs have for the most part tried to keep it that way. The reason for this is obvious enough: TNCs "legally" evade paying taxes by taking advantage of loopholes and gaps deriving from the complex and inconsistent structure of international business taxation, and they often prefer ad hoc, closed-door negotiations conducted by corporate tax lawyers and government officials which determine how much they are to pay.[60] In an economic context in which, first, TNCs often possess surprising mobility and, second, attracting TNC investment seems essential to economic well-being, corporate representatives possess obvious strategic advantages when engaging in ad hoc negotiations with tax official even from rich countries. In a similar manner TNCs (with political support from their home countries) thus far have managed to ward off even modest attempts to set up enforceable international legal codes promulgating proper forms of business conduct. United Nations–sponsored plans to challenge an onerous history of TNC meddling in the internal affairs of host countries have been beaten back, and cautious attempts by the International Chamber of Commerce and Organization for Economic Cooperation and Development (OECD)—hardly principled critics of international business—have resulted in recommendations possessing at best the character of soft law.[61] In this sphere as well TNCs for the most part prefer a global regulatory scenario plagued by inconsistencies and discrepancies, because its inchoate structure provides loopholes galore for maximizing the privileges enjoyed by the TNC in the global economy.

TNCs also have less to fear from the possibility of arbitrary government than small and medium-sized firms lacking their vast resources and mobility. The mere specter of "unfair" or "discriminatory" treatment by a host country often suffices as a disincentive to invest there in the first place. And, even after the decision has been made to invest in a particular locality, TNCs may exhibit few reservations about closing down and moving elsewhere at signs of a worsening "investment climate." Because especially small and medium-sized states increasingly depend on TNC investment for economic development, their interest in undertaking hostile forms of "arbitrary" action against foreign capital is substantially reduced from the outset. On the contrary, the centrality of TNC investment for successful economic development means that prospective host states typically compete to attract foreign investment by promising what in effect amount to special rights and privileges, such as tax breaks, direct and indirect subsidies, government outlays for research.[62] Accordingly, many anxieties experienced by TNCs today stem not from the traditional specter of discretionary or arbitrary state intervention hostile to the pursuit of profits but, instead, from the prospect that the special incentives they enjoy may be less generous than those gained by competitors operating elsewhere. From the perspective of the TNCs government "discretion" is often a problem only to the extent that it may be insufficiently lucrative.

Of course, defenders of the World Trade Organization envision one of its main tasks as the construction of a global rule of law which purportedly would put an end to such practices.[63] The WTO clearly represents an attempt to develop a "hard" legal shell for the global economy, and there is no question that its enforcement procedures have been substantially strengthened in recent years. The WTO's dispute resolution devices hardly conform to traditional models of formal legality, however, despite the organization's self-advertised loyalty to the rule of law. The WTO Agreement is "riddled with exceptions—grandfather clauses, waivers, balance-of-payment exception," along with vague and open-ended clauses, loopholes, and sectoral exemptions.[64] It provides substantial room for a highly discretionary process of adjudication, and many of its decisions are likely to strike even those familiar with the complex norms making up the WTO legal system as controversial. WTO tribunals are confidential as well, and opinions expressed in the tribunal reports remain anonymous. This failing not only represents a violation of the modern idea of the publicity of law, but it works in conjunction with the WTO's discretionary system of norms to raise the specter of a deeply irregular system of adjudication whose chief commitment is to the core neoliberal economic beliefs presently driving the organization's policy.[65] Anyone who takes the time to study the massive body of available WTO legal materials is inevitably reminded of the legal "Egyptian hieroglyphics" that so worried Bentham.[66]

This situation is clearly distinct from that envisioned by classical liberal theorists who wrote so convincingly of the dangers of political arbitrariness to commercial life. Such perils remain real for segments of the business community unable to neutralize political authority by "playing off" nation-states against one another. Yet for an increasingly significant sector of the global economy the classical protective functions of the rule of law lack the overriding significance they once possessed. If Czech authorities fail to enforce laws requiring the protection of a struggling mom-and-pop grocery store unable to pay protection money to the Mafia, the store probably will go under. In contrast, if Coca-Cola gains word of recalcitrant officials who refuse to enforce anti-Mafia laws, it may threaten Czech authorities with the prospect of opting for another location for its next plant. On the basis of such threats Coca-Cola not only will be to make sure that anti-Mafia laws are enforced but may be able to garner an array of additional lucrative privileges. Of course, similar threats from the local grocery store are likely to gain nothing but a dismissive glance from a lower-level civil servant.

When early modern thinkers such as Locke and Montesquieu first described the protective functions of the rule of law, capitalist enterprise for the most part was small-scale and necessarily tied to a specific geographical location; from the perspective of the fledgling entrepreneur, the political authorities who exercised sovereignty within that locality were a force to be reckoned with. At the start of the twenty-first century the scope and scale of capitalist production reduces both the de facto and de jure authority of the sovereign power of the nation-state and thereby diminishes the importance of the traditional protective functions of the rule of law for the largest and most mobile units of capital. The main problem posed by globalization is less that transnational business can only preserve its autonomy by limiting state power by means of the rule of law than that the democratic nation-state can only hope to maintain its independence in relation to global business by counteracting the virtually universal competitive rush to provide transnational firms with special rights and privileges. This competition contains worrisome implications for the regulatory capacity of the liberal democratic state, let alone its ability to achieve a necessary minimum of social cohesion: the rush to provide capital with investment incentives contributes to a "race to the bottom" in which states embrace a now-familiar coterie of neoliberal reforms, including corporate tax cuts, the rollback of the welfare state, and relaxed social and environmental regulation. In an astonishing historical reversal discretionary authority for the sake of global business now threatens the liberal democratic nation-state, whereas international business often gains directly from nongeneral, irregular regulations (e.g., special tax cuts for foreign investors). States need increased generality, consistency, and stability within international regulation in order to preserve their integrity, whereas privileged international economic interests oftentimes seem perfectly happy with legal inconsistency and irregularity among states forced to court them.[67]

Impact on the Calculative Functions of the Rule of Law

Social acceleration also raises difficult questions about the calculative ethos of the capitalist enterprise which Weber and subsequent scholars influenced by him considered constitutive of its kinship to the rule of law. Earlier I alluded to the fact that Weber's picture of the capitalist entrepreneur has long been subject to a series of major criticisms. Joseph Schumpeter, for example, early on suggested that Weber's model obscured the core of capitalist entrepreneurship—that is, the ability to act in unforeseen ways that often seem irrational from the perspective of preexisting forms of economic behavior. Weber's exaggerated focus on the calculative ethos of the capitalist entrepreneur allegedly stumbles because "the nature of the innovation process, the drastic departure from existing routines, is inherently one that cannot be reduced to mere calculation, although subsequent imitation of the innovation, once accomplished, can be so reduced."[68] For Schumpeter the *differentia specifica* of capitalist entrepreneurship—namely, the capacity to pursue economic innovation by piercing the crust of worn-out commercial routine—is captured poorly by a model of capitalism in which predictability and calculability are seen as its predominant principles. For Schumpeter the classical entrepreneur is a heroic and even charismatic figure precisely because he shatters predictable and calculable modes of economic activity.

This is not the place to take sides in one of the great debates in twentieth-century economic theory. Yet recalling Schumpeter's critique of Weber brings attention to the fact that one influential statement of the idea of an elective affinity between capitalism and the rule of law potentially relies on a historically contingent model of capitalist enterprise. What, then, is the status of the calculative ethos described by Weber in the context of economic globalization? Recall again David Harvey's view that a recent bout of innovation in information, communication, and transportation technologies engenders far-reaching shifts in the workings of the contemporary capitalist enterprise. Novel economic possibilities provided by new technologies place a special "premium on 'smart' and innovative entrepreneurship, aided and abetted by all the accoutrements of swift, decisive, and well-informed decision-making."[69] New opportunities for simultaneity and instantaneousness make flexibility in the labor process, labor markets, production, and consumption possible on a scale that would have stunned earlier generations of entrepreneurs.[70] Successful capitalist enterprises today are characterized by their prowess at rapidly adapting to new information and new techniques: social acceleration not only provides increased chances for flexibility and mobility in economic life, but the successful capitalist exploits them properly.

We would probably be well advised to take Harvey's model of entrepreneurship as describing major trends within the global economy but being hardly the whole story; relatively traditional forms of entrepreneurship continue to operate in contemporary capitalism. Nonetheless, his account provides a helpful starting point for making sense of a number of recent legal trends.

Atiyah, for example, refers to the "pace of change in modern society" as one of the sources for the decline of classical forms of free contract.[71] As Atiyah notes, contracts in the twentieth century, in some distinction to their nineteenth-century predecessors, increasingly tended to provide ample possibilities for parties engaged in an economic exchange to renegotiate their agreement "on terms which are open to continuous adjustment as long as the relationship lasts."[72] Possibilities for flexibility are now built into the structure of contracts, suggesting to Atiyah that a "growing recognition that the opportunity to change one's mind is a valuable right" has played an important role in the transformation of freedom of contract.[73] Yet the acknowledgment of a right "to change one's mind" is surely in part motored by ongoing changes in the structure of capitalist enterprise, according to which flexibility and the possibility of rapid-fire adjustments become decisive to economic success. Contracts allow for economic actors to revise their expectations in part because the right to change one's mind is ever more indispensable in an economy characterized by the growing importance of exploiting opportunities provided by instantaneousness and simultaneity. Atiyah obscures this feature of the story because he attributes the decay of classical "executory" contracts chiefly to the rise of the welfare state and the growth of public enterprise. Although accurate, this view fails to explain sufficiently why flexibility within contract law is increasingly common in areas of law in which neither public enterprise nor the welfare state plays an important role.[74]

In fact, recent legal literature on globalization and contract law rests on a growing consensus that transnational exchanges must be free of the excessively "static" as well as "inflexible and irrevocable legal remedies" presumably characteristic of earlier forms of contract law.[75] This is hardly surprising: global players thus far have proven most capable at making use of new information, communication, and transportation technologies, and they come closest to fitting the model of the contemporary capitalist enterprise described by Harvey. Accordingly, they are most comfortable with legal practices providing generous possibilities for flexible modes of conflict resolution, particularly when decision makers sympathize with the basic ideological orientation of the international business community as a whole. Economic globalization has spawned a number of ambitious recent attempts to harmonize contract law in order to facilitate cross-border transactions. In this vein the U.N. Commission on International Trade Law (UNICTRAL), International Institute for the Unification of Private Law (Unidroit), and the Commission on European Contract Lawyers have been busily undertaking reforms of contract law so as to make it better suited to the dictates of a global economy. A pervasive theme in the burgeoning legal literature on the harmonization of transnational contracts is the need for dynamism, along with growing skepticism concerning the virtues of traditional forms of codification: "many of us are becoming increasingly sensitive to the extent that codification of commercial law has not proven to be the most desirable goal."[76] Legal practitioners are no less unambiguous when describing the motivating force behind the general movement toward increased dependence on open-ended principles in transnational contracts: the changing contours of contract law are "primarily driven by business practice, not the grand theoretical structures of legal scholars" too often influenced by (allegedly) anachronistic and formalistic legal notions.[77] Commercial practice should directly shape contracts, and business practice in the global economy increasingly requires elasticity in the law:

> If a contract appears insufficiently explicit to furnish a direct statement of the parties' rights, duties, powers, and liberties, then the arbitrators will construct it and fill the gaps in it by recourse to their own knowledge of how commerce works in practice, and how commercial men [*sic*] in the relevant field express themselves . . . What is important is the arbitrator should keep constantly in mind that he is concerned with international commerce, with all the breadth of horizon, flexibility, and practicality of approach which that demands.[78]

In a similar vein most analysts of the burgeoning field of international business arbitration agree that its decision-making structure remains flexible and highly discretionary, characterized by a surprising absence of the classical legal virtues of generality, publicity, clarity, prospectiveness, and stability. Nonetheless, international arbitration services are flourishing today, and global business is opting, in surprising numbers, to resolve conflicts by means of arbitration services over traditional forms of court-based adjudication. A popular how-to literature tailored for the international business community praises arbitration as superior to costly, time-consuming, and purportedly rigid forms of "bureaucratic" adjudication.[79] Traditional liberal law, it seems, has become too inflexible and unwieldy for global entrepreneurs hoping to make optimal use of the economic possibilities provided by social acceleration. In a context in which economic success requires speedy reactions to complex, fast-moving economic shifts, a system of legal coordination offering substantial opportunities for discretionary decision making contains some obvious advantages for entrepreneurs in need of multiple chances to "change their minds." Economic transactions today take place rapidly; sudden market changes demand flexibility and fast reactions. Legal forms permitting flexible decision making potentially provide a framework in which economic actors can adjust effectively to the ever-changing dynamics of the marketplace. As an international business lawyer recently noted, TNCs are hostile to hard uniform regulation because "advanced technology and organizational techniques permit MNCs [multinational corporations] to transmit information, shift production, alter marketing strategy, and otherwise adapt to changing business conditions on a scale and a pace unthinkable only a decade or two earlier."[80]

Although international business arbitration appears to be undergoing a process of change in which its limited legalistic features have undergone fortification, it remains a system of dispute resolution in which confidentiality (and even secrecy) is far-reaching, and recourse to clear legal rules or precedent remains relatively limited.[81] Nonetheless, the enthusiasm evinced by global players for business arbitration seems to confirm the claim of one academic observer that "formalistic facades are not necessary to achieve the sensible results dictated by a commercial ethic."[82] A substantial body of literature also suggests that the ascent of international commercial arbitration is having a greater impact on domestic legal systems than first might seem obvious. Most national legal systems today not only are striving to free international arbitrators from many traditional legal restraints on their activities, but they also are tolerating an expanded reliance on arbitration devices at home.[83] Courts are finding it difficult to distinguish clearly between national and transnational forms of economic activity, and thus the embrace of arbitration in the realm of international business dispute resolution makes arbitration ever more pervasive even in areas of the economy traditionally considered domestic in character.[84]

The rise of international business arbitration has many sources,[85] but one of them arguably confirms the theoretical diagnosis offered here. Arbitration's "procedural norms emphasize speed," and many global entrepreneurs evidently believe that the economic advantages to be gained by the fast-paced character of arbitration outweigh any of the disadvantages stemming from its informality.[86] An omnipresent theme in the literature on business arbitration is the promise of rapid-fire forms of dispute resolution free of the relatively time-consuming technicalities and formalities of traditional adjudication. Much of the academic literature tends to accept this view as well: for example, legal sociologist Reza Banaker characteristically refers to the "relatively subtle and swift procedures" characteristic of international business arbitration.[87] Revealingly, those touting the merits of international business arbitration typically worry that legalistic trends within its development threaten to undermine the relatively speedy character of arbitration and thereby destroy one of its main attractions to the global business community.[88] Although it would be a mistake to exaggerate the degree to which arbitration has come to institutionalize time-consuming procedural refinements, it nonetheless is striking that arbitration now faces a whole range of competitors (including variants of mediation and conciliation geared toward the needs of business) united by one common denominator: each promises an even faster mode of conflict resolution than that provided by arbitration.[89] In turn, defenders of arbitration have responded with a panoply of reform proposals aimed at minimizing its purportedly wasteful use of the precious commodity of time, and they are now energetically promoting the virtues of what they describe as fast-track arbitration, premised on the possibility of a mode of "accelerated justice" in which entrepreneurs can expect quick answers even in the most difficult disputes.[90]

Whether or not arbitration or its rivals are in fact as speedy as its enthusiasts and many academic commentators assert requires careful empirical scrutiny. But, even if such claims turn out to be exaggerated, it still remains relevant for the purposes of the argument here that one of the main selling points of arbitration is the promise of speed: in itself this highlights a surprising trend— namely, the global business community's apparent readiness to sacrifice traditional legal virtues for the promise of "getting things done" at a rapid pace.

Arbitration and its "accelerated" rivals share one additional feature attractive to business in the age of speed. The reduced emphasis on legal precedent and preexisting standing rules implies that legal continuity and stability mean less than in traditional forms of adjudication. Classical models of the relationship between capitalism and law would lead us to expect entrepreneurs to strive to overcome this state of affairs for the sake of ensuring legal predictability. Nonetheless, the global business community generally seems satisfied with the extreme situation-specific focus of decision making within arbitration and "alternative dispute resolution." Who can blame them given a global economy in which speed and flexibility are so crucial to economic success? Precisely this situation-specific focus renders both arbitration and its competitors less past oriented than traditional modes of legal regulation, thereby minimizing the impact of a legal past that increasingly seems irrelevant in the face of fast-moving economic trends. For their part those aggressively marketing alternatives to traditional adjudication intuitively grasp this point as well, at least to the extent that they note the degree to which nontraditional forms of dispute resolution seem well suited to situations in which the cultivation of long-term relations with business partners is of paramount significance. Litigation concerned first and foremost with assigning guilt to one party in reference to a past act may be less useful economically than a relatively quick compromise emphasizing positive lessons to be learned for both sides for the sake of maintaining cordial ties in the future.[91]

Earlier I argued that the unitary executive was the most likely institutional beneficiary of social acceleration. Subsequent discussions of constitutional change and the motorization of statutory legislation tended to confirm that expectation for the domestic arena. The lack of an effective global executive means, however, that similar possibilities for institutional adaptation are probably foreclosed beyond the confines of the nation-state. I also pointed to the possibility that new forms of discretionary adjudication, profoundly different from those sought by classical liberalism, might emerge in response to the need for rapid-fire decision making. In this alternative courts would become instruments for speedy conflict resolution but only at the cost of abandoning the normative and institutional attributes traditional liberalism deemed essential to their legitimacy. Their decision making might become discretionary and even unpredictable in character, as they abandoned a narrow retrospective temporal orientation and freed themselves from traditional legal formalities. The ascent of international business arbitration offers initial empirical confirmation for the potential appeal of this alternative path of institutional adaptation to social speed: arbitration provides high-speed conflict resolution while sacrificing traditional legal virtues that liberal democrats long envisioned as indispensable to legitimate adjudication.

Economic Globalization and Executive Prerogative

Economic globalization is also intimately tied to legal trends on the domestic scene which conflict with traditional liberal democratic expectations. Not only does economic globalization fail to strengthen liberal legal forms abroad, but it also undermines them at home. Earlier I briefly suggested that legal forms originally envisioned as best suited for warding off foreign foes (most important, executive prerogative) increasingly "collapse inward" on the legal system as a whole, as social acceleration contributes to the blurring of the traditional division between emergency and ordinary regulation. One of the most widely noted features of economic globalization, as well as an obvious offshoot of the compression of space via high-speed social activity, is the growing incapacity to distinguish clearly between domestic and international economic policy. In part because of their implicit endorsement of the orthodox view that flexible, high-speed executive prerogative represents our best hope for navigating the stormy waters of foreign affairs, policy makers are responding to a growing dilemma—the difficulty of distinguishing domestic from foreign economic policy—by taking legal recourse to the traditional legal paraphernalia of executive prerogative in foreign affairs. In an environment in which foreign economic affairs increasingly impinge on every facet of domestic economic life, the traditional notion of the primacy of the unitary executive in foreign affairs can only work to dismantle the law-based state. Here, too, empirical trends widely associated with economic globalization provide a vivid illustration of the general claim that social acceleration challenges liberal democracy. Its impressive political and economic muscle would seem to leave the United States particularly well positioned to grapple with the exigencies of globalization. Yet even in the United States the rule of law finds itself on the defensive, and forms of executive and administrative discretion, long considered by liberals suitable to the foreign sphere but inappropriate to the domestic arena, are gaining in significance in those policy arenas most intensely affected by economic globalization.

In U.S. law traditional rule of law standards are relaxed in reference to the executive's activities in the sphere of international economic policy. In accordance with the traditional notion of foreign affairs as constituting a lawless sphere necessitating the exercise of high-speed executive prerogative, U.S. courts have generally proven chary of restricting the president's economic policy making in the foreign realm.[92] As a result, unilateral action undertaken by the president in accordance with his "inherent" constitutional authority, as well as action set in motion under the auspices of generous congressional delegations of discretionary authority, are often left unchecked by U.S. courts. Delegations of power to the president in this realm have often been shielded by the "acquiescence doctrine," according to which congressional failure to challenge executive prerogative provides a sufficient constitutional justification for broad exercises of executive discretion.[93] As Supreme Court Justice William Rehnquist noted with characteristic bluntness in justifying presidential economic sanctions against Iran in 1981, "Past practice does not, by itself, create power, but 'long-continued practice, known to and acquiesced in by Congress, would raise a presumption that the [action] had been taken in pursuance of its consent.' "[94] The Administrative Procedures Act (APA) of 1946, which guarantees the maintenance of some rule of law virtues within the administrative apparatus,[95] does not generally apply to foreign and military affairs, and courts have been ready to place executive economic international policy making in this category. The consequences of excluding this realm of executive activity from the APA have often been far-reaching. In 1993, for example, judges relied on the exception clauses of APA to rule that the North American Free Trade Agreement (NAFTA) need not be accompanied by an "environmental impact statement," a necessary complement to every legislative act since passage of the National Environmental Policy Act of 1970. According to the justices, the APA does not apply to the president's foreign policy affairs, and thus NAFTA need not undergo the same environmental scrutiny to which most legislation is now subject.[96] In light of the profound environmental ramifications of the free trade treaty and similar international economic agreements, the court's ruling is obviously an eye-opener. Yet it represents a far-too-typical example of judicial subservience to the unitary executive in the realm of international economic policy making.

Such judicial reticence might be tolerable if the scope of executive international economic policy making were relatively limited and clearly circumscribed. Yet economic globalization makes it increasingly difficult to distinguish effectively between domestic and foreign economic policy; NAFTA represents a paradigmatic case of the increasingly tenuous character of this classical distinction. The speed-up of the global capitalist economy means that foreign economic matters now impact directly on the domestic economy of even the richest and most powerful capitalist states; in this very immediate sense "the world seems to collapse inward upon us."

Before the 1930s the U.S. Congress was generally the main site for foreign economic policy, which consisted chiefly in hammering out tariffs and trade rules, and Congress periodically undertook this task by means of a series of colorful political brawls in which competing regional and economic interests vied for political favors. Yet the last half of the twentieth century witnessed a remarkable shift in this authority from Congress to the executive, as evinced by at least three key institutional shifts.

First, even though the U.S. Constitution explicitly gives Congress power to regulate foreign commerce, since passage of the 1934 Reciprocal Trade Agreements Act (RTAA) Congress has tended to delegate much of this power to the president. Lawyers and political scientists continue to debate the precise scope of executive power vis-à-vis the legislature in international trade and commerce, in part because Congress has on occasion successfully placed procedural restraints on the exercise of presidential prerogative. Nonetheless, few today question the fact of presidential dominance in the area of international trade. The international lawyers John H. Jackson and William J. Davey probably speak for the majority of experts in the field when they comment that congressional delegations of authority in international economic policy "often are so general or ambiguous as to give the President considerable freedom to act."[97] One might expect growing public anxiety in recent years about the global economy to have led to a reassertion of congressional control, but Congress, for the most part, has continued to delegate generous powers to the executive. Despite occasional bouts of protectionism and sporadic evidence suggesting that Congress might rethink its sweeping delegations of international economic policy making to the executive, most academic specialists agree that it thus far has "refrained from reclaiming, directly, the primary trade power granted by the Constitution."[98]

Even protectionist calls to defend domestic industry have often strengthened the general trend toward executive discretion rather than curbing it: Congress occasionally responds to anxieties about excessive presidential prerogative exercised for the sake of advancing global free trade by providing the executive with additional powers to protect domestic industry. As a result, there is now a plethora of statutes on the books authorizing the president to undertake retaliatory trade actions. The president possesses impressive discretionary power to undertake reprisals against "unfair" trade practices (Section 301 Complaints Procedure Legislation)[99] as well as more limited but nonetheless significant authority to limit imports that constitute a "substantial cause of serious injury" to American industry (Section 201 Escape Clause), add duties to imports below the price at which such goods are sold on their home market (Anti-dumping Laws), and add duties to offset subsidies that imported goods enjoy (Countervailing Duty Laws). The president can also authorize duty-free imports from developing countries if he so chooses (Trade Act of 1974), and he has broad power to control imports and exports deemed a danger to "national security."[100]

Second, since midcentury the executive has become the main player in the realm of foreign agreements, despite the fact that the Constitution expressly requires that all treaties be approved by a two-thirds vote of the Senate. U.S. policy makers have gotten around this quaint leftover from our legalistic Enlightenment heritage by establishing a separate category of "executive agreements," in which traditional constitutional treaty-making procedures are abrogated and presidents have even been allowed to act unilaterally. Although taking different forms, "executive agreements" possess one common denominator: they reduce the traditional legislative authority of the Senate and increase presidential discretion in an ever more vital area of governmental policy.[101] Notwithstanding their suspect constitutional basis, executive agreements have proliferated. Whereas under Franklin Roosevelt the U.S. entered into 105 treaties and 123 executive agreements, during the Truman Administration ten times more executive agreements than treaties were approved; under Nixon 846 agreements were issued by the executive, but only 63 treaties were passed by the Senate. According to a recent empirical survey, 88 percent of all international agreements accepted by the United States between 1934 and 1988 took the form of an executive proclamation; a plurality of them (37 percent) concerned economic matters.[102] One immediate result of this trend is that some international economic agreements lack a clear-cut statutory basis. The most important international economic agreement endorsed by the United States in this century, the 1947 General Agreement on Tariffs and Trade (GATT), was initially done so in the form of an executive agreement; its chief legislative basis was a set of open-ended clauses in the Reciprocal Trade Agreements Act of 1945 calling for the expansion of "foreign markets for the products of the United States" and regulation of the "admission of foreign goods into the United States in accordance with the characteristics and needs of various branches of American production so that foreign markets will be made available to those branches of American production."[103] The Bretton Woods Agreement, as well as many other trade agreements, was similarly put into effect by specific variants of the executive agreement. Most recently, both NAFTA and the World Trade Organization were approved by means of one version of the executive agreement, the "congressional-executive agreement," according to which a simple majority of both houses of Congress suffices to pass a foreign treaty.

The problem here is less that such trends contradict an "originalist" reading of the U.S. Constitution than the general dangers they pose for self-government and the rule of law.[104] Although the NAFTA debate was relatively lively and freewheeling, the case of NAFTA simply reinforces the familiar saying about the exception proving the rule: too often, the executive's preference for entering into international economic agreements resting on a meager legal basis and subject to limited congressional, let alone meaningful public scrutiny, bodes poorly for the U.S. version of liberal democracy. Polls repeatedly show that the overwhelming majority of Americans today lack even minimal knowledge of their country's international economic commitments and entanglements; international economic policy making by means of executive agreement probably exacerbates this problem. Moreover, apathy represents a disturbingly understandable response to a political system in which free elections too often seem to have at most a limited impact on international economic policies having far-reaching implications for ordinary Americans.

Third, as noted earlier, the president controls sweeping emergency powers in the sphere of international economic policy as well. For example, the International Emergency Economic Powers Act of 1977 (IEEPA) authorizes the president to declare a national emergency in the face of "any unusual and extraordinary threat, which has its source in whole or substantial part outside the United States, to the national security, foreign policy, or economy of the United States." Upon declaration of an emergency, the president is allowed to undertake a diversity of economic sanctions, including cutting off exports and imports or restricting private financial transactions. Congress formally has authority to override the president's declaration of emergency powers, but the standards that Congress must meet to do so are strict; according to most commentators, they have failed so far to halt the expansion of executive prerogative. As one international lawyer describes IEEPA, "the criterion for invoking it are vague, Congress has very little to say about its use, and there is no effective way to terminate a use that becomes inappropriate as time passes."[105] Not surprisingly, presidents have made ready use of the generous provisions of IEEPA, relying on it to declare that the United State faced "extraordinary threats" from countries such as Iran, Nicaragua, and Libya before unleashing a series of economic weapons against them. The tragedy of IEEPA is that legal reformers cognizant of the perils of excessive executive discretion originally envisioned it as an improvement over a sad state of affairs in which the president, by the early 1970s, was able to rely on any of hundred of legislative delegations of emergency power. By eliminating many of them during the mid-1970s and replacing them with IEEPA, congressional reformers hoped to rein in what contemporaries were then widely describing as the "imperial presidency." The IEEPA has failed to live up to the admirable aspirations of those who helped initiate it, and presidential emergency economic power is probably no less awesome today than in the early 1970s.[106]

Congress surely could do more to limit executive prerogative in the sphere of foreign economic policy. And judges would do well to rethink the notion that the purportedly foreign character of some types of economic policy justifies substantial executive prerogative. At the same time economic globalization generates real difficulties for those hoping to revitalize the rule of law. As we have seen, social acceleration dramatically exacerbates a traditional jurisprudential problem—namely, the fact that legal rules necessarily "force the future into the categories of the past."[107] Where social settings are characterized by relatively slow-paced changes in social and economic conditions, the dilemma of a time lag between statutes and social and economic reality possesses limited practical significance. As capitalism revolutionizes the temporal horizons of social life, however, this familiar enigma necessarily takes on a dramatically heightened significance. Consequently, even relatively recent statutes quickly look like relics from a distant past irrelevant to the latest economic requirements, and legislatures seek to compensate for this failing by providing the executive and administration with substantial room to engage in discretionary, flexible forms of situational decision making.

Possible Critical Responses and Political Implications

In this chapter I have argued that capitalism's once intimate relationship to the rule of law seems ever more distant and estranged. The elective affinity endorsed by so many legal analysts on both the Left and Right increasingly belongs to the trashcan of legal and intellectual history. Although it remains true that every functioning capitalist economy requires some minimum of legal protections (private property, contracts, a system of binding dispute resolution), even that minimum is more pliable than generally acknowledged. By no means can we endorse the orthodox view that capitalism and a robust rule of law—based on a system of clear, general, stable, prospective, public norms—are likely to go hand in hand. On the contrary, economic globalization flourishes precisely where such legal forms are lacking. The overlap between economic globalization and social acceleration helps explain why. The temporal mismatch between economic activity and traditional forms of adjudication is particularly acute within global law because of the striking employment there of new possibilities for high-speed social action. Economic globalization is also rightly associated with the blurring of the border between domestic and foreign economic policy. To the extent that policy makers continue to envisage the unitary executive as best equipped to tackle the exigencies of foreign affairs, economic globalization provides them with an additional justification for dramatically expanding executive prerogative at home. Unfortunately, the tendency to do so further undermines the rule of law precisely where liberal theory long considered it most secure.

What, then, of other arenas of global law? After all, social acceleration is motored by interstate competition and rivalry, no less so than by modern capitalism; at least that was one of the claims proffered in chapter 1. If the general thesis that social acceleration undermines traditional forms of liberal law holds water, it therefore should also obtain for noneconomic arenas of global law in which social acceleration is no less acute. For example, areas of public international law directly concerned with interstate relations—in particular, warfare—should probably exhibit the same lacuna of rule of law virtues that we find in the context of economic globalization. Yet a substantial body of literature now suggests that this is not the case. According to one widely endorsed interpretation of the development of public international law over the course of the last fifty years, the rule of law has celebrated major victories in the international arena since the conclusion of World War II and the cessation of the Cold War between the United States and Soviet Union.[108] Since the Nuremberg and Tokyo Trials, international human rights protections have advanced the cause of a global order based on the rule of law; international tribunals against Slobodan Milosevic, as well the establishment of the International Criminal Court, presumably represent recent examples of the trend toward a heightened commitment to legality in international affairs. The founding of the United Nations, as well as its recent success in undertaking "humanitarian intervention" against outlaw states, might similarly suggest that interstate relations increasingly exhibit core features of the rule of law.

To the extent that this counterargument takes note of the unsuitability of classical depictions of the international arena as a lawless state of nature, it provides a useful intellectual service. In addition, by underscoring the normative and political potential advantages of radical shifts in interstate relations, it deserves our careful attention. From the argumentative perspective outlined here, such transformations would be truly momentous: fundamental changes in interstate relations—most important, a reduction in interstate rivalry—would potentially undermine one of the main structural sources of social acceleration, opening the door to far-reaching changes in the temporal contours of contemporary social existence. One of the main driving forces behind social acceleration, interstate competition, would no longer directly function, and new possibilities for overcoming the temporal gap between liberal democracy and high-speed society might appear on the horizon. Many of the dilemmas described in previous chapters would suddenly seem less obtrusive.

Nonetheless, we should avoiding confusing our normative and political preferences with the empirical facts of public international law.[109] Changes in international law over the course of the last half-century have undoubtedly been complex and multifaceted, and there is indeed evidence of progress toward a rule of law–based international system. It would be a mistake, however, to overstate the existence of such trends. Most obviously, ours is still an international political order in which the great powers not only write many of the rules of international politics and enforce them to serve their own power interests, as well, but also openly insist on exception clauses that allow them to avoid falling subject to precisely those norms that they (inconsistently) enforce against lesser powers. The shocking refusal of the United State to accept the jurisdiction of the International Criminal Court, as well as the obsequiousness with which its European allies agreed to exempt the United States, are only two examples of this trend. The move toward humanitarian military intervention under the auspices of powerful transnational organizations (the U.N.-backed war against Iraq in 1991 or the NATO war in Yugoslavia), widely interpreted as evidence of a growing commitment to rule of law virtues in the global community, is no less ambivalent from a traditional legal perspective. To the extent that humanitarian intervention still relies on a highly selective, politicized, and ad hoc system of application and enforcement, it conflicts with the ideal of the generality of law and potentially undermines international law's certainty and stability. The great powers simply are not subject to the same rules as lesser states, and the application of key international law norms remains intensely politicized to a degree that meshes badly with a defensible liberal democratic conception of adjudication. The tendency to undertake military action under the auspices of controversial and oftentimes open-ended moral appeals, in exchange for an abandonment of the traditional notion of the legal equality of all sovereign states, is similarly ambiguous from the perspective of the basic notion of the rule of law.[110] Despite its widely noted limitations, the modern notion of the legal equality of states helps guarantee a modicum of predictability and certainty in international politics, and violations of it by the great powers risk generating onerous legal and political consequences. Some attempts in the past to do so have exacerbated rather than counteracted instability and uncertainty in international law.[111] In addition, international war crime tribunals potentially conflict with the principle of the non-retroactivity of law, and their ad hoc character similarly raises difficult questions from the perspective of the rule of law. The fact that it is difficult to imagine military representatives of a great power such as the United States being forced to appear before a war crimes tribunal continues to speak volumes about the limitations of the existing international legal order.[112]

Despite the deleterious trends described in this chapter, the rule of law remains essential to liberal democracy. Clear, general, stable, prospective, public norms serve as a necessary aid in the struggle to tame arbitrary power and prevent tyranny. The fact that the rule of law is no longer essential to some segments of global business hardly makes it any less important as a basic assurance of legal security for liberal democratic citizens. I have also tried to suggest here that the rule of law today is gaining in utility as a protection for liberal democratic polities subject to the whims of giant economic interests; discretionary decision making, for the benefit of transnational business, poses a growing threat to the political effectiveness of the liberal democratic state. If we are to ward off the specter of an international economic tyranny, in which mammoth economic interests employ their structural advantages to dictate economic and social policy to the rest of us, we need to consider new legal possibilities for counteracting the disastrous trend among nation-states to engage in the legally dubious parceling out of special privileges to the largest and most mobile units of capital. If they are to prove effective, new forms of regulation are going to have to take many of the attributes of legality described by classical jurisprudence: in light of the structural advantages enjoyed today by international business, it often remains best positioned to exploit ambiguities and discrepancies within legal and regulatory standards. When rules are vague or unclear or when they fail to provide "fair warning" by allowing for a multitude of inconsistent interpretations, oftentimes it is those possessing the greatest de facto economic (or political) power who gain. Of course, if legal materials exhibit the classical virtues of legality, this hardly ensures their socially progressive character; a vast range of (potentially conflicting) political and economic goals are consistent with the notion that law should take a general, public, prospective, and relatively clear and stable form.[113] Nonetheless, classical rule of law virtues make up indispensable prerequisites for the successful operation of any system of enforceable norms. Lon Fuller once relied on a wonderful metaphor to make this simple yet crucial point: the "art" of legality, like carpentry, can serve either good or bad purposes; clear, prospective, stable, general norms can advance either immoral or moral policies, just as a carpenter can use his skills to build either an orphans' asylum or a racially exclusionary country club. "But it still remains true that it takes a carpenter . . . to build an orphans' asylum, and that it will be a better asylum if he is a skilled craftsman equipped with tools that have been used with care and kept in proper condition."[114] Similarly, the effective pursuit of progressive public policy at the transnational level will typically require use of the classical attributes of legality.[115]

The precise nature of the relationship between traditional forms of national authority and the emerging modes of transnational business regulation described here is a complicated matter. Yet the ascent of international business arbitration, proliferation of soft law and self-regulation, and establishment of the WTO arguably constitute attempts to minimize the potential impact of the democratic nation-state over the supervision of transnational business. Forms of legal regulation meshing poorly with the ideal of the rule of law have obviously been commonplace in the welfare and regulatory states. They were undertaken, however, by political bodies resting on liberal democratic procedures and committed to the advancement of equal opportunity and social justice. Whatever the legal ills of the regulatory and welfare state from the standpoint of traditional liberal democratic jurisprudence, they have often served as a worthwhile trade-off in the quest to ensure democratic legitimacy and social stability. The same cannot generally be said about most present-day forms of transnational business regulation. Where economic and technological innovations permit large-scale business to reduce the de facto and de jure significance of national regulation while simultaneously opting for an alternative supranational regulatory system lacking the minimal preconditions of legality, we risk abandoning precisely those features of liberal democracy which allow it to rein in privileged economic interests. Some evidence suggests that vague deformalized law in economic and social policy is best exploited by the most organized and economically privileged interests in the domestic political economy.[116] Those perils are even greater in the global arena, in which mechanisms capable of providing representation to lower- and middle-income groups are missing and possibilities for counteracting the potential dangers of vague, open-ended regulation are either underdeveloped or nonexistent as well.

Needless to say, the struggle for new forms of legal regulation is sure to face fierce opposition from both privileged economic interests and wealthy nation-states that have the most to gain from the legal status quo. Yet those of us who remain appreciative of one of liberalism's most impressive weapons against arbitrary power, the rule of law, have no choice but to throw ourselves into the battle at hand. I hope that I have made an initial contribution to that battle in this chapter by discrediting outdated illusions about the purported kinship between capitalism and the rule of law. When writing about the negative impact of laissez-faire ideas on modern liberal democracy, John Dewey commented that "traditional ideas are more than irrelevant. They are an encumbrance."[117] This is true of the traditional notion of an elective affinity between capitalism and the rule of law as well.

Those of us committed to preserving the rule of law will need to consider how we can do so while developing forms of coordination and regulation properly suited to the dictates of a high-speed economy. The fundamental paradox at hand is clear enough: we need the rule of law, yet social acceleration appears to undermine it. Writing in the heyday of the postwar regulatory and welfare states, Fuller once remarked that the task "of finding the most apt institutional design for governmental control over the economy has been acute for a long time. In the future this problem is, I think, bound to become more pressing and pervasive."[118] Amid the contours of the ongoing process of economic globalization, Fuller's comments are more timely than they were in 1964.

CHAPTER SIX

Liberal Democracy in a High-Speed World

What, then, is to be done about liberal democracy in a high-speed age? Can it overcome the institutional pathologies bedeviling it and be revitalized? Or must we make our peace with the discouraging status quo and abandon any hope of renewing core liberal democratic institutional aspirations?

Yet maybe the institutional status quo is more attractive than suggested thus far. Perhaps *institutional conservatism* offers the most plausible response to the temporal misfit between liberal democracy and social acceleration, and my account has simply exaggerated the ills of present-day liberal democracy. Arguing against this option, I will consider the prospect that only a fundamental transformation of the temporal horizons of human experience might revive liberal democracy. From this alternative perspective liberal democracy requires a drastic deceleration of fundamental social and economic processes, and nothing less than a *temporal revolution* can put liberal democratic institutions back on the right track. Countering this position, in turn, I will highlight the virtues of an *institutional and temporal reformism,* according to which we need to start from the assumption that core features of social acceleration represent irrevocable facets of contemporary existence. Social speed is here to stay, that is, and we need to pursue institutional reforms that leave liberal democracy better adept at grappling with it.

Institutional Conservatism?

The expansion of executive prerogative, decline of elected legislatures, and fragility of liberal constitutionalism and rule of law have long made up central intellectual preoccupations of prominent critics of liberal democracy. For some readers the story that I have tried to tell must sound irritatingly reminiscent of the one-sided accounts of liberal democratic decay which were so popular in the last century among both left- and right-wing writers. From the Frankfurt School, on the Left, to Carl Schmitt and Friedrich Hayek, on the Right, such critics delighted in chronicling the distempers of recent institutional transformation in order to discredit the liberal democratic status quo.[1] Evoking the legacy of these critics, my argument relies on a favorable portrayal of traditional liberal democratic ideals—in particular, the temporal separation of powers. In the process have I unfairly conjured up an image of a long-lost but probably mythical (temporal) golden age in order to discredit the relatively unattractive working realities of contemporary liberal democracy? If so, the main argument developed in this book suffers from the same methodological sleight of hand which plagued so many twentieth-century critics of liberal democracy: real-life liberal democratic institutions are unfairly contrasted to an ambitious set of liberal democratic ideals in order misleadingly to imply that liberal democratic institutions have undergone deterioration. The problem with this view, of course, is that real-life liberal democracy may never have offered a compelling instantiation of the temporal separation of powers in the first place. Notwithstanding the original ideals of classical liberal democratic theory, nineteenth-century liberal democratic reality possibly conflicted with the dictates of social temporality no less than its twenty-first-century successor.

This suspicion would gain further support if it turned out that the account provided here elides key facets of institutional transformation. For example, one might plausibly argue that core facets of liberal democracy have already undergone a successful acceleration that effectively counteracts the temporal misfit between liberal democracy and contemporary society. For example, the rise of the mass media arguably means that political deliberation in liberal democracy has long taken no less high-speed forms than rapid-fire social and

economic processes: since the nineteenth century new forms of communication and information exchange (newspapers, telegraph, radio, and television)
have permitted fast-paced political exchange and deliberation, and political
debate now occurs at just as speedy a pace as many other facets of social and
economic life.[2] In contrast to claims advanced earlier, the tempo of political
life in liberal democracy has intensified no less strikingly than that of many
other facets of social existence. Does it make sense to picture freewheeling
democratic deliberation as "lagging behind" social and economic processes
when a panoply of high-velocity technologies (most important, television)
allows liberal democratic citizens to express and exchange views, and squabble
over competing interests, at unprecedented speeds?

Along similar lines one might point out that the account offered earlier in
this volume downplays the significance of crucial shifts in the institutional core
of liberal democracy (the executive, judiciary, and legislature) which offer
potential remedies to the dangers diagnosed. For example, my criticism of an
increasingly executive-driven political system may slight the democratization
of the executive which took place in many political systems in the twentieth
century. Implicitly relying on a nineteenth-century picture of the executive, in
which the executive branch was typically dominated by political and social
interests hostile to an increasingly democratic elected legislature, anxieties
about executive discretion rest on potentially anachronistic assumptions about
its necessarily antidemocratic bias. In an age of mass-based plebiscitarianism
executive discretion hardly constitutes, a priori, an attack on democratic legitimacy. Liberal democracy has also developed an array of impressive institutional instruments for counteracting the potentially deleterious consequences
of unmitigated executive discretion: ombudsmen, administrative hearings and
various quasi-judicial procedures, new forms of client participation in administrative decision making, and legislative oversight of administrative bodies
function to guarantee that the exercise of political power is consistent with
liberal democratic procedures and principles even where the law is vague and
unsettled. Even if it remains true that social acceleration engenders heightened
executive and administrative discretion, such discretion is considerably less
threatening to liberal democracy than implied by the discussion of executive-
dominated constitutional change or the pathologies of motorized lawmaking.

In short, the assertion that social acceleration undermines liberal democracy may rest on a historical myth, and the temporal dilemmas posed for
contemporary liberal democracy by social speed are probably overstated.

Throughout its history liberal democracy has adapted effectively to the challenges of social speed, and many facets of contemporary liberal democracy suggest that it will continue to do so. Of course, future adjustments may be necessary. There is neither pressing reason for alarm, however, nor sufficient grounds for positing the necessity of far-reaching social or political reform.

Although this critical response underscores worthwhile qualifications to the original argument, it nonetheless obfuscates the central issues at hand. We need not rely on the tired fiction of liberal democratic decay in order to worry about the clash between present-day liberal democracy and its underlying normative aspirations. Deliberative representative legislatures as the main site for lawmaking; the rule of law as a device for humanizing the exercise of political power; clarity and relative stability in constitutional law—each of these traditional ideals remains normatively admirable, and the burden of proof remains with those who would jettison them. The fact that nineteenth-century political life exhibited countless pathologies of its own hardly makes core traditional liberal democratic aspirations any less attractive. Moreover, there is substantial empirical evidence that liberal democracy has in fact changed in dramatic and unexpected ways; earlier I tried to explain how social acceleration can help us explain some of these changes, including the increasingly executive-centered face of decision making. Of course, it is true that executive power now possesses a different political and social meaning than in the nineteenth century, when its domination in parts of Europe by openly antiliberal and antidemocratic political and social constituencies made it an easy target for those hoping to advance liberal democracy. And liberal democracy has indeed developed numerous institutional weapons for redressing troublesome expressions of executive power. By the same token far too much empirical evidence continues to suggest that executive and administrative discretion remain significant in contemporary liberal democracy. Even if the growth of discretionary government derives in part from the rise of mass plebiscitarianism, its democratic origins fail to provide a sufficient justification: in a liberal democracy not simply the origins of government action but also its form must accord with liberal and democratic ideals. As executive discretion undermines publicity and transparency in government, it also violates core democratic political ideals. By paving the way for irregular and inconsistent state action, it threatens the rule of law and undermines the private autonomy essential to liberalism.

More considerable is the accusation that this discussion disregards ways by which liberal democracy has already acclimated itself to the imperatives of a high-speed social world. My tendency to emphasize the institutional (and formal-legal) core of liberal democracy, rather than public life or civil society, means that some parts of the story, including the place of high-speed mass media, assuredly have been neglected. At the same time, it seems implausible to assert that the present-day organization of the mass media offers optimal possibilities for high-speed political exchange and deliberation. This is not the place to revisit a massive literature documenting the failings of the contemporary mass media. For now it suffices to point out that communication and information media subject to powerful plutocratic interests, with a noticeable preference for reducing complex public issues to petty personal disputes and superficial "sound bites," probably does not represent an employment of new high-speed technologies sufficiently supportive of the liberal democratic ideal of government by discussion and debate.[3] Transnational conglomerates (e.g., Bertelsmann, Rupert Murdoch's News Corporation, Italian prime minister Silvio Berlusconi's Finivest, Time AOL Warner) today dominate the mass media in many parts of the liberal democratic universe. The effective monopolization of the necessary tools of high-speed public debate in the hands of a small group of firms contributes to the fact that the main sources for news increasingly spill out the same lightweight mush of sensationalism and "human interest" stories, with an increasing percentage of news coverage devoted to "infotainment."[4] According to some evidence, the dependence of large media conglomerates on advertising revenue systematically drives them to avoid challenging widely held political biases, let alone even address substantive political issues in the first place.[5] In the United States the rollback of Federal Communication Commission (FCC) regulations since the 1980s has exacerbated long-standing tendencies favoring an episodic and fragmentary portrayal of political events which exaggerates the significance of particular events and individuals. The appearance of "around-the-clock" cable television news tends to deepen these trends rather than correct for them, since its emphasis on "breaking" news typically leads journalists to neglect complex chains of social and political causality. Instead of offering a path beyond the political perils of high-speed society, the contemporary mass media reproduces many of the pathological political consequences of social acceleration described earlier in this book. As sociologist Herbert J. Gans observes: "thanks to the invention of new electronic media, journalists must now produce a constantly changing product . . . What is called the perpetual news cycle therefore requires, more than ever before, that a fresh product be manufactured in the fastest, most routinized, and efficient way possible."[6] Televised political discourse, for example, has been dramatically accelerated, with the time allotted to uninterrupted political speech falling from 42.3 seconds in 1968 to less than 9 seconds by 1992.[7] In part because commercially driven journalists are necessarily obsessed with novelty, they tend to favor "hard" (i.e., coverage of events that have occurred in last twenty-four hours) but often superficial news: "abrupt developments are regarded as more newsworthy than chronic conditions,"[8] and news tends to become an "endless stream of emergencies" possessing an "artificial short-lived intensity."[9] This trend also heightens journalists' dependency on top government officials, who "have the power and staffs to create newsworthy events"—such as decisions, news conferences, reports, and ceremonies—"regularly and quickly."[10] No wonder that the contemporary mass media so often appears to be fueling the rise of a personalistic style of plebiscitary rule à la Berlusconi or the Texas businessman and former presidential candidate H. Ross Perot: its implicit vision of the political world as one plagued by disruptive and fast-moving emergencies plays into the hands of would-be executives who promise quick resolutions to crises for which slow-going deliberative legislatures seem ill equipped.

Even if one remains unconvinced by these counterarguments, a final point deserves attention. Defenders of the institutional status quo probably still need to acknowledge a gap between the actual temporal workings of our institutions and traditional liberal democratic assumptions about that temporality. The contemporary executive is not the high-speed institutional actor described by the classics of modern political thought; executive action is oftentimes likely to be complex, unwieldy, and time-consuming, and the traditional dogma of the energetic executive rests on historically specific preconditions that no longer readily accord with the realities of political life. Acknowledging this point suggests why social acceleration requires even ardent defenders of real-existing liberal democracy to consider the possibility of political reform: a sizable range of existing policies presupposes the myth of the high-speed executive, and intellectual integrity demands that even the most adamant defender of the institutional status quo think hard about the suitability of these policies.[11]

Temporal Revolution?

In chapter 4 I criticized Carl Schmitt and more recent U.S. common lawyers for undertaking to combat social acceleration by decelerating judicial practice, arguing that this antidote was likely to exacerbate the existing ills of liberal democratic decision making rather than eliminate them. The flaw with this approach, I argued, was that it focuses on legal manifestations of social acceleration while overlooking the broader social trends that engender "motorized legislatures" in the first place. Because it fails to address the original sources of legislative acceleration, the dilemma of a temporal disconnect between liberal democracy and social acceleration would probably increase if vast decision-making power were placed in the hands of slow-going common law–oriented courts. Why not, then, salvage liberal democracy by eliminating the root temporal cause of so many of its weaknesses? The most impressive answer to the institutional dilemmas chronicled in this book would also seem to be the most obvious: the misfit between liberal democracy and social acceleration could be overcome by decelerating fundamental social and economic processes. If liberal democracy operated in an environment in which technological acceleration, the rate of social change, as well as the pace of everyday life were substantially slowed down, many of the institutional enigmas described here might be ameliorated. Legislatures would have fewer reasons to "pass the buck" to the executive; for its part the executive might possess reduced opportunities to claim that the "lightning speed" of contemporary life necessitates awesome accretions of executive prerogative. The traditional aspiration for stable and clear constitutional law—as well as a body of statutory law embodying the rule of law attributes of generality, publicity, prospectiveness, and stability—might again seem realizable. Perhaps it would also become less far-fetched to envision a legal substructure for the global economy resting on a substantial dose of traditional liberal democratic legal and political ideals. Neoliberal rhetoric about an emerging rule of law for economic globalization might finally step off the policy pronouncements and public relations Web sites of powerful international organizations and instead become basic to the reality of international law.

The appeal of this strategy should be evident for another reason as well. A decent society surely might seek to discard certain manifestations of social acceleration. Those of us forced to load our pocket calendars with an unachievable variety of tasks hardly need a reminder of the tensions generated by the acceleration of everyday life. No less harried than the rest of us, businesspeople obsessed with catching up to the latest economic and technological innovations hardly seem to represent the paragons of individual autonomy celebrated by classical economic liberalism; overworked employees often lack sufficient time for their loved ones, let alone the obligations of citizenship; the rapid pace of social change might legitimately lead even the least conservative among us to worry about the lack of stability and constancy in core areas of social existence. Not surprisingly, social scientists concerned with the high-speed tempo of contemporary society tend to picture social deceleration as the only suitable antidote to speed.[12] What better way not only to revitalize liberal democracy but also to help provide real possibilities for a less harried and potentially more humane existence than by slowing down the temporal fundaments of contemporary society? In light of disturbing evidence that speed may now be overtaxing our basic physical and mental capacities, this response might appear to be sheer biological necessity.[13]

Despite the drawing power of this response, it oversimplifies the intellectual tasks at hand. Social acceleration represents an ambivalent process. As political theorist William Connolly observes, speed can "jeopardize freedom," yet "the crawl of slow time contains injuries, dangers, and repressive tendencies too. It may be wise therefore to explore speed as an ambiguous medium that contains some positive possibilities."[14] A society subject to limited change is unlikely to provide a sufficient terrain for the personal experimentation essential to freedom; a dramatic reduction in the pace of technological acceleration might easily have a debilitating impact on attractive forms of social and economic dynamism; the deceleration of everyday existence could simply mean reducing the impressive array of choices for realizing self-chosen life plans we now enjoy. Static and homogeneous societies are less subject to social acceleration than our own, but they provide fewer opportunities for personal autonomy as well. Notwithstanding its many pathologies, social speed contributes directly to the liberties that we moderns take for granted, and a frontal assault on social acceleration risks becoming an attack on modernity's most worthwhile accomplishments. To be sure, we need to think hard about how to make social acceleration consistent with a decent society, and we should strive to eliminate its more disturbing faces. Doing so successfully means starting from the assumption that elements of social speed represent an indispensable component of modernity, however, rather than an unambiguously negative ailment we can discard at will.

Notwithstanding much of the existing literature on speed, it is also naive to believe that deceleration could ever succeed without a fundamental reorganization of contemporary society.[15] As I argued in chapter 1, modern capitalism and the modern system of states represent two of the central structural driving forces behind social acceleration. Although plausible arguments can be marshaled in defense of experimenting with alternative forms of economic organization as well as radically reshuffling interstate relations, both seem unlikely in the present political context. For better or worse, the fundamental structural motors behind social acceleration will probably continue to operate for some time. And, even if we were to succeed in undertaking desirable alterations to these structural mechanisms, it remains the case that at least some facets of social acceleration will undoubtedly continue to haunt us well into the future. Any viable economic alternative to present-day capitalism, for example, will undoubtedly make use of markets and other competitive mechanisms.[16] An appealing model of a postcapitalist economy is sure to exhibit at least some of the same mechanisms that buttress contemporary capitalism's contributions to social acceleration in the present era: any dynamic and thus desirable economy will need to be characterized by relatively high rates, for example, of technological acceleration.

The point is not that we should abandon ambitious attempts to restructure social temporality. But such experiments need to "explore speed as an ambiguous medium that contains some positive possibilities." How, then, might we undertake such explorations? A viable political system, outfitted with rich possibilities for freewheeling deliberation and inclusive interest representation, still constitutes our best chance for doing so. A vibrant liberal democracy, able to explore new possibilities for social and economic organization, offers us the best hope for determining which facets of social speed can be modified or even discarded in contrast to those that we must keep. Unless we can improve the decision-making operations of liberal democracy, it remains unlikely that we can successfully negotiate the challenges of social speed. The question of institutional design therefore takes on special significance even for those of us sympathetic to a radical reorganization of social temporality.

Institutional and Temporal Reformism

For those of us hoping to reform liberal democracy, one recent trend in contemporary political and legal theory seems especially promising. Substantial energy and intellectual creativity have been devoted to outlining a model of deliberative democracy, and a growing number of scholars have begun to analyze its appropriate institutional moorings, including fundamental alterations to the traditional separation of powers described in chapter 2. Notwithstanding some striking weaknesses, the debate about deliberative democracy potentially points the way to an appropriate response to social acceleration.

Deliberative democracy represents a flourishing academic cottage industry, with its defenders now offering diverse (communitarian, critical theory inspired, liberal, and republican) models of it.[17] For the limited purposes of this discussion crucial to this debate is (1) a shared normative assumption that the legitimacy of political decision making in liberal democracy rests on meaningful possibilities for testing reasons and interests in free and open public debate; and (2) a common diagnostic concern that the paucity of significant political debate in contemporary liberal democracy suggests a drying up of political legitimacy. Despite the significant differences separating its various proponents, advocates of deliberative democracy are concerned with revitalizing liberal democracy by unleashing new and dormant possibilities, both in formal institutions and the "informal" sphere of public life at large, for uncoerced communication and dialogue. Deliberative democracy's critical bite stems from its theorists' tendency to conceptualize deliberation in a manner that underscores its unrealized character in contemporary society. Although the specific details depend on the particular philosophical framework in which it is situated, deliberative democracy is often associated with relatively demanding normative ideals of liberty and equality: an authentic deliberative democracy is sometimes envisioned as one in which all citizens would possess free and equal chances to debate and respond to the arguments of the peers and in which oftentimes arbitrary sources of inequality (stemming, e.g., from class, gender, or race) would no longer be permitted to infringe unnecessarily on political debate. Participants "strive to reach agreement solely on the basis of the better argument, free of coercion, and open to all competent speakers."[18] Free public exchange requires that reasons "must be communicated in such a way that any other citizen might be able to understand them, and freely respond to them on his or her own terms. Reasons formed in this way are more likely to result in decisions that everyone may consider legitimate in a special sense: even if there is no unanimity, citizens agree sufficiently to cooperate in deliberation."[19]

Although sometimes neglectful of institutional questions, recent proponents of deliberative democracy have also suggested ways in which liberal democratic institutions might better advance free and uncoerced political debate. The late Argentine legal theorist Carlos Santiago Nino argued persuasively that deliberative democracy is incompatible with the trend towards executive-dominated government. In executive-centered presidential regimes political debate during electoral campaigns is likely to focus on the executive's personal attributes, rather than public ideals or substantive political proposals.

Presidentialism tends to polarize political deliberation (one is either for or against a particular candidate for the presidency) to a degree that impoverishes political exchange and makes useful argumentative give-and-take difficult. Nor can the single person of the executive ever realistically succeed in providing meaningful representation to the multiplicity of voices and interests found in modern pluralistic society. In contrast, in political systems in which a representative parliament constitutes the central site for decision making, electoral campaigns are more likely to focus on significant ideological and policy differences separating the parties, and, especially in those systems providing real opportunities for minority parties to gain an institutional foothold, one can generally expect campaigns to encourage a relatively diverse expression of political viewpoints. Finally, a key advantage of parliamentary government for deliberative democracy is that a numerous and multivocal elected parliament offers an indispensable device by means of which the political community at large can reasonably delegate the authority "to continue the deliberation that has taken place among the citizens before the representatives have been elected."[20] Although deliberative democracy requires thriving debate and exchange in society at large, it also needs institutions that effectively translate the broader process of deliberation into binding legislation. The broad-based character of elected legislatures makes them better suited to this task than either the executive or judiciary: "representatives must deliberate so as to come as close as possible to the deliberation that the electors themselves would have carried out. But the best way to ensure this dynamic is to have a body which is a highly accurate sample of the values and interests of the larger unit."[21]

On a more creative institutional note, some working within the paradigm of deliberative democracy have proposed a rethinking of the traditional tripartite (legislative, executive, and judiciary) separation of powers. However normatively appealing, the attempt to return all legislative rule making to a central parliament, this argument goes, is probably unrealistic given the vast activities of contemporary government. Nonetheless, we would do well to preserve the core intuition of the traditional liberal democratic ideal of legislation, according to which binding laws require the reasonable and considered consent of those affected by them. The superior representative character of central legislatures means that they should still determine how particular policy tasks are best tackled, even if that now requires of the legislature that it sometimes carefully delegate decision-making authority to alternate institutional sites.

In this vein the German social philosopher Jürgen Habermas provocatively argues for a restatement of the traditional idea of a separation of powers between different institutions in terms of a distinction between alternative modes of communication as well as different ways of making use of arguments and reasons. The conventional emphasis on distinct institutions no longer accurately expresses the core differences separating the basic activities with which they traditionally have been associated. Regardless of their specific location within the apparatus of government, types of activity deserve to be described as "legislative," "administrative," and "judicial" to the degree that they make use of different forms of argumentation, which Habermas interprets as capturing the essence of what classical liberal democratic theory implicitly conceived by means of each of the individual institutional instances composing the separation of powers.[22] In turn, such forms of action should be institutionalized so as to correspond to the fundamental logic of the type of communication at hand.

In this account legislative power is best conceived as resting on a model of communication concerned with the justification of norms. Political deliberation of this type can take many different forms and typically should be as inclusive as possible. In Habermas's terminology moral, ethical, and pragmatic forms of discourse can be appropriate when the justification of norms is at stake: moral discourse concerns matters of moral fairness and is guided by a demanding neo-Kantian criterion of universalizability; ethical discourse deals with issues of cultural value and identity, in which strict standards of universalizability are relaxed; pragmatic discourse is a compromise-oriented activity in which we strive to give equal weight to all relevant interests. Whereas legislative power draws its normative energy from diverse communicative sources, administrative power rests on a relatively circumscribed mode of strategic and instrumental-rational communication: "The legitimating ideals of administration are accuracy and efficiency. Administrators are to discover and undertake those actions that will be instrumental to the achievement of specific ends" to be determined by broader processes of deliberation which should culminate in binding legislation.[23] Administrative discourse is narrowly "tailored to the choice of technologies and strategies that, under the given circumstances (such as limited resources, deadlines, resistance in acceptance, and other restrictions), are suitable for realizing the values and goals previously set by the legislature."[24] The gist of Habermas's argument is that too much of what presently passes for administration in fact constitutes legislation and thus must be made subject to broad-based forms of deliberation presently missing in the state bureaucracy. When problems require a legislative resolution—for example, when administrators face a choice between mutually incompatible goals in such a way as to explode the boundaries of traditional conceptions of administrative activity—forms of deliberation suited to the justification of norms are normatively desirable. In this view legislation already takes place at many different interstices of the apparatus of government. It is now time to acknowledge this fact by allowing central parliaments openly to delegate legislative authority to the "administration" and then subsequently organize it in such a way as to subordinate it to genuinely deliberative democratic mechanisms. Thus, in a far more self-conscious manner than hitherto has been the case, the legislature should be required to reflect carefully about when legislative delegation is called for and how it can be rendered consistent with the requirements of deliberative democratic legitimacy. For example, an administrative body faced with the daunting task of tackling environmental problems in a particular locality might initiate public hearings and local meetings at which those affected by environmental legislation would be encouraged to participate in rule making. Devices ensuring that those affected would possess a meaningful impact on environmental lawmaking would have to be developed: citizens' review boards, as well as many other imaginable forms of citizen representation in administration rule making, might be required by the central legislature.[25]

From the conceptual perspective developed earlier, the appeal of deliberative democracy should be evident enough. To their credit its theorists frankly concede that the traditional liberal democratic vision of a polity governed by thriving deliberative legislature rarely accords with present-day political reality. Despite their many philosophical differences, they also have been creatively preoccupied with the task of reformulating the noble liberal ideal of government by discussion so as to make it better attuned to contemporary conditions. Some defenders of deliberative democracy also corroborate anxieties expressed earlier about the trend toward executive-centered government. Even though its proponents have sometimes been lax in identifying the legal problems posed by executive discretion, they convincingly suggest that executive-dominated government meshes poorly with a normatively attractive vision of deliberative democracy. Finally, deliberative democrats have offered thoughtful proposals for how we might rethink the separation of powers so as to adjust it to contemporary political necessities while maintaining a healthy fidelity to traditional intuitions. For example, Habermas not only accurately acknowledges a normatively ambivalent trend—namely, the migration of decision making into nonlegislative bodies, but he also offers a useful conceptual starting point for reforming administrative bodies that presently engage in ambitious forms of decision making. Perhaps one way by which we might begin to combat deleterious tendencies toward insufficiently transparent and accountable forms of state activity would be by institutionalizing deliberative democratic mechanisms and procedures in the very core of the burgeoning administrative and executive apparatus.

The account provided in previous chapters also points, however, to an Achilles' heel plaguing the contemporary debate on deliberative democracy. Whereas classical liberal democratic theory included an open acknowledgment of the unavoidably time-consuming character of wide-ranging deliberation, both within political life at large and representative legislatures, the recent theoretical discussion seems oblivious to temporal concerns altogether. Deliberative democrats have had little to say about temporality, and, when they have addressed the temporal presuppositions of deliberative democracy, their ideas generally seem quaint and anachronistic.[26] Yet, as I have argued, the misfit between the relatively slow-going temporality of liberal democratic politics, on one hand, and the high-speed dynamics of modern capitalism and the modern state system, on the other, represents a main source of the fragility of deliberative politics. Any attempt to explain why deliberation fails to determine lawmaking needs to pay attention to the key role played by social temporality. By failing to do so, deliberative democrats deny themselves a satisfactory explanation for the political ills that represent the most direct inspiration for their own normative and diagnostic concerns. Contemporary theorists typically envision deliberation in even more demanding normative terms than classical liberal democratic theory; they picture legitimate political debate as requiring political exchange in accordance with strict normative ideals of equality, reciprocity, and openness, and they insist that it needs to be substantially more inclusive than the "bourgeois" public of property owners which eighteenth- and nineteenth-century liberal theorists often had in mind. Deliberation along these lines is probably destined to be even more slow going, especially in large and pluralistic polities, than it was in the days of Madison or Mill.[27]

If social acceleration clashes with even the modest ideals of traditional liberal democracy, how might these vastly more ambitious views of deliberation ever gain a successful footing in our high-speed society? Might not proposals, such as that offered by Habermas, to democratize the administrative apparatus unwittingly contribute to the paralysis of state activity? As noted earlier, legislative delegation to the executive or administration often takes place as an understandable response to the immense time pressures of prospective legislative rule making. But, if the administration is now to be rendered subject to demanding forms of time-consuming deliberation not unlike those found in parliament, what is to prevent it from suffering from the same temporal pressures? Was not the original point of delegating decision making to the executive or administration a legitimate concern with getting a "fast" resolution?

Once again, the quest to ameliorate the tensions between liberal democracy and social speed seems to have taken us to a dead end. Might there be a path beyond this impasse?

Earlier I intimated that finding such a path requires us to rethink the commonsense association of popular and legislative deliberation with slowness, arguing against a dogmatic fidelity to traditional temporal presuppositions about liberal democracy. The free ebb and flow of discussion requires sufficient opportunities to respond as well as speak, of taking turns so that participants in deliberation possess equal chances to express their views and interests as well as to answer opposing arguments and be heard. It also requires sufficient time to ensure that expressed preferences will be sufficiently well considered and reflective. Deliberation's normative fundaments, as well as its intrinsically sequential character, undoubtedly place some restraints on how fast the give-and-take of political exchange ideally should be. Yet pathbreaking shifts in the temporal contours of human existence have also generated unexpected opportunities for eliminating historically contingent forms of unnecessary or excess slowness in political deliberation. When new communication and information technologies allow for useful interaction among citizens, provide vast information resources at a moment's notice, and permit fruitful communication across distances that once precluded it, conventional presuppositions about the necessarily slow character of deliberation seem increasingly suspect. For these reasons free, public, and reciprocal deliberation should be able to take relatively speedy forms that would surprise our historical predecessors no less than our increasingly fast-paced capitalism or fast-moving state system. As a conceptual matter, there seems to be no a priori reason for eliminating the possibility of a temporally efficient as well as normatively

legitimate deliberative democracy. By implication, corresponding modifications of the separation of powers, including the heightened scrutiny of administrative rule making by deliberative mechanisms, might be possible as well.

Can we concretize this vague suggestion? In the following section I point to
some ways by which we might begin to do so. Given the daunting institutional
challenges at hand, my answers will necessarily seem insufficient. But perhaps
they can get the ball rolling by initiating a much-needed debate about the
dilemmas posed by social speed for liberal democracy.

What Is to Be Done?

Let me suggest three arenas for reform. First, liberal democracy needs to
make sure that high-speed communication and information technologies sus-
tain broad public debate and deliberation. Without lively deliberative publics
operating at a multiplicity of societal interstices, liberal democracy cannot
thrive. Second, we might consider how lawmaking procedures could better
exploit novel possibilities for speed. Given that some traditional criticisms of
direct democracy have been rendered obsolete by social acceleration, liberal
democracy would do well to undertake careful experiments with forms of
direct popular lawmaking which rest on extensive debate and deliberation. In a
similar vein I devote special attention to creative recent proposals for what has
been described as *reflexive law* as one possible way to update legislation in
accordance with the imperatives of our high-speed society.

High-Speed Deliberation

A successful liberal democracy relies on the free flow of ideas and arguments: this simple but crucial intuition lies at the core of classical liberal theory
as well as present-day debates about deliberative democracy. Unfortunately,
the contemporary mass media often does a miserable job sustaining the deliberative exchange required by liberal democracy. Can we make better use of the
possibilities for high-speed political debate and exchange presently available
to us?

A number of potentially helpful proposals are already on the table. The
watering down of legal regulation mandating that broadcasters guarantee representation to a diversity of political viewpoints and perspectives, as well as
requiring "quality" programming, needs to be reversed; in the United States
the Federal Communications Commission "fairness doctrine" will have to be

revitalized and updated in accordance with a media and technological environment dramatically different from that in which it initially emerged.[28] For example, requiring major media outlets to provide chunks of free time for political debate might help generate heightened interest in substantive political issues, particularly if the time available were used in creative and potentially unpredictable ways (e.g., question-and-answer sessions between politicians and a randomly selected audience). In this spirit network and cable news could be allotted time for what political theorist James Fishkin describes as "deliberative opinion polls," in which an audience determined by pollsters to be representative of public opinion as a whole meets at a particular location and subsequently engages in intense group discussion on a particular set of political issues (such as health care policy).[29] Ambitious proposals for countering the negative consequences of the corporate character of the mass media also demand careful consideration. Some countries have banned television advertising altogether; others make it difficult for advertisers to influence programming by preventing networks from selling advertising spots for a particular program or time slot. In a pathbreaking study of the negative impact of advertising on the media, C. Edwin Baker proposes a tax on advertising that would then be used to subsidize media use by readers or viewers. Advertisers would still possess legitimate venues to hawk their wares, and advertising revenue would continue to help finance the exorbitant expenses of the contemporary mass media and thereby reduce costs to those serviced by it. Yet a well-structured system of taxation might minimize the inordinate influence of corporate advertisers on editorial content and news coverage, while tax-generated subsidies distributed on the basis of readership (or viewership) could work to increase responsiveness to audience.[30]

Only a direct assault on growing evidence of media concentration can provide the necessary institutional presuppositions for generating appropriately freewheeling high-speed political exchange. As long as a tiny club of large corporations dominates the media landscape, it will remain subject to the familiar economic pressures of large-scale capitalist enterprise. These pressures not only systematically undermine the media's capacity to generate the public good of political debate,[31] but they also lie at the root of many of the pathologies afflicting the contemporary mass media noted by observant critics. As we saw in chapter 1, capitalism represents a major driving force behind the process of social acceleration; many of the most striking attributes of acceleration are intimately linked to the structural requirements of capitalism. Is it no surprise, then, that the same obsession with novelty, change, and speed which we see at work in other arenas of capitalist economic activity characterizes news and political coverage provided by large corporate media (e.g., the sound bite or episodic reporting that reduces complex chains of causality to "breaking" emergencies)? Only diversity in ownership and control—achievable in part by substantial subsidies to existing as well as novel public and quasi-public media—can guarantee a corresponding diversity in political content. A "mixed economy" in the mass media able to exploit the dynamism of capitalism while counteracting its problematic side effects offers us a reasonable chance that existing information and communication technologies effectively serve liberal democracy.

Along similar lines liberal democracy needs to exploit the deliberative potential of novel high-speed interactive technologies. The Internet has already demonstrated its impressive potential as an organizational tool for social movements and nongovernmental organizations (NGOs), and this experience has encouraged some to argue that its effective democratic employment requires universal access.[32] The extension of computer and Internet access can only successfully buttress liberal democracy, however, if the Internet is prevented from becoming an overwhelmingly commercial device. Otherwise, it is likely to deepen trends toward civic privatism and further emaciate liberal democracy's already scarce deliberative energies. Public subsidies for Web sites offering a forum for political debate and exchange represent one possible initiative. Requiring Web sites to adhere to strict rules of disclosure—for example, news sites that are required by law to disclose potential conflicts of interest—might be another.[33] Finally, more attention needs to be paid to the difficult question of how best to update familiar speech and broadcasting regulations such as the fairness doctrine to new information and communication technologies. Perhaps a revitalized fairness doctrine should be interpreted to require Web sites to include links that would facilitate access to substantive questions and contrary views.[34] One legal scholar has innovatively suggested that the Internet should be treated in a manner akin to public streets, sidewalks, and parks, which in U.S. law are conceived as "public forums" where citizens should be able to assemble, speak with one another, and challenge their fellow citizens with (oftentimes unwanted) political messages. Since cyberspace now functions as a public site much as sidewalks and parks once did, perhaps it needs to be similarly regulated so as to provide meaningful communicative access for interested participants. This might entail permitting speakers to gain the attention of select Internet users, just as the public forum doctrine allows speakers to confront their fellow citizens with political messages on sidewalks, parks, and other public spaces.[35]

High-Speed Decision Making

Can we better integrate high-speed information and communication technologies into lawmaking? If we were able to achieve this, it might be possible to reduce the tension between slow-going deliberative lawmaking and the rapid-fire pace of contemporary society.

It appears that many elected legislatures are already doing so, though generally in modest ways. Parliaments are using the Internet to provide citizens with access to basic information about the workings of government, records of legislative debates and votes, and "position papers." Rudimentary evidence suggests that the Internet is contributing to the openness and transparency of government decision making.[36] Much remains to be done. Public interest advocate Ralph Nader regularly points out that U.S. Congress Web sites, for example, make it unduly difficult for users to figure out how their elected representatives actually voted. There is also some evidence that the Internet has improved the legislature's ability to respond to crises: in the face of sudden public outcry in 1999 over genetically modified (GM) food, the British Labour Party was able to e-mail its MPs a series of reliable scientific reports that they then relied on in order to respond quickly to public anxiety.[37] In the immediate aftermath of the fall 2001 anthrax attacks on the U.S. Congress, "members were kept up to date by their leadership on floor scheduling, caucus meetings, health alerts, and building closure developments via computer, cell phone, pager, and Palm Pilot."[38] Even though many congressional officers were forced to close, Congress continued operating. Although easily overlooked, experiences of this type contain far-reaching implications: to the extent that new technologies support the legislature in undertaking rapid-fire responses to unexpected crises, they directly undermine the traditional temporal justification for the supremacy of executive power during a crisis.

Legislators have also begun to use the Internet as a serious forum for debate and consultation. Tony Blair's government endorsed an online debate on the meaning of the "third way," and the results of the debate were passed along to the prime minister in a written report and via a policy seminar.[39] It is now technically possible for constituents to watch simultaneous broadcasts of legislative debates while downloading relevant policy papers and other substantive materials and then quickly communicate their views to their fellow citizens or elected representatives.[40] One might imagine the Internet serving as an effective tool for public and ultimately legislative oversight of the administrative apparatus: administrative agencies should probably be required to place significant chunks of information online, thus making them readily available to journalists, legislators and their staff, as well as the public at large.[41]

Over the course of the last decade a lively debate also has erupted over the possibility of employing high-speed computer technology as an instrument of (1) broad popular deliberation and exchange followed by (2) direct citizen lawmaking.[42] Although experiments with new types of direct democracy should only be undertaken with great caution, sound reasons suggest that they might help redress the temporal difficulties described earlier. Since high-speed communication technology compresses space, traditional geographical barriers to direct democracy no longer obtain. In contrast to earlier forms of high-speed communications technology such as television, some new technologies allow for fast-paced lateral communication and hence the deliberative give-and-take essential to democratic politics in a way that previous proposals for direct democracy (via televised debate followed by a push-button vote, e.g.) could not.[43] Unless there are convincing reasons for privileging the immediacy of face-to-face deliberation in democratic politics, there would seem to be no necessary reason for excluding the possibility that new technologies might provide a forum for meaningful popular debate followed by direct participation in legislation. To be sure, immediate forms of deliberation and participation remain desirable. In light of the fact that existing representative democracy typically only offers physically direct deliberation a limited role in the immediate process of lawmaking anyway, however, it seems disingenuous to criticize defenders of computerized direct democracy for potentially devaluing face-to-face political interaction. In addition, many familiar flaws of direct democracy remain unaffected by the new technologies.[44] Initiatives and referenda can fail to provide sufficient room for the compromise and negotiation typically better accomplished in smaller collegial bodies. The fact that citizens ultimately have to vote yes or no on a particular legislative proposal risks simplifying complicated issues that call for no less complex forms of legislation along with the political give-and-take that requires legislative compromise. Advocates of direct democracy will need to think hard about how it might combat ubiquitous trends toward executive-centered government: a long history of executive manipulation of popular referenda suggests that the difficulties may be significant.[45] Even more problematic, increased possibilities for direct democracy would undoubtedly require a substantial use of the scarce resource of time. High-speed communication technology undoubtedly minimizes the time-consuming character of popular deliberation across sizable distances. Yet increased demands on citizens to undertake direct involvement in legislation would simultaneously offset some of these temporal gains. Given the temporal pressures of contemporary society, new possibilities for direct democracy can only succeed if unnecessary temporal pressures can be reduced so as to provide citizens with sufficient leisure time with which to pursue political interests.[46] An increased reliance on direct democracy will have to be accompanied by at least some deceleration of the pace of everyday life, and political reform must go hand in hand with complementary social reforms that alter some features of present-day social temporality.

For these and other reasons direct democracy should be seen as a supplement to deliberative legislatures. Nonetheless, it may be possible to extend the scope of direct citizen lawmaking in more ambitious ways than has been accomplished thus far. As long as they are properly structured so as to guarantee broad access as well as the expression of well-considered political views, new electronic media might provide impressive possibilities for relatively direct forms of popular rule. In this spirit Ian Budge has proposed the universal distribution of new interactive communication technologies, followed by "the organization of this network by some kind of central committee or moderator, for it to transmit a political discussion in which all those nominated by the organizer(s) could speak. The techniques for organizing such discussions are already well known from television and radio chat-shows and video conferences. Only official approval and possibly a secretariat similar to those which now serve legislatures are necessary to give this kind of electronic discussion an authoritative voice in making political decisions. If this were done it would institutionalize direct democracy in a modern form."[47] Budge sketches out the details of this proposal over the course of an entire volume, but the core intuitions behind it remain straightforward enough. Representative bodies would continue to function in many familiar ways, but parliament would now take on a heightened role as an "advisory, investigative and debating committee informing popular discussion and voting."[48] Although universal access to computers would allow for extensive interactive political debate and deliberation, in order to ensure that a fair sample of views and interests gains expression, a moderator or coordinating committee would be required to guarantee the representation of a fair sample, just as existing norms and procedures mandate that the speaker of the house or president of the legislative chamber allow for the expression of a broad variety of ideas and interests.

The legal regulation of the moderator's activities might also easily build on familiar forms of media regulation such as the fairness doctrine. Ground rules guaranteeing the necessary independence of the coordinating committee from immediate partisan pressures as well as universal access to electronic debate would be required, but similar tasks already face representative democracy as well: "If the electronic media are to be used as a forum for debate and voting, like a legislative chamber, they require a similar support apparatus to permit them to serve as a medium of discussion. No one would think of turning legislators into a hall and then expecting them to have ordered discussion and voting without a President and secretariat, no regulations limiting the participation of outside bodies, no criteria for apportioning time among participants, no rules for how long debates could continue and for voting—without even rules and committees for revising the rules in light of experience!"[49] According to Budge, many criticisms of direct democracy stem from a caricatured association of it with a legally untamed popular demiurge, able to exert its will at a moment's notice and thereby destined to lack the requisite thoughtfulness that competent self-government requires. But, if we admit the possibility of a direct democracy compatible with procedures chosen on the basis of their capacity to encourage the formulation of well-considered political views, rather than momentary expressions of unreflective political preferences, the theoretical foundations of traditional criticisms of direct democracy begin to seem suspect.

Budge's proposal raises numerous unanswered questions. For example, it would be useful to imagine some specific institutional "test" as a way of being reasonably sure that computerized deliberation not only has taken on a high-speed character but also has been adequately well considered and thought out. To the extent that such tests (e.g., requiring majority support for a referendum in two separate votes undertaken over a given period of time) might decelerate direct decision making, they counteract the temporal advantages of high-speed technology. Here, again, we need to acknowledge the sound intuition that "fast is often bad, [and] slow sometimes good" in popular deliberation.[50] Nonetheless, it seems unjustifiably dogmatic to exclude the possibility of achieving a more satisfactory balance between the unavoidable laggardness of popular deliberation and the growing necessity for high-speed deliberative decision making. Determining precisely where and when "slowness" is appropriate to political deliberation remains a legitimate object of responsible institutional experimentation, rather than a rigid historical given requiring unthinking fidelity to the institutional status quo. Although the quest to reduce unnecessary or surplus slowness in deliberative politics will have to proceed by careful experimentation and according to the well-worn principle of "trial and error," it seems at least possible that we can achieve a more acceptable balance than existing liberal democracy. Direct democracy may have a role to play in our quest to achieve that balance.

Budge is right to claim that some critics of direct democracy simply reproduce antidemocratic biases inconsistent with a robust commitment to liberal democracy, direct or otherwise; even Plato might blush at the hyperbolic claims about the inevitable irrationality of computerized popular decision making now commonplace in the literature on democracy and the Internet. Budge is also correct to observe that critics sometimes unfairly commence from a caricatured picture of an untamed (and potentially irrational) *demos,* without considering the obvious point that any representative institution lacking in necessary ground rules and norms would soon appear no less irrational. Successful possibilities for direct democracy, like thriving representative institutions, will need to make use of institutional filtering mechanisms that encourage inclusive freewheeling debate as well as the formulation of thoughtful and well-considered opinions. Alternately, some critics of direct democracy via new technology rely on a classical republican preference for face-to-face political activity that risks romanticizing simple and long bygone forms of political decision making while conveniently ignoring the manner in which decision making even within small groups depends on indirect forms of (technologically mediated) interaction: representative assemblies themselves "now rely heavily on electronic devices like microphones, internal television and voting buttons."[51] It also remains unclear what relevance any attempt to privilege the physical immediacy of face-to-face decision making ultimately possesses given the trends toward globalization described in chapter 5. The pressing need for democratically legitimate and legally sound forms of transnational regulation is probably a priori unachievable if we start from the traditional bias that authentic self-rule can only occur in small groups whose members must interact in direct and immediate ways. Whatever its normative appeal, the republican critique of computerized democracy represents an institutional dead end.

Reflexive Law

If liberal democracy is to thrive in the age of speed, we need to consider additional possibilities for supplementing conventional lawmaking. A number of thoughtful proposals for doing so are presently on the table.[52] For now I focus in depth on one conspicuous candidate for developing both an institutionally realistic and normatively legitimate form of legislation suited to the dictates of speed. For two decades legal scholars have been discussing the merits of the *reflexive paradigm of law*, as first outlined in a series of innovative essays by the German legal scholar Gunther Teubner in the mid-1980s. Conceived initially as a potential answer to the widely noted ills of certain forms of regulatory and welfare state–type law, reflexive law has since garnered broad attention among scholars working in many different legal fields, and recent literature suggests its potential relevance to the regulatory challenges posed by labor, consumer protection, and sexual harassment law.[53] Perhaps reflexive law can help us tackle social acceleration as well.

Reflexive law was initially conceived as a potential alternative to two competing models of legal regulation whose limitations have been widely discussed in the literature on the legal structure of the welfare state. In Teubner's original account classical *formal law*, according to which state action must be rule bound, clear, general, prospective, and applied deductively, while aspiring to establish autonomous "spheres of activity for private actors" within the context of a classical liberal market economy, necessarily plays a limited role within the operations of the modern regulatory and welfare states.[54] Teubner accepts the widely shared assumption of an "elective affinity" between economic liberalism and formal law, and thus he considers calls to resuscitate formal law retrograde attempts to roll back the welfare state and its unfinished quest to compensate for the inadequacies of capitalism.[55] Yet the movement away from formal law to more complex forms of state regulation, closely tied to the growth of state regulation and the rise of the welfare state, has hardly proven unproblematic. Forms of what Teubner describes as *substantive law* are by necessity particularized and purposive in character, aiming to overcome economic and social inequality by means of goal-oriented forms of state intervention directed at generating particular policy outcomes. Welfare state–type substantive law typically relies on open-ended and ambiguous norms, principles, and standards, thereby generating "grave consequences for the [traditional] conceptual construction of doctrinal legal systems."[56] In addition, "this mode of juridification wields a heavy hand. It is intrusive, substantive, authoritative, and meant to be so."[57] Substantive law sometimes proves inflexible and ineffective, since it undertakes to regulate complex social spheres without an adequate knowledge of the particular characteristics of the activities at hand. Inspired by the systems theory of Niklas Luhmann, Teubner argues that both formal and substantive law are ill equipped to deal with the pressures of societal complexity. Both mistakenly presuppose the anachronistic notion that society can be "steered" from one central site, thereby necessarily obscuring the difficulties for state regulation posed by the differentiation of modern society into competing modes of social activity (in the terminology of systems theory: competing "subsystems") possessing distinct internal logics or rationalities. In this theoretical account "centralized social integration is effectively ruled out today," given the "conditions of extreme function differentiation" in which any attempt "to maximize the rationality of one subsystem is to create insoluble problems in other functional systems."[58] Teubner insists that any attempt to coordinate social activities by means of a central lawmaker inevitably risks succumbing to this danger. In order to avoid contributing to a regressive attack on modernity, forms of "reflexivity" counteracting the potentially negative side effects of specific institutional practices need to be fostered and realized within their internal operations. Otherwise, continued dependence on centralized modes of formal or substantive law inevitably means that regulation will prove "poorly suited to the internal social structure of the regulated spheres of life" at hand.[59]

Reflexive law aims at avoiding both the Charybdis of formal law and the Scylla of vague and open-ended substantive law. The core intuition behind Teubner's model is that legislative policies today are only likely to prove effective if they limit themselves to specifying procedures and basic organizational norms geared toward fostering self-regulation within distinct spheres of social activity. Reflexive law aims to offer a more abstract and less direct form of legal coordination than substantive law. Like substantive law, however, it is guided by the aim of subordinating social and economic activities to broader regulatory purposes. Yet it hopes to do so without dictating specific outcomes and thereby contributing to the rigidity and ineffectiveness of some existing forms of regulatory law. The omniscient "central steering" characteristic of both formal and substantive law is to be jettisoned in favor of more indirect decision-making devices: as long as key (legislatively determined) basic procedural and organizational norms are respected, social actors can seek whatever outcomes they desire. Reminiscent of classical formal law, reflexive law hopes to preserve the relative autonomy of distinct social spheres. Yet it breaks with laissez-faire notions of a "natural" market economy by acknowledging the existence of inequalities endemic to modern capitalism. By focusing on key organizational variables and providing substantial decision-making autonomy to those potentially affected by regulatory activity, reflexive law also endorses the notion that legislation should be "self-limiting." Its self-limiting character derives from the goal of achieving a more effective use of what Teubner describes as the "scarce resource" of political power, not from a mythical belief in the virtues of preserving the pristine workings of an autonomous market economy.[60]

Teubner generally interprets the proliferation of vague, open-ended, and occasionally moralistic legal standards ("unconscionable," "in good faith," "in the public interest"), widely lamented by liberal thinkers from Weber to Hayek, as a potential evolutionary gain for modern legal development: vague and ambiguous legal clauses often buttress decentralized forms of "regulated self-regulation."[61] In this view the vague legal standards and principles essential to modern forms of collective bargaining—the historical paradigm inspiring many of Teubner's abstract theoretical reflections—have been instrumental in facilitating trends toward an identifiably reflexive mode of legal regulation in the sphere of labor relations.[62] Labor law is important for Teubner for another reason as well. Reflexive law rests on an attempt to reform legislation "so as to achieve salutary egalitarian purposes by institutionalizing appropriate incentives, norms, and guidelines while incorporating flexibility and respect for social autonomy and initiatives."[63] In more concrete terms regulated self-regulation needs to rest on basic legal procedures and organizational norms working to equalize the bargaining power of those parties affected by specific arenas of social activity. Teubner expressly distinguishes his version of decentralized self-regulation from radical democratic models in which the maximization of popular participation and some ideal or "absolute" equalization of power are taken to be overriding goals. The equalization of bargaining positions is only valued here to the extent that it contributes to the "reflexive" character of regulatory law, which for Teubner chiefly refers to the notion that distinct arenas of self-regulation (or subsystems) need to become "sensitive to the outside effects of their attempts to maximize internal rationality."[64] Nonetheless, reflexivity generally is dependent on reducing power asymmetries by procedural devices.

When properly designed, the regulation of self-regulation generates effective internal control structures such that the pursuit of internal goals can be accompanied by an internalized "conscience" able to counteract the potentially deleterious consequences of particular institutional activities. Reflexive law is predicated on the possibility of making decision-making structures sensitive to externalities and side effects, and it does so by achieving institutional designs in which groups negatively affected by the pursuit of the "rationality" of a particular activity (e.g., labor or consumer groups affected by certain business practices) are guaranteed representation.[65] The legal framework of collective bargaining and workplace codetermination exhibit the fundamental outlines of reflexive law to the extent that they rest on decentralized decision-making structures involving participation by those affected by specific workplace activities. The legal procedures making up the framework of collective bargaining and codetermination aspire to diminish inequalities in bargaining power between capital and labor—in order to heighten reflexivity, which in this context amounts to balancing the internal imperatives of the business enterprise (the quest for profits) with the interests of labor.

According to Teubner, there is no necessary reason for assuming that specific forms of regulated self-regulation cannot develop internal "sensors" able to correct for the potentially negative consequences of their actions; the problem at hand is chiefly one of proper institutional design. A great deal of his intellectual energy accordingly has been devoted to the task of underlining trends within lawmaking which anticipate the possibility of encouraging what we might describe as "socially sensitive" or "public-minded" forms of regulation.[66] Most provocative of all, Teubner believes that the legal institutionalization of internal sensors need not pose a fundamental challenge to the logic or rationality of distinct forms of social activity. For instance, even economic activities should in principle be consistent with internal restrictions (requiring, e.g., the consideration of ecological concerns) because the unregulated and unlimited pursuit of profit "is itself paradoxical from the organization's own point of view" to the extent that it may undermine the long-term interests of a business enterprise.[67]

How might reflexive law tackle the demands of social acceleration? As I have tried to argue, social acceleration raises many fundamental questions for liberal democracy. Traditional forms of lawmaking are rapidly rendered out-of-date given the dynamic character of social and economic change, and the half-life of formal and even more flexible "substantive" legal norms appears to be experiencing a dramatic decline: in the age of speed "law will be easily trapped in the dilemma: either to remain static and be ignored, or to keep up with social dynamics and be devalued as a normative reference."[68] By reconfiguring the relationship between centralized and decentralized forms of lawmaking, reflexive law potentially points the way toward a legal resolution of the enigmas posed by speed. Of course, any model of legal activity faces the possibility that it may fail to provide sufficient resources to grapple effectively with the imperatives of social acceleration. Some forms of legal coordination are more vulnerable to this failing, however, than others. Most today would rightly consider any attempt to return to traditionalist notions of a customary "good old law" inconsistent with the dynamism of modern social and economic life. Adaptability to change is only allowed within customary law to the extent that legal decision making can be packaged as a mere restoration of the good old law. Customary law thus sharply limits the range of acceptable political and legal decisions. Indeed, the emergence of positive law can be attributed at least in part to its temporal virtues, to the extent that legislated positive law "made it possible to bring rapidly fluctuating situations and behavior within the scope of the law."[69] In this simple yet decisive way positive law proved better suited to social acceleration than customary law.

Similarly, one might plausibly interpret the transition from formal to substantive law (i.e., from one mode of positive law to another) in part as a result of the latter's superiority from the perspective of the acceleration of modern capitalism. Formal parliamentary lawmaking relied chiefly on a central legislature to make sure that law "adapted" to economic and social change; according to classical liberal doctrine (and to some extent nineteenth-century liberal reality as well), judges and administrators were to exercise minimal legislative functions. Formal parliamentary law surely represented an evolutionary gain from the perspective of customary law, but its achievements nonetheless seem to have been rendered problematic by the dynamics of a long-term process in which the temporal horizons of modern capitalism have been constantly revolutionized. Arguably, substantive law provides superior possibilities for legal actors to overcome potential gaps between "static" legal norms and constantly altering social and economic patterns: by relying on open-ended standards and norms that can be interpreted in many different ways while condoning judicial and administrative creativity, substantive law potentially represents a more dynamic mode of legal regulation than its historical predecessors. Notwithstanding its normative failings from the perspective of traditional models of the rule of law, that dynamism surely arguably helped render substantive law a more "realistic" legal paradigm in the twentieth century than its predecessors.

Reflexive law may be even better suited to the imperatives of high-speed social and economic activity. Central legislation in the reflexive paradigm of law is chiefly limited to the tasks of (1) determining the general direction of regulatory policy; and (2) institutionalizing procedures so as to heighten reflexivity within specific institutional spheres. Reflexive law still aspires to coordinate complex social practices according to liberal and democratic ideals. For example, it conceivably offers a credible legal framework for contemporary models of deliberative democracy: decentralized sites for decision making could be structured so as to provide extensive possibilities for those affected by policies to debate and argue about them. Not only does reflexive law rest on an open acknowledgment of the limitations of centralized forms of lawmaking in a context characterized by "changing business conditions on a scale and at a pace unthinkable only a decade or two earlier,"[70] but it also recognizes the need to correct for the ills of existing forms of "flexible" (substantive) legal regulation. Untrammeled administrative and judicial discretion too often has been allowed to play a key role within the regulatory and welfare states. Reflexive law forthrightly concedes the need for highly flexible forms of specialized decision making, but it strives to provide a firm legal shell for regulated self-regulation via institutionalized legal procedures and organizational norms. In this subtle yet decisive way reflexive law exhibits fidelity to the traditional quest to provide a sturdy legal framework for social and economic activity—for the sake of buttressing social activities conducive to the realization of human autonomy. Reflexive law also aims to counteract the democratic deficit plaguing forms of substantive law where far-reaching discretionary authority is left in the hands of administrators and judges. By insisting that law institutionalize devices geared toward the equal representation of voices and interests of those affected by particular forms of regulated activity, reflexive law takes a step toward overcoming that deficit.

Yet might not reflexive law require us to abandon basic rule of law virtues? Teubner's willingness to defend the growth of vague, open-ended, moralistic legal clauses occasionally suggests as much. If so, would we not again face the familiar dilemma of achieving new high-speed forms of lawmaking only at the cost of sacrificing traditional liberal democratic legal ideals?

More than a decade ago the German political theorist Ingeborg Maus argued that Teubner's tendency to belittle classical rule of law attributes (especially clarity and cogency within the law) left his model of reflexive law unnecessarily vulnerable to manipulation by privileged social and economic interests. Maus observed that, especially when legislation concerns antagonistic economic interests, vague and open-ended legal norms too often are exploited by those in possession of the greatest de facto economic power: when the rules of the game are ambiguous and open-ended, it is often the biggest boys and girls on the block who succeed in enforcing their interpretation on other players. From this perspective defenders of reflexive law would do well to insist on preserving certain elements of classical formal law.[71] According to Maus, Teubner is right to seek an alternative to substantive law and its widely acknowledged pathologies, and he is also justified in arguing that certain forms of centralized parliamentary lawmaking are no longer suited to the tasks of regulation. She also agreed that the central legislator would do well to delegate far-reaching forms of decision making to new, decentralized legislative sites. Accordingly, we need to supplement central legislatures with new decentralized bodies and initiate a division of labor between the two

> according to the degree of the generality of the applicability of a mode of legal regulation. Legal norms directed at only a very limited number of addressees or which only have regional consequences could be conferred about and determined in legislative arrangements in which the parties to the conflict directly confront each other and are equipped with symmetrical negotiation-positions so as to compensate legally for the asymmetries of social power . . . All this presupposes that the parliamentary center stays responsible for the most general function: the determination of procedural norms, according to which the contents of law emerge in decentralized legislative processes.[72]

Yet this recalibration of lawmaking can only prove immune to illegitimate manipulation by privileged interests if we make sure that procedural devices not only equalize the bargaining positions of affected groups but also that they do so by means of legal devices exhibiting the classical legal virtues of clarity and cogency. According to Maus, procedural and organizational norms taking a clear and cogent form alone can realistically be employed for the sake of reining in powerful economic interests; in this novel way traditional liberal legal virtues still have a vital role to play within a socially sensitive and authentically democratic form of reflexive law. Because of Teubner's tendency to consider formal law a fundamentally anachronistic mode of legal regulation unsuited to present-day regulatory needs, however, he ignores this crucial point. In contrast to Teubner, we would do well not to overstate the existence of an "elective affinity" between classical market capitalism and core elements of classical formal law.[73] By insisting on the need to decentralize substantial regulatory authority, Maus's reformulation of reflexive law, like Teubner's original model, provides sufficient room for fluidity and flexibility within regulatory decision making; in this crucial respect it seems well adapted to the imperatives of social acceleration. At the same time, Maus convincingly argues that the legal framework of regulated self-regulation will still have to respect some traditional liberal legal ideals if reflexive law can meaningfully hope to counteract the advantages often enjoyed by the economically privileged.

One might counter that any attempt to give law an "enduring form" necessarily renders regulation problematic in an age of speed. Yet, if law is to continue to serve the indispensable function of coordinating and channeling social and economic activities and not be reduced to a mere cover for the exercise of untamed authority by privileged social interests, we would do well to maintain an appropriate distance between law's normative structure and key facets of social and economic life. The virtue of a properly conceived version of reflexive law is that it offers a realistic starting point for confronting the dynamic and fast-paced character of contemporary social and economic experience without subordinating legal regulation to the sorry empirical realities of growing economic inequality.

Reflexive Law and the Challenges of Globalization

This brief discussion of reflexive law is likely to raise at least as many questions as it answers. A number of impressive criticisms have already been leveled against reflexive law.[74] Most important for our concerns, empirical confirmation is still needed that reflexive law offers an appropriate device for achieving high-speed lawmaking while preserving a satisfactory quotient of rule of law virtues. An obvious dilemma is that reflexive law's call for the involvement of those affected by policy would necessitate time-consuming deliberation and thereby counteract its temporal merits. No magic wand is available with which we can simply wave away the difficult, toilsome temporal challenges of legitimate liberal democratic decision making in the age of speed. Nonetheless, cautious experiments with reflexive law would be helpful as a way of determining whether it might reduce the gap between social speed and liberal democracy.

For now I focus on the potential merits of the paradigm of reflexive law as a basis for confronting the legal challenges of globalization. Globalization is not only intimately tied to social acceleration, as noted in chapter 5, but the growing significance of globalization for a vast range of political and legal activities also suggests that any serious attempt to reform liberal democracy will have to pay careful attention to questions of transnational legal regulation. Although Teubner and others inspired by him originally envisioned the paradigm of reflexive law as a basis for reforming nationally based state economic regulation, it contains some unexpected fruits for those struggling to outline a satisfactory legal framework for the global economy.

First, reflexive law acknowledges that centralized legislatures need to play a different role than prescribed by classical liberal democratic theory: in order to make sure that regulation is well suited to the logic of regulated activities, substantial decision-making authority sometimes should be left in the hands of actors most familiar with the distinctive traits of those activities. Although centralized political bodies still must provide meaningful guidance to social actors, traditional models of government "steering" requires reconsideration. For starters we need to figure out how internal mechanisms can be achieved in particular arenas of delegated regulatory authority so as to heighten their sensitivity to potentially negative side effects, particularly in light of the fact that it is unlikely, given the complexity of tasks at hand, that any central lawmaking body will (1) possess the requisite knowledge for effective forms of direct regulation and (2) thus succeed in grappling with the negative side effects of particular activities.

This argument is even more telling at the transnational than the national level. The attempt to develop an authentically transnational system of economic regulation dramatically underscores the Achilles' heel of the classical model of an elected legislature outfitted with the task of undertaking the direct regulation of a host of distinct social activities. If the notion that the legislature can serve as an omniscient source of central steering already evinces signs of decay within the confines of the nation-state, the intense pace of social acceleration in the global economy implies that its weaknesses would inevitably be even greater there. Of course, no such global parliament exists or is likely to exist, in the near future anyway. Even the most ambitious models of "cosmopolitan democracy" presently under consideration typically embrace the notion of global decision making as ultimately resting in a complex "network of [democratized] regional and international agencies and assemblies that cut across spatially delimited locales."[75] Emerging forms of global economic law are unlikely to derive from a consolidated world-state or one central legislative body. To the extent that they are likely to appear, a complex variety of institutional sites will play a decisive role in that process, and at least for the foreseeable future these institutions will continue to suffer from democratic deficits more severe than those at the level of national governments. To be sure, this situation raises difficult questions for any attempt to conceive of the appropriate form democratic legitimacy might take at the transnational level. The quest to employ reflexive law as a model for reconfiguring transnational economic regulation ultimately will need to face such questions: in reflexive law democratic legitimacy still entails the necessity of a (general and thereby legitimate) determination of precisely which norms and procedures are to make up the framework within which self-regulation is to be conducted.[76]

Second, the paradigm of reflexive law may also be immediately useful to the extent that it stimulates us to consider how democratic deficits at the global level might at least be partially compensated for by developing reflexive models of decentralized self-regulation able to "balance" the needs of particular forms of activity (e.g., the profitability of business enterprise) with a sensitivity toward their potentially deleterious side effects. Even global bankers have an interest in maintaining the long-term stability of the global financial system and thus in developing regulation capable of contributing to financial stability. There is no manifest reason why global bankers should be unwilling to endorse regulatory forms able to counter the specter of global financial disaster.

Third, some trends within transnational regulation already seem reminiscent of Teubner's vision of regulated self-regulation: where social acceleration is most pronounced, legal development accords with key elements of reflexive law. Although it would be Pollyannaish to claim that existing global regulation exhibits full-fledged legal reflexivity, some striking features of the emerging system of regulation anticipate it.

As noted earlier, G-10 central bank authorities faced with the task of coordinating high-speed global finance are moving away from the conventional model of imposing "strict, uniform, quantitative limits on the activities of the banks" in favor of "outsourcing" some regulatory activities to the banks themselves.[77] In light of the "growing complexity and dynamism of the global financial services industry," G-10 banking regulators have acknowledged that, "provided certain qualitative and quantitative safeguards were present, the banks' own control and risk management mechanisms would prove superior to any that the regulators could impose," and political authorities are making sure that substantial decision making is placed in the hands of "those actors better equipped, trained, and experienced to execute" regulatory functions.[78] G-10 central bank authorities still play a key role in overseeing facets of this emerging system, yet relatively indirect controls and incentives are increasingly decisive.[79] In accordance with Teubner's expectations, regulatory activity in global finance now depends on providing "legal incentives for self-regulation that will lead social actors to comply with general legislative goals."[80] An additional advantage of this approach is that it minimizes the significance of territorial boundaries: by relying on (globally operating) banks' own internal control and risk management devices, regulation is better equipped to grapple with the transnational character of financial activity. In this way, too, reflexive law seems especially well suited to the imperatives of legal regulation in our high-speed age, which requires decision-making devices able to produce legitimate outcomes across borders.[81]

Reza Banakar has similarly observed that the booming business of international business arbitration anticipates features of reflexive law. International business arbitration represents an increasingly significant mode of decentralized self-regulation: "arbitration illustrates signs of 'legal reflexivity,' in the sense that it appears to establish norms of procedure, organization, membership, and competence . . . sensitive to the needs of the disputing parties."[82] Prominent labor lawyers have also noted that aspects of the emerging system of transnational labor regulation may constitute nascent manifestations of reflexive law.[83]

Unfortunately, each of these arenas of transnational economic regulation also suffers from profound flaws. Despite the relatively broad impact of the G-10 banking norms on a diverse array of social groups, nonbanking interests thus far have been excluded from the coterie of interests involved in the emerging system of regulated self-regulation in global finance. G-10 procedures and organizational norms were approved by nation-states with little debate in either parliament or civil society; a serious democratic deficit plagues them. Not surprisingly, given its failure to institutionalize devices for the representation of a broad array of affected social interests, the emerging system of banking self-regulation can hardly be described as socially sensitive or public minded. Indeed, global bankers typically exhibit excessive caution when it comes to undertaking regulatory reforms that even those close to the global financial community now consider long overdue.[84] By no stretch of the imagination has global financial law developed sufficient internal sensory mechanisms able to counteract negative externalities.

Nor does business arbitration constitute a successful instantiation of Teubner's vision of socially sensitive, public-minded reflexive law. The legal status of international business arbitration rightly remains controversial, in part because its open-ended, amorphous character (e.g., in the *Lex Mercatoria*) suggests the existence of a highly discretionary system of legal coordination tailored to the interests of privileged economic interests.[85] Many commentators legitimately worry that the universal acceptance by the international political community of relatively far-reaching authority by arbitration bodies amounts to a troubling sacrifice of too much of the traditional authority of individual nation-states. Existing arbitration procedures fail sufficiently to integrate the concerns of nonbusiness groups likely to be affected by arbitration decisions involving transnational businesses. In fact, one of the obvious reasons for the growing popularity of arbitration is that it represents a mode of self-regulation not only attuned to the specialized practical needs of specific branches of global commerce but that it also minimizes the possibility of decisions hostile to the material and ideological interests of global business: those institutions that presently provide arbitration services, such as the International Chamber of Commerce, typically make sure that global players hardly need worry about the prospect of arbitrators pursuing an aggressively anti-business orientation. Environmentalists, labor activists, and socialists are rare indeed in this global rendition of "arbitration under chamber of commerce auspices."[86]

Should such experiences lead us to abandon reflexive law as a starting point for envisioning effective forms of transnational regulation? Perhaps not. Yet those who are sympathetic to reflexive law will have to tackle a series of difficult questions if they can legitimately hope to employ it successfully for the purposes of reforming global law.

For starters defenders of reflexive law will need to figure out how nascent forms of reflexive law might be cleansed of their unattractive features. Maus's reformulation of reflexive law offers a first step toward doing so. "Global players" often prefer soft and open-ended legal regulation because it allows them to negotiate the dilemmas posed by social acceleration. Yet they also opt for soft economic regulation because it occasionally permits them to engage in nontransparent forms of highly discretionary activity having potentially negative consequences for less-privileged social and economic interests. Like Teubner, Maus rightly underlines the tenuous character of the notion that a central legislature can be solely responsible for steering regulatory activities. Yet we also need to worry about the specter of vague and soft forms of law functioning as a legal front for effectively untamed expressions of global economic power. A model of reflexive law committed to achieving clear procedures and strict organizational norms designed to counteract illegitimate economic privilege might help overcome some of the present ills of transnational economic regulation.

Economic globalization calls attention to the existence of additional difficulties for defenders of reflexive law. Who should be represented in decentralized arenas of regulated self-regulation and why? As we saw earlier, a system of global banking regulation in which large financial interests are disproportionately influential presents some obvious problems; this is surely one reason why global banking regulation has yet to develop effective internal checks on its less attractive side effects. So, who else should be represented in some modified system of reflexive law within global finance? The notion that global regulation "must ensure that all parties that have an interest in the issue also have access to the process" seems normatively impeccable, yet its concrete institutional implications remain ambiguous.[87] After all, the global banking system arguably affects most (if not all) of humanity today in far-reaching ways. In many areas of global regulation the demand that all affected parties participate in self-regulation potentially undermines one of the most striking advantages of self-regulation—namely, its preference for placing substantial regulatory authority in the hands of those constituencies most familiar with a particular set of specialized activities. Given that it also seems to imply the necessity of a time-consuming deliberative exchange involving a potentially vast range of affected social actors, it would also undermine the temporal advantages of reflexive law vis-à-vis competing conceptions of legal regulation. An immediate consequence of the compression of distance via social acceleration is that many seemingly "local" decisions (e.g., a municipality's failure to finance public transportation, resulting in increased reliance on private automobiles) now immediately take on global repercussions (e.g., the depletion of the ozone layer). Maus sensibly suggests that decisions having a general impact should remain the monopoly of centralized legislative devices, whereas those having a more limited or specialized significance should be decentralized.[88] Even if we ignore the fact that it remains unclear which political institutions might legitimately serve as a stand-in for the democratic legislature at the global level, however, the border between "general" and "particular" legislative matters often seems blurred. To be sure, we can begin to imagine some potential paths beyond this quagmire. Perhaps reflexive law could institutionalize procedures acknowledging the manner in which regulatory decisions affect different groups with varying degrees of intensity. For example: global banking regulations impact at least indirectly on most of humanity, but they clearly are of special interest to bankers and their customers and clients. How, then, might reflexive law institutionalize that decisive difference? Given the difficulties of measuring intensity in such matters, the normative and institutional tasks at hand remain formidable.

Finally, any serious attempt to rely on the idea of reflexive law to reform transnational economic regulation will have to confront a series of weighty political dilemmas. As we saw earlier, reflexive law aims to realize a self-limiting mode of law to the extent that it transforms the would-be omniscient legislator into a body chiefly concerned with laying the groundwork for situation-specific forms of decentralized decision making. In addition, reflexive law holds out the promise of genuinely egalitarian lawmaking; for this reason the possibility of achieving internal, socially sensitive sensors is seen by Teubner as dependent on the reduction of power asymmetries. Yet the realization of an authentically egalitarian mode of reflexive law in global economic regulation can only be achieved by means of a determined political challenge to the privileged social and economic groups presently gaining most from the on-going process of economic globalization. Recall the historical inspiration for so many of Teubner's own theoretical reflections: where labor law and codetermination came to embody elements of legal reflexivity, they only did so because of a century of heated and even violent political struggle waged by labor unions and left-wing social movements. Of course, there is no a priori reason to exclude the possibility of similar struggles culminating in the achievement of heightened levels of egalitarian reflexive law at the global level. Yet contemporary social movements are effectively deprived of some of the most important political tools employed by labor and socialist movements in their historic struggle to establish collective bargaining and codetermination in many areas of the industrialized world. Reflexive labor law was only achieved because labor movements and their political allies were able to exert substantial influence on the institutions of the sovereign nation-state. These gains were only made possible because a significant number of workers saw the nation-state as a meaningful site for political engagement. Political engagement of this type, in turn, presupposed a long and complex history in which political identities, notwithstanding the internationalist rhetoric of modern socialism, in many ways often gained decisive national overtones: the gradual development of citizenship famously chronicled by T. H. Marshall in his account of the emergence of modern social rights was always citizenship within the confines of the nation-state.[89] What new forms of political identity might replace the primarily nation-state-based identities of traditional labor and socialist movements? What political identities might emerge among subordinate social groups under present-day conditions? Whether these groups will develop such an identity and then succeed in marshaling sufficient political influence for the sake of establishing egalitarian forms of global reflexive law remains an unanswered question.

Some forms of twentieth-century labor law and codetermination may in fact have been reflexive and self-limiting in the fashion described by Teubner, but their enforcement always rested on the impressive power capacities of the sovereign nation-state. In light of the immense difficulties of even a modest invigoration and democratization of transnational decision-making bodies, how might such institutions function as the nation-state once did to secure the efficacy of egalitarian modes of reflexive law? The political muscle of the sovereign nation-state often proved indispensable in the struggle to humanize some features of labor relations and often relied heavily on the institutions of the central state for the enforcement of labor law. What new political institutions might perform this task, given the improbability as well as undesirability of a consolidated world-state?

Proposals for reflexive law offer no easy answers to these tough questions. But they do provide a helpful framework for trying to answer them. In the process perhaps we can take a modest step toward recalibrating liberal democracy in accordance with our age of speed.

Conclusion

Social acceleration places many familiar legal and political concerns in a fresh light. A proper understanding of traditional liberal democratic institutional aspirations, including the separation of powers, deliberative representative legislatures, constitutionalism, and the rule of law, requires us to pay careful attention to their temporal presuppositions. Many widely discussed institutional trends—the rise of the executive, dramatic shifts in the separation of powers, threats to traditional visions of constitutionalism and rule of law, a general speed-up of legislation, the ongoing globalization of law—can be fruitfully reinterpreted, at least in part, as institutional adaptations to social acceleration. Social acceleration also forces us to think creatively about liberal democracy's prospects in the new century. Might we successfully reconfigure liberal democracy for a temporal context distinct from that in which its eighteenth- and early-nineteenth-century defenders first hinted at the possibility of its realization? Can we revive traditional liberal democratic ideals of "government by discussion," the closely related notion of a freewheeling deliberative legislature, the separation of powers, constitutionalism, and the rule of law? A substantial dose of institutional imagination is called for if we are to update liberal democracy to make it mesh with the dictates of speed. Although my own contribution here to a revitalization of liberal democracy has undoubtedly been a modest one, I hope at the very least to encourage others to confront the difficult unanswered questions posed by changes in the temporality of contemporary society for political life. Thus far, it has generally been anthropologists, geographers, and sociologists who have dealt with questions of social temporality. It is now time for political and legal scholars—as well as citizens and policy makers—to situate the problem of social speed at the top of their agenda.

Perhaps it is fitting that my discussion of reflexive law tentatively raised the issue of transnational democracy. For no more basic intellectual and political challenge of social speed faces us than the need to consider the possibility of extending liberal democracy beyond national borders. As I hinted at earlier, the prospect of achieving reflexive law within global economic regulation may ultimately depend on institutionalizing effective transnational forms of liberal democratic state authority. Reflexive law as a possible paradigm for tackling the legal challenges of social acceleration can only take an initial step toward grappling with the broader and more demanding enterprise of achieving transnational liberal democracy. One striking implication of the compression of space generated by high-speed social activity is a long-term trend by which key social and economic activities are "stretched" and intensified across preexisting political boundaries. For those of us committed to liberal democracy, the "shrinking" of the world via speed probably calls for the advancement of liberal democracy on the transnational arena as well as within the boundaries of existing nation-states. At the same time, social acceleration threatens to undermine even modest attempts to establish transnational liberal democratic institutions (e.g., the rule of law). Speed cries out for transnational governance while simultaneously undermining normatively acceptable forms of it.

Fortunately, a formidable body of scholarly literature shows that many scholars are already busy at work on the difficult normative and institutional questions posed by the possibility of transnational forms of liberal democracy.[1] Unless the concept of social acceleration plays a pivotal role in that debate, however, its participants are likely to misconstrue many core issues at hand. Only by placing the concept of social acceleration at the center of their analyses can they successfully shift thinking about globalization and liberal democracy onto fruitful terrain. For example, it is surely inadequate simply to extend existing liberal democratic institutions to the transnational level because, as I have argued, these institutions are already plagued by serious faults that derive from social acceleration. It is incumbent on those who defend the idea of a "cosmopolitan democracy," for example, to explain exactly how their oftentimes provocative proposals can help counteract the deeply rooted anti-liberal and antidemocratic developmental trends thematized here. How might the invigoration of international supranational political bodies manage the challenge of social acceleration more effectively than the existing nation-state? What evidence exists that they might provide a better basis for regulating an increasingly high-speed capitalism?

If I am not mistaken, much more than the deepening of (existing) liberal democratic institutions on the global level will be necessary if we are to ward off the more worrisome features of social acceleration. It is probably no less mistaken to see the growing impotence of many elected legislatures as a relatively sudden and even unprecedented development resulting from the ongoing transnationalization of capitalist production and financial markets, unparalleled movements of immigrants and refugees, and cross-border environmental problems. The recent losses of democratic sovereignty lamented by many scholars of globalization are simply the latest chapter in a long-term erosion of democratic legitimacy directly linked to the revolutionary implications of social acceleration long evident within nation-state-based capitalist liberal democracy. The defensive tone of even relatively critical recent contributions to the debate on globalization and democracy is probably misplaced. In his recent essays on globalization, for example, Habermas at times seems primarily concerned with the task of *preserving* the existing constellation of welfare state liberal democracy in the face of transnational pressures to weaken liberal democracy and dismantle social programs.[2] Alas, this preoccupation obscures the seriousness of the ills plaguing existing liberal democratic institutions. We undoubtedly should strive to ward off irresponsible attacks on the welfare state, and the sad liberal democratic status quo is preferable to the technocratic political fantasies of some contemporary defenders of laissez-faire. But we also need to devote more attention to a question whose significance Habermas and many other analysts of the impact of globalization on liberal democracy downplay: how can we refigure liberal democratic institutions so that they have a real chance of successfully confronting the awesome problems posed by social acceleration?

Perhaps the present volume can help convince scholars as well as citizens and policy makers of the pressing nature of this question.

Notes

Introduction

1. Anthony Giddens, *The Nation-State and Violence* (Berkeley: University of California Press, 1987), 12. There are some important exceptions. My study builds, for example, on Sheldon Wolin's suggestive insight that the temporality of democracy is inconsistent with the temporal dynamics of contemporary capitalism ("What Time Is It?" *Theory & Event* 1 [1997]: 1–4). William E. Connolly (*Neuropolitics: Thinking, Culture, Speed* [Minneapolis: University of Minnesota Press, 2002]) has also played a decisive role in introducing socio-theoretical discussions of speed into political theory, as has Michael J. Shapiro (see, e.g., "Time, Disjuncture, and Democratic Citizenship," in *Democracy and Vision: Sheldon Wolin and the Vicissitudes of the Political*, ed. Aryeh Botwinick and William E. Connolly [Princeton: Princeton University Press, 2001], 232–55). Like Connolly and Shapiro, I rely on recent social theory on temporality to illuminate questions traditionally of interest to political scientists. In addition, I share especially Connolly's assessment of the fundamentally ambivalent normative character of social speed, for reasons sketched out later in this book. My study devotes substantially more energy, however, to the task of excavating assumptions about temporality found in the mainstream of modern liberal democratic political and legal thought. In addition, the present work is more anxious than the existing literature about the deleterious consequences of acceleration for basic liberal democratic legal and political institutions, many of which I consider indispensable to a legitimate political order. Many classic works in political theory ably describe how assumptions about time figure prominently in the history of political philosophy. Yet these works have little to say about the institutional implications of the temporality of contemporary society for liberal democracy. See John G. Gunnell, *Political Philosophy and Time* (Middletown, Conn.: Wesleyan University Press, 1968); J. G. A. Pocock, *Politics, Language and Time: Essays in Political Thought and History* (New York: Athenaeum, 1973); Sheldon Wolin, *Politics and Vision: Continuity and Innovation in Western Political Thought* (Boston: Little, Brown, 1960).

2. Of course, such comments should always be made in a comparative spirit. As we will see, attempts to jettison liberal democracy because of its limited temporal efficiency have consistently resulted not only in political disaster, but they also have failed to offer more effective institutional approaches for tackling the challenges of speed. Some of the reasons for this are discussed in subsequent pages, especially in chapters 2–4.

3. During the course of my argument my usage of the term *liberal democracy* should become clear. By way of an initial definition let me just say that I consider liberal

democracy consistent with a broad range of institutional variations. At its core, however, it refers to a constitutionally based (primarily) representative government, resting on the separation of powers and rule of law. Based also on the principle of the accountability of power holders to the people, it requires free and relatively frequent elections as well as the effective protection of basic civil liberties. Ultimately, liberal democracy must rest on a plausible conception of the fundamental equality of all human beings. Note that this preliminary definition is chiefly political and legal in character. Thus, liberal democracy entails no necessary commitment to capitalism. Indeed, to the extent that capitalism represents one of the main driving forces behind social acceleration, capitalism potentially conflicts with liberal democracy. Many recent social democratic defenders of liberal democracy—most famously Norberto Bobbio, Jürgen Habermas, Hans Kelsen, and Franz Neumann—have similarly insisted on a clear analytical separation between liberal democracy as a political (and legal) system and capitalism. The account provided here of social acceleration tends to confirm one of their main reasons for doing so—namely, the fact that they saw capitalism as a highly problematic economic system in contrast to the fundamentally attractive normative core of liberal democracy.

Some scholars (e.g., see John S. Dryzek, *Deliberative Democracy and Beyond: Liberals, Critics, Contestations* [Oxford: Oxford University Press, 2000]) are likely to consider the defensive spirit of my discussion of liberal democracy inconsistent with a critical theory of society. This is a complicated matter, but let me just say for now that I consider a (creative) defense and temporally minded reformulation of traditional liberal democratic aspirations anything but politically quiescent in an age characterized by rampant executive prerogative, disdain for constitutional government and the rule of law, and growing authoritarian tendencies.

4. Readers who would like a more rigorous definition of the rule of law are encouraged to jump ahead and first read the second section of chapter 5, "Elective Affinities?" in which I offer one.

5. Richard Kay, "Constitutional Chronomy," *Ratio Juris* 13 (2000): 33.

6. In a previous volume (*Carl Schmitt: The End of Law* [Oxford: Rowman & Littlefield, 1999]) I have undertaken to credit Schmitt for his more astute insights, while simultaneously criticizing the terrible intellectual and political uses for which those insights were employed. In the same spirit here chapter 4 acknowledges the strengths of Schmitt's account of legislative "motorization" while striving to locate the misleading facets of his account which generated Schmitt's embrace of right-wing dictatorship.

O N E : Social Acceleration

1. James Gleick, *Faster: The Acceleration of Just About Everything* (New York: Pantheon Books, 1999). See also "Read This Slowly," *New York Times*, September 28, 2002, A16.

2. For a recent survey of literature, see Barbara Adam, *Time and Social Theory* (Cambridge: Polity Press, 1990).

3. David Harvey, *Justice, Nature and the Geography of Difference* (Oxford: Blackwell, 1996), 211.

4. E. P. Thompson, "Time, Work-Discipline, and Industrial Capitalism," *Past and Present* 38 (1967): 6–97.

5. Richard Sennett, *The Corrosion of Character: The Personal Consequences of Work in the New Capitalism* (New York: Norton, 1998), 23.

6. For a famous statement of the contrast between the contrasting tempos of urban and rural life, see Georg Simmel, "The Metropolis and Mental Life" (1902–3), in *The Sociology of George Simmel*, ed. Kurt H. Wolff (New York: Free Press, 1950), 410–11. Empirical studies have confirmed Simmel's impressions about the relatively fast pace of urban life. See Marc H. and Helen G. Bornstein, "The Pace of Life," *Nature* 259 (1976): 557–59; Marc H. Bornstein, "The Pace of Life: Revisited," *International Journal of Psychology* 14 (1979): 83–90. For national differences, see Robert Levine, *A Geography of Time* (New York: Basic Books, 1997).

7. Georges Gurvitch, *The Spectrum of Social Time* (Dordrecht, Holland: D. Riedel, 1964), 13.

8. Ibid., 13. In a similar vein, see David Harvey, *Justice, Nature and the Geography of Difference*, 241.

9. Marshall McLuhan, *Understanding Media: The Extensions of Man* (New York: McGraw-Hill, 1964), 103.

10. See Bauman on the significance of the "new speed" in *Globalization: The Human Consequences* (Cambridge: Polity Press, 1998); Manuel Castells on "timeless time" in the role of information technology and contemporary capitalism in *The Rise of Network Society* (Oxford: Blackwell, 1996); David Harvey on "time and space compression" in *The Condition of Postmodernity* (Cambridge: Blackwell, 1989), 201–326; Anthony Giddens on "time-space convergence" in *A Contemporary Critique of Historical Materialism*, vol. 2: *The Nation-State and Violence* (Berkeley: University of California Press, 1987); and on the rapid pace of change of modern society in *The Consequences of Modernity* (Stanford: Stanford University Press, 1990). Also see Reinhart Koselleck's pathbreaking piece on the "acceleration of history," "Gibt es eine Beschleunigung der Geschichte?" (1976), in *Zeitschichten* (Frankfurt: Suhrkamp, 2000), 150–76; Paul Virilio on "dromology" in *Speed and Politics*, trans. Mark Polizzotti (New York: Semiotexte, 1986); and Hartmut Rosa's impressive recent discussion of social acceleration. In "Social Acceleration: Ethical and Political Consequences of a Desynchronized High-Speed Society," *Constellations* 10 (2003): 3–33. I rely extensively on Rosa's account at many junctures in this chapter.

11. Matthias Eberling, *Beschleunigung und Politik* (Frankfurt: Peter Lang, 1996), 84. Also see Hans Jonas, *From Ancient Creed to Technological Man* (Englewood Cliffs, N.J.: Prentice-Hall, 1974), 5.

12. Thomas Hylland Eriksen, *Tyranny of the Moment: Fast and Slow Time in the Information Age* (London: Pluto, 2001).

13. Lewis Mumford, *The Pentagon of Power* (New York: Harcourt Brace Jovanovich, 1970), 148.

14. For vivid illustrations of this thesis, see Eriksen, *Tyranny of the Moment*, 49–77.

15. Ibid., 14–15.

16. Those whose lives may be untouched directly by new workplace technologies are affected by it in other ways: "Even an unemployed persons with eons of 'time to kill,' is sucked up by the side-effects of acceleration the moment he or she turns on the TV or opens the newspaper" (ibid., 148).

17. The timely phrase is from Anthony Giddens, *Runaway World* (New York: Routledge, 2000).

18. Montesquieu, *Persian Letters*, trans. C. J. Betts (London: Penguin, 1973 [1721]), 168 [letter 87].

19. See, for example, Alexis de Tocqueville, *Democracy in America*, ed. Phillips Bradley (New York: Vintage, 1990), 2:136–39 (chap. 13), 228–29 (chap. 17).

20. Cited in Harvey, *Justice, Nature and the Geography of Distance*, 242.

21. Cited in Wolfgang Schivelbusch, "Railroad Space and Railroad Time," *New German Critique* 14 (1978): 34.

22. Henry Adams, "The Law of Acceleration" (1904), in *The Education of Henry Adams* (New York: Modern Library, 1931), 489–98.

23. Stephen Kern, *The Culture of Time and Space, 1880–1918* (Cambridge: Harvard University Press, 1983). Also see Peter Conrad, *Modern Times, Modern Places* (New York: Alfred Knopf, 1999), 91–97.

24. Filippo Tommaso Marinetti, *Marinetti: Selected Writings*, ed. R. W. Flint (New York: Farrar, Strauss and Giroux, 1972), 41, 81. Also see the conclusion to chapter 2.

25. John Dewey, *The Public and Its Problems* (Athens, Ohio: Swallow Press, 1954 [1927]), 140; Theodor Adorno, *Minima Moralia*, trans. E. F. N. Jephcott (London: Verso, 1999 [1951]), 162; Hannah Arendt, *The Human Condition* (Chicago: University of Chicago Press, 1958), 250, 261 (I am grateful to Jim Farr for bringing these passages to my attention). Heidegger describes the "abolition of distance" as a result of high-speed technologies, in "The Thing" (1950), in *Poetry, Language, Thought*, trans. Albert Hoftstadter (New York: Harper & Row, 1970), 165–66.

26. For examples: Ilya Ehrenburg, *The Life of the Automobile*, trans. Joachim Neugroschel (London: Pluto, 1976); Ernst Jünger, *The Glass Bee*, trans. Louise Bogan and Elizabeth Mayer (New York: New York Review of Books, 2000 [1960]), esp. 92–93; Milan Kundera, *Slowness*, trans. Linda Asher (New York: Harper and Row, 1996).

27. In this vein, see, Eriksen, *Tyranny of the Moment*, 30–31; Harvey, *Condition of Postmodernity;* Manuel Castells, *End of Millennium* (Oxford: Blackwell, 1998), 356. I am not convinced that the question of periodization, notwithstanding the understandable attention it gains from social theorists and historians, is crucial for my inquiry here: regardless of the exact timing of social acceleration, we need to figure out how liberal democracy can grapple with it.

28. Harvey, *Justice, Nature & the Geography of Difference*, 240–41.

29. Harvey, *Condition of Postmodernity*, 240. For an alternative non-Marxist account, see James R. Beniger, *The Control Revolution: Technological and Economic Origins of the Information Society* (Cambridge: Harvard University Press, 1986).

30. Harvey, *Condition of Postmodernity*, 157, 147.

31. Castells, *Rise of Network Society*, 93; Castells, *End of Millennium*, 356.

32. Erica Schoenberger, "Competition, Time, and Space in Industrial Change," in *Commodity Chains and Global Capitalism*, ed. Gary Gereffi and Miguel Korzeniewicz (Westport, Conn.: Greenwood, 1994), 59. See also Scott Lash and John Urry, *Economies of Signs and Space* (Thousand Oaks, Calif.: Sage, 1994).

33. Castells, *Rise of Network Society*, 84.

34. Eberling, *Beschleunigung und Politik*, 41. By relying on the notion of an objectively measurable unit of time, these formulations might seem to contradict the discussion earlier in this chapter of the social and historical constitution of time. That conclusion, however, would be incorrect. First, the preliminary definition of *acceleration* provided here hardly contradicts the insight of anthropologists, sociologists, and

historians that what we now widely consider to be an objectively measurable unit of time was not so in earlier moments of history or in other cultures. For the sake of our discussion here (which is concerned with offering an adequate conceptualization of the temporal dynamics of contemporary society and especially contemporary Western society) those differences are of secondary importance. Second, this initial definition by no means precludes the possibility that the subjective perception of social acceleration may vary in accordance with social and cultural factors. Just to mention one example: the fact that a workplace is now capable of producing more goods in any given unit of time is likely to have a different psychological impact on the worker than the CEO, notwithstanding the fact that both are in important senses subject to social acceleration.

35. The tripartite conceptualization that follows is taken directly from Rosa, "Social Acceleration"

36. Jonas, *From Ancient Creed to Technological Man,* 5.

37. Eriksen, *Tyranny of the Moment,* 72; Gleick, *Faster,* 87.

38. John P. Robinson and Geoffrey Godbey, *Time for Life: The Surprising Ways Americans Use Their Time* (University Park: Penn State University Press, 1997), 40.

39. Beniger, *Control Revolution,* 186–92; Koselleck, *Zeitschichten,* 157–58; Schivelbusch, "Railroad Space, Railroad Time," 31–32.

40. James R. Beniger's *The Control Revolution* provides many examples of this and related phenomena since the industrial revolution.

41. On this facet of social acceleration, see also Robinson and Godbey, *Time for Life,* 46–48.

42. For an example, see John Dewey, *Liberalism and Social Action* (New York: Capricorn, 1963 [1935]), 57–58, in which Dewey moves quickly from a discussion of rapid changes in "industrial habits" to those in "political relations."

43. Laslett distinguishes between different sites of change (e.g., production, political institutions, culture [aesthetics and intellectual life]), different paces of change, and different patterns (e.g., repetitive, reversible, or cyclical). Whatever the merits of Laslett's specific typology, this is an important undertaking. Notwithstanding repeated references by historians and social scientists to the concept of social change, it remains woefully unclear. Peter Laslett, "Social Structural Time: An Attempt at Classifying Types of Social Change by Their Characteristic Paces," in *The Rhythms of Society,* ed. Michael Young and Tom Schuller (London: Routledge, 1988), 20–21. Similarly, we can read Marx as suggesting that we need to distinguish between different forms and rates of social change: changes at the level of the superstructure (e.g., law or morality) lag behind social change at the level of the relations and forces of production.

44. This example, as well as the earlier one of changing jobs during a single life course, come from Rosa, "Social Acceleration."

45. For example, see Eriksen, *Tyranny of the Moment,* 1–6, 56–77.

46. Marx, *Communist Manifesto,* in *Marx-Engels Reader,* 476.

47. Hermann Lübbe, "Gegenwartsschrumpfung," in *Die Beschleunigungsfalle oder der Triumph der Schilkroete,* ed. Klaus Backhaus and Holger Bonus (Stuttgart: Schaeffer-Poeschel, 1998), 263–93.

48. Indeed, by the time you read this, my examples may already be anachronistic.

49. Marx, *Communist Manifesto,* in *Marx-Engels Reader,* 476. The German sociologist Manfred Garhammer speculates that the limited half-life of previous experience is

one of the sources of the ubiquitous fatalism and apathy that seem to characterize contemporary political consciousness (*Wie Europäer ihre Zeit nutzen. Zeitstrukturen und Zeitkulturen im Zeichen der Globalisierung* [Berlin: Sigma, 2001], 482–83).

50. Dewey, *Public and Its Problems*, 140.

51. Staffan Burenstam Linder, *The Harried Leisure Class* (New York: Columbia University Press, 1970), 1.

52. For example, see Jeremy Rifkin, *Time Wars: The Primary Conflict in Human History* (New York: Henry Holt, 1987).

53. This is one of the many thoughtful observations in Linder, *Harried Leisure Class*.

54. Garhammer offers a useful survey of data available from Japan, the United States, and Western Europe; he concludes that acceleration (*Beschleunigung*) has occurred, at least since 1965, when the first major time-budget studies of human behavior were conducted (*Wie Europäer ihre Zeit nutzen*, 466–70). Focusing on extensive U.S. data (including time-budget studies done by the University of Michigan since 1965 and the University of Maryland in 1985), Robinson and Godbey dispute many of the individual conclusions reached by Garhammer, but they similarly defend the general postulate of an ongoing "speedup of life" (Robinson and Godbey, *Time for Life*, 24–42, 314). They do, however, claim that the empirical evidence for the mid-1990s suggests a leveling off and maybe even deceleration in the general pace of life.

55. Garhammer offers a detailed survey of relevant time-budget studies from Germany, Japan, Spain, Sweden, the United Kingdom, and the United States, in *Wie Europäer ihre Zeit nutzen*, 373–79. Robinson and Godbey challenge this claim for the United States (*Time for Life*, 113).

56. Empirical studies show that the U.S. pattern of "fast food" is the trendsetter for the rich countries of Western Europe, as the average time spent by West Europeans (in Germany, Spain, Sweden, and the UK) enjoying meals home declined from 1.3 hours daily in 1965 to 1 hour in the 1990s. Garhammer, *Wie Europäer ihre Zeit nutzen*, 382–86.

57. Of course, the data on the length of the workday is complex. The general pattern (in Germany, Japan, Spain, Sweden, the UK, and the United States) is probably for overall declines in the length of the paid workday since 1965, but in some countries (in particular, Japan and the United States) the general length of the workday may have increased in the last ten or fifteen years. For a detailed analysis of the data, see Garhammer, *Wie Europäer ihre Zeit nutzen*, 293–345, 396. Robinson and Godbey dispute the finding that either paid or unpaid labor time has increased in the United States since 1965 (*Time for Life*, 81–109).

58. Garhammer, *Wie Europäer ihre Zeit nutzen*, 389–92. Robinson and Godbey challenge this finding as well (*Time for Life*, 97–109).

59. Garhammer, *Wie Europäer ihre Zeit nutzen*, 405–6, 429–35.

60. Robinson and Godbey, *Time for Life*, 124–153, 167–86. Americans now devote approximately 40 percent of their free time to watching television (an increase of 10.4 hours per week, to 15.1 in 1985).

61. Robinson and Godbey, *Time for Life*, 231; Levine, *Geography of Time*, 145–46.

62. Harvey, *Condition of Postmodernity*, 121–326.

63. Giddens, *Nation-State and Violence*, 2.

64. Koselleck, *Zeitschichten*, 157–58.

65. Virilio, *Speed and Politics*; James der Derian, ed., *The Virilio Reader* (Oxford:

Blackwell, 1998). Inspired by Virilio, der Derian is one of a tiny number of political scientists who have begun to think through the implications of social acceleration. See "The Space of International Relations: Simulation, Surveillance, and Speed," *International Studies Quarterly* 34 (1990): 295–310. Virilio wavers uneasily between a *marxisant* interpretation of military conflict and an alternative line of inquiry in which the technology of modern warfare is conceived as an independent factor in the compression of space by speed.

66. Max Weber, *The Protestant Ethic and the Spirit of Capitalism*, trans. Talcott Parsons (London: Routledge, 1992 [1930]), 17. I should add that many different (e.g., Marxist, Weberian, Schumpeterian, or Hayekian) conceptions of capitalism are consistent with the claim that capitalism motors social acceleration.

67. These are the pointed questions raised by Justin Rosenberg in *The Follies of Globalisation Theory* (London: Verso, 2000). Rosenberg criticizes the growing reliance on spatiotemporal categories in discussions of globalization.

68. This claim still has to be demonstrated, as I hope to accomplish in subsequent chapters.

69. Rosa, "Social Acceleration." The fact that technical acceleration may produce, albeit paradoxically, unintended slow-downs in activity (e.g., a traffic jam resulting from too many cars trying to reach the same destination at a high speed or a breakdown of the university computer services because too many students and faculty try to send e-mail simultaneously) hardly contradicts this argument. On the contrary, when a slow-down of this type occurs, the result is likely to be increased anxiety about "falling behind," followed by a search for even faster forms of technology (faster cars and wider freeways or computer servers with greater capacity).

70. Rosa neglects this side of the story. To be sure, my account of the broader driving forces behind social acceleration may not be complete. I believe, however, that modern capitalism and the modern state system provide two fundamental sources of acceleration.

71. For a concise discussion of the Westphalian system's core attributes, see David Held, *Democracy and the Global Order: From the Modern State to Cosmopolitan Governance* (Stanford: Stanford University Press, 1995), 77–83.

72. John Herz, *The Nation-State and the Crisis of World Politics* (New York: David McKay, 1976), 94–95.

73. Otto Hintze, *The Historical Essays of Otto Hintze*, ed. Felix Gilbert (New York: Oxford University Press, 1975).

74. Charles Tilly, *Coercion, Capital, and European States, A.D. 990–1992* (Oxford: Blackwell, 1990), 14–15. See also Bruce M. Downing, *The Military Revolution and Political Change: Origins of Democracy and Autocracy in Early Modern Europe* (Princeton: Princeton University Press, 1992).

75. In a related vein Anthony Giddens suggests that the organizational superiority and historical triumph in modernity of the nation-state rests on its effectiveness at marshaling administrative power and making effective use of military force. In contrast to Tilly, however, Giddens clearly grasps that these achievements require us to pay proper "conceptual attention to the timing and spacing of human activities." The control of information is intimately tied to the structuring of time and space: the invention of writing, followed by printing, electronic communication and, more recently, advanced information technology allow for the realization of a core feature of

administrative power, namely *surveillance,* defined by Giddens as "the control of information and the superintendence of the activities of some groups by others." The manner in which surveillance is nested within a particular temporal and spatial context is crucial for understanding its scope as well as its contribution to the effectiveness of administrative power. Giddens correctly notes that a host of recent high-speed technological innovations "considerably expands the range" of information that can be stored by power-holders and thereby significantly heighten possibilities for surveillance in modernity (*Nation-State and Violence,* 2, 12, 14).

76. William H. McNeill, *The Pursuit of Power: Technology, Armed Force, and Society since A.D. 1000* (Chicago: University of Chicago Press, 1982), 130.

77. Paul Virilio and Sylvere Lotringer, *Pure War,* trans. Mark Polizzotti (New York: Semiotext[e], 1983), 20.

78. For example, the defeat of Prussia by Napoléon in 1806. On Prussia's conservatism in contrast to French military modernity, see McNeill, *Pursuit of Power,* 171–73.

79. Max Weber, *Economy and Society,* trans. Gunther Roth and Klaus Wittich (Berkeley: University of California Press, 1978), 979.

80. In this vein, see Castells's discussion of the trend toward "instant, surgical, secluded, technology-driven wars" (*Rise of the Network Society,* 459). This also seems to be Virilio's view, at least on some occasions.

81. Some of the empirical material discussed here from recent time-budget studies of human activity potentially lends support to this suspicion as well, at least to the extent that it documents a relatively recent intensification of the pace of some human activities. Of course, my claim by no means denies the indisputable point that contemporary society is also subject to slow-downs—for example, an economic crisis in which instances of deceleration seem far more widespread than acceleration. Interestingly, there has been some recent speculation that social acceleration is essential for understanding the changing pattern of deceleration as well. No other than Fed chairman Alan Greenspan has suggested that the increased significance of high-speed communication and information technologies in the economy is important for understanding the no less rapid character of recent economic downturns. What Greenspan refers to as "faster adjustment time" means that business behavior—some of which may be conducive toward a sudden downturn—is compressed into a "shorter time frame," thereby potentially contributing to economic volatility. One consultant compares the pace of business before the use of new computer technology to driving in city traffic at twenty miles an hour: "If somebody slams on the brakes, everybody can slow down." Given the accelerated speed of crucial economic activities, however, which is akin "to running stock cars at 200 miles an hour, a slight misstep can cause a pileup with great carnage." New technologies, for example, potentially open the door to rapid-fire overreactions to bad economic news, thereby generating widespread panic (John Schwartz, "Business on Internet Time," *New York Times,* Mar. 30, 2001, C2.)

82. Virilio, *Speed and Politics,* 139.

83. "Fehler führte 1983 fast zu atomaren Schlagabtausch," *Frankfurter Rundschau,* September 23, 1998, 2.

84. The report also noted that "the average time between finding a target and hitting it dropped to 15 minutes in Afghanistan a year ago from 45 minutes in the Persian Gulf war of 1991." John H. Cushman Jr., "Pentagon's Urgent Search for Speed: At the Pentagon, an Urgent Push for Faster and Smarter Weapons," *New York Times,* December 1, 2001, 3:1, 13.

85. Virilio, *Speed and Politics*, 139.
86. Ronald Deibert, "Harold Innis and the Empire of Speed," *Review of International Studies* 25 (1999): 289–90.
87. To be sure, this claim requires careful comparative historical and sociological scrutiny.
88. In Robert Levine's recent cross-cultural study of the pace of life in thirty-one countries, Japan ranks fourth (*Geography of Time*, 131).
89. Weber, *Protestantic Ethic and the Spirit of Capitalism*, 48.
90. Charles Taylor, *The Ethics of Authenticity* (Cambridge: Harvard University Press, 1991); and *Sources of the Self: The Making of Modern Identity* (Cambridge: Harvard University Press, 1989).
91. Rosa, "Social Acceleration."

T W O : Liberal Democracy's Time

1. Publius [James Madison], *Federalist Papers*, ed. Clinton Rossiter (New York: NAL Penguin, 1961), 321–22 (Federalist 51).
2. Ibid., 322. For Locke the legislative and executive powers should be distinct "because it may be too great a temptation to human frailty, apt to grasp at power, for the same persons who have the power of making laws to have also in their hands the power to execute them" (*Second Treatise of Government*, in *Political Writings of John Locke*, ed. David Wootton [New York: Mentor, 1993]), 335 (para. 143).
3. M. J. C. Vile, *Constitutionalism and the Separation of Powers*, 2d ed. (Indianapolis: Liberty Press, 1998), 17–18. To be sure, temporally minded institutional analysis might legitimately analyze many other attributes of modern liberal democracy (e.g., federalism). I follow the traditional view, however, by interpreting the separation of powers as liberal democracy's linchpin.
4. Montesquieu, *The Spirit of the Laws*, trans. Thomas Nugent (New York: Hafner, 1949), 150 (vol. 1, bk. 11, chap. 6).
5. Ibid.
6. Ibid.
7. Revealingly, William B. Gwyn observes that "the earliest proponents of the separation of powers were republicans, quite willing to see supreme (but not total) political power vested in a unicameral elected legislature" (*The Meaning of the Separation of Powers: An Analysis of the Doctrine from Its Origin to the Adoption of the United States Constitution* [New Orleans: Tulane University Press, 1965], 27.) My analysis of the temporal presuppositions of the separation of powers resembles what Gwyn describes as the "efficiency argument" in favor of it.
8. As Francis D. Wormuth has noted, "the separation of powers was a corollary of the proposition that law is necessarily general and prospective" (*The Origins of Constitutionalism* [New York: Harper & Bros., 1949], 193). A clear delineation of legislative rule making (in reference to a general category of potential cases) from (particular, individual case-oriented) executive and judicial application of the law was widely seen by the theoretical forerunners to liberal democracy as essential to decent government. As soon as the legislature is understood in overtly democratic terms, the separation of powers necessarily plays a central role in the quest to subordinate the operations of government to rules made by and for the people.
9. My account of the temporal separation of powers can be read fruitfully along the

lines of a Weberian "ideal-type." That is, many deviations can be found from it in actual liberal democratic systems. Nonetheless, it should still help provide an understanding of the fundamental temporal dynamics of traditional liberal democracy. The account here is not meant to suggest that classical liberal democracy endorsed an idealized parliamentary model of rule; this is clearly not the case for the United States, for example. It is important to note that even in the early U.S. model, however, it was generally believed that the Congress would rightly occupy the dominant place in lawmaking. There is absolutely no question that the original powers attributed to the U.S. executive, though by no means insignificant, were vastly less weighty than what he soon came to possess.

10. See Douglas V. Verney, "Parliamentary Government and Presidential Government," in *Parliamentary versus Presidential Government*, ed. Arend Lijphart (Oxford: Oxford University Press, 1992), 38–39. For this reason I do not focus here on the (in many respects pivotal) institutional differences between parliamentarism and presidentialism.

11. My argument here builds on the brief but suggestive observations of an Austrian social theorist whose interest in political theory is indisputably peripheral. See Helga Nowotny, *Time: The Modern and Postmodern Experience*, trans. N. Plaice (Cambridge, UK: Polity Press, 1994), 148–49. There are important historical predecessors to this tripartite temporal structure in the separation of powers. In Aristotle's *Rhetoric*, for example, he distinguishes between and among three types of speech—deliberation, which is described as concerned with the future; forensic (roughly: judicial), which is backward looking and concerned with the past; and "display," which not only is described in terms that anticipate some aspects of the representation of executive power but is interpreted by Aristotle as being present oriented (Aristotle, *The Art of Rhetoric*, trans. H. C. Lawson-Tancred [New York: Penguin, 1991], 80–82).

12. It is important not to read twentieth-century notions of state-driven social engineering, according to which society can be "made" or at least fundamentally transformed via state activity, into early liberal democratic ideals of legislation. The early modern architects of liberal democracy clearly did not share such notions. The classical model probably did not exclude, however, the possibility that state activity, to a limited degree, might modify future social trends. Yet, in accordance with its commitment to traditional conceptions of limited government, government's role was generally conceived in reactive terms.

13. Locke, *Second Treatise*, 344–45 (para. 160).

14. Richard H. Fallon, "'The Rule of Law' as a Concept in Constitutional Discourse," *Columbia Law Review* 97 (1997): 8.

15. Fritz Kern, *Kingship and Law in the Middle Ages* (Oxford: Blackwell, 1948). This tradition, though hardly in an unmodified form, remained influential into the nineteenth century. Recall, for example, the influence of common lawyers on the U.S. model of the separation of powers (James R. Stoner, *Common Law and Liberal Theory: Coke, Hobbes, and the Origins of American Constitutionalism* [Lawrence: University Press of Kansas, 1992], 177–225).

16. Niklas Luhmann, *Rechtssoziologie* (Hamburg: Rowohlt, 1972), 190–226, 294–353.

17. Elaine Spitz, *Majority Rule* (Chatham, N.J.: Chatham House, 1984), 94–95. New technologies pose difficult questions for this traditional notion of the necessary rever-

sibility of majority decisions. An atomic power plant cannot simply be closed down and the environment freed of all traces of it, in part because the plutonium cycle operates for thousands of years; future generations will not be able to reverse revolutionary changes made in the life cycle by present-day genetic research. See Bernd Guggenberger and Claus Offe, eds., *An den Grenzen der Mehrheitsdemokratie* (Opladen: Westdeutscher Verlag, 1984).

18. Locke, "Fundamental Constitutions for Carolina," in *Political Writings of John Locke*, 226, 232.

19. For the historical and intellectual story, see David E. Kyvig, *Explicit and Authentic Acts: Amending the U.S. Constitution, 1776–1995* (Lawrence: University Press of Kansas, 1996), 1–109.

20. In this critical spirit, see Sanford Levinson, ed., *Responding to Imperfection: The Theory and Practice of Constitutional Amendment* (Princeton: Princeton University Press, 1995). In chapter 3 I discuss the implications of social acceleration for constitutional amendment, as well as the peculiarities of the U.S. model, in greater depth.

21. Richard S. Kay, "Constitutional Chrononomy," *Ratio Juris* 13 (2000): 33.

22. Vilhelm Aubert, "Law as a Way of Resolving Conflicts: The Case of a Small Industrialized Society," 287; also see Laura Nader, "Styles of Court Procedure: To Make the Balance," 87, both in *Law in Culture and Society*, ed. L. Nader (Berkeley: University of California Press, 1969).

23. Recall how deeply rooted hostility to judicial discretion was in classical liberal jurisprudence. Locke, Montesquieu, Beccaria, Voltaire, and Bentham saw it as a terrible evil that needed to be fought off. For some of them this critique was also tied to a preference for statutory over customary or common law, which was interpreted as inviting judicial arbitrariness. In response to my general account here, one might argue that, in common law adjudication, rules can never be fully retrospective because they are typically crafted with consideration toward future cases. The fact that (oftentimes prospective) common law adjudication has always remained influential in Anglo-American liberal democracies might also generate legitimate worries about the accuracy of the temporal separation of powers as depicted here. Nonetheless, the traditional dogma in common law adjudication was that adjudication should be fundamentally retrospective because judges were merely supposed to apply past precedent. We would do well to avoid anachronistically reading more recent understandings of the common law into the past. Although undoubtedly deceptive, it would be a mistake to ignore the central place of this self-understanding of common lawyers well into the recent past. Moreover, even Anglo-American liberal democracy was influenced by Enlightenment critics of the common law, along with the relatively formalistic conception of jurisprudence endorsed by the mainstream of the Enlightenment tradition. Even those who underscore the common law background (e.g., Stoner, *Common Law and Liberal Theory*) concede this point. Although space restraints prevent me from adequately defending this claim, for now it must suffice to recall that the influence of Enlightenment critics of judicial discretion (including Beccaria) was profound even among most of the U.S. founders.

24. See, in particular, Cesare Beccaria, *On Crimes and Punishments* (Indianapolis: Hackett, 1986 [1764]), 10–13.

25. Montesquieu, *Spirit of the Laws*, 158 (vol. 1, bk. 11, chap. 6). In a more recent translation the relevant passage reads: "executive power is always exercised on immedi-

ate things" (Montesquieu, *Spirit of the Laws,* ed. and trans. Anne. M. Cohler, Basia Carolyn Miller, and Harold Samuel Stone [Cambridge: Cambridge University Press, 1989], 162. The original French reads: "outre que la puissance exécutrice s'exerce toujours sur les choses momentanées" (*De l'esprit des lois,* book 1, ed. Robert Derathe [Paris: Editions Garnier Frères, 1973], 175). In a similar vein the U.S. founders conceived of the executive as "directed to, and bound by the necessities of, decisive, and often immediate, action" (Joseph M. Bessette, *The Mild Voice of Reason: Deliberative Democracy and American National Government* [Chicago: University of Chicago Press, 1994], 31).

26. Not surprisingly, one of the key intellectual architects of the modern executive, Machiavelli, focused on this feature of political leadership.

27. I am thinking here of those voices in the liberal democratic tradition who have been hostile to executive power. Vile argues that such voices were common among French defenders of the separation of powers (see *Constitutionalism and the Separation of Powers,* 193–232). Many of the Anti-Federalists shared this hostility as well.

28. Locke, *Second Treatise,* 334 (para. 142), 341–42 (para. 156 and 157).

29. Ibid., 344–45 (para. 160).

30. Ibid., 342–43 (para. 158). Perhaps this is also why Locke's account of the separation of powers emphasizes that the executive is a "power always in being" (335–36 [para. 144]).

31. Ibid., 342 (para. 157). Locke adds that "people, riches, trade, power change their stations; flourishing mighty cities come to ruin and prove in time neglected, desolate corners, whilst other unfrequented places grow into populous countries, filled with wealth and inhabitants."

32. Ibid., 344 (para. 160). For a discussion of the influence of French reason of state theorists on the Lockean conception of prerogative powers, see Daniel Engster, *Divine Sovereignty: The Origins of Modern State Power* (Dekalb: Northern Illinois University Press, 2001), 111; and John Dunn, *The Political Thought of John Locke: An Historical Account of the Argument of the "Two Treatises of Government"* (Cambridge: Cambridge University Press, 1969), 161–64. The reason of state literature is similarly concerned with the dilemmas generated by the static character of law.

33. The liberal view of the legislature as a deliberative body can probably be traced in part to the influence of Montesquieu. See Montesquieu, *The Spirit of the Laws* (vol. 1, bk. 11, chap. 6), 155. Of course, liberals have conceived of legislative deliberation in many different ways and as serving many different functions. A particularly succinct version of the argument can be found in John Stuart Mill, *Considerations on Representative Government* (Buffalo: Prometheus, 1991), 97–119. For now it suffices to point out that the basic idea of a deliberative representative legislature has been well nigh universal within liberalism, at least until the advent of "realist" democratic theory in the twentieth century. C. Wright Mills captured the central place of this view succinctly when he observed that liberalism was committed to "the free ebb and flow of discussion . . . which the legislative organ enacts into law, thus lending to it legal force. Congress, or Parliament, as an institution, crowns all the scattered publics; it is the archetype for each of the little circles of face-to-face citizens discussing their public business (*The Power Elite* [New York: Oxford University Press, 1956], 298–99).

34. Publius [Alexander Hamilton], *The Federalist Papers,* 426–27 (Federalist 70). As Bessette observes, "Congress was designed to be the principal locus of deliberation in American national government" (*Mild Voice of Reason,* 3). Bessette interprets the

framers' original vision as a legislative-centered model of "deliberative democracy," according to which "deliberation calls for a collegial institution in which those of roughly equal rank voice a variety of contrasting views as they argue and reason together to promote common interests" (31).

35. Publius [Hamilton], *Federalist Papers*, 431–33 (Federalist 71).

36. Robert Dahl and Edward Tufte, *Size and Democracy* (Stanford: Stanford University Press, 1973), 72.

37. Jürgen Habermas, *The Structural Transformation of the Public Sphere*, trans. Frederick Lawrence (Cambridge: MIT Press, 1989), 57–88.

38. Harvey C. Mansfield Jr., *Taming the Prince: The Ambivalence of Executive Power* (New York: Free Press, 1989), 142. Mansfield overstates the debt of modern executive power to the least attractive elements of Machiavelli's political theory. Yet he is right to see Machiavelli as an important influence. For example, Machiavelli points out in the *Discourses* that assemblies are ill suited to "remedying a situation which will not brook delay," arguing that the executive is better suited to the imperatives of rapid-fire government. While elected representatives "have to consult with one another, and to reconcile their diverse views takes time," the single person of the executive can act speedily and avoid the "temporizing" that necessarily plagues large assemblies. Situations that "will not brook delay" (e.g., a dire and perhaps unexpected crisis) thus call for immediate, high-speed executive action (Machiavelli, *Discourses*, trans. L. J. Walker [London: Penguin, 1970], 194–95).

39. Montesquieu, *Spirit of the Laws* (vol. 1, bk. 11, chap. 6), 156; *Federalist Papers* (Federalist 70), 424. Following Machiavelli, Locke and Hamilton assume that popular assemblies are inherently slow moving, whereas the executive possesses a built-in capacity for fast-paced action. See Locke, *Second Treatise*, 344 (para. 160); Publius [Hamilton and Jay], *Federalist Papers*, 392–93, 426–27, 431–33 (Federalists 64, 70–71).

40. Some systems, however—for example, Uruguay—have experimented with a plural executive. See Harry Kantor, "Efforts Made by Various Latin American Countries to Limit the Power of the President," in *Parliamentary versus Presidential Government*, 102–4.

41. Locke, *Second Treatise*, 344 (para. 159).

42. Ibid., 344 (para. 160).

43. Ibid., 316 (para. 108), 336–37 (para. 146–48).

44. For a useful discussion of executive discretion and foreign policy in early liberalism see Vile, *Constitutionalism and the Separation of Powers*, 96–106. Jay's discussion of the role of the proposed U.S. presidency in foreign affairs is revealing as well (Publius [Jay], *Federalist Papers*, 392–93 [Federalist 64]). An important place in this argument is occupied by the traditional metaphor of the political community as a concrete "body politic," pictured in Locke's account as situated within a fundamentally lawless and perilous international realm: Locke's influential picture of international relations as constituting a "state of nature" immediately suggests a picture of individual commonwealths strikingly akin to the individual persons who populate Locke's state of nature before the establishment of what he calls "political society" (*Second Treatise*, 335–36 [para. 145–47]). To be sure, Locke was chiefly underscoring the point that sovereign states should be seen as legal or juridical persons, and the "analogy of sovereign commonwealths in a state of nature to individual men in that state is not meant to be taken too literally" (Richard H. Cox, *Locke on War and Peace* [Oxford: Claren-

don, 1960], 147). Nonetheless, the corporeal analogy helps explain the conventional view that potential existential threats to the physical community require rapid-fire executive-led action. In foreign affairs, but also during domestic "accidents" posing a serious danger to the polity, high-speed executive discretion is necessary because the stakes are so high. Why are the stakes high? Because the political community constitutes a body politic strikingly akin to the individual human body, and, as we all know, even relatively modest physical invasions of our corporeality represent violations of our physical integrity and potentially dangerous threats to our existence. By allowing others to assault us physically, we place our physical well-being and perhaps even our existence in alien hands. At least implicitly, key strands in early modern liberalism thus rely on seemingly credible preconceptions about physical self-defense in order to justify executive preeminence in the face of dire crises: when vulnerable to physical assault, individuals lack the luxury of debating with their peers or allies about the best conceivable response. Instead, they must move quickly to ward off immediate threats to their physical well-being, and such moments call for action rather than deliberation, dispatch instead of delay. If physical violence is imminent or already at hand, self-preservation can only be achieved by the imperatives of physical self-defense, in which agility and swiftness are at a premium. In the political universe the unitary executive, and not a numerous assembly, is the most likely source of such agility and swiftness.

45. Publius [Hamilton], *Federalist Papers*, 431 (Federalist 71). Congressional terms of office also mesh with the temporal account provided here. For example, House terms of office (two years) were conceived as a device for ensuring the broadly representative character of the House: in order to replicate the broad-based process of deliberation in society at large within government as well as effectively mirror the configuration of interests found within society at large, the House would not only be relatively large but also would face the specter of frequent elections. But might not frequent elections counteract the quest for successful prospective (or long-term) legislation? Perhaps. For this reason the Senate was conceived as having terms of office even longer than those of the presidency. What better way to ensure the proper long-term legislative orientation and circumspection required by prospective lawmaking?

46. Montesquieu, *Spirit of the Laws*, 77 (vol. 1, bk. 6, chap. 5). On Montesquieu, see also Vile, *Constitutionalism and the Separation of Powers*, 98. Also see Tocqueville's praise for the legal profession for "applying an invisible brake which slows down" popular decision making (Tocqueville, *Democracy in America*, trans. George Lawrence [New York: Harper & Row, 1969], 268).

47. Beccaria, *On Crimes and Punishments*, 15.

48. Montesquieu, *Spirit of the Laws*, 156, 159 (vol. 1, bk. 6, chap. 6).

49. Beccaria, *On Crimes and Punishments*, 6–37.

50. For a discussion of this facet of the Federalist position, see Louis Fischer, "The Efficiency Side of Separated Powers," *Journal of American Studies* 5 (1971): 113–31.

51. Publius [Madison], *Federalist Papers*, 379 (Federalist 62). On bicameralism as an instrument for preventing a "mere mob" from being rapidly swayed, see David Hume, "Idea of a Perfect Commonwealth," in Hume, *Political Essays*, ed. Charles Hendel (Indianapolis: Bobbs-Merrill, 1953), 153.

52. Montesquieu, *Spirit of the Laws*, 154–55 (vol. 1, bk. 11, chap. 6).

53. Hamilton describes representative bodies as "acquainted with the general ge-

nius, habits, and modes of thinking of the people at large" (Publius, *Federalist Papers*, 217 [Federalist 35]). When Mill reflects on the impossibility of direct democracy, he might be interpreted as acknowledging its temporal impracticality. See Mill, *Considerations on Representative Government*, 80.

54. Locke, *Second Treatise*, 375 (para. 223).

55. Publius [Madison], *Federalist Papers*, 59–61 (Federalist 10).

56. To pretend that we can understand our institutions and practices without making sense of their implicit temporal and philosophical assumptions is myopic. One of the reasons why some of the traditional temporal ideas discussed here now seem quaint is because social acceleration has probably helped contribute to major transformations of traditional liberal democratic practice.

57. Might a revival of economic liberalism ward off these temporal dilemmas? Probably not. Recent political experience (in Thatcher's Britain and George W. Bush's United States, e.g.) shows that neoliberal reform requires extensive state activity in the economy. For this simple reason the problems plaguing legislation in the context of social acceleration should concern neoliberals as much as they do defenders of the welfare state, since both ultimately need to be concerned with the proper form of effective state action in a fast-paced economy.

58. Kay, "Constitutional Chrononomy," 44–47.

59. Locke, *Second Treatise*, 344–45 (para. 160). We know from the vast secondary literature that Locke's relationship to modern economic institutions remains a controversial matter. For now let me just mention that some passages in the *Second Treatise*— for example, his reference to constant "flux" (para. 157)—imply an impeccably modern view of social and economic dynamism. In the final analysis, it seems to me that Locke is ambivalent on this point.

60. In a similar vein, see Sheldon Wolin, *The Presence of the Past: Essays on the State and Constitution* (Baltimore: Johns Hopkins University Press, 1989), 170.

61. Mill, *Considerations on Representative Government*, 109.

62. Ibid. Woodrow Wilson similarly remarked in 1885 that "time would fail it [i.e., the House of Representatives] to discuss all the bills brought in, for they every session number thousands; and it is to be doubted whether, even if time allowed, the ordinary processes of debate and amendment would suffice to sift the chaff from the wheat in the bushels of bills every week piled upon the clerk's desk" (*Congressional Government* [New York: Meridian, 1960 [1885]), 62.

63. Mill, *Considerations on Representative Government*, 109–10.

64. Ibid., 100.

65. Niklas Luhmann, "Die Knappheit der Zeit und die Vordringlichkeit des Befristeten," *Politische Planung. Aufsätze zur Soziologie von Politik und Verwaltung* (Opladen, Ger.: Westdeutscher, 1971), 150–56.

66. Presidency scholars now speak of the "plural presidency," arguing that a more appropriate emphasis than traditional notions of the unitary executive "is the plural nature of the presidency, its policy environment, and the demands placed upon the institution by different groups and nations" (Gary King and Lyn Ragsdale, *The Elusive Executive: Discovering Statistical Patterns in the Presidency* [Washington, D.C.: Congressional Quarterly, 1988], 11).

67. Jules Lobel, "Emergency Powers and the Decline of Liberalism," *Yale Law Journal* 98 (1989): 1400–1421.

68. Kenneth R. Mayer, *With the Stroke of a Pen: Executive Orders and Presidential Power* (Princeton: Princeton University Press, 2001), 26.

69. Carl Schmitt, *Die Lage der europäischen Rechtswissenschaft* [*The Situation of European Jurisprudence*] (Tübingen: Universitäts-Verlag, 1950), esp. 18. I discuss this text in depth in chapter 4.

70. For example, see Beccaria, *On Crimes and Punishments*, 10–13.

71. Cass Sunstein points out that open-ended language (*feasible*, e.g., or *public policy*) in statutes sometimes means that "Congress has invited interpretation over time" in order to avoid the specter of statutory obsolescence (*After the Rights Revolution: Reconceiving the Regulatory State* [Cambridge: Harvard University Press, 1990], 178).

72. Jerome Frank, *Law and the Modern Mind* (New York: Doubleday, 1963 [1930]), 6–7.

73. Harvey, *Justice, Nature, and the Geography of Difference*, 240–41.

74. These are familiar criticisms of Frank's early brand of Legal Realism. For example, Franz Neumann observes that Frank "denies any certainty of the law . . . the assertion that law is certain is for him a mere myth" (*The Rule of Law: Political Theory and the Legal System in Modern Society* [Leamington Spa, UK: Berg, 1986]), 229.

75. Benjamin Barber, "Three Scenarios for the Future of Technology and Strong Democracy," *Political Science Quarterly* 113 (1998–99): 579.

76. See Dahl and Tufte, *Size and Democracy*.

77. Sennett, *Corrosion of Character*, esp. 130–35.

78. Robinson and Godbey, *Time for Life*, 47. In their extensive study of time use among U.S. citizens, Robinson and Godbey find a significant decline since 1965 in the amount of time devoted to associational activity, including political activity (175–76).

79. They may also tend to favor substantive policies that offer a privileged position to the executive as a way of guaranteeing "fast results." The criminologist David Garland argues that we have witnessed exactly this development in the last twenty years in the realm of penal policy: "the essential and abiding attractiveness of the 'sovereign' [i.e., executive-centered] response to crime (and above all of retaliatory laws that create stronger penal sanctions or police powers) is that it can be represented as an immediate, authoritative intervention. Such action gives the impression that *something is being done*—here, now, swiftly and decisively" (*The Culture of Control: Crime and Social Order in Contemporary Society* [Chicago: University of Chicago Press, 2001], 134–35).

80. For some communitarians, for example, the most recent one seems to be easy or "no-fault" divorce laws, which they see as complicit in an astonishing variety of contemporary social and political ills. Is it so surprising that cultural conservatives— including many communitarians—are now seeking to turn the family into a bastion of constancy and stability, given the ongoing intensification of social acceleration which seems so widespread? The family might appear to offer a final refuge from the pressures of our high-speed lives. Alas, the data discussed in chapter 1 suggests that this is an empirically dubious expectation. Its normative undertones are problematic as well, since it potentially implies the virtues of "freezing" traditional (and sometimes unjust) gender and familial patterns.

81. Dewey, *Public and Its Problems*, 140–41.

82. C. Neal Tate and Torbjoern Vallinder, "The Global Extension of Judicial Power: The Judicialization of Politics," in *The Global Expansion of Judicial Power*, ed. Tate and Vallinder (New York: New York University Press, 1995), 2.

83. C. Neal Tate, "Why the Expansion of Judicial Power?" in Tate and Vallinder, *Global Expansion of Judicial Power*, 31–32.

84. Lawrence B. Solum, "Indeterminacy," in *A Companion to Philosophy of Law and Legal Theory*, ed. Dennis Patterson (Oxford: Blackwell, 1996), 488–502.

85. Suzanne Berger, "Politics and Anti-Politics in Western Europe," *Daedalus* 108 (1979): 46–47; Claus Offe, *Contradictions of the Welfare State*, ed. John Keane (Cambridge, Mass.: MIT Press, 1984), 166–67; Gianfranco Poggi, *The State: Its Nature, Development, and Prospects* (Stanford: Stanford University Press, 1990), 128–44. On legislative decay in the United States, see Theodore Lowi, *The End of Liberalism* (New York: Norton, 1979).

86. George E. Connor and Brice I. Oppenheimer, "Deliberation: An Untimed Value in a Timed Game," in *Congress Reconsidered*, ed. Lawrence C. Dodd and Brice I. Oppenheimer, 5th ed. (Washington, D.C.: Congressional Quarterly Press, 1993), 327.

87. Michael Crozier, Samuel P. Huntington, and Joji Watanuki, *The Crisis of Democracy: Report on the Governability of Democracies to the Trilateral Commission* (New York: New York University Press, 1975). The cause of "ungovernability," however, is not democracy per se or the political acrimony of the 1960s but, instead, fundamental temporal shifts that make it difficult for slow-moving, deliberate legislatures to operate effectively in an increasingly fast-paced society.

88. Hernando do Soto, "Some Lessons in Democracy—For the U.S.," *New York Times*, April 1, 1990, 4:A2.

89. Administrative rule making in the United States is subject to the Administrative Procedures Act (APA), which mandates some minimal rule of law standards. U.S. presidents regularly rely on various types of executive orders, proclamations, memoranda, and national security directives in order to act "expeditiously." Unfortunately, the exemption of some of these forms of executive rule from the APA raises difficult questions for procedural regularity and predictability. For an excellent survey, see Phillip J. Cooper, *By Order of the President: The Use and Abuse of Executive Direct Action* (Lawrence: University Press of Kansas, 2002), 58.

90. For a neo-Marxist account of antiformal trends in the law, see Franz L. Neumann, "The Change in the Function of Law," in *The Rule of Law under Siege: Selected Essays of Franz L. Neumann and Otto Kirchheimer*, ed. William E. Scheuerman (Berkeley: University of California Press, 1996), 101–41; for a free market analysis, see Friedrich Hayek, *Law, Liberty, and Legislation*, vols. 1–3 (London: Routledge & Kegan Paul, 1976); from a Critical Legal Studies perspective, see Roberto Mungabeira Unger, *Law in Modern Society* (New York: Free Press, 1976).

91. D. J. Galligan, *Discretionary Powers: A Legal Study of Official Discretion* (Oxford: Clarendon, 1990).

92. Perhaps we can also interpret the much-discussed rise of independent central banks as a particularly striking facet of this trend. How better to allow for financial regulation of our high-speed capitalism than by minimizing the direct interventionist instruments of slow-moving legislatures while outfitting a group of financial experts with significant discretionary power to respond to fast-moving markets shifts?

93. Steven G. Calabresi and Saikrishna B. Prakash, "The President's Power to Execute Laws," *Yale Law Journal* 104 (1994): 541–665. For a discussion of how U.S. presidents since Ronald Reagan have pursued this approach, see Elena Kagan, "Presidential Administration," *Harvard Law Review* 114 (2002): 2245–2385. Notably, critics of an executive-dominated administrative state express concerns about the contemporary

relevance of the traditional picture of the unitary energetic executive similar to those articulated here. See Martin S. Flaherty, "The Most Dangerous Branch," *Yale Law Journal* 105 (1996): 1725–1839.

94. "Sunset laws" are one example of this trend.

95. Frank Church and Charles Matthias, "Foreword," in *A Brief History of Emergency Powers in the United States: A Working Paper Prepared for the Special Committee on National Emergencies and Delegated Emergency Powers, United States Senate* (Washington, D.C.: U.S. Government Printing Office, 1974), vi.

96. Church and Matthias, "Foreword," *Brief History of Emergency Powers*, vi. Also see Jules Lobel, "Emergency Powers and the Decline of Liberalism"; Arthur S. Miller, "Crisis Government Becomes the Norm," *Ohio State Law Journal* 39 (1978): 736–51.

97. Ernst Frankel, ed., *Der Staatsnotstand* (Berlin: Colloquium, 1964); Clinton Rossiter, *Constitutional Dictatorship: Crisis Government in Modern Democracies* (New York: Harcourt Brace Jovanovich, 1964); more recently, see Oren Gross, "The Normless and Exceptionless Exception: Carl Schmitt's Theory of Emergency Powers and the 'Norm-Exception' Dichotomy," *Cardozo Law Review* 21 (2000): 1825–68.

98. Although outdated, the classic statement on the growth of the U.S. executive remains Arthur Schlesinger's *The Imperial Presidency* (Boston: Houghton Mifflin, 1973). For more recent discussions of the expansion of executive decision making, see Cooper, *By Order of the President;* Louis Fisher, *Constitutional Conflicts between Congress and the President,* 3d ed. (Lawrence: University Press of Kansas, 1991); Louis Fisher, *Presidential War Power* (Lawrence: University Press of Kansas, 1995); Philip B. Kurland, "The Rise and Fall of the 'Doctrine' of the Separation of Powers," *Michigan Law Review* 85 (1987): 592–613; Harry P. Monaghan, "The Protective Power of the Presidency," *Columbia Law Review* 93 (1993): 1–74; Gordon Silverstein, *Imbalance of Powers: Constitutional Interpretation and the Making of American Foreign Policy* (New York: Oxford University Press, 1997); Cass R. Sunstein, "An Eighteenth-Century Presidency for a Twenty-First Century World," *Arkansas Law Review* 48 (1995): 1–22. Mayer describes the enormous accretion of executive authority via (constitutionally suspect) unilateral "executive orders." The president's ability to "act first" has played a significant role in the expansion of executive orders (*With the Stroke of a Pen,* 26).

99. This statement appears in Roosevelt's March 1933 inaugural address. Cited in William M. Goldsmith, *The Growth of Presidential Power: A Documented History* (New York: Chelsea House, 1974), 1553.

100. Cited in ibid.

101. See *The United States v. Curtiss-Wright,* 299 U.S. 304 (1936), in which Sutherland argues that the "international field must often accord the President a degree of discretion and freedom from statutory restriction which would not be admissible were domestic affairs alone involved." He affirms an 1816 U.S. Senate Foreign Relations Committee assertion that executive "success frequently depends on secrecy and dispatch." Sutherland's decision is widely cited in subsequent constitutional jurisprudence. For a discussion, see Fisher, *Constitutional Conflicts between Congress and the President,* 91–93.

102. See Attorney General Robert Jackson, "Decision Submitted to President Roosevelt Asserting the Legality of Certain Presidential Actions [in particular, military support for Great Britain], August 27, 1940" in Goldsmith, *Growth of Presidential Power,* 1763–64.

103. Franklin Delano Roosevelt, "Annual Message to Congress, January 4, 1939," in

Goldsmith, *Growth of Presidential Power,* 1737. See also Roosevelt's anxious observation that "new range and speed" characterizes war making in the twentieth century.

104. Theodore J. Lowi, "Afterword: The Paradox of Presidential Power," in Martin Fausold and Alan Shank, eds., *The Constitution and the American Presidency* (Albany: SUNY Press, 1991), 238–39. Lowi prefers the slow-track separation of powers model. Richard Neustadt links the postwar U.S. presidency to what he similarly identifies as a nexus between emergency government and what I have described as social acceleration. In his view "what distinguishes mid-century can be put very briefly: emergencies in policy with politics as usual . . . By present standards what would once have been emergency is commonplace. Policy dilemmas throughout the postwar period resemble past emergencies in one respect, their difficulty and complexity for government. Technological innovation, social and political change abroad, and population growth at home impose enormous strains not only on the managerial equipment of our policymakers but also on their intellectual resources. The gropings of mature men at midcentury remind one of the intellectual confusions stemming from depression, thirty yeas ago, when men were pushed past comprehension by the novelty of their condition. In our time innovation keeps us constantly confused; no sooner do we start to comprehend than something new is added and we grope again" (*Presidential Power and the Modern Presidents* [New York: Free Press, 1990], 5). My claims about temporality and executive power may also shed light on Stephen Skowronek's view of the U.S. presidency as a "blunt disruptive force" for political change (see *The Politics Presidents Make: Leadership from John Adams to Bill Clinton* [Cambridge: Harvard University Press, 1997], 5). In a high-speed social universe conceptions of executive speed are likely to augment executive power, thereby providing the presidency with increased possibilities for routinely jolting the institutional status quo.

105. Lowi, "Afterword: The Paradox of Presidential Power," 234.

106. For example, executive action on behalf of guaranteeing the civil rights of racial minorities has been justified by the executive conjuring up the specter of an emergency requiring swift executive reaction. Along these lines, see Harry Truman's defense of his decision to establish a President's Committee on Civil Rights in 1946 (Goldsmith, *Growth of Presidential Power,* 1568). For a vivid illustration of the "domestic emergency" defense of executive power, see John F. Kennedy, "The Challenges of the Modern Presidency" (Address to the National Press Club, January 14, 1960), in ibid., 1621–65, in which he promises a return to the "fast-moving, creative Presidential rule" of the Roosevelt and Truman eras while praising Lincoln as a model of a successful president who "did not hesitate. He did not equivocate. For he was the President of the United States" (1621, 1625).

107. Lowi, "Afterword: The Paradox of Presidential Power," 237.

108. K. D. Ewing and C. A. Gearty, *Freedom under Thatcher: Civil Liberties in Modern Britain* (Oxford: Clarendon, 1990), 5, 7.

109. On the growth of presidential government in Europe, see Robert Elgie, ed., *Semi-Presidentialism in Europe* (Oxford: Oxford University Press, 1999). The resurgence of executive-dominated liberal democracies is critically analyzed in Guillermo O'Donnell, "Delegative Democracy," *Journal of Democracy* 5 (1994): 55–69; also see Juan Linz, "Presidential or Parliamentary Democracy: Does It Make a Difference?" in *The Failure of Presidential Democracy: Comparative Perspectives,* ed. Juan Linz and Arturo Valenzuela (Baltimore: Johns Hopkins University Press, 1994), 3–87.

110. We should, however, avoid throwing the baby out with the bathwater, as demo-

cratic "realists" inspired by Joseph Schumpeter do (see *Capitalism, Socialism, and Democracy*, 3d ed. [New York: Harper, 1950]). The unappealing "democratic method" that they favor over classical liberal democracy reifies the worst consequences of speed for liberal democracy.

111. Marinetti, *Marinetti*, 41, 81.

112. Ibid., 94.

113. Ibid., 74, 153.

114. Filippo Tomasso Marinetti, "The Florence Address," in *A Primer of Italian Fascism*, ed. Jeffrey T. Schnapp (Lincoln: University of Nebraska Press, 2000), 269.

115. Marinetti, *Marinetti*, 158–59.

THREE: Constitutionalism in an Age of Speed

1. James Bryce, *Constitutions* (New York: Oxford University Press, 1901), x.

2. John R. Vile, *The Constitutional Amending Process in American Political Thought* (New York: Praeger, 1992), 137–56.

3. David E. Kyvig, *Explicit and Authentic Acts: Amending the U.S. Constitution, 1776–1995*, 216–314; Daniel Lazare, *The Frozen Republic* (New York: Harcourt Brace Jovanovich, 1996).

4. Kay, "Constitutional Chrononomy," 33.

5. The concept of constitutionalism remains contested. See Larry Alexander, ed., *Constitutionalism: Philosophical Foundations* (Cambridge: Cambridge University Press, 1998); Jon Elster and Rune Slagstad, eds., *Constitutionalism and Democracy* (Cambridge: Cambridge University Press, 1988); Thomas Grey, "Constitutionalism: An Analytic Framework," in *Nomos XX: Constitutionalism*, ed. John W. Chapman and J. Roland Pennock (New York: New York University Press, 1979), 189–209. As will become clear, I take the written character of constitutional government seriously; I also believe that there are good reasons for distinguishing between higher (constitutional) and lower (ordinary) legislation and for conceptualizing constitutionalism in liberal democratic terms. In these respects I think that all students of constitutionalism remain indebted to the Enlightenment legal tradition and, more specifically, the U.S. founders, who played a major role in initiating the distinction between ordinary and constitutional legislation. But my account is meant to be applicable to a relative diversity of constitutional systems and normative interpretations thereof. My tendency to rely on U.S. examples is not intended to suggest the superiority of the existing U.S. system of constitutionalism. On the contrary, a central theme of this chapter is that, in part because of its failure to develop a satisfactory model of constitutional change, the present-day U.S. constitutional system is plagued by many ills, and thus others would do well before rushing to imitate it. A recent study by Jed Rubenfeld (*Freedom and Time: A Theory of Constitutional Government* [New Haven: Yale University Press, 2001]) also focuses on the temporal contours of modern constitutionalism. Unfortunately, Rubenfeld neglects the problem of social speed.

6. Kay, "Constitutional Chrononomy," 33.

7. In chapter 4 I examine the problem of statutory obsolescence.

8. John Locke, "Fundamental Constitutions for Carolina," in Wootton, *Political Writings of John Locke*, 232.

9. See Michael Hamburger, "The Constitution's Accommodation of Social Change," *Michigan Law Review* 88 (1988): 239–327; Morton Horwitz, "The Constitution of

Change: Legal Fundamentality without Fundamentalism," *Harvard Law Review* 107 (1993): 30–117.

10. Locke's "Fundamental Constitutions for Carolina" is lengthy and detailed.

11. Stephen Macedo, *The New Right v. the Constitution* (Washington, D.C.: Cato Institute, 1986), 18.

12. Kay, "Constitutional Chrononomy," 41.

13. Ibid.

14. Karl Marx, "Communist Manifesto," in Tucker, *Marx-Engels Reader,* 469.

15. Sunstein, *After the Rights Revolution,* 174–75.

16. Sklar is speaking more generally of the relationship between the legal system as a whole and capitalism (*The Corporate Reconstruction of American Capitalism, 1890–1916* [Cambridge: Cambridge University Press, 1988], 89).

17. For a classic discussion of the merits (and also limits) of stability and clarity in the law, see Lon Fuller, *The Morality of Law* (New Haven: Yale University Press, 1964), 63–65, 79–81. Only extreme views of legal indeterminacy are inconsistent with my attempt to take the notion of a written constitution, as well as the traditional legal virtues of constancy and clarity, seriously. For a critique of such views, see Lawrence B. Solum, "On the Indeterminacy Crisis: Critiquing Critical Dogma," *University of Chicago Law Review* 54 (1987): 462–503.

18. Bryce, *Constitutions,* 80.

19. See Albert L. Sturm, "The Development of American State Constitutions," *Publius* 12 (1982): 57–98. Also see John Dinan, " 'The Earth Belongs Always to the Living Generation': The Development of State Constitutional Amendment and Revision Procedures," *Review of Politics* 62 (2000): 645–74; Donald S. Lutz, "Toward a Theory of Constitutional Amendment," in Levinson, *Responding to Imperfection,* 237–74.

20. This rejoinder is inspired by the provocative reflections of Stephen Griffin (*American Constitutionalism: From Theory to Politics* [Princeton: Princeton University Press, 1996]), who attributes many of the problematic facets of recent U.S. constitutional development to the emergence of the interventionist and welfare states.

21. For Dworkin's distinction between rules and principles, see *Taking Rights Seriously* (Cambridge: Harvard University Press, 1977). Christopher L. Eisgruber (*Constitutional Self-Government* [Cambridge: Harvard University Press, 2001], 10–45) relies on Dworkin's insight that the U.S. Constitution contains open-ended moral principles to defend the rigidity of Article 5. In Eisgruber's view Article 5's toilsome procedures provide a sensible embodiment of the worthy liberal quest for stability and constancy in constitutional law. At the same time, the Constitution's numerous expressions of abstract moral principle permit substantial flexibility via judicial interpretation. Thus, the United States is blessed with the best of both worlds: substantial legal stability as well as impressive possibilities for flexibly applying fundamental constitutional principles to changing circumstances. Eisgruber's argument probably only makes sense, however, if we exclude the possibility that judicial reinterpretations of abstract moral principles oftentimes effectively constitute fundamental changes to the constitutional order. In my reading of U.S. constitutional history, this assumption is implausible (see n. 26). In effect, Eisgruber endorses constitutional alteration via the Supreme Court while relying on a problematic notion of constitutional principle to veil the Court's use of the amendment power.

22. Sanford Levinson, "How Many Times Has the United States Constitution Been

Amended? (A) < 26; (B) 25; (c) 27; (D) > 27: Accounting for Constitutional Change," in Levinson, *Responding to Imperfection*, 14–24. Levinson offers a helpful starting point for developing a conceptual account of how we might delineate constitutional interpretation from constitutional alteration: the former is "linked in specifiable ways to analyses of the text or at least to the body of materials conventionally regarded within the ambit of the committed constitutionalist," whereas the latter "signifies something out the ordinary, something truly *new*" (15).

23. William J. Stuntz, "The Substantive Origins of Criminal Procedure," *Yale Law Journal* 105 (1995): 395. As Stuntz notes: "the substantive issues that shaped Fourth and Fifth Amendment law are long since settled . . . We have taken a privacy ideal formed in heresy cases and railroad regulation disputes, an ideal that had no connection to ordinary criminal law enforcement, and used it as the foundation for much of the vast body of law that polices the police. Predictably, the combination has not worked out very well" (396). The Fourth Amendment protects against unreasonable searches and seizures; the Fifth Amendment says that no one shall "be deprived of life, liberty, or property, without due process of law."

24. Robert Justin Lipkin, *Constitutional Revolutions: Pragmatism and the Role of Judicial Review in American Constitutionalism* (Durham: Duke University Press, 2002). As Lipkin shows, constitutional courts often operate as the constituent or constitution-making power. Lipkin points out that "American constitutional practice is replete with constitutional revolutions" (22), that is, fundamental court-based transformations to the preexisting legal order possessing at most a tenuous basis to previous constitutional doctrine and practice. Two prominent examples are *Marbury v. Madison* (which initiated judicial review) and *Brown v. Board of Education* (which attacked U.S.-style apartheid), but Lipkin provides an excellent reinterpretation of many other famous Supreme Court rulings as well. "The original constitutional principle of limited government was altered through both the Marshall Court and the New Deal Court decisions. The principle of the original role of the presidency has been altered drastically in the twentieth century. The advent of the administrative state as a fourth branch of governmental authority is not in the original Constitution" (219). Yet in each case the Supreme Court played a decisive role in generating fundamental institutional change.

25. In this vein, see Antonin Scalia, *A Matter of Interpretation: Federal Courts and the Law* (Princeton: Princeton University Press, 1997), 47.

26. Cass Sunstein points out that statutory obsolescence rests on various sources, including the possibility that "a statutory provision may no longer be consistent with widely held social norms," and "the legal background [to a particular statute] may have changed dramatically as a result of legislative and judicial innovations" (*After the Rights Revolution*, 174). Similarly, constitutional obsolescence undoubtedly has diverse roots. Nonetheless, the phenomenon of social and economic acceleration makes up an important source of the problem, thus my emphasis on it here. What Sunstein describes as changing "factual assumptions" underlying an original legal norm (e.g., the introduction of new technology) is contained in the notion of social and economic acceleration used here.

27. One might also add a further option to this list—namely, the possibility that popular revolution is the only appropriate response to the inevitable decay of all constitutions. During the U.S. Revolution some radical republicans endorsed this approach (Michael Lienesch, *New Order of the Ages: Time, the Constitution, and the*

Making of Modern American Political Thought [Princeton: Princeton University Press, 1988], 67). I neglect it here for the reason that social acceleration suggests that revolutions of this type would have to be a more or less permanent affair, given the intense pace of social change and the necessity of frequent constitutional change. Surely, no defender of liberal democratic constitutionalism wants permanent revolution.

28. For background, see Kyvig, *Explicit and Authentic Acts,* 9–109; Vile, *Constitutional Amending Process,* 23–78. The procedural core of Article 5 reads as follows:

> The Congress, whenever two thirds of both Houses shall deem it necessary, shall propose Amendments to this Constitution, or, on the Application of the Legislatures of two thirds of the several States, shall call a Convention for proposing Amendments, which, in either Case, shall be valid to all Intents and Purposes, as part of this Constitution, when ratified by the Legislatures of three fourths of the several States, or by Conventions in three fourths thereof, as the one or the other Mode of Ratification may be proposed by the Congress.

Despite its seeming clarity, Article 5 continues to inspired heated debate. See Akhil Reed Amar, "Popular Sovereignty and Constitutional Amendment"; as well as Walter F. Murphy, "Merlin's Memory: The Past and Future Imperfect of the Once and Future Polity," both in Levinson, *Responding to Imperfection,* 89–116, 163–90.

29. Bruce Ackerman, *We the People: Foundations* (Cambridge: Harvard University Press, 1991), 6. Ackerman's views have generated a wide-ranging debate that, unfortunately, I cannot discuss here. See especially Andrew Arato, *Civil Society, Constitution, and Legitimacy* (Lanham, Md.: Rowman & Littlefield, 2000); also see the special issue of *Ethics* 104 (1994) devoted to Ackerman's work. For now let me just say that I find the outlines of Ackerman's model of constitutional dualism appealing, especially his insight that there are "important reasons why constitutional politics can and therefore should involve a wider and more democratic form of participation than normal politics" (Arato, *Civil Society, Constitution, and Legitimacy,* 134; more generally, 135–38). Nonetheless, there are many reasons for criticizing Ackerman's own defense of the manner in which constitutional dualism in the United States has taken unexpected institutional paths. We need to separate Ackerman's core intuitions about constitutional dualism from the particular form it has taken in the United States. The latter has been more problematic than Ackerman generally concedes. Like Arato, I am more skeptical than Ackerman of constitutional adaptation "outside of legality," and my discussion presupposes a normatively and institutionally more appreciative view of legal paths to constitutional change (xiv).

30. Ackerman, *We the People: Foundations,* 9.

31. David R. Dow, "The Plain Meaning of Article V," in *Responding to Imperfection: The Theory and Practice of Constitutional Amendment,* 128; also see Donald S. Lutz, "Toward a Constitutional Amendment," 239. The inflexibility of Article 5 in part derives from the fact that the U.S. founders may have been closer to Locke's notion of an "unalterable" constitution than many modern commentators acknowledge. Michael Hamburger has argued plausibly that the founders were deeply hostile to constitutional change, tending to envision Article 5 as a device for completing or perfecting what they conceived as a fundamentally timeless doctrine. By no means did they picture Article 5 as an instrument for adapting the constitution to social and economic change ("Constitutions's Accommodation of Social Change," 301).

32. Recall Madison's claim that in a large republic "communication is always checked" (or *slowed down*), which contributes to the reasonable character of popular deliberation. Excessive speed in popular debate, it seems, is not conducive to well-considered outcomes. Publius [Madison], *Federalist Papers* (Federalist 10), 83.

33. See the discussion of traditional liberal democratic theory in chapter 2. Of course, the U.S. founders were influenced by many of the ideas described there.

34. Article 5 allows as few as thirteen of ninety-nine state legislative bodies to defeat the ratification of a proposed amendment, and "the requirement for such extraordinary majorities means that, in the case of structural amendments, any significant political bloc possesses an effective veto" (Sundquist, *Constitutional Reform and Effective Government* [Washington, D.C.: Brookings Institution, 1992], 17). For an empirical discussion of Article 5, see Lutz, "Toward a Theory of Constitutional Amendment," in Levinson, *Responding to Imperfection*, 237. Only the Russian amendment procedures may be more toilsome than those in the United States. For a useful collection of new East European constitutional clauses concerning amendment, see the "Appendix: Amending Provisions of Selected New Constitutions in Eastern Europe," in Levinson, *Responding to Imperfection*, 319–23. With the Russian exception, most new amendment rules avoid the U.S. and Australian models.

35. This is a theme of many of the essays collected in ibid. The rigidity of Article 5 was anticipated by some of the Anti-Federalists (Federal Farmer, "Letter IV," in *The Anti-Federalist: Writings by Opponents of the Constitution*, ed. Herbert J. Storing [Chicago: University of Chicago Press, 1981], 59–60).

36. Beyond Madison's hope that a large republic would "check" (or decelerate) mass debate, recall Locke's famous discussion of the "dissolution of government" in the "Second Treatise," in which he suggests that revolutionary politics is only well considered after a tyrannized people has patiently tolerated a "long train of abuses." Patience and even procrastination are essential preconditions of reasonable popular deliberation (in *Two Treatises of Government*, ed. D. Wootton, 375 [para. 223]).

37. See Levinson, *Responding to Imperfection*. The most important amendments (13–15) were approved during the Reconstruction period and were forced upon the southern states by northern bayonets and rifles.

38. Cited in Kyvig, *Explicit and Authentic Acts*, 306. Kyvig suggests that the New Deal failure to gain formal constitutional status may be one of the reasons for its fragility in recent decades.

39. On some matters the Australian Constitution requires unanimous agreement by all six states. See Lutz, "Towards a Theory of Constitutional Amendment," in Levinson, *Responding to Imperfection*, 266.

40. Griffin notes that "constitutional scholars have become increasingly aware of the importance of developing a theory of constitutional change" (*American Constitutionalism*, 10). A revealing illustration of the pervasive skepticism toward formal amendment found among contemporary (especially left-liberal) legal scholars is an article by Morton Horwitz on constitutional change in one of the nation's premier legal reviews, in which formal amendment is ignored altogether ("Constitution of Change").

41. The distinction between constitutional interpretation and constitutional alteration introduced here might be taken as one way by which we might plausibly delineate law (interpretation) from politics (alteration).

42. For examples, see Lipkin, "Anatomy of Constitutional Revolutions," 734–39. Also see Stephen M. Griffin, *American Constitutionalism*, 9–58. Creative reinterpretation of constitutional norms has played a decisive role, to a far greater extent than Article 5, in many if not most of the major legal and constitutional transformations of the U.S. system in the last century (the guarantee of civil rights to racial minorities, the rise of the welfare state, and the transformation of the United States from a regional into a world power).

43. Benjamin N. Cardozo, *The Nature of the Judicial Process* (New Haven: Yale University Press, 1921), 28.

44. Ibid., 161. Jerome Frank similarly observed that "we have practically insisted on a flexible construction of its words to permit the legalization of social changes which were never contemplated by our forefathers who drafted and adopted the sacred instrument" of the U.S. Constitution (*Law and the Modern Mind* [New York: Doubleday, 1963 (1930), 324]). There are reasons for suspecting that the U.S. founders would have been skeptical of the trend toward court-based constitutional adaptation via flexible exegesis. See Raoul Berger, *Government by Judiciary: The Transformation of the Fourteenth Amendment* (Cambridge: Harvard University Press, 1977), 363–64, 377–80. Those who believe that the contemporary United States should pay homage to the founders on this point fail to explain how we can adequately calibrate constitutional law to the imperatives of high-speed social change.

45. Bryce, *Constitutions*, 73. Bryce's insight about the relationship between flexible constitutional interpretation and rigid amendment procedures is empirically supported by Donald Lutz, "Towards a Theory of Constitutional Amendment," 237–74.

46. Brian Bix, *Jurisprudence: Theory and Context*, 2d ed. (London: Sweet & Maxwell, 1999), 86.

47. See Hamburger, " Constitution's Accommodation of Social Change."

48. Louis Henkin and Albert J. Rosenthal, *Constitutionalism and Rights: The Influence of the United States Constitution Abroad* (New York: Columbia University Press, 1990).

49. In this vein, see Kay, "Constitutional Chrononomy," 44–47.

50. Ackerman, *We the People: Transformations* (Cambridge: Harvard University Press, 1998), 406.

51. Woodrow Wilson, cited in Hannah Arendt, *On Revolution* (New York: Penguin, 1963), 200. Arendt seems to have been enamored of this ambivalent model of constitutional change.

52. In Ackerman's terminology this model of constitutional change represents the paradigmatic case of "constitutional monism," for which the "British design captures the essence of democracy" (*We the People: Foundations*, 8).

53. Bryce, *Constitutions*, x.

54. Stephen Holmes and Cass R. Sunstein, "The Politics of Constitutional Revision in Eastern Europe," in Levinson, *Responding to Imperfection*, 285.

55. Ibid., 295.

56. Publius [Hamilton], *Federalist Papers* (Federalist 70), 426–27.

57. For example, see Andras Sajo's comments on contemporary Hungary (*Limiting Government: An Introduction to Constitutionalism* [New York: Central European University Press, 1999], 39–40).

58. Bryce, *Constitutions*, 13, 22.

59. Ibid., 31.
60. Ibid., 18, 35.
61. Ibid., 45–36.
62. Holmes and Sunstein speak vaguely (and unconvincingly) of the "salutary filtering effect of elected representatives." See "Politics of Constitutional Revision in Eastern Europe," 298.
63. Arendt, *On Revolution*, 163. Here I am interested in executive-dominated constitutional change within the context of functioning liberal democracies. Of course, in dictatorships this is common practice, as Pakistan's authoritarian leader, General Pervez Musharraf, recently reminded the world when he unilaterally tore up the existing Pakistan Constitution in favor of a new one that vastly augmented his power. Appearing at a news conference, General Musharraf proudly announced that parliament would have no power to overrule his changes, including dramatic reductions in its authority: "This is part of the Constitution," he told the assembled journalists. "I am hereby making it part of the Constitution" (qtd. in David Rohde, "Musharraf Redraws Constitution, Blocking Promise of Democracy," *New York Times*, Aug. 22, 2002, A1).
64. Otto Kirchheimer, "Constitutional Reaction in 1932," in *Politics, Law, and Social Change: Selected Essays of Otto Kirchheimer*, ed. Frederic S. Burin and Kurt Shell (New York: Columbia University Press), 88–109.
65. In this vein, see Bruce Ackerman and David Golove, *Is NAFTA Constitutional?* (Cambridge: Harvard University Press, 1995); Griffin, *American Constitutionalism*, 82; Koh, *National Security Constitution*, esp. 93–98; Silverstein, *Imbalance of Powers*.
66. For a political contemporary's subtle analysis of this shift, see Kirchheimer, "France From Fourth to the Fifth Republic," in Burin and Shell, *Politics, Law, and Social Change*, 197–211.
67. Putin has reportedly toyed with the idea of "a draft law on the Constitutional Assembly that, if enacted, would allow the executive branch to change the constitution virtually at whim" (Sergei Kovalev, "The Putin Put-On," *New York Review of Books*, Aug. 9, 2001, 29–30).
68. Kirchheimer, "Constitutional Reaction in 1932," in Burin and Shell, *Politics, Law, and Social Change*, 78. Schmitt's main arguments on executive-based constitutional change are found in his *Der Hüter der Verfassung* (Tübingen: Mohr, 1931); *Legalität und Legitimität* (Berlin: Duncker & Humblot, 1932).
69. For the sordid details, see Scheuerman, *Carl Schmitt*, 85–180.
70. This is one of the more familiar reasons for the privileged legislative status of elected representative bodies vis-à-vis the executive in traditional liberal democratic theory.
71. Arato, *Civil Society, Constitution, and Legitimacy*, 235.
72. Publius [Hamilton], *Federalist Papers* (Federalist 70), 424.
73. "Speed is of the essence, administration officials say [in justifying a broad range of unilateral executive actions], arguing that even a wartime Congress would not move fast enough to help the authorities counter new terrorism threats" (Robert Toner and Niel A. Lewis, "White House Push on Security Steps Bypass Congress: New Executive Orders—Administration Urges Speed in Terror Fight, but Some See Constitutional Concern," *New York Times*, Nov. 15, 2001, A1).
74. Cited in Koh, *National Security Constitution*, 119. The case is *United States v. Curtiss-Wright Export Co.* (299 U.S. 304 [1936]), which helped redefine the constitu-

tional structure of U.S. foreign policy making. Of course, this example reminds us that executive-based constitutional change is oftentimes assisted by other institutions (in this case the courts). My typology of constitutional change tends to minimize the empirical complexity of most cases of constitutional change. Nonetheless, traditional temporal presuppositions about executive power justified the court's support for heightened executive discretion in foreign affairs. The same notion of an energetic rapid-fire executive paved the way for vast executive discretion in international economic policy. As Ackerman and Golove note, New Dealers helped provide the U.S. president with heightened authority over foreign trade by arguing that the "country's chief rivals were constitutionally equipped for rapid action. Their chief executives could act promptly . . . It followed that Congress must empower the executive branch to move decisively to make the most of the nation's economic opportunities" (*Is NAFTA Constitutional?* 48).

75. In describing the origins of the French Fifth Republic, Kirchheimer nicely captures the political imagery typically employed by executives as they undertake constitutional reform during moments of crisis. Describing the self-understanding of de Gaulle and his supporters, Kirchheimer notes that the president is to function "as guarantor of the whole national establishment. He is cast in the role of *deus ex machine*, the demiurge, removed from the daily strife of factions, who by some intermittent but well-aimed strokes puts the world in order" (Kirchheimer, "France from Fourth to Fifth Republic," 221). The contrast between the dynamic executive and slow-going legislature has repeatedly played a central role during moments of executive-based constitutional alteration.

76. Publius [Hamilton], *Federalist Papers* (Federalist 70), 427–29.

77. Think, for example, of the countless cases of prime ministers or presidents successfully linking ministers or members of the cabinet to unpopular policies in order to minimize political costs, before proceeding to replace them.

78. See Eriksen, *Tyrannny of the Moment*, 144.

79. Andrew Arato, "The New Democracies and American Constitutional Design," *Constellations* 7 (2000): 319.

80. Ackerman, *We the People: Transformations*, 410–14.

81. Until recently, Ackerman seemed to favor exporting U.S model of executive-led constitutional change (*The Future of Liberal Revolution* [New Haven: Yale University Press, 1992]). A more recent publication suggests that he is now revising that view (Ackerman, "The New Separation of Powers," *Harvard Law Review* 113 [2000]: 634–729).

82. For a critical discussion of Ackerman in this spirit, see Arato, "New Democracies and American Constitutional Design," 325. Arato worries about the dangers of U.S.-style presidentialism in Eastern Europe. One might also recall many unsuccessful borrowings from the United States by failed Latin and South American regimes. For a survey of the lively debate about presidentialism, see Lijpjart, *Parliamentary versus Presidential Government.*

83. Sanford Levinson, "Designing an Amendment Procedure," in *Constitutional Culture and Democratic Rule,* ed. John Ferejohn, Jack N. Rakove, and Jonathan Riley (Cambridge: Cambridge University Press, 2001), 284.

84. Lutz, "Toward a Theory of Constitutional Amendment," 265.

85. Arato, "New Democracies and American Constitutional Design," 324.

86. Ibid., 334–35.

87. For an account highlighting the sluggishness and inefficiency of Nazi dictatorship, see Franz L. Neumann, *Behemoth: The Structure and Practice of National Socialism, 1933–44* (New York: Harper & Row, 1944).

88. King and Ragsdale, *Elusive Executive.*

89. See chapter 2, note 44.

90. Theodore K. Rabb, *The Struggle for Stability in Early Modern Europe* (Oxford: Oxford University Press, 1975).

91. Held, *Democracy and the Global Order*, 73–120.

92. I take this to be close to John Dewey's point when he concludes his brief discussion of the impact of the "mania for motion and speed" (*Public and Its Problems*, 142).

93. Ian Budge, *The New Challenge of Direct Democracy* (Cambridge, UK: Polity Press, 1996), 24. In the concluding chapter I say more about the proper role of new technologies in revitalizing democracy.

94. Barber, "Three Scenarios," 585.

95. Budge, *New Challenge of Direct Democracy*, 1.

96. Barber, "Three Scenarios," 584.

F O U R : The Motorization of Lawmaking

1. Carl Schmitt, *Die Lage der europäischen Rechtswissenschaft* (*The Situation of European Jurisprudence*), 18. All translations are the author's own.

2. Ibid., 20.

3. Most recent scholarship neglects the phenomenon of emergency economic authority. Even the most important recent studies of emergency powers barely mention their use as a tool of economic regulation (Daniel P. Franklin, *Extraordinary Measures: The Exercise of Prerogative Powers in the United States* [Pittsburgh: University of Pittsburgh Press, 1991]; John M. Carey and Matthew S. Shugart, eds., *Executive Decree Authority* [Cambridge: Cambridge University Press, 1998], 254–73), in stark contrast to earlier works (see Clinton Rossiter, *Constitutional Dictatorship: Crisis Government in the Modern Democracies;* and Winifried Dallmayr and Robert S. Rankin, *Freedom and Emergency Powers in the Cold War* [New York: Appleton-Century-Croft, 1964]).

4. Rossiter, *Constitutional Dictatorship*, 29–61, 91–103, 151–83, 240–65.

5. See Roosevelt's 1933 inaugural address, cited in *Brief History of Emergency Powers in the United States*, 55–56. "The tangible merits of the Hundred Days were a group of emergency statutes delegating the President unprecedented power to wage war on the economic front. Taken as a whole, the dozen or so important statutes enacted in the special session constitute the largest instance of delegated power in American history" (Rossiter, *Constitutional Dictatorship*, 260).

6. Otto Kirchheimer, "Decree Powers and Constitutional Law in France under the Third Republic" in Burin and Shell, *Politics, Law, and Social Change*, 130.

7. *Brief History of Emergency Powers in the United States*, 87–118.

8. Joel B. Harris and Jeffrey P. Bialos, "The Strange New World of United States Export Controls under the International Emergency Economic Powers Act," *Vanderbilt Journal of Transnational Law* 18 (1985): 71–108; Harold H. Koh, "Why the President

(Almost) Always Wins in Foreign Affairs: Lessons of the Iran-Contra Affair," *Yale Law Journal* 97 (1988): 1263–65.

9. See Carey and Shugart, *Executive Decree Authority.*

10. The first example refers to a 1971 presidential proclamation (*Summary of Emergency Power Statutes: A Working Paper Prepared by the Staff of the Special Committee on the Termination of the National Emergency, United States Senate* [Washington, D.C.: U.S. Government Printing Office, 1973], 74); the latter refers to a 1970 enabling law passed by the Congress (cited in Joel L. Fleishman and Arthur H. Auses, "Law and Orders: The Problem of Presidential Legislation," *Law and Contemporary Problems* 40 [1976]: 26–27).

11. On "conservative" economic policies pursued in the interwar years by means of emergency authority, see Rossiter, *Constitutional Dictatorship*, 51–53 (in Germany), 122–24 (France), 179 (Britain). On the role of emergency laws in postwar social democracy, see Francis Sejersted, "From Liberal Constitutionalism to Corporate Pluralism: The Conflict over the Enabling Acts in Norway after the Second World War and the Subsequent Constitutional Development," in *Constitutionalism and Democracy*, ed. Jon Elster and Rune Slagstad (Cambridge: Cambridge University Press, 1989), 275–303.

12. Friedrich A. Hayek, *The Road to Serfdom* (Chicago: University of Chicago Press, 1944), 63–96.

13. This is an important theme in Franz L. Neumann's account of the decline of traditional forms of liberal legislation ("Change in the Function of Law in Modern Society," 122–32). Some evidence for it can be located in the accounts provided by Scott Parish, "Presidential Decree Authority in Russia, 1991–1995," 72–73, 88, 99; Gregory Schmidt, "Presidential Usurpation or Congressional Preference? The Evolution of Executive Decree Authority in Peru," 124, both in Carey and Shugart, *Executive Decree Authority.*

14. On Italy, see Vincent Della Sala and Annie Kreppel, "Dancing without a Lead: Legislative Decrees in Italy"; on France, see John D. Huber, "Executive Decree Authority in France," both in Carey and Shugart, *Executive Decree Authority*, 175–96, 233–53.

15. An influential version of the former was advanced by Hayek; of the latter, by the Frankfurt School jurists Otto Kirchheimer and Franz. L. Neumann as well as their interlocutor, Ernst Fraenkel.

16. See the many examples collected in a report put together by the attorney general of the United States in 1918, J. Reuben Clark Jr., *Emergency Legislation Passed prior to December, 1917 Dealing with the Control and Taking of Private Property for the Public Use, Benefit, or Welfare* (Washington, D.C.: U.S. Government Printing Office, 1918).

17. *Brief History of Emergency Powers in the United States*, 1–40; George M. Dennison, "Martial Law: The Development of a Theory of Emergency Powers, 1776–1861," *American Journal of Legal History* 18 (1974): 52–79.

18. On the European context, see Hans Boldt, "Ausnahmezustand," in *Geschichtliche Grundbegriffe*, ed. Otto Brunner, Werner Conze, and Reinhart Koselleck (Stuttgart: Klett, 1972), 355–56, 369, 373.

19. Karl Marx, *The Eighteenth Brumaire of Louis Bonaparte* (New York: International Press, 1963), 30, 34–35.

20. Charles Fairman, "Martial Law in the Light of *Sterling V. Constantin*," *Cornell Law Quarterly* 19 (1934): 29.

21. Ernst Fraenkel, "'Martial Law' und Staatsnotstand in England und USA," in Fraenkel, *Der Staatsnotstand*, 154–64. Martial law was employed against the labor movement in the United States well after the end of World War II. See Dallmayr and Rankin, *Freedom and Emergency Powers in the Cold War*, 172–87.

22. On the New Deal and its ideological ties to the experience of economic planning in World War I, see Michael S. Sherry, *In the Shadow of War: The United States since the 1930s* (New Haven: Yale University Press, 1993), 19–20.

23. This does not mean that emergency economic regulation exclusively reproduces the class-disciplinary character of emergency power as an instrument of class domination.

24. Rossiter, *Constitutional Dictatorship*, 172–74.

25. Ibid., 45–49, 120–21.

26. For example, Roosevelt's emergency banking regulations of 1933 were passed under the rubric of the Trading with the Enemy Act.

27. Sherry, *In the Shadow of War*, 15–63. Use of martial law against the labor movement was often justified in the United States with reference to the "foreign" or "alien" character of labor radicalism. In many liberal democracies, of course, rule of law standards have typically been relaxed in the spheres of foreign policy.

28. On the U.S. case, see *Brief History of Emergency Powers in the United States*, 87, 90–91, 106–7.

29. Dallmayr and Rankin, *Freedom and Emergency Powers in the Cold War*.

30. Sejersted, "From Liberal Constitutionalism to Corporate Pluralism," 298. In a similar vein, the Constitutional Council in France has played an important role in restraining executive decree authority. See Huber, "Executive Decree Authority in France," 241. Many other examples can be identified as well.

31. Church and Matthias, "Foreword," *Brief History of Emergency Powers in the United States*, vi.

32. Lobel, "Emergency Power and the Decline of Liberalism," 1412–21. Also see Oren Gross, "Chaos and Rules: Should Response to Violent Crises Always Be Constitutional?" *Yale Law Journal* 112 (2003): 1014–1134. The constitutional issues are complex. It is telling, however, that legal scholars question the long-term impact on postwar practice of the landmark case of *Youngstown Sheet & Tube v. Sawyer*, 343 U.S. 579 (1952), in which presidential emergency economic power was directly challenged by the Supreme Court. See Neal Devins and Louis Fisher, "The Steel Seizure Case: One of a Kind?" *Constitutional Commentary* 19 (2002): 75–83.

33. O'Donnell, "Delegative Democracy," 63.

34. On the weaknesses of Russian courts, see Parish, "Presidential Decree Authority in Russia," 81, 91–95; on weak courts in Argentina, see Delia Ferreira Rubio and Mattheo Goretti, "When the President Governs Alone: The *Decretazo* in Argentina, 1989–93," 55–56; in Peru, see Schmidt, "Presidential Usurpation or Congressional Preference?" 130–31; in Venezuela, see Brian F. Crisp, "Presidential Decree Authority in Venezuela," 142–74, all in Carey and Shugart, *Executive Decree Authority*.

35. Catherine Conaghan, James Malloy, and Luis Abugattas, "Business and the 'Boys': The Politics of Neoliberalism in the Central Andes," *Latin American Research Review* 25 (1990): 3–29; Adam Przeworski, *Democracy and the Market: Political and Economic Reforms in Eastern Europe and Latin America* (Cambridge: Cambridge University Press, 1991), 183–87.

36. Renato Cristi, *Carl Schmitt and Authoritarian Liberalism* (Cardiff: University of Wales Press, 1998); John P. McCormick, "The Dilemmas of Dictatorship: Carl Schmitt and Constitutional Emergency Powers," in *Law as Politics: Carl Schmitt's Critique of Liberalism,* ed. David Dyzenhaus (Durham, N.C.: Duke University Press, 1998), 217–51.

37. The pervasiveness of emergency economic power is described in Carl Schmitt, "Vergleichender überblick über die neueste Entwicklung des Problems der gesetzgeberischen Ermächtigungen; 'Legislative Delegationen,'" in *Positionen und Begriffe im Kampf mit Weimar-Genf-Versailles* (Positions and Concepts in the Struggle with Weimar-Genf-Versailles) (Hamburg: Hanseatische Verlagsanstalt, 1940), 214; *Die Lage der europäischen Rechtswissenschaft,* 18–21. At least some of the latter work seems to have been conceived and even written before 1944.

38. Carl Schmitt, *Der Hüter der Verfassung* (*Guardian of the Constitution*) (Tübingen: Mohr, 1931), 131.

39. Schmitt, "Vergleichender überblick über die neueste Entwicklung," 212, 224–25. Schmitt's *Der Hüter der Verfassung* is also critical of attempts to tame Weimar's crisis by judicial means.

40. This element of Schmitt's argument is expertly explicated in David Dyzenhaus, *Legality and Legitimacy: Carl Schmitt, Hans Kelsen and Hermann Heller in Weimar* (Oxford: Oxford University Press, 1997), 58–70.

41. Schmitt, *Der Hüter der Verfassung,* 63; also see Carl Schmitt, *Die Verfassungslehre* (Munich: Duncker & Humblot, 1928), 143–57.

42. Schmitt, *Die Lage der europäischen Rechtswissenschaft,* 15.

43. Ibid., 14–18. This is another reason why Schmitt opts for the expression *motorization.* The term is meant to capture not only the accelerated character of present-day legislation but also its "mechanical" (or "value-free") contours, resulting from the (alleged) influence of legal positivism.

44. Carl Schmitt, *The Crisis of Parliamentary Democracy,* trans. Ellen Kennedy (Cambridge, Mass.: MIT Press, 1985). Alas, history rarely comports with the conceptual underpinnings of political or legal theory.

45. Schmitt, *Der Hüter der Verfassung,* 81, 127.

46. Carl Schmitt, "Die Rechtswissenschaft im Führerstaat," *Zeitschrift der Akademie für Deutsches Recht* 7 (1935): 438–39.

47. Ibid., 439; Schmitt, "Vergleichender überblick über die neueste Entwicklung," 219–20.

48. Schmitt, "Die Rechtswissenschaft im Führerstaat," 439–40; also see Schmitt, "Vergleichender überblick über die neueste Entwicklung," 227, in which the Nazis are praised for moving beyond the inconsistencies of twentieth-century liberal democracy.

49. Schmitt, "Die Rechtswissenschaft im Führerstaat," 439.

50. Frederick Schauer, "Legal Formalism," *Yale Law Review* 97 (1988): 542. Also see Alan Watson, *Society and Legal Change,* 2d ed. (Philadelphia: Temple University Press, 2001).

51. On the American case, see Lawrence M. Friedman, *The History of American Law,* 2d ed. (New York: Simon & Schuster, 1985), 177–78, 192–93.

52. Schmitt, *Die Lage der europäischen Rechtswissenschaft,* 18–21.

53. Ibid., 14–18, 30.

54. Ibid., 20.

55. Harvey, *Justice, Nature and the Geography of Difference,* 240–41.

56. Harvey, *Condition of Postmodernity,* 240.

57. Ibid., 157.

58. Gross, "Normless and Exceptionless Exception," 1827.

59. More will be said about this matter in chapter 5, in which I examine globalization.

60. George Kateb, *The Inner Ocean: Individualism and Democratic Culture* (Ithaca, N.Y.: Cornell University Press, 1992), 22.

61. Jules Lobel, "Emergency Power and the Decline of Liberalism"; Gross, "Normless and Exceptionless Exception," 1853–68. In his analysis at midcentury on the general trend toward the "garrison state," Harold Lasswell observed that legislatures would tend to "go out of use" in the context of the perpetual preparation for war that characterizes contemporary political life (*Essays on the Garrison State* [New Brunswick, N.J.: Transaction, 1997, 65). Also see Edward S. Corwin, *Total War and the Constitution* (New York: Knopf, 1947). The Bush Administration's interpretation of the heinous terrorist attacks of September 11, 2001, as an act of war has opened the door to a vast expansion of executive prerogative (Andrew Arato, "The Bush Tribunals and the Specter of Dictatorship," *Constellations* 9 [2002]: 450–76; Michael Stokes Paulsen, "*Youngstown* Goes to War," *Constitutional Commentary* 19 [2002]: 250–53).

62. Virilio, *Speed and Politics,* 139.

63. High-speed air warfare was seen by Schmitt as playing a crucial role in a "spatial revolution" (*Raumrevolution*), according to which traditional nation-state borders are rendered porous. See Schmitt, "Die Raumrevolution," *Das Reich,* September 29, 1940, 3; "Reich und Raum. Elemente eines neuen Völkerrechts," *Zeitschrift der Akademie für Deutsches Recht* 7 (1940): 201–2; "Das Meer gegen das Land," *Das Reich,* March 9, 1941, 17–18; "Raum and Grossraum im Völkerrecht," *Zeitschrift für Völkerrecht* 24 (1941): 145–49. On the demise of traditional state structures, see Schmitt, "Staat als konkreter, an eine geschichtliche Epoche gebundener Begriff" (1941), in *Verfassungsrechtliche Aufsätze aus den Jahren, 1924–1954* (Berlin: Duncker & Humblot, 1973), 375–85. Schmitt's ideas about the impact of high-speed forms of weapons technology (in particular, air warfare) on the nation-state probably influenced the fascinating study by John Herz, *The Nation-State and the Crisis of World Politics* (New York: McKay, 1976), which salvages plausible facets of Schmitt's observations while cleansing them of the heinous purposes for which Schmitt used them.

64. Grant Gilmore, "Putting Senator Davies in Context," *Vermont Law Review* 4 (1979): 239. It would be useful to have more "hard" data demonstrating the existence of accelerated lawmaking. Such data are hard to find, in part because they are difficult to quantify (e.g., legal obsolescence). A substantial legal literature, however, documents many of the empirical trends described here. For a discussion of accelerated statute making in recent tax law, for example, see Richard L. Doernberg and Fred S. McChesney, "On the Accelerating Rate and Decreasing Durability of Tax Reform," *Minnesota Law Review* 21 (1987): 913–62. Similarly, it would be helpful to know if the institutional adaptations to social acceleration described here in fact successfully speed up decision making or, instead, fail to do so. My expectation is that some of them do succeed at least in terms of allowing for quick state action, whereas others prove unsuccessful. Although this is an important empirical issue calling for systematic scrutiny, just as important for my purposes here is the fact that the institutional

strategies discussed under the rubric of motorized lawmaking (e.g., delegations of legislative power to the executive) rest on traditional assumptions about temporality which continue to influence liberal democratic political practice.

65. Grant Gilmore, *The Ages of American Law* (New Haven: Yale University Press, 1977), 95.

66. Guido Calabresi, *A Common Law for the Age of Statutes* (Cambridge: Harvard University Press, 1982), 5. One of the most prominent jurists of his generation, Calabresi served as dean of the Yale Law School. His widely discussed volume garnered a prestigious prize from the American Bar Association; it may be the most important critical English-language discussion of statutory legislation written in the last twenty years, thus the attention paid to it here. Calabresi is presently a judge on the United States Court of Appeals for the Second Circuit. I am not trying to rekindle the tired game of guilt by association. It is illuminating, however, to rely on Schmitt to underscore potential weaknesses in contemporary jurisprudence, notwithstanding the vast normative and political distance separating Schmitt from the U.S. scholars I discuss.

67. Ibid., 79. Calabresi seems to have coined the term *statutorification*. As we will see in just a moment, Schmitt similarly invents an expression, *Vergesetzlichung*, to capture many of the same trends. Statutorification contains the same negative connotations captured by the German word *Vergesetzlichung*, which suggests to the native German speaker that statutory legislation now takes a distorted and even perverse form, and thus I will translate Schmitt's term *Vergesetzliching* as identical with *statutorification*.

68. Ibid., 73; more generally, 72–77, 133.

69. Ibid., 163.

70. Of course, the growth of statutory legislation predates the twentieth century (David Lieberman, *The Province of Legislation Determined: Legal Theory in Eighteenth-Century Britain* [Cambridge: Cambridge University Press, 1989]). Nonetheless, the evidence collected by Calabresi, Gilmore, and others suggests that, first, this growth has been particularly dramatic in the twentieth century and, second, it has indeed oftentimes been tied to the experience of political or economic "crisis," real or otherwise. See also Jack Davies, "A Response to Statutory Obsolescence: The Nonprimacy of Statutes Act," *Vermont Law Review* 4 (1979): 209–12.

71. Luhmann, *Rechtssoziologie*, 190–226, 294–353. Schmitt also describes the decay of customary law as a precondition of legislative motorization (*Die Lage der europäischen Rechtswissenschaft*, 14–18).

72. Gerald Postema, *Bentham and the Common Law Tradition* (Oxford: Clarendon Press, 986), 4.

73. Karl N. Llewellyn, *The Common Law Tradition* (Boston: Little, Brown, 1960). One of the ways by which the common law has adapted to contemporary temporal necessities is by embracing an unabashedly creative and prospective orientation.

74. Marx, "Communist Manifesto," 469.

75. Roscoe Pound, "Common Law and Legislation," *Harvard Law Review* 21, no. 6 (1908): 404. Pound also pointed to growing evidence for the "excessive output of legislation in all our jurisdictions" (383).

76. Cardozo, *Nature of the Judicial Process*, 28.

77. Schmitt, *Die Lage der europäischen Rechtswissenschaft*, 14, in which he describes

nineteenth-century attacks on natural law and the rise of legal positivism. Although worried that the decay of natural law prepares the way for motorized legislation, he seems to consider that decay irreversible.

78. Luhmann, *Rechtssoziologie*, 216.

79. Max Weber, *Max Weber on Law in Economy and Society*, trans. Max Rheinstein (New York: Simon & Schuster, 1967), 5, 298, 350.

80. Ibid., 298.

81. Luhmann, *Rechtssoziologie*, 209.

82. Schmitt, *Die Lage der europäischen Rechtswissenschaft*, 28.

83. Cited in John Dinwiddy, *Bentham* (New York: Oxford University Press, 1989), 58.

84. Calabresi, *Common Law for the Age of Statutes*, 2, 133.

85. Grant Gilmore, "On Statutory Obsolescence," *Colorado Law Review* 39 (1967): 472. Cass Sunstein argues that open-ended terms (*feasible*, e.g., or *public policy*) in statutes means that "Congress has invited interpretation over time" in order to circumvent the specter of statutory obsolescence (*After the Rights Revolution*, 178). On the proliferation of open-ended law as a consequence of the altered temporal preconditions of statutory activity, see Erhard Denninger, *Der gebändigte Leviathan* (Baden-Baden: Nomos, 1990), 36–38.

86. As T. Alexander Aleinikoff suggests, the U.S. Supreme Court ruling in *Chevron, USA, Inc. v. NRDC* (467 U.S. 865–66 [1984]) may legitimize this approach ("Updating Statutory Interpretation," *Michigan Law Review* 87 [1988]: 42–45).

87. Calabresi, *Common Law for the Age of Statutes*, 44–58.

88. John Locke, "Fundamental Constitutions for Carolina," 226.

89. Calabresi, *Common Law for the Age of Statutes*; Gilmore, "On Statutory Interpretation"; Werner Hugger, "Legislative Effektivitätssteigerung. Von den Grenzen der Gesetzesevaluierbarkeit zum Gesetz auf Zeit," *Politische Vierteljahresschrift* 20 (1979): 202–20; Harald Kindermann, "Erfolgskontrolle durch Zeitgesetz," in *Rationalisierung der Gesetzgebung*, ed. Heinz Schaeffer and Otto Triffterer (Baden-Baden: Nomos, 1982), 133–50.

90. Calabresi, *Common Law for the Age of Statutes*, 6–7.

91. William N. Eskridge, "Dynamic Statutory Interpretation," *University of Pennsylvania Law Review* 135 (1987): 1479.

92. This is a central concern of Schmitt's *Die Lage der europäischen Rechtswissenschaft*.

93. Ibid., 20, in which he bluntly announces the "impossibility" of the judiciary accelerating its activities while maintaining its proper professional identity.

94. Richard Posner (*The Federal Courts* [Cambridge: Harvard University Press, 1996], 124–89) provides a survey of research suggesting that an increased federal caseload works to accelerate numerous facets of judicial decision making.

95. Ibid., 185.

96. Schmitt, *Die Lage der europäischen Rechtswissenschaft*, 21, 24.

97. Ibid., 25. Schmitt's discussion revolves around Savigny's celebrated attack on statutory legislation and legal codes, *Vom Beruf unser Zeit für Gesetzgebung und Rechtswissenschaft* (Freiburg: Akademische Verlagsbuchhandlkung, 1892 [1814]).

98. Schmitt, *Die Lage der europäischen Rechtswissenschaft*, 22.

99. This emphasis on the importance of legal professionals for constructing an alternative to the liberal democratic legal status quo runs like a red thread through

much of Schmitt's jurisprudence. See Scheuerman, *Carl Schmitt*, 15–39, 113–40. An adequate discussion of the relationship between Schmitt's Nazi era vision of an identifiably German "legal estate" and his preference in the postwar *Situation of European Jurisprudence* for a revitalized mode of customary law takes us beyond the scope of this study. Some of the argumentative connections, however, should already be clear. Schmitt worried that economic emergency powers necessarily overburdened (and disfigured) liberal democratic courts. The *Situation of European Jurisprudence* might be interpreted as part of an attempt to develop a vision of a postliberal judiciary suited to contemporary regulatory needs yet able to preserve traditional legal virtues.

100. Schmitt, *Die Lage der europäischen Rechtswissenschaft*, 25.

101. Wolfgang Friedmann, *Legal Theory* (New York: Columbia University Press, 1967), 209. See also James Q. Whitman, *The Legacy of Roman Law in the German Romantic Era: Historical Vision and Legal Change* (Princeton: Princeton University Press, 1990), 108–10. The relevant passages from Savigny are in *Vom Beruf unser Zeit für Gesetzgebung und Rechtswissenschaft*, 7–8. Schmitt neglects this facet of Savigny.

102. Schmitt uses the English term *due process*, describing it as an "indestructible kernel without which there can be no law" (*Die Lage der europäischen Rechtswissenschaft*, 30). There is a profound irony here: during the Nazi period Schmitt polemicized bitterly against notions of due process.

103. Ibid., 29. There are many echoes in Schmitt's brief reflections on the role of jurists in Western rationalism of Weber's account of the key role played by legal experts in Western law, which Weber also considered a core attribute of occidental rationalism.

104. Ibid., 24; Savigny, *Vom Beruf unser Zeit für Gesetzgebung und Rechtswissenschaft*, 3. The target is legal positivism.

105. Calabresi is the most outspoken member of this camp, but his arguments have been repeated by many others, including Davies and Gilmore. See also Robert C. Berry, "Spirits of the Past—Coping with Old Laws," *University of Florida Law Review* 19 (1966): 24–44. William Blatt has also underscored the revival of traditionalistic (in his terminology "pre-classical") ideas about the law in the work of Calabresi, Gilmore, and other recent scholars interested in the problem of legal obsolescence ("The History of Statutory Legislation," *Cardozo Law Review* 6 [1985]: 839–40).

106. Recall that "pre-20th century common law judges used to conceptualize the law not only as a science but also as a custom . . . to which judges had better access than legislators." Jurists commonly argued that "courts were democratic bodies . . . because they incorporated into law the law those customs that prevailed in society" (William D. Popkin, *Materials on Legislation: Political Language and the Political Process* [New York: Foundation Press, 2001], 401). As we will see, Calabresi is deeply indebted to these traditional ideas about the common law. The relationship between common and customary law is a complex matter. Nonetheless, relevant for this discussion is "the enduring idea that the heart of common law is not in specific decisions or in rules distilled from them but in broad notions which are difficult to unify or systematize, but which may be 'woven into the fabric of life'" (Roger Cotterrell, *Politics of Jurisprudence: A Critical Introduction to Legal Philosophy* [Philadelphia: University of Pennsylvania Press, 1990], 24).

107. Calabresi, *Common Law for the Age of Statutes*, 82.

108. Abner J. Mikva, "The Shifting Sands of Legal Topography," *Harvard Law Review* 96 (1982): 539.

109. Calabresi, *Common Law for the Age of Statutes,* 163.

110. Davies, "Response to Statute Obsolescence," 211–12.

111. Calabresi, *Common Law for the Age of Statutes,* 91–119.

112. Schmitt, *Die Lage der europäischen Rechtswissenschaft,* 29.

113. Mikva, "Shifting Sands of Legal Topography," 535.

114. Calabresi, *Common Law for the Age of Statutes,* 95, 163–64. Also see Davies, "Response to Statutory Obsolescence," 209, 222–23.

115. For a classic description of Savigny as a political reactionary, see Hermann Kantorowicz, *Was ist uns Savigny?* (Berlin: Carl Heymann, 1912), 36.

116. Schmitt's own reactionary proclivities make him uninterested in formulating an identifiably democratic justification for customary law. Yet at least he accedes to a sober assessment of the normative and political credentials of judge-centered customary law.

117. Mikva, "Shifting Sands of Legal Topography," 540.

118. Calabresi, *Common Law for the Age of Statutes,* 13.

119. Ibid., 98.

120. On the intellectual background, see Postema, *Bentham and the Common Law Tradition* (Oxford: Clarendon Press, 1986), 3–38. Even those who are sympathetic to the common law often hesitate to underscore its democratic virtues (Friedrich A. Hayek, *The Constitution of Liberty* [Chicago: University of Chicago Press, 1960], 58, 103–17).

121. Cited in Whitman, *Legacy of Roman Law in the German Romantic Era,* 110.

122. Schmitt, *Die Lage der europäischen Rechtswissenschaft,* 24–25.

123. Calabresi, *A Common Law for Statutes,* 98.

124. Ibid., 99–100.

125. See Frank M. Coffin, "The Problem of Obsolete Statutes: A New Role for Courts?" *Yale Law Journal* 91 (1982): 838–39.

126. Calabresi, *Common Law for Statutes,* 240 n. 20.

127. Coffin, "Problem of Obsolete Statutes," 834.

128. The phrase is James Madison's (Publius, *Federalist Papers* [Federalist 10], 59–61).

129. On Schmitt's problematic critique of democratic legislatures, see Scheuerman, *Carl Schmitt,* 39–60. In fairness this strand of antidemocratic thinking remains underdeveloped in the work of Calabresi and other recent U.S. jurists, who are principled liberal democrats. In contrast to Schmitt, they are intent on emphasizing the liberal democratic credentials of their proposals for legislative reform. Yet there are occasional echoes of the long-standing hostility in Western political thought to popularly elected legislatures in their work as well. Calabresi, for example, tends to underscore the superior reasonableness of common law rules and doctrines vis-à-vis majority decisions made by elected legislatures, and he seems overly dismissive of constructive proposals to reform our legislatures (*Common Law for the Age of Statutes,* 59–68, 103).

130. Mikva, "Shifting Sands of Legal Topography," 544.

131. Calabresi, *Common Law for the Age of Statutes,* 75. Calabresi is also right to point out that social dynamism is here to stay, and hence "it is unrealistic to believe that one can turn the clock back" (77).

132. Waldron, *Dignity of Legislation* (Cambridge: Cambridge University Press, 1999),

1–2. This description fits Schmitt, who tends to describe legislatures as dominated by selfish interest groups and privileged social blocs, as well as Calabresi, who claims that the "interplay of interests" in legislative bodies means that legislative-based solutions to statutorification are destined to fail (*Common Law for the Age of Statutes*, 62).

133. Publius [Alexander Hamilton], *Federalist Papers* (Federalist 70), 426–27.

134. For an early defense of sunset legislation, see Lowi, *End of Liberalism*, 309–10.

135. Mikva, "Shifting Sands of Legal Topography," 543.

F I V E : Globalization and the Fate of Law

1. Max Weber, *Economy and Society*, trans. Gunther Roth and Claus Wittich (Berkeley: University of California Press, 1978), 162. For a useful survey of Weber's legal thought, see Anthony Kronman, *Max Weber* (Stanford: Stanford University Press, 1983).

2. Hayek, *Road to Serfdom*.

3. See Unger, *Law in Modern Society*.

4. In this spirit, former U.S. trade representative Charlene Barshefsky recently justified U.S. support for permanent trading rights for China by noting that the rule of law is the "most important aspect" of the U.S. trade agreement with China. "Prosperity, security, and international respect" come from an "economic opening to the world and ultimately development of the Rule of Law" ("U.S. Trade Policy and the Trading System," speech delivered at the Johns Hopkins University School of Advanced International Studies, Washington, D.C., March 2, 2000 [www.chinpntry.gov/speeches/barshefsky0302.htm]). In a similar vein, see Jeffrey Sachs, "Consolidating Capitalism," *Foreign Affairs* 98 (1995): 50–64; as well as more systematic arguments by academics and lawyers, on both the Left and Right: Francis M. Neate, "The SBL [Section of Business Law] and the Rule of Law," *International Business Lawyer* 23 (1995): 344–45; Michael Zürn, "Sovereignty and the Law in a Denationalized World," in *Rules and Networks: The Legal Culture of Global Business Transactions*, ed. Richard P. Appelbaum, William Felstiner, and Volkmar Gessner (Oxford: Hart, 2001), 39–72.

5. On the United States, see Morton Horwitz, *The Transformation of American Law, 1780–1860* (Cambridge: Harvard University Press, 1977); on Britain, see P. S. Atiyah, *The Rise and Fall of Freedom of Contract* (Oxford: Clarendon Press, 1979); on Germany, see Franz Wieacker, *Industriegesellschaft und Privatrechtsordnung* (Kronberg: Scriptor, 1974).

6. I claim no originality here, since theorists of globalization have widely acknowledged the significance of social speed for their endeavors. Perhaps, however, I can add some clarity to an often confusing discussion of the nexus between globalization and speed.

7. Jan Aart Scholte, "Beyond the Buzzword: Towards a Critical Theory of Globalization," in *Globalization: Theory and Practice*, ed. Eleonore Kofman and Gillians Young (London: Pinter, 1996), 45.

8. Jan Aart Scholte, *Globalization: A Critical Introduction* (New York: St. Martin's, 2000).

9. John Tomlinson, *Globalization and Culture* (Cambridge, UK: Polity Press, 1999), 9.

10. David Held, Anthony McGrew, David Goldblatt, and Jonathan Perraton, *Global Transformations: Politics, Economics and Culture* (Stanford: Stanford University Press, 1999), 15.

11. Dewey, *Public and Its Problems*, 140.

12. Harvey, *Condition of Postmodernity*, 147.

13. Ibid., 156; Schoenberger, "Competition, Time, and Space in Industrial Change," 51–66.

14. Harvey, *Condition of Postmodernity*, 171.

15. In other words, the rule of law serves both liberal and democratic purposes. I elaborate on these familiar virtues of the rule of law during the course of my exposition.

16. As we saw in chapter 2, some (especially early modern) political thinkers did come close to defending an overstated legal formalism. I should also note that defenders of the rule of law, despite the hostility to the common law found among some of them, often see its components as inhering, though often in different ways and to varying degrees, in both common law and civil law systems. Common law systems possess functional equivalents (e.g., the notion of a binding precedent) for the more obviously formalistic features of the civil law.

17. On "limited indeterminacy," see Scheuerman, *Carl Schmitt*, 1–14.

18. Judith N. Shklar, *Legalism: Law, Morals, and Political Trials* (Cambridge: Harvard University Press, 1986), 43. At least implicitly, Shklar was responding to writers such as Ronald Dworkin, for whom the failure of the positivist quest to guarantee a strict separation of morality from legality means that a traditional rule-centered model of the law is best replaced by a right-based interpretation in which moral principles play a pivotal role (*Taking Rights Seriously* [Cambridge: Harvard University Press, 1977]; and *A Matter of Principle* [Cambridge: Harvard University Press, 1985]). For her direct critique of Dworkin, see "Political Theory and the Rule of Law," in *Political Thought and Political Thinkers* (Chicago: University of Chicago Press, 1998), 32–36. I think that Shklar was right to be skeptical of this move in Dworkin's theory. It is, of course, possible to defend traditional rule of law virtues without ignoring their ethical qualities.

19. Compare, for example, Joseph Raz, *The Authority of Law* (Oxford: Clarendon Press, 1979), 210–29; and Fuller, *Morality of Law*, 33–94. This is not to deny the point that fundamental jurisprudential differences generate differences in competing models of the rule of law. But for my purposes here such differences are of peripheral significance. Admittedly, the rudimentary model of the rule of law offered here may not satisfy all of its proponents. Most notably, I purposefully ignore Michael Oakeshott's insistence on the need to distinguish between "rules instrumental to achieving various substantive purposes and noninstrumental 'rules of the game' regulating the activities of subjects, no matter what their purposes" (Terry Nardin, *The Philosophy of Michael Oakeshott* [University Park: Penn State University Press, 2001], 197). Oakeshott's definition of the rule of law privileges noninstrumental rules. Contemporary social life requires, however, a vast range of instrumental rules. If we are to shape these rules in a normatively satisfactory manner, we need to pay attention to their formal structure. The basic definition of the rule of law offered here suggests how we can begin to do so.

20. Weber, *Protestant Ethic and the Spirit of Capitalism*, 18–19.

21. Ibid., 181.

22. Ibid., 181.

23. Ibid., 20–21.

24. Weber's formulation here has exercised an enormous impact especially on Continental European legal thought.

25. Weber, *Economy and Society*, 7.

26. David M. Trubek, "Max Weber on Law and the Rise of Capitalism," *Wisconsin Law Review* 3 (1972): 743.

27. This argument is made by Harold J. Berman's provocative *Law and Revolution: The Formation of the Western Legal Tradition* (Cambridge: Harvard University Press, 1983), which criticizes Weber for exaggerating the legal formalism requisite to the flourishing of capitalism. At least to the extent that we both ultimately question the existence of an elective affinity along the lines described by Weber, Berman's argument complements my own here.

28. For Weber essential to the rationalization of Western society is that it drives "magic" from the world while systematically rendering social and natural processes increasingly predictable and calculable in character. Modern capitalism and the rule of law are two interrelated components of this process. Since growing calculability is built into Weber's concept of rationalization, it is hardly surprising that he tends to emphasize—and probably exaggerate—the growing predictability of both its economic and legal manifestations.

29. For accounts of the common law influenced by Weber, see Franz L. Neumann, *The Rule of Law: Political Theory and the Legal System of Modern Society* (Leamington Spa, UK: Berg, 1986), 239–52; Otto Kahn-Freund, "Einführung," in Karl Renner, *Die Rechtsinstitute des Privatrechts und ihre soziale Funktionen* (Stuttgart: Gustav Fischer Verlag, 1965), 8–16.

30. Hayek, *Road to Serfdom*, 72.

31. Harvey, *Condition of Postmodernity*, 240–59.

32. Harvey, *Justice, Nature and the Geography of Difference*, 240–41.

33. Malcolm Waters, *Globalization* (New York: Routledge, 1995), 55.

34. Martin Shapiro, "The Globalization of Law," *Indiana Journal of Global Legal Studies* 1 (1993): 7. For recent discussions of economic globalization and legal development, see Richard Appelbaum, "The Future of Law in a Global Economy," *Social and Legal Studies* 7 (1998): 171–92; Richard Appelbaum, William Felstiner, and Volkmar Gessner, eds., *Rules and Networks: The Legal Culture of Global Business Transactions* (Oxford: Hart, 2001); A. Claire Cutler, Tony Porter, and Virginia Haufler, eds., *Private Authority and International Affairs* (Albany: SUNY Press, 199); Volkmar Gessner and Ali C. Budak, eds., *Emerging Legal Certainty: Empirical Studies on the Globalization of Law* (Aldershot, UK: Dartmouth, 1994); Wolf Heydebrand, "Globalization and the Rule of Law at the End of the Twentieth Century," *European Yearbook in the Sociology of Law* (2000), 25–127; Kanishka Jayasuriya, ed., *Law, Capitalism, and Power in Asia: The Rule of Law and Legal Institutions* (New York: Routledge, 1999); Carol Jones, "Capitalism, Globalization and Rule of Law: An Alternate Trajectory of Legal Change in China," *Social & Legal Studies* 3 (1994): 95–214; Sol Picciotto and Ruth Mayne, eds., *Regulating International Business: Beyond Liberalization* (New York; St. Martin's, 199); Gunther Teubner, ed., *Global Law without a State* (Aldershot, UK: Dartmouth, 1997). See also the special issue of *Constellations* (8, no. 4 [2001]) devoted to economic globalization and the rule of law.

35. Jarrod Wiener, *Globalization and the Harmonization of Law* (London: Pinter, 1999).

36. Yves Dezalay and Bryant G. Garth, *Dealing in Virtue: International Commercial*

Arbitration and the Construction of a Transnational Legal Order (Chicago: University of Chicago Press, 1996).

37. John Braithwaite and Peter Drahos, *Global Business Regulation* (Cambridge: Cambridge University Press, 2000), 30. Braithwaite and Drahos point out that the "recurrently most effective actors" in global regulation are presently large corporations (27). Picciotto also notes the growth of "soft law" and the "indeterminacy of abstract legal rules" in global economic regulation ("Introduction: What Rules for the World Economy?" in Picciotto and Mayne, ed., *Regulating International Business*, 15, 21).

38. Susan Strange, *Casino Capitalism* (Oxford: Blackwell, 1986).

39. Wolfgange H. Reinicke, *Global Public Policy: Governing without Government?* (Washington, D.C.: Brookings Institution Press, 1998), 120. Reinicke is describing the Basel-based system of banking regulation undertaken by the major industrial powers making up the Group of Ten (G-10) countries. Also see Tomaso Padoa-Schioppa and Fabrizio Saccomanni, "Managing a Market-Led Global Financial System," in *Managing the World Economy: Fifty Years after Bretton Woods,* ed. Peter B. Kenen (Washington, D.C.: Institute for International Economics, 1994), esp. 259–60.

40. Ethan Kapstein, *Governing the Global Economy: International Finance and the State* (Cambridge: Harvard University Press, 1994), 50.

41. See John Eatwell and Lance Taylor, *Global Finance at Risk: The Case for International Regulation* (New York: New Press, 2000).

42. See Philip B. Evans and Thomas R. Wurster, "Strategy and the New Economics of Information," *Harvard Business Review* 75 (1997): 71–82.

43. Insufficiently appreciative of the liberal rule of law, the legal sociologist Boaventura de Sousa Santos nonetheless captures the enigma at hand when he notes that the "speed and social acceleration" of contemporary social and economic life means that "law will be easily trapped in the dilemma: either to remain static and be ignored, or to keep up with social dynamics and be devalued as a normative reference" ("The Postmodern Transition: Law and Politics," in *The Fate of Law,* ed. Austin Sarat and Thomas Kearns [Ann Arbor: University of Michigan Press, 1993], 115).

44. Fuller, *Morality of Law,* 171–72.

45. Ibid., 171–72.

46. Ibid., 173.

47. Lon L. Fuller, "The Forms and Limits of Adjudication," in *The Principles of Social Order: Selected Essays of Lon L. Fuller,* ed. Kenneth I. Winston (Durham: Duke University Press, 1981), 112.

48. Fuller, *Morality of Law,* 174–75.

49. Schauer, "Legal Formalism," 542. Carl Schmitt's account of a "time lag" plaguing liberal democratic adjudication, described in chapter 4, also anticipated these problems.

50. Laura Nader, "Styles of Court Procedure: To Make the Balance," 87; Vilhelm Aubert, "Law a Way of Resolving Conflicts: The Case of A Small Industrialized Society," 287, both in Nader, *Law in Culture and Society.*

51. Oligopolistic tendencies are more pervasive in the global economy than generally acknowledged by neoliberal rhetoric (John Stopford and Susan Strange, *Rival States, Rival Firms: Competition for World Market Shares* [Cambridge: Cambridge University Press, 1991], 6–72, 92–97).

52. Industry leaders in international marine insurance, for example, are a main source of international rules, and large firms have played a decisive role in the stan-

dardization of international sales terms. In addition, "home states are increasingly prepared to formulate both domestic and economic policy with the interests of their home-based MNCs in mind," which often amounts to ensuring legal mechanisms tailored to suit their preferences. Peter Muchlinski, " 'Global Bukowina' Examined: Viewing the Multinational Enterprise as a Transnational Lawmaking Community," in Teubner, *Global Law without a State*, 85–89, 91. NAFTA grants firms rights hitherto generally limited to nation-states: Chapter 11 (B) allows private businesses to submit complaints against member states to a three-member tribunal, one of whose members is chosen by an affected member state, another by the firm, and the third jointly by two parties. NAFTA thereby effectively grants states and corporations equal authority in some crucial decision-making matters. In a revealing contrast the procedures making up NAFTA's labor "side agreement" deny similar rights to organized labor.

53. "Giant corporate groups dominate international economic flows: notably, about one-third of inter-state trade consists of internal flows between affiliates of such groups" (Sol Picciotto, "Introduction: What Rules for the World Economy?" in Picciotto and Mayne, *Regulating International Business*, 6). Picciotto is relying on data provided by the United Nations.

54. Muchlinski, " 'Global Bukowina' Examined," 82.

55. The last decade has witnessed a proliferation of voluntary "codes of conduct" detailing safe and healthy work conditions, grievance procedures, antidiscrimination norms, and bans on child labor and substandard wages.

56. See the *International Labor Organization Working Party on the Social Dimensions of Liberalization of International Trade Report* (1998) [www.ilo.org/public/english/20gb/docs/gb273/sdl-1.htm#]. For more support for this critical interpretation of voluntary codes of conduct, see William E. Scheuerman, "False Humanitarianism? U.S. Advocacy of Transnational Labor Standards," *Review of International Political Economy* 8 (2001): 359–88. I have gained greatly from Harry Arthurs, "Private Ordering and Workers' Rights in the Global Economy: Corporate Codes of Conduct as a Regime of Labor Market Regulation," in *Labour Law in an Era of Globalization: Transformative Practices and Possibilities*, ed. Joanne Conaghan, Michael Fischl, and Karl Klare (Oxford: Oxford University Press, 2002), 471–87.

57. Muchlinski, " 'Global Bukowina' Examined," 83.

58. Atiyah, *Rise and Fall of Freedom of Contract*, 724.

59. Outside the wealthy countries of the North, foreign direct investment (FDI) tends to flow to an elite group of a dozen or so developing countries (including Argentina, China, and Singapore). But other developing countries are eager to join that group. See V. N. Balasubramanyam, "Foreign Direct Investment to Developing Countries," in Picciotto and Mayne, *Regulating International Business*, 29–46.

60. Sol Picciotto, *International Business Taxation: A study in the Internationalization of Business Regulation* (London: Weidenfeld & Nicolson, 1992). Also see Susan Strange, *The Retreat of the State: The Diffusion of Power in the World Economy* (Cambridge: Cambridge University Press, 1996), 60–65, 77.

61. A large legal literature is available. For an introduction, see Muchlinski, " 'Global Bukowina' Examined," 90–96. Also see Muchlinski, "Brief History of Business Regulation," 53–55.

62. This is the "new pragmatism" between host states and foreign capital described by Stopford and Strange in *Rival States, Rival Firms*.

63. The WTO's record here is at best mixed. See Ernest H. Preeg, *Traders in a Brave*

New World: The Uruguay Round and the Future of the International Trading System (Chicago: University of Chicago Press, 1995).

64. David Kennedy, "The International Style in Postwar Law and Policy: John Jackson and the Field of International Economic Law," *American University Journal of International Law and Policy* 10 (1995): 685. More generally on the legal structure of the WTO, see John H. Jackson, *The World Trading System: Law and Policy of International Economic Relations* (Cambridge, Mass.: MIT Press, 1999). Obviously, much more could be said about the complex legal structure of the WTO. My point here is merely that we need to be skeptical about unsubstantiated claims that it already embodies a substantial quotient of rule of law virtues.

65. L. Wallach and L. Sforza, *Whose Trade Organization? Corporate Globalization and the Erosion of Democracy* (Washington, D.C.: Public Citizen, 1999), 198.

66. The General Agreement on Tariffs and Trade (GATT) Agreement, on which WTO builds, consisted of 22,000 pages and weighed 424 pounds. At a U.S. Senate hearing in 1951, Senator Milliken commented that "anyone who reads GATT is likely to have his sanity impaired." The jurist R. Gardner commented in 1966 that "only ten people in the world understand it, and they are not telling anyone" (qtd. in Antonio Cassese, *International Law in a Divided World* [Oxford: Clarendon Press, 1986], 340). These comments would be no less appropriate in the context of the contemporary WTO.

67. This reversal hardly renders the protective functions of the rule of law wholly anachronistic. My point here is simply that it does so for the most privileged segments of the corporate world.

68. Nathan Rosenberg, "Joseph Schumpeter: Radical Economist," in *Schumpeter in the History of Ideas*, ed. Mark Perlan and Yuichi Shionoyo (Ann Arbor: University of Michigan Press, 1994), 48. For textual support for this reading, see Joseph Schumpeter, *The Theory of Economic Development* (Cambridge: Harvard University Press, 1934), 79–83.

69. Harvey, *Condition of Postmodernity*, 157. Alternative interpretations of the economic impulses behind social acceleration could serve my purposes equally well. For example, see Michael J. Piore and Charles F. Sabel, *The Second Industrial Divide: Possibilities for Prosperity* (New York: Basic Books, 1984).

70. Harvey, *Condition of Postmodernity*, 147.

71. Atiyah, *Rise and Fall of Freedom of Contract*, 713.

72. Ibid., 717. For example, "the modern commercial transaction is, in practice, apt to include provision for varying the terms of exchange to suit the conditions applicable at the time of performance. Goods ordered for future delivery are likely to be supplied at prices ruling at the time of delivery; rise and fall clauses in building or construction works are the rule and not the exception; currency-variation clauses may well be included in international transactions" (714).

73. Ibid., 756

74. For examples, see ibid., 759.

75. Peter Schlechtriem, *Uniform Sales Law: The UN Convention on Contracts for the International Sale of Goods* (Vienna: Manzsche Verlags- und Universitätsbibliothek, 1986), 1. See the symposium on commercial law in the *American Journal of Comparative Law* 40 (1992).

76. Arthur Rosett, "Unification, Restatement, Codification and Reform in International Commercial Law," *American Journal of Comparative Law* 40 (1992): 687.

77. Ibid., 695.

78. Lord Justice Mustill, "The New *Lex Mercatoria:* The First Twenty-Five Years," *Arbitration International* 4 (1988): 118–19.

79. Jeswald W. Salacuse, *Making Global Deals: Negotiating in the International Marketplace* (Boston: Houghton Mifflin, 1991), 128–30.

80. John Kline, "Advantages of International Regulation: The Case for a Flexible Pluralistic Framework," in *International Regulation: New Rules for a Changing World Order,* ed. Carol Adelman (San Francisco: Institute for Contemporary Studies, 1988), 36.

81. A. Claire Cutler, "Global Capitalism and Liberal Myths: Dispute Settlement in Private International Trade Law," *Millennium: Journal of International Studies* 24 (1995): 384; Henry P. DeVries, "International Commercial Arbitration: A Transnational View," *Journal of International Arbitration* 1 (1984): 7–20; Yves Dezaley and Bryant G. Garth, *Dealing in Virtue: International Commercial Arbitration and the Construction of a Transnational Legal Order* (Chicago: University of Chicago Press, 1996); Albert Jan van den Berg, ed., *International Dispute Resolution: Towards an International Arbitration Culture* (The Hague: Kluwer, 1998).

82. Thomas Carbonneau, "The Remaking of Arbitration: Design and Destiny," in *Lex Mercatoria and Arbitration,* ed. Carbonneau (Dobbs Ferry, N.Y.: Transnational Juris Publications, 1990), 13.

83. Linda Hirschman, "The Second Arbitration Trilogy: The Federalization of Arbitration Law," *Virginia Law Quarterly* 71 (1985): 1305–78; Richard B. Lillich and Charles N. Brower, eds., *International Arbitration in the 21st Century: Towards Judicialization and Uniformity?* (Irvington, N.Y.: Transnational, 1994); John T. McDermott, "Significant Developments in the United States Law Governing International Commercial Arbitration," *Connecticut Journal of International Law* 1 (1985–86): 111–50.

84. Thomas Carbonneau, "The Exuberant Pathway to Quixotic Internationalism: Assessing the Folly of *Mitsubishi*," *Vanderbilt Journal of International Law* 19 (1987): 265–98; *Alternative Dispute Resolution: Melting the Lances and Dismounting the Steeds* (Urbana: University of Illinois Press, 1989); "National Law and the Judicialization of Arbitration: Manifest Destiny, Manifest Disregard, and Manifest Error," in Lillich and Brower, *International Arbitration in the 21st Century.* From the perspective of the account of motorized legislation provided earlier, this is a revealing trend. Domestic courts' willingness to grant substantial autonomy to forms of international business arbitration widely considered speedier than traditional forms of adjudication represents another example of the general quest for accelerated lawmaking.

85. On one level the growth of arbitration confirms Shklar's observation that the "resort to arbitration under chamber of commerce auspices" has been a widely held preference for business groups throughout the history of capitalism. "Capitalist entrepreneurs have their own interest in stability and calculability, but the excessive formalities of lawyers' law are [often] uncongenial to them" (*Legalism,* 16–17). For an account of the complicated history of commercial arbitration in the United States which confirms Shklar's comments, see Jerold Auerbach, *Justice without Law* (Oxford: Oxford University Press, 1983). A major selling point for commercial arbitration throughout its history has always been the promise of a speedy resolution to business disputes. Nonetheless, we still need to explain why "lawyer's law" has become especially uncongenial to global business groups in contemporary capitalism.

86. Cutler, "Global Capitalism and Liberal Myths," 385; "Public Meets Private: The International Unification and Harmonization of Private International Trade Law," *Global Society* 13 (1999): 31.

87. Reza Banakar, "Reflexive Legitimacy in International Arbitration," in Gessner and Budak, *Emerging Legal Certainty*, 370.

88. Van den Berg, *International Dispute Resolution*.

89. Ellen Joan Pollock, "Arbitrator Finds Role Dwindling as Rivals Grow," *Wall Street Journal*, April 28, 1993, B10; Linda Singer, *Settling Disputes: Conflict Resolution in Business, Families, and the Legal System* (Boulder: Westview, 1994).

90. Eva Müller, "Fast-Track Arbitration: Meetings the Demands of the New Millennium," *Journal of International Arbitration* 15 (1998): 5–18; Arthur M. Rovine, "Fast-Track Arbitration: A Step Away from Judicialization of International Arbitration?" in Lillich and Brower, *International Arbitration in the 21st Century*; Michael Schneider, "Combing Arbitration with Conciliation," in van den Berg, *International Dispute Resolution*.

91. Singer, *Settling Disputes*, 74–75.

92. For the doctrinal history, see Thomas Franck, *Political Questions/Judicial Answers: Does the Rule of Law Apply to Foreign Affairs?* (Princeton: Princeton University Press, 1992).

93. Barry E. Carter, "International Economic Sanctions: Improving the Haphazard U.S. Legal Regime," *California Law Review* 75 (1987): 1242–48; John H. Jackson and William J. Davey, *Legal Problems of International Economic Relations*, 2d. ed. (St. Paul, Minn..: West Publishing, 1986), 132–33.

94. Quoted in Carter, "International Economic Sanctions," 1245. Rehnquist cites a 1915 court ruling, *United States v. Midwest Oil Co.*, 236 U.S. 459, 474.

95. For example, the APA requires administrative standards to be announced publicly.

96. Sharyn O'Halloran, *Politics, Process, and American Trade Policy* (Ann Arbor: University of Michigan Press, 1994), 168–70.

97. Jackson and Davey, *Legal Problems of International Economic Relations*, 128.

98. I. M. Destler, *American Trade Politics* (Washington, D.C.: International Institute for International Economics, 1995), 207.

99. Ibid., 126–27.

100. Jackson and Davey, *Legal Problems of International Economic Relations*, 131–32; Carter, "International Economic Sanctions," 1183–1229.

101. Here, too, judges have demonstrated leniency when evaluating the constitutionality of executive agreements. For a typology of different forms of executive agreements, see Jackson and Davey, *Legal Problems of International Economic Relations*, 113–14.

102. Fourteen percent were military, and the remainder procedural (O'Halloran, *Politics, Process and American Trade Policy*, 72). Also see Harold H. Koh, "Why the President (Almost) Always Wins in Foreign Affairs: Lessons of the Iran-Contra Affair," *Yale Law Journal* 97 (1988): 1261–63.

103. Jackson and Davey, *Legal Problems of International Economic Relations*, 119.

104. The most important defense of the procedures according to which NAFTA was approved has been formulated by the constitutional scholars Bruce Ackerman and David Golove, for whom the congressional-executive agreement and fast track are

"merely variations on the institutional and doctrinal themes developed by the New Dealers" in the 1930s and 1940s ("Is NAFTA Constitutional," 109). Ackerman and Golove trace the immediate historical roots of the decline of senatorial power over foreign policy to the rise of the New Deal. Unfortunately, they misleadingly claim that the Senate's demise stems from a popular revolution, in which ordinary Americans self-consciously engaged in a bout of "foundational politics" resulting in fundamental alterations in our constitutional system's approach to foreign policy questions. Yet most Americans (both during the period described by Ackerman and Golove and more recently) would surely be surprised by the news that they have recently initiated revolutionary changes in the way foreign policy is made. If there was a popular revolution in this constitutional area during the mid-1940s, it seems to have been a stealth revolution that most of the American people curiously seem to have overlooked. This raises some serious questions about the popular character of the revolution in foreign policy making which occurred over the course of the second half of the twentieth century; Ackerman and Golove are correct in describing how dramatic the changes have been, but they are describing a revolution made with little conscious popular consent. They conveniently downplay the facts that (1) the decline of the Senate as a force in foreign policy too often has simply prepared the way for a strengthening of the executive, whose policies have often been anything but a continuation of the New Deal; (2) executive agreements have played a key role in the well-known excesses of postwar American foreign policy; and (3) NAFTA and the WTO presuppose an uncritical faith in the "free market" which the New Dealers refused to endorse.

105. Carter, "International Economic Sanctions," 1229, 1234. Also see Joel B. Harris and Jeffrey P. Bialos, "The Strange New World of United States Export Controls under the International Emergency Economic Powers Act," *Vanderbilt Journal of Transnational Law* 18 (1995): 72–108; and Koh, "Why the President (Almost) Always Wins," 1268.

106. Jackson and Davey, *Legal Problems of International Economic Relations*, 130–31.

107. Schauer, "Formalism," 542.

108. This argument is commonly found among defenders of "cosmopolitan democracy." See, for example, David Held, *Democracy and the Global Order: From the Modern State to Cosmopolitan Governance;* also see Daniele Archibugi, David Held, and Martin Koehler, eds., *Re-imagining Political Community: Studies in Cosmopolitan Democracy* (Stanford: Stanford University Press, 1998).

109. The same tendency plagues political discourse on the rule of law in the global economy. Too often, representatives of the World Bank, WTO, and IMF confuse their own preference for a rule of law with the somewhat less attractive realities of contemporary global law.

110. Danilo Zolo, *Invoking Humanity: War, Law, and Global Order* (London: Continuum, 2000), 6–91. One need not accept a cultural relativist interpretation of human rights in order to acknowledge the potentially controversial character of appeals to them as a justification for military intervention.

111. Writing in the context of the Nazi attack on the classical ideal of the universal legal equality of states, the Frankfurt School legal theorist Franz Neumann defended its "progressive" functions (*Behemoth*, 166–71).

112. See the powerful polemic by Zolo, *Invoking Humanity*, 122–23. Zolo's Realist views on international relations need not be endorsed in order to appreciate his legiti-

mate skepticism about recent trends in international public law. Also see Zolo, *Cosmopolis: Prospects for World Government* (Cambridge, UK: Polity Press, 1997).

113. Along these lines, see David Schneiderman, "Investment Rules and the Rule of Law," *Constellations* 8 (2001): 521–37.

114. Fuller, *Morality of Law*, 155–56.

115. Scheuerman, "False Humanitarianism?"; also see Patrick Macklem, "Labour Law beyond Borders," *Journal of International Economic Law* 5 (2002): 605–45.

116. William E. Scheuerman, "The Rule of Law and the Welfare State: Towards a New Synthesis," *Politics and Society* 22 (1994): 195–213.

117. Cited in John Patrick Diggins, *The Promise of Pragmatism: Modernism and the Crisis of Knowledge and Authority* (Chicago: University of Chicago Press, 1994), 264.

118. Fuller, *Morality of Law*, 175.

s i x : Liberal Democracy in a High-Speed World

1. Hayek attributed legal and parliamentary decay to the rise of the welfare state and socialism; Franz Neumann and the young Jürgen Habermas described similar trends but argued that structural transformations of the capitalist economy were the root cause (see Scheuerman, ed., *The Rule of Law under Siege: Collected Essays of Franz L. Neumann and Otto Kirchheimer*; Habermas, *Structural Transformation of the Public Sphere*); as discussed earlier, Carl Schmitt chronicled the demise of parliamentarism and the rule of law (*The Crisis of Parliamentary Democracy*, trans. Ellen Kennedy [Cambridge: MIT Press, 1990]).

2. Lawrence K. Grossman, *The Electronic Republic: Reshaping Democracy in the Information Age* (New York: Penguin, 1995), 69–119.

3. Even the former president of NBC News and PBS has acknowledged these ills (ibid., 173–86, 225–28).

4. In the United Kingdom, for example, four large media groups presently control 92 percent of the circulation of national daily newspapers (John B. Thompson, *The Media and Modernity: A Social Theory of the Media* [Stanford: Stanford University Press, 1995], 77–78).

5. See C. Edwin Baker, *Advertising and a Democratic Press* (Princeton: Princeton University Press, 1994). There is also evidence of a growing right-wing bias among media monopolies. For example, Clear Channel, owner of a significant number of radio stations in the United States, aggressively supported the U.S. invasion of Iraq (John Schwartz and Geraldine Frabrikant, "War Puts Radio Giant on the Defensive," *New York Times*, Mar. 31, 2003, C1, C7), as did Rupert Murdoch's vast media empire (David D. Kirkpatrick, "Mr. Murdoch's War: Global News Empire Marches to Chairman's Political Drum," *New York Times*, Apr. 7, 2003, C1, C7).

6. Herbert J. Gans, *Democracy and the News* (Oxford: Oxford University Press, 2003), 50.

7. Cass Sunstein, *Democracy and the Problem of Free Speech* (New York: Free Press, 1993), 61.

8. Thomas E. Patterson, "Time and News: The Media's Limitations as an Instrument of Democracy," *International Political Science Review* 19 (1998): 57.

9. James Fallows, qtd. in Patterson, "Time and News," 59.

10. Gans, *Democracy and the News*, 50.

11. The legal response to the terrorist attacks of September 11, 2001, which has resulted in a vast expansion of executive prerogative, rests on the dogma of the high-speed executive (Scheuerman, "Rethinking Crisis Government," *Constellations* 9 [2002]: 492–505). Elaine Scarry has argued that preconceptions about the high-speed character of present-day warfare have "been used to legitimize an increasingly centralized, authoritarian model of defense" ("Citizenship in Emergency: Can Democracy Protect Us against Terrorism?" *Boston Review* 27 [2002]: 4).

12. For example, see Eriksen, *Tyranny of the Moment*, 147–64. Unfortunately, much of this literature depicts the choice for "slowness" as a lifestyle choice akin to our preference for one variety of ice cream over another. Such an approach ignores the structural sources of acceleration.

13. Radhakamal Mukerjee, "Time, Technics, and Society," in *The Sociology of Time*, ed. John Hassard (New York: St. Martin's, 1990), 47–55.

14. William E. Connolly, "Speed, Concentric Circles, and Cosmopolitanism," *Political Theory* 28, no. 5 (2000): 598.

15. In a similar vein, see Eberling, *Beschleunigung und Politik*, 110–53.

16. Alec Nove, *The Economics of Feasible Socialism* (London: Routledge, 1983).

17. For a useful survey, see James Bohman, "The Coming of Age of Deliberative Democracy," in *Journal of Political Philosophy* 6 (1998): 400–425. Also see Rainer Forst, "The Rule of Reasons: Three Models of Deliberative Democracy," *Ratio Juris* 14 (2001): 345–78.

18. James Bohman, *Public Deliberation: Pluralism, Complexity, and Democracy* (Cambridge: MIT Press, 1996), 7. Bohman is summarizing Habermas's view.

19. Ibid., 26.

20. Carlos Santiago Nino, *The Constitution of Deliberative Democracy* (New Haven: Yale University Press, 1996), 171.

21. Ibid. Dennis Thompson and Amy Gutmann have criticized theorists of deliberative democracy for neglecting the pivotal role of the central legislature while falsely envisioning constitutional courts as a privileged site for deliberation (*Democracy and Disagreement* [Cambridge: Harvard University Press, 1996], 45–47, 128–64).

22. At times Habermas seems to conflate the executive branch with administrative power. He typically describes a clearly circumscribed executive, "which is not supposed to have control over the normative grounds of legislation and adjudication, is subordinate in its activity both to parliamentary oversight and to judicial review, whereas the opposite relation, a supervision of the two branches by the executive, is excluded" (*Between Facts and Norms*, trans. William Rehg [Cambridge, Mass.: MIT Press, 1996], 240–41). Perhaps his skepticism about executive power can be interpreted as presciently acknowledging the anachronistic character of many traditional ideas about it.

23. Jerry Mashaw, cited in ibid., 187.

24. Ibid., 186. Also see William E. Scheuerman "Between Radicalism and Resignation: Democratic Theory in *Between Facts and Norms*," in *Discourse and Democracy: Essays on Habermas' Between Facts and Norms*, ed. Kenneth Baynes and Rene von Schomberg (Albany: SUNY Press, 2002), 61–88.

25. See Bohman, *Public Deliberation*, 190–91, for an account of what Habermas's proposals might entail. Also see Christian Hunold, "Corporatism, Pluralism, and Democracy: Toward a Deliberative Theory of Bureaucratic Accountability," *Governance* 14 (2001): 151–67.

26. For example, Bruce Ackerman has recently offered a persuasive critique of the classical tripartite separation of powers as well as a number of creative institutional suggestions for updating the separation of powers. But his account is marred by dogmatic fidelity to the idea of the energetic high-speed unitary executive (" New Separation of Powers," 679).

27. The contemporary debate suggests that pluralism requires problem solving via deliberation. Given the enormous moral, religious, and political divides characteristic of contemporary society, this would seem to suggest a greater role for (time-consuming) deliberation than was probably necessary in the relatively homogeneous political communities presupposed by classical liberal democratic theory.

28. Sunstein, *Democracy and the Problem of Free Speech*, 77–88.

29. Britain's Channel Four has successfully televised facets of one deliberative opinion poll; the Internet would provide a forum as well (James S. Fishkin, *The Voice of the People: Public Opinion and Democracy* [New Haven: Yale University Press, 1995], 134–81).

30. Baker focuses on the print media, but his basic arguments might apply to other media sources as well (*Advertising and a Democratic Press*, 83–117).

31. See Sunstein, *Democracy and the Problem of Free Speech*, in which the point is made from a classical Madisonian perspective. Also see Gans, *Democracy and the News*, 49–55.

32. See Javier Corrales, "Lessons from Latin America," in *Democracy and the Internet: Allies or Adversaries*, ed. Leslie David Simon, Javier Corrales, and Donald R. Wolfensberger (Washington, D.C.: Woodrow Wilson Center Press, 2002), 30–66.

33. In fact, disclosure rules might be an effective device for overseeing any news provider, Internet based or otherwise.

34. Cass Sunstein, *republic.com* (Princeton: Princeton University Press, 2001), 167–90.

35. Noah Zatz, "Sidewalks in Cyberspace: Making Space for Public Forums in the Electronic Environment," *Harvard Journal of Law & Technology* 12 (1998): 151–240. Might this approach prove intrusive? "Attempting to have access to the website of *Time* magazine, they might find themselves opening a page to Citizens for Control of Nuclear Power as well . . . But is it much different from daily life on a street or in a park? . . . Because it is so easy to close a web page, any intrusion on Internet users seems far more trivial than those introduced via public forums" (Sunstein, *republic.com*, 189).

36. Pippa Norris, *Digital Divide: Civic Engagement, Information Poverty, and the Internet Worldwide* (New York: Cambridge University Press, 2001), 132–47.

37. Anne Campbell, Andrew Harrop, and Bill Thompson, "Towards the Virtual Parliament—What Computers Can Do for MPs," in *Parliament in the Age of the Internet*, ed. Stephen Coleman, John Taylor, and Wim van de Donk (New York: Oxford University Press, 1999), 32–33.

38. Donald R. Wolfensberger, "Congress and the Internet: Democracy's Uncertain Link," in Simon, Corrales, and Wolfensberger, *Democracy and the Internet*, 69.

39. Blair dubbed the experience a "unique experiment in political debate, [which] has shown the potential of the new medium to be serious, constructive, and imaginative" (Campbell, Harrop, and Thompson, "Towards the Virtual Parliament," 39).

40. Bert Mulder, "Parliamentary Futures: Re-Presenting the Issue Information, Technology and the Dynamics of Democracy," in Coleman, Taylor, and van de Donk, *Parliament in the Age of the Internet*, 195–96.

41. There seems to be anecdotal evidence that journalists, in particular, are already benefiting from having government records and documents available online.

42. See Darin Barney, *Prometheus Wired: The Hope for Democracy in the Age of Network Technology* (Chicago: University of Chicago Press, 2000); Norris, *Digital Divide;* Ian McLean, *Democracy and New Technology* (Cambridge: Polity Press, 1989).

43. R. P. Wolff, *In Defense of Anarchism* (New York: Harper & Row, 1970).

44. See George Kateb, "The Moral Distinctiveness of Representative Democracy," *Ethics* 91 (1981): 357–74. I am not convinced, however, that greater direct democracy necessitates the Rousseauian excesses vividly described by Kateb.

45. For a balanced survey, see Thomas E. Cronin, *Direct Democracy: The Politics of Initiative, Referendum, and Recall* (Cambridge: Harvard University Press, 1989).

46. Budge suggests that direct democracy requires a shortening of the workday (*New Challenge of Direct Democracy,* 64–65).

47. Ibid., 27, in which Budge observes that the "union of computing with telephone and television and the likely presence of such a device in every household" in the near future contains opportunities for direct democracy.

48. Ibid., 181.

49. Ibid., 115.

50. Barber, "Three Scenarios," 585.

51. Budge, *New Challenge of Direct Democracy,* 31. For an example of this republican genre of criticism, see Hubertus Buchstein, "Bytes That Bite: The Internet and Deliberative Democracy," *Constellations* 4 (1997): 260, in which he claims that "questions of ethical self-understanding, the interpretation of needs, or issues of social policy, depend to some degree on the dimension of direct confrontation, personal experience, and visibility." Of course, direct interaction has a role to play in each of these processes. The question, however, is whether the need for such immediacy precludes the possibility of computerized direct democracy, as Buchstein seems to conclude.

52. For example, see Michael C. Dorf and Charles F. Sabel, "A Constitution of Democratic Experimentalism," *Columbia Law Review* 98 (1998): 267–473. Dorf and Sabel start with a realistic depiction of our high-speed capitalism before considering possibilities for how we might subject it to effective regulatory devices.

53. On the virtues of reflexive law as a regulatory solution to a host of difficult questions concerning intimacy and sexuality, see the excellent study by Jean L. Cohen, *Regulating Intimacy: A New Legal Paradigm* (Princeton: Princeton University Press, 2002). Cohen offers the best general account of the debate about reflexive law available in any language. Also see Jean L. Cohen and Andrew Arato, *Civil Society and Political Theory* (Cambridge, Mass.: MIT Press, 1992), 480–97; Arato, "Procedural Law and Civil Society: Interpreting the Radical Democratic Paradigm," in *Habermas on Law and Democracy: Critical Exchanges,* ed. Arato and Michel Rosenfeld (Berkeley: University of California Press, 1998), 26–36. Habermas has engaged with Teubner's ideas, as evinced by his "proceduralist" model of legal regulation (*Between Facts and Norms,* 388–446).

54. Gunther Teubner, "Substantive and Reflexive Elements in Modern Law," *Law & Society Review* 17 (1983): 256. Teubner's intellectual biography is a complex one. Although influenced by the systems theorist Luhmann, Teubner hopes to show how Luhmann's concerns could be rendered compatible with concerns deriving from theoretical traditions less hostile to "old European" forms of rationalistic normative argumentation. Teubner's theoretical trajectory has also undergone significant transformations since the mid-1980s. Since my chief interest here lies in the potential merits of

reflexive law for tackling social speed, I neglect these shifts. In the crudest terms Teubner has been seeking to develop a theory of legal "autopoiesis" emphasizing the radical autonomy of legal discourse: law is a distinct discourse that generates its own object and validity of criteria while simultaneously taking information from—and transferring information to—an environment consisting of separate distinct systems (including politics, science, and the economy). For critical discussions of problems resulting from Teubner's attempt to synthesize Luhmann and Habermas, see Cohen, *Regulating Intimacy*, 156–57; and, more generally, 151–79; also see Ingeborg Maus, "Perspektiven 'reflexiven Rechts' im Kontext gegenwärtige Deregulierungstendenzen," *Kritische Justiz* 19 (1986): 390–405.

55. Gunther Teubner, "After Legal Instrumentalism? Strategic Models of Post-Regulatory Law," in *Dilemmas of Law in the Welfare State*, ed. G. Teubner (New York: de Gruyter, 1985), 306–7.

56. Teubner, "Substantive and Reflexive Elements in Modern Law," 254. Teubner relies Weber's famous account of the growth of antiformal trends in the law (*Economy and Society*, 2:882–89). Weber described the movement away from "formal legality" to "materialized" law, which in his view helped buttress growing state involvement in the economy at the price of sacrificing traditional rule of law virtues (e.g., clarity and generality in the law). Teubner's concept of substantive law overlaps substantially with Weber's description of the "materialization" of law.

57. Jean L. Cohen, "Dilemmas of Harassment Law," *Constellations*. 6 (1999): 461.

58. Teubner, "Substantive and Reflexive Elements in Modern Law," 272.

59. Ibid., 274.

60. Teubner, "After Legal Instrumentalism," 317.

61. Hayek, *Road to Serfdom*, 80–96; Weber, *Economy and Society*, 2:882–89. As noted in chapter 5, economic globalization appears to be exacerbating antiformal trends in the law.

62. Teubner, "Substantive and Reflexive Elements in Modern Law," 277.

63. Cohen, "Dilemmas of Harassment Law," 461.

64. Teubner, "Substantive and Reflexive Elements in Modern Law," 278. On occasion, however, Teubner suggests that there may be no necessary connection between equalizing bargaining positions and reflexivity in law: "dynamic, flexible institutions with strong asymmetric [*sic*] power relations can, under certain circumstances, be more responsive to human needs than self-enclosed, power-symmetrical, equilibrium institutions" ("After Legal Instrumentalism?" 318). But he tends to posit a relatively close tie between reflexivity and the reduction of power inequalities. Matters are complicated by the fact that Teubner oscillates between different understandings of *reflexivity*. See Cohen, *Regulating Intimacy*, 155–56.

65. Teubner, "After Legal Instrumentalism?" 316; and "Verrechtlichung—Begriffe, Merkmale, Grenzen, Auswege" in *Verrechtlichung von Wirtschaft, Arbeit und sozialer Solidarität*, ed. Hans F. Zacher (Frankfurt: Suhrkamp, 1985), 342.

66. Teubner, "Verrechtlichung—Begriffe, Merkmale, Grenzen, Auswege," 333–44. This is one of many reasons why it is simply not correct to characterize Teubner as an advocate of "deregulation" along free market lines.

67. Cohen and Arato, *Civil Society and Political Theory*, 483.

68. Santos, "Postmodern Transition," 115.

69. Niklas Luhmann, *The Differentiation of Society*, trans. Stephen Holmes and Charles Larmore (New York: Columbia University Press, 1982), 101.

70. Kline, "Advantages of International Regulation," 36.

71. Maus, "Perspektiven 'reflexiven Rechts,'" 400–405. Robert Goodin has argued that state actors in "positions of power—legislators, judges, administrators, and so on"—are unlikely to "pass up opportunities for binding their inferiors and successors to precise rules and precedents" given the fact that they possess an eminently political interest in limiting the choices available to inferiors. After all, "power is the essence of politics, and the essence of power lies in restricting the choices available to others" (*Political Theory and Public Policy* [Chicago: University of Chicago Press, 1982], 71). Yet political actors often tolerate vague and open-ended legal forms because they face significant pressures from privileged economic interests that prefer antiformal legal practices as a way of buttressing their de facto power advantages.

72. Ingeborg Maus, "Sinn und Bedeutung der Volkssouveränität in der modernen Gesellschaft," *Kritische Justiz* 24 (1991): 148–49.

73. This criticism meshes with Erhard Blankenburg's observation that Teubner develops a misleading "evolutionist" account of law which obscures the messy complexities of modern legal development, in which formal, substantive, and reflexive legal forms typically coexist ("The Poverty of Evolutionism: A Critique of Teubner's Case for 'Reflexive Law,'" *Law & Society Review* 18 [1984]: 273–89).

74. See Cohen, *Regulating Intimacy*, 151–79.

75. Held, *Democracy and the Global Order*, 237.

76. In his more recent work the paucity of effective democratic institutions on the global level seems to have encouraged Teubner to argue that any emerging system will need to take the form of a "global law without the state." He thereby abandons his earlier aspiration to rely on coordinated political authority in order to guarantee a general legal framework for self-regulation. Teubner sees global law as emerging from "self-organized processes" operating in autonomous sectors "independently of the laws of nation-states" and now seems skeptical of attempts to subject these processes to even the relatively limited forms of traditional state-based legal coordination described in his earlier ideas about reflexive law. Given his skepticism concerning the prospects of an effective mode of state-based global governance, however, it is no longer clear how power inequalities are to be compensated for (and reflexivity within law achieved), especially in light of Teubner's own admission that many facets of the emerging global law without a state presently favor privileged economic interests. See Teubner, " 'Global Bukowina,'" 4, 8, 19.

77. Reinicke, *Global Public Policy*, 120.

78. Ibid., 120.

79. Ibid., 122.

80. Cohen, "Dilemmas of Harassment Law," 461.

81. John Dryzek, "Transnational Democracy," *Journal of Political Philosophy* 7 (1999): 30–51, 43.

82. Banakar, "Reflexive Legitimacy in International Arbitration," in Gessner and Budak, *Emerging Legal Certainty*, 349.

83. Harry Arthurs, "Corporate Self-Regulation: Political Economy, State Regulation, and Reflexive Labor Law," MS, Osgood Law School, Toronto, 2002.

84. Reinicke, *Global Public Policy*, 99–100, 114, 125–26.

85. See chapter 5.

86. Shklar, *Legalism*,

87. Reinicke, *Global Public Policy*, 101.

88. Maus, "Sinn und Bedeutung der Volkssouveranität," 148–49.

89. T. H. Marshall, *Citizenship and Social Class, and Other Essays* (Cambridge: Cambridge University Press, 1950). On national identity and the origins of the modern welfare state, see Pierre Rosanvallon, *The New Social Question: Rethinking the Welfare State* (Princeton: Princeton University Press, 2000), 37–40.

Conclusion

1. See Archibugi, Held, and Koehler, *Re-imagining Political Community;* Held, *Democracy and the Global Order;* Ian Shapiro and Casiano Hacker-Cordon, eds., *Democracy's Edges* (Cambridge: Cambridge University Press, 2000).

2. Jürgen Habermas, *The Postnational Constellation: Political Essays* (Cambridge, Mass.: MIT Press, 2001).

Index